Cameron B.
Mrs. Gordon

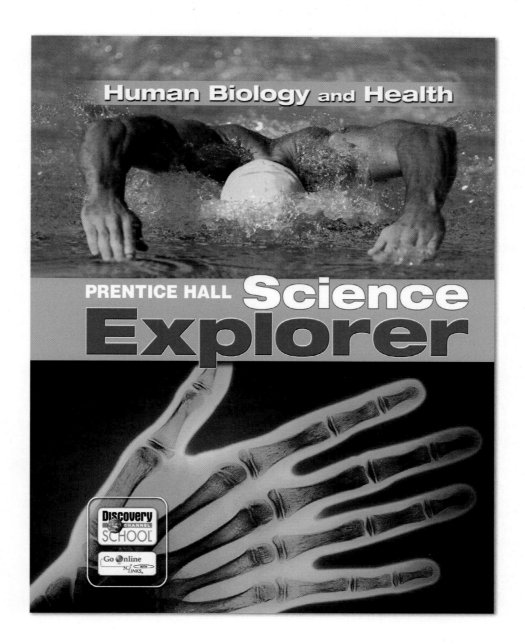

Human Biology and Health

PRENTICE HALL Science Explorer

PEARSON

Boston, Massachusetts
Glenview, Illinois
Shoreview, Minnesota
Upper Saddle River, New Jersey

PRENTICE HALL **Science Explorer**

Human Biology and Health

Book-Specific Resources

Student Edition
StudentExpress™ CD-ROM
Interactive Textbook Online
Teacher's Edition
All-in-One Teaching Resources
Color Transparencies
Guided Reading and Study Workbook
Student Edition in MP3 Audio
Discovery Channel School® Video
Consumable and Nonconsumable Materials Kits

Program Print Resources

Integrated Science Laboratory Manual
Computer Microscope Lab Manual
Inquiry Skills Activity Books
Progress Monitoring Assessments
Test Preparation Workbook
Test-Taking Tips With Transparencies
Teacher's ELL Handbook
Reading Strategies for Science Content

Differentiated Instruction Resources

Adapted Reading and Study Workbook
Adapted Tests
Differentiated Instruction Guide for Labs and Activities

Program Technology Resources

TeacherExpress™ CD-ROM
Interactive Textbooks Online
PresentationExpress™ CD-ROM
ExamView®, Test Generator CD-ROM
Lab zone™ Easy Planner CD-ROM
Probeware Lab Manual With CD-ROM
Computer Microscope and Lab Manual
Materials Ordering CD-ROM
Discovery Channel School® DVD Library
Lab Activity Video Library—DVD and VHS
Web Site at PearsonSchool.com

Spanish Print Resources

Spanish Student Edition
Spanish Guided Reading and Study Workbook
Spanish Teaching Guide With Tests

Acknowledgments appear on p. 292, which constitutes an extension of this copyright page.

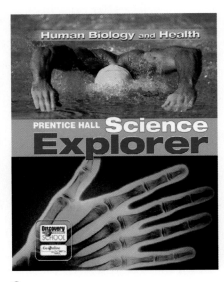

Cover
Swimmer (top) and a close-up of a colored X-ray of a hand (bottom)

13-digit ISBN 978-0-13-365103-4
10-digit ISBN 0-13-365103-7
10   V063   12

PEARSON

Program Authors

Michael J. Padilla, Ph.D.
Associate Dean and Director
Eugene T. Moore School of Education
Clemson University
Clemson, South Carolina

Michael Padilla is a leader in middle school science education. He has served as an author and elected officer for the National Science Teachers Association and as a writer of the National Science Education Standards. As lead author of Science Explorer, Mike has inspired the team in developing a program that meets the needs of middle grades students, promotes science inquiry, and is aligned with the National Science Education Standards.

Ioannis Miaoulis, Ph.D.
President
Museum of Science
Boston, Massachusetts

Originally trained as a mechanical engineer, Ioannis Miaoulis is in the forefront of the national movement to increase technological literacy. As dean of the Tufts University School of Engineering, Dr. Miaoulis spearheaded the introduction of engineering into the Massachusetts curriculum. Currently he is working with school systems across the country to engage students in engineering activities and to foster discussions on the impact of science and technology on society.

Martha Cyr, Ph.D.
Director of K–12 Outreach
Worcester Polytechnic Institute
Worcester, Massachusetts

Martha Cyr is a noted expert in engineering outreach. She has over nine years of experience with programs and activities that emphasize the use of engineering principles, through hands-on projects, to excite and motivate students and teachers of mathematics and science in grades K–12. Her goal is to stimulate a continued interest in science and mathematics through engineering.

Book Author

Elizabeth Coolidge-Stolz, M.D.
Medical Writer
North Reading, Massachusetts

Contributing Writers

Douglas E. Bowman
Health/Physical Education Teacher
Welches Middle School
Welches, Oregon

Patricia M. Doran
Science Instructional Assistant
State University of New York at Ulster
Stone Ridge, New York

Jorie Hunken
Science Consultant
Woodstock, Connecticut

Consultants

Reading Consultant

Nancy Romance, Ph.D.
Professor of Science
    Education
Florida Atlantic University
Fort Lauderdale, Florida

Mathematics Consultant

William Tate, Ph.D.
Professor of Education and
    Applied Statistics and
    Computation
Washington University
St. Louis, Missouri

Reviewers

Teacher Reviewers

David R. Blakely
Arlington High School
Arlington, Massachusetts

Jane E. Callery
Two Rivers Magnet Middle
School
East Hartford, Connecticut

Melissa Lynn Cook
Oakland Mills High School
Columbia, Maryland

James Fattic
Southside Middle School
Anderson, Indiana

Dan Gabel
Hoover Middle School
Rockville, Maryland

Wayne Goates
Eisenhower Middle School
Goddard, Kansas

Katherine Bobay Graser
Mint Hill Middle School
Charlotte, North Carolina

Darcy Hampton
Deal Junior High School
Washington, D.C.

Karen Kelly
Pierce Middle School
Waterford, Michigan

David Kelso
Manchester High School Central
Manchester, New Hampshire

Benigno Lopez, Jr.
Sleepy Hill Middle School
Lakeland, Florida

Angie L. Matamoros, Ph.D.
ALM Consulting, INC.
Weston, Florida

Tim McCollum
Charleston Middle School
Charleston, Illinois

Bruce A. Mellin
Brooks School
North Andover, Massachusetts

Ella Jay Parfitt
Southeast Middle School
Baltimore, Maryland

Evelyn A. Pizzarello
Louis M. Klein Middle School
Harrison, New York

Kathleen M. Poe
Fletcher Middle School
Jacksonville, Florida

Shirley Rose
Lewis and Clark Middle School
Tulsa, Oklahoma

Linda Sandersen
Greenfield Middle School
Greenfield, Wisconsin

Mary E. Solan
Southwest Middle School
Charlotte, North Carolina

Mary Stewart
University of Tulsa
Tulsa, Oklahoma

Paul Swenson
Billings West High School
Billings, Montana

Thomas Vaughn
Arlington High School
Arlington, Massachusetts

Susan C. Zibell
Central Elementary
Simsbury, Connecticut

Safety Reviewers

W. H. Breazeale, Ph.D.
Department of Chemistry
College of Charleston
Charleston, South Carolina

Ruth Hathaway, Ph.D.
Hathaway Consulting
Cape Girardeau, Missouri

Douglas Mandt, M.S.
Science Education Consultant
Edgewood, Washington

Activity Field Testers

Nicki Bibbo
Witchcraft Heights School
Salem, Massachusetts

Rose-Marie Botting
Broward County Schools
Fort Lauderdale, Florida

Colleen Campos
Laredo Middle School
Aurora, Colorado

Elizabeth Chait
W. L. Chenery Middle School
Belmont, Massachusetts

Holly Estes
Hale Middle School
Stow, Massachusetts

Laura Hapgood
Plymouth Community
Intermediate School
Plymouth, Massachusetts

Mary F. Lavin
Plymouth Community
Intermediate School
Plymouth, Massachusetts

James MacNeil, Ph.D.
Cambridge, Massachusetts

Lauren Magruder
St. Michael's Country
Day School
Newport, Rhode Island

Jeanne Maurand
Austin Preparatory School
Reading, Massachusetts

Joanne Jackson-Pelletier
Winman Junior High School
Warwick, Rhode Island

Warren Phillips
Plymouth Public Schools
Plymouth, Massachusetts

Carol Pirtle
Hale Middle School
Stow, Massachusetts

Kathleen M. Poe
Fletcher Middle School
Jacksonville, Florida

Cynthia B. Pope
Norfolk Public Schools
Norfolk, Virginia

Anne Scammell
Geneva Middle School
Geneva, New York

Karen Riley Sievers
Callanan Middle School
Des Moines, Iowa

David M. Smith
Eyer Middle School
Allentown, Pennsylvania

Gene Vitale
Parkland School
McHenry, Illinois

Contents

Human Biology and Health

Discovery
CHANNEL
SCHOOL
VIDEO
Fighting
Disease

Discovery
CHANNEL
SCHOOL
VIDEO
The Nervous
System

Discovery
CHANNEL
SCHOOL
VIDEO
The Endocrine
System and
Reproduction

Activities

VIDEO

Web Links

Enhance understanding through dynamic video.

Preview Get motivated with this introduction to the chapter content.

Field Trip Explore a real-world story related to the chapter content.

Assessment Review content and take an assessment.

Get connected to exciting Web resources in every lesson.

Find Web links on topics relating to every section.

Active Art Interact with selected visuals from every chapter online.

Planet Diary® Explore news and natural phenomena through weekly reports.

Science News® Keep up to date with the latest science discoveries.

Experience the complete text-book online and on CD-ROM.

Activities Practice skills and learn content.

Videos Explore content and learn important lab skills.

Audio Support Hear key terms spoken and defined.

Self-Assessment Use instant feedback to help you track your progress.

A Steely Athletic Trainer

"When I was young in Japan, I wanted to be a professional athlete," says National Football League athletic trainer Ariko Iso. "I was hoping to play sports forever." But all of that changed in one fateful moment on the basketball court. "I was playing junior high basketball, when I tore the anterior cruciate ligament (ACL) in my knee. I was 14."

"I was in the hospital for about seven weeks for recovery and rehabilitation. It was nearly a year before I played basketball again. I did play, but I was never the same as before. I was never as fast or as quick."

The experience changed Ariko's career plans. "I decided if I couldn't play sports, I would choose a profession where I could help athletes." Today, Ariko is the assistant athletic trainer for the Pittsburgh Steelers. Ariko is neither big nor tall, but she plays a vital role on the team. It's her job to help 200–300-pound athletes stay in the best condition possible. For Ariko, it's a dream job.

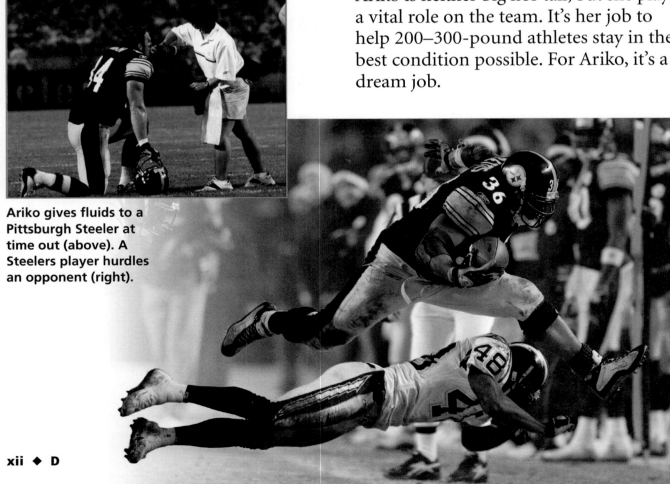

Ariko gives fluids to a Pittsburgh Steeler at time out (above). A Steelers player hurdles an opponent (right).

Ariko applies electric stimulation to a Pittsburgh Steelers's knee. The technology helps control swelling and reduce pain after surgery.

Career Path

Ariko Iso Ariko Iso grew up in Japan. She came to the United States to attend Oregon State University, where she received a bachelor's degree in Exercise and Sport Science. She earned a master's degree from San Jose State University in California. Ariko was an assistant athletic trainer for Portland State University in Oregon for six years. Currently, she is the assistant trainer for the NFL's Pittsburgh Steelers.

Talking With
Ariko Iso

? What brought you to the United States?

Twenty years ago in Japan, athletic training was fairly new. There was no four-year college degree in athletic training. Furthermore, the techniques are from the West. I wanted to learn the science. Also, I had always wanted to go to a new country and learn a new language. My parents told me they would support my going overseas. So I ended up at Oregon State University.

? What science courses should a trainer take?

First, you have to learn about the human body. Anatomy and physiology are key courses to our education. In anatomy class, I learned all the bones and muscles in the body. I also learned the other parts of the body. But to an athletic trainer, the bone and muscle structures are the most important.

I studied physiology to learn how the different parts of the body function. Later, I studied kinesiology, or body movement. Kinesiology involves physics as well as anatomy and physiology.

? Why is kinesiology important?

When you throw a ball, for instance, you want to know the most efficient way to do it. That means you need to know the best angle of the shoulder and which muscles move the shoulder in a throwing motion. You also need to know and understand the internal rotation of the shoulder. It's helpful to analyze each joint, its motion, and the muscles that make a movement happen. Then you know which muscles to train in order to improve that motion.

How did you get the job with the Steelers?

I started out at Portland State University in Oregon as the women's basketball assistant athletic trainer. Later, when I became the football athletic trainer, I attended an NFL football-injury conference. There I met the head athletic trainer for the Pittsburgh Steelers. He told me to apply to the Steelers' summer internship program for athletic trainers. I ended up working at the Steelers' training camp for two summers. Then in the spring of 2002, the Steelers called and asked if I would be interested in a full-time job.

In the Steelers' training center, Ariko monitors the recovery of injured players.

What do you do as an athletic trainer?

I do a little bit of everything. I will tape up ankles before a practice or a game. If someone needs help loosening up his muscles, I'll lend a hand. I make sure that the players drink plenty of fluids. If someone gets a small cut, I'll close it up. When someone is injured on the field, it's my job to evaluate the injury and to perform whatever emergency treatment is appropriate. I also need to be able to tell when to call for a doctor or other specialist.

Off the field, my duties include helping the athletes avoid injury. But if a player does get injured, I make sure that his rehabilitation goes as well as possible. An athlete recovering from an anterior cruciate ligament (ACL) injury, for instance, can take up to a year to be completely healthy. It's my job to monitor his progress and make sure he is doing everything he can to speed his recovery.

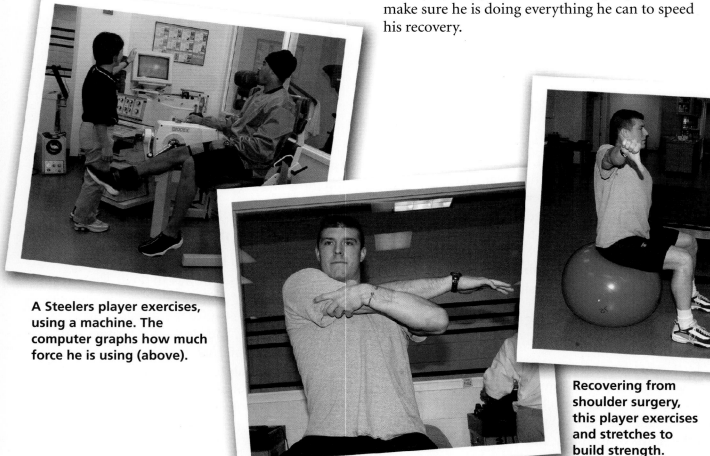

A Steelers player exercises, using a machine. The computer graphs how much force he is using (above).

Recovering from shoulder surgery, this player exercises and stretches to build strength.

What rehabilitation do you give for an ACL injury?

Tearing the anterior cruciate ligament is a big injury. If you sprain your ankle, there is usually no need to operate. But if you tear your anterior cruciate ligament in your knee, reconstruction is recommended. With my athletes, the focus during the first 24 to 48 hours after the surgery is on controlling the pain and swelling with compression and ice. As soon as the pain is bearable, the patient is expected to exercise to regain a range of motion in the knee. The player is walking with crutches within about three days and without crutches within two weeks.

The tissue needs a certain time to heal before beginning rehabilitation. I would probably start with really light weights as soon as the pain and swelling go down and then watch the knee carefully. You begin with no weight, work up to a five-pound weight, and increase the amount of weight from there.

What's the best part of your job?

I like working with athletes over a long time. I can tend to their aches and pains, monitor their training, and oversee their rehabilitation. It's a mentally challenging job, too. It demands a detailed knowledge of how the body works and how best to take care of it. I'd choose this job again!

This Steelers player is exercising with weights in the whirlpool.

Writing in Science

Career Path Ariko says that it's important for an athletic trainer to know the science of bone and muscle structures. Think of one simple motion that you use in an activity, such as walking, running, or swimming. In a paragraph, describe the bones and muscles you use and what you'd like to learn about improving your motion.

For: More on this career
Visit: PHSchool.com
Web Code: ceb-4000

Chapter 1

Bones, Muscles, and Skin

The BIG Idea
Structure and Function

 How do the systems of the human body work together?

Chapter Preview

No matter your age or ability level, ▶ playing sports is fun and healthful.

Lab zone™ Chapter **Project**

Design and Build a Hand Prosthesis

A prosthesis is an artificial device that replaces a human body part. Designing artificial replacements, such as prosthetic hands, can be a challenging task. This is because even a simple act, such as picking up a pen, involves a complex interaction of body parts.

Your Goal To design, build, and test a replacement for a human hand

Your prosthesis must

● grasp and lift a variety of objects
● be activated by pulling a cord or string
● spring back when the cord is released
● be built following the safety guidelines in Appendix A

Plan It! Before you design your prosthetic hand, study the human hand. Watch how the fingers move to pick up objects. Make a list of devices that mimic the ability of the hand to pick up objects. Examples include tongs, tweezers, pliers, and chopsticks. Then, choose materials for your hand and sketch your design. When your teacher has approved your design, build and test your prosthetic hand.

Body Organization and Homeostasis

Reading Preview

Key Concepts
- What are the levels of organization in the body?
- What is homeostasis?

Key Terms
- cell • cell membrane
- nucleus • cytoplasm
- tissue • muscle tissue
- nervous tissue
- connective tissue
- epithelial tissue
- organ • organ system
- homeostasis • stress

Target Reading Skill

Outlining An outline shows the relationship between main ideas and supporting ideas. As you read, make an outline about body organization and homeostasis. Use the red headings for the main ideas and the blue headings for the supporting ideas.

Body Organization and Homeostasis
I. Cells
A. Structures of cells
B.
II. Tissues

Discover Activity

How Does Your Body Respond?

1. Stack one book on top of another one.
2. Lift the two stacked books in front of you so the lowest book is about level with your shoulders. Hold the books in this position for 30 seconds. While you are performing this activity, note how your body responds. For example, how do your arms feel at the beginning and toward the end of the 30 seconds?
3. Balance one book on the top of your head. Walk a few steps with the book on your head.

Think It Over

Inferring List all the parts of your body that worked together as you performed the activities in Steps 1 through 3.

The bell rings—lunchtime! You hurry down the noisy halls to the cafeteria. The unmistakable aroma of hot pizza makes your mouth water. At last, you balance your tray of pizza and salad while you pay the cashier. You look around the cafeteria for your friends. Then, you walk to the table, sit down, and begin to eat.

Think about how many parts of your body were involved in the simple act of getting and eating your lunch. Every minute of the day, whether you are eating, studying, walking, or even sleeping, your body is busily at work. Each part of the body has a specific job to do. And all the different parts of your body usually work together so smoothly that you don't even notice them.

This smooth functioning is due partly to the way in which the body is organized. **The levels of organization in the human body consist of cells, tissues, organs, and organ systems.** The smallest unit of organization is the cell. The next largest unit is tissue; then, organs. Finally, the organ system is the largest unit of organization.

Cells

A **cell** is the basic unit of structure and function in a living thing. Complex organisms are composed of many cells in the same way a brick building is composed of many bricks. The human body contains about 100 trillion cells. Cells are quite tiny, and most cannot be seen without a microscope.

Structures of Cells Most animal cells, including those in the human body, have a structure similar to the cell in Figure 1. The **cell membrane** forms the outside boundary of the cell. Inside the cell membrane is a large structure called the nucleus. The **nucleus** is the control center that directs the cell's activities and contains the information that determines the cell's form and function. When the cell divides, or reproduces, this information is passed along to the newly formed cells. The material within a cell apart from the nucleus is called the **cytoplasm** (SYT uh plaz um). The cytoplasm is made of a clear, jellylike substance containing many cell structures called organelles.

Functions of Cells Cells carry on the processes that keep organisms alive. Inside cells, for example, molecules from digested food undergo chemical reactions that release energy for the body's activities. Cells also grow and reproduce. And they get rid of waste products that result from these activities.

 **Reading Checkpoint** **What is the function of the nucleus?**

Lab zone Try This **Activity**

How Is a Book Organized?

In this activity, you will analyze the levels of organization in a book.

1. Examine this textbook to see how it is subdivided— into chapters, sections, and so on.
2. Make a concept map that shows this pattern of organization. Place the largest subdivision at the top of the map and the smallest at the bottom.
3. Compare the levels of organization in this textbook to those in the human body.

Making Models Which level of organization in the textbook represents cells? Which represents tissues? Organs? Organ systems?

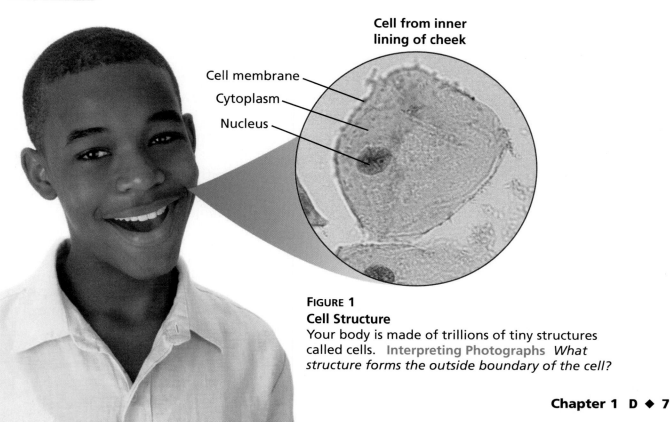

Cell from inner lining of cheek

Cell membrane
Cytoplasm
Nucleus

FIGURE 1
Cell Structure
Your body is made of trillions of tiny structures called cells. **Interpreting Photographs** *What structure forms the outside boundary of the cell?*

FIGURE 2
Types of Tissues

Your body contains four kinds of tissues: muscle, nervous, connective, and epithelial.

Comparing and Contrasting *How is the function of nervous tissue different from that of epithelial tissue?*

Muscle Tissue
Every movement you make depends on muscle tissue. The muscle tissue shown here allows your body to move.

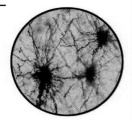

Nervous Tissue
Nervous tissue, such as the brain cells shown here, enables you to see, hear, and think.

Connective Tissue
Connective tissue, such as the bone shown here, connects and supports parts of your body.

Epithelial Tissue
Epithelial tissue, such as the skin cells shown here, covers the surfaces of your body and lines your internal organs.

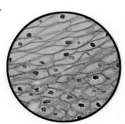

Tissues

The next largest unit of organization in your body is a tissue. A **tissue** is a group of similar cells that perform the same function. The human body contains four basic types of tissue: muscle tissue, nervous tissue, connective tissue, and epithelial tissue. To see examples of each of these tissues, look at Figure 2.

Like the muscle cells that form it, **muscle tissue** can contract, or shorten. By doing this, muscle tissue makes parts of your body move. While muscle tissue carries out movement, **nervous tissue** directs and controls the process. Nervous tissue carries electrical messages back and forth between the brain and other parts of the body. Another type of tissue, **connective tissue,** provides support for your body and connects all its parts. Bone tissue and fat are connective tissues.

The surfaces of your body, inside and out, are covered by **epithelial tissue** (ep uh THEE lee ul). Some epithelial tissue, such as your skin, protects the delicate structures that lie beneath it. The lining of your digestive system consists of epithelial tissue that allows you to digest and absorb the nutrients in your food.

 **Reading Checkpoint** **What is the job of muscle tissue?**

Organs and Organ Systems

Your stomach, heart, brain, and lungs are all organs. An **organ** is a structure that is composed of different kinds of tissue. Like a tissue, an organ performs a specific job. The job of an organ, however, is generally more complex than that of a tissue. The heart, for example, pumps blood throughout your body, over and over again. The heart contains all four kinds of tissue—muscle, nervous, connective, and epithelial. Each type of tissue contributes to the organ's overall job of pumping blood.

Each organ in your body is part of an **organ system,** which is a group of organs that work together to perform a major function. Your heart is part of your circulatory system, which carries oxygen and other materials throughout the body. Besides the heart, blood vessels are major structures in the circulatory system. Figure 3 shows some of the major organ systems in the human body.

FIGURE 3
Organ Systems

The human body is made up of eleven organ systems. Eight of the systems are shown here.

Interpreting Diagrams *Which two systems work together to get oxygen to your cells?*

Circulatory System
Transports materials to and from cells.

Skeletal System
Supports and protects the body.

Digestive System
Breaks down food and absorbs nutrients.

Nervous System
Detects information from the environment and controls body functions.

Endocrine System
Controls many body processes by means of chemicals.

Respiratory System
Takes in oxygen and eliminates carbon dioxide.

Muscular System
Enables movement of the body and internal organs.

Excretory System
Removes wastes.

Go Online

SC*i*LINKS™ NSTA

For: Links on body systems
Visit: www.SciLinks.org
Web Code: scn-0411

Homeostasis

The different organ systems work together and depend on one another. When you ride a bike, you use your muscular and skeletal systems to steer and push the pedals. But you also need your nervous system to direct your arms and legs to move. Your respiratory, digestive, and circulatory systems work together to fuel your muscles with the energy they need. And your excretory system removes the wastes produced while your muscles are hard at work.

All the systems of the body work together to maintain **homeostasis** (hoh mee oh STAY sis), the body's tendency to keep an internal balance. **Homeostasis is the process by which an organism's internal environment is kept stable in spite of changes in the external environment.**

Homeostasis in Action To see homeostasis in action, all you have to do is take your temperature when the air is cold. Then, take it again in an overheated room. No matter what the temperature of the air around you, your internal body temperature will be close to 37°C. Of course, if you become sick, your body temperature may rise. But when you are well again, it returns to 37°C.

Maintaining Homeostasis Your body has various ways of maintaining homeostasis. For example, when you are too warm, you sweat. Sweating helps to cool your body. On the other hand, when you are cold, you shiver. Shivering occurs when your muscles rapidly contract and relax. This action produces heat that helps keep you warm. Both of these processes help your body maintain homeostasis by regulating your temperature.

FIGURE 4
Maintaining Homeostasis
Regardless of the surrounding temperature, your body temperature remains fairly constant at about 37°C. Sweating (left) and shivering (right) help regulate your body temperature.
Applying Concepts *What is the term for the body's tendency to maintain a stable internal environment?*

Stress and Homeostasis Sometimes, things can happen to disrupt homeostasis. As a result, your heart may beat more rapidly or your breathing may increase. These reactions of your circulatory and respiratory systems are signs of stress. **Stress** is the reaction of your body to potentially threatening, challenging, or disturbing events.

Think about what happens when you leave the starting line in a bike race. As you pedal, your heart beats faster and your breathing increases. What is happening in your body? First, your endocrine system releases a chemical called adrenaline into your bloodstream. Adrenaline gives you a burst of energy and prepares your body to take action. As you pedal, your muscles work harder and require more oxygen. Oxygen is carried by the circulatory system, so your heart beats even faster to move more blood to your muscles. Your breath comes faster and faster, too, so that more oxygen can get into your body. Your body is experiencing stress.

If stress is over quickly, your body soon returns to its normal state. Think about the bike race again. After you cross the finish line, you continue to breathe hard for the next few minutes. Soon, however, your breathing and heart rate return to normal. The level of adrenaline in your blood returns to normal. Thus, homeostasis is restored after just a few minutes of rest.

FIGURE 5
Stress
Your body reacts to stress, such as the start of a bike race, by releasing adrenaline and carrying more oxygen to body cells.

 **Reading Checkpoint** **What is stress?**

Section 1 Assessment

Target Reading Skill Outlining Use the information in your outline to help you answer the questions below.

Reviewing Key Concepts

1. a. Identifying List the four levels of organization in the human body from smallest to largest. Give an example of each level.
   b. Comparing and Contrasting What is the difference between tissues and organs?
   c. Applying Concepts What systems of the body are involved when you prepare a sandwich and then eat it?

2. a. Defining What is homeostasis?
   b. Explaining How does stress affect homeostasis?
   c. Relating Cause and Effect Describe what happens inside your body as you give an oral report in front of your class.

Writing in Science

Summary Write a paragraph that explains what body systems are involved when you sit down to do your homework. Be sure to begin your paragraph with a topic sentence and include supporting details.

The Skeletal System

Reading Preview

Key Concepts
- What are the functions of the skeleton?
- What role do joints play in the body?
- What are the characteristics of bone, and how can you keep your bones strong and healthy?

Key Terms
- skeleton • vertebrae • joint
- ligament • cartilage
- compact bone • spongy bone
- marrow • osteoporosis

Target Reading Skill
Asking Questions Before you read, preview the red headings. In a graphic organizer like the one below, ask a *what* or *how* question for each heading. As you read, answer your questions.

The Skeletal System

Question	Answer
What does the skeleton do?	The skeletal system provides shape . . .

Lab zone Discover Activity

Hard as a Rock?
1. Your teacher will give you a rock and a leg bone from a cooked turkey or chicken.
2. Use a hand lens to examine both the rock and the bone.
3. Gently tap both the rock and the bone on a hard surface.
4. Pick up each object to feel how heavy it is.
5. Wash your hands. Then make notes of your observations.

Think It Over
Observing Based on your observations, why do you think bones are sometimes compared to rocks? List some ways in which bones and rocks are similar and different.

A high rise construction site is a busy place. After workers have prepared the building's foundation, they begin to assemble thousands of steel pieces into a frame for the building. People watch as the steel pieces are joined to create a rigid frame that climbs toward the sky. By the time the building is finished, however, the building's framework will no longer be visible.

Like a building, you also have an inner framework, but it isn't made up of steel. Your framework, or **skeleton,** is made up of all the bones in your body. The number of bones in your skeleton, or skeletal system, depends on your age. A newborn has about 275 bones. An adult, however, has about 206 bones. As a baby grows, some of the bones in the body fuse together. For example, as you grew, some of the bones in your skull fused together.

What the Skeletal System Does

Just as a building could not stand without its frame, you would collapse without your skeleton. **Your skeleton has five major functions. It provides shape and support, enables you to move, protects your organs, produces blood cells, and stores minerals and other materials until your body needs them.**

Shape and Support   Your skeleton determines the shape of your body, much as a steel frame determines the shape of a building. The backbone, or vertebral column, is the center of the skeleton. Locate the backbone in Figure 6. Notice that the bones in the skeleton are in some way connected to this column. If you move your fingers down the center of your back, you can feel the 26 small bones, or **vertebrae** (VUR tuh bray) (singular: *vertebra*), that make up your backbone. Bend forward at the waist and feel the bones adjust as you move. You can think of each individual vertebra as a bead on a string. Just as a beaded necklace is flexible and able to bend, so too is your vertebral column. If your backbone were just one bone, you would not be able to bend or twist.

Reading Checkpoint **Why is the vertebral column considered the center of the skeleton?**

FIGURE 6
The Skeleton
The skeleton provides a framework that supports and protects many other body parts. Comparing and Contrasting *In what ways is the skeleton like the steel framework of a building? In what ways is it different?*

Skull

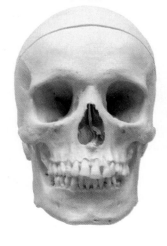

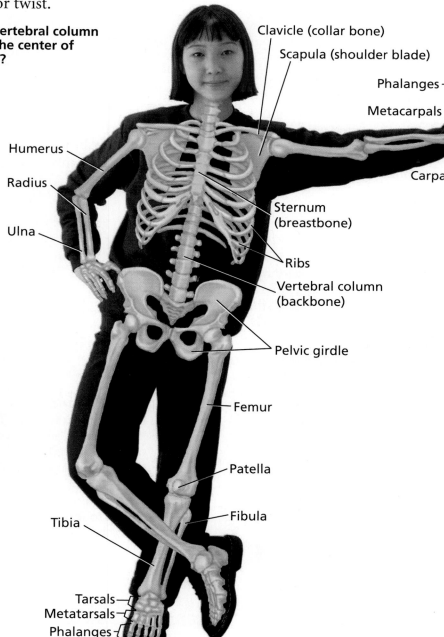

Clavicle (collar bone)

Scapula (shoulder blade)

Phalanges

Metacarpals

Humerus

Radius

Carpals

Ulna

Sternum (breastbone)

Ribs

Vertebral column (backbone)

Pelvic girdle

Femur

Patella

Fibula

Tibia

Tarsals

Metatarsals

Phalanges

Movement and Protection Your skeleton allows you to move. Most of the body's bones are associated with muscles. The muscles pull on the bones to make the body move. Bones also protect many of the organs in your body. For example, your skull protects your brain, and your breastbone and ribs form a protective cage around your heart and lungs.

Production and Storage of Substances Some of your bones produce substances that your body needs. You can think of the long bones of your arms and legs as factories that make certain blood cells. Bones also store minerals such as calcium and phosphorus. When the body needs these minerals, the bones release small amounts of them into the blood.

Joints of the Skeleton

Suppose that a single long bone ran the length of your leg. How would you get out of bed or run for the school bus? Luckily, your body contains many small bones rather than fewer large ones. A **joint** is a place in the body where two bones come together. **Joints allow bones to move in different ways.** There are two kinds of joints—immovable joints and movable joints.

Go Online
active art

For: Movable Joints activity
Visit: PHSchool.com
Web Code: cep-4012

FIGURE 7
Movable Joints

Without movable joints, your body would be as stiff as a board. The different kinds of joints allow your body to move in a variety of ways. Comparing and Contrasting *How is the movement of a hinge joint different from that of a ball-and-socket joint?*

Hinge Joint
A hinge joint allows forward or backward motion. Your knee is a hinge joint that allows you to bend and straighten your leg. Your elbow is also a hinge joint.

Ball-and-Socket Joint
Ball-and-socket joints allow the greatest range of motion. The ball-and-socket joint in your shoulder allows you to swing your arm freely in a circle. Your hips also have ball-and-socket joints.

Immovable Joints Some joints in the body connect bones in a way that allows little or no movement. These joints are called immovable joints. The bones of the skull are held together by immovable joints.

Movable Joints Most of the joints in the body are movable joints. Movable joints allow the body to make a wide range of movements. Look at Figure 7 to see the variety of movements that these joints make possible.

The bones in movable joints are held together by strong connective tissues called **ligaments.** Most joints have a second type of connective tissue, called **cartilage** (KAHR tuh lij), which is more flexible than bone. Cartilage covers the ends of the bones and keeps them from rubbing against each other. For example, in the knee, cartilage acts as a cushion that keeps your femur (thighbone) from rubbing against the bones of your lower leg. In addition, a fluid lubricates the ends of the bones, allowing them to move smoothly over each other.

 **Reading Checkpoint** How are movable joints held together?

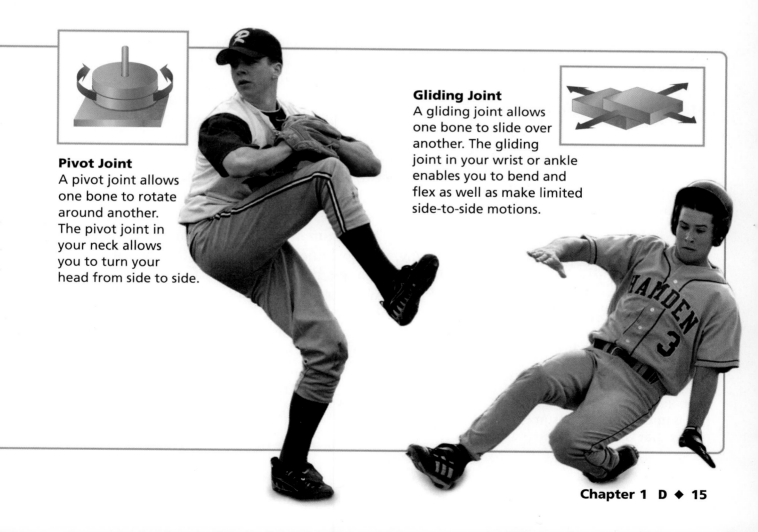

Pivot Joint
A pivot joint allows one bone to rotate around another. The pivot joint in your neck allows you to turn your head from side to side.

Gliding Joint
A gliding joint allows one bone to slide over another. The gliding joint in your wrist or ankle enables you to bend and flex as well as make limited side-to-side motions.

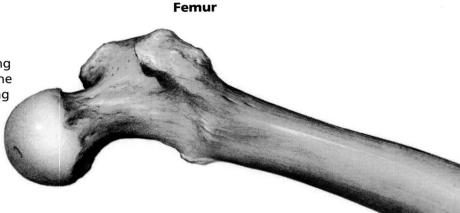

Femur

FIGURE 8

Bone Structure

The most obvious feature of a long bone, such as the femur, is its long shaft. Running through the compact bone tissue within the shaft is a system of canals. The canals bring materials to the living bone cells.

Interpreting Diagrams *What different tissues make up the femur?*

Try This Activity

Soft Bones?

In this activity, you will explore the role that calcium plays in bones.

1. Put on protective gloves. Soak one clean chicken bone in a jar filled with water. Soak a second clean chicken bone in a jar filled with vinegar. (Vinegar causes calcium to dissolve out of bone.)

2. After one week, put on protective gloves and remove the bones from the jars.

3. Compare how the two bones look and feel. Note any differences between the two bones.

Drawing Conclusions Based on your results, explain why it is important to consume a diet that is high in calcium.

Bones—Strong and Living

When you think of a skeleton, you may think of the paper cutouts that are used as decorations at Halloween. Many people connect skeletons with death. The ancient Greeks did, too. The word *skeleton* actually comes from a Greek word meaning "a dried body." The bones of your skeleton, however, are not dead at all. **Bones are complex living structures that undergo growth and development.**

Bone Structure Figure 8 shows the structure of the femur, or thighbone. The femur, which is the body's longest bone, connects the pelvic bones to the lower leg bones. Notice that a thin, tough membrane covers all of the bone except the ends. Blood vessels and nerves enter and leave the bone through the membrane. Beneath the bone's outer membrane is a layer of **compact bone,** which is hard and dense, but not solid. As you can see in Figure 8, small canals run through the compact bone. These canals carry blood vessels and nerves from the bone's surface to the living cells within the bone.

Just inside the femur's compact bone is a layer of spongy bone. Like a sponge, **spongy bone** has many small spaces within it. This structure makes spongy bone tissue lightweight but strong. Spongy bone is also found at the ends of the bone.

The spaces in many bones contain a soft, connective tissue called **marrow.** There are two types of marrow—red and yellow. Red bone marrow produces most of the body's blood cells. As a child, most of your bones contained red bone marrow. As a teenager, only the ends of your femurs, skull, hip bones, and sternum (breastbone) contain red marrow. Your other bones contain yellow marrow. This marrow stores fat that can serve as an energy reserve.

✓ **Reading Checkpoint** What are the two types of bone marrow?

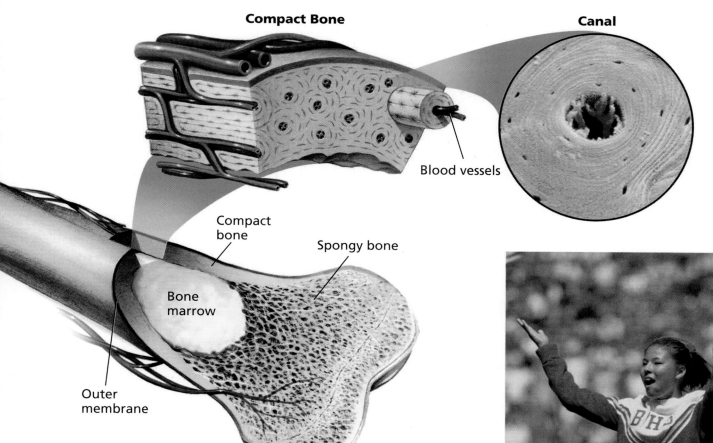

Compact Bone

Canal

Blood vessels

Compact bone

Spongy bone

Bone marrow

Outer membrane

Bone Strength The structure of bone makes it both strong and lightweight. In fact, bones are so strong that they can absorb more force without breaking than can concrete or granite rock. Yet, bones are much lighter than these materials. In fact, only about 20 percent of an average adult's body weight is bone.

Have you ever heard the phrase "as hard as a rock"? Most rock is hard because it is made up of minerals that are packed tightly together. In a similar way, bones are hard because they contain minerals—primarily phosphorus and calcium.

Bone Growth Bones are alive—they contain cells and tissues, such as blood and nerves. Because they are alive, bones also form new bone tissue as you grow. Even after you are grown, however, bone tissue continues to form within your bones. For example, every time you play soccer or basketball, some of your bones absorb the force of your weight. They respond by making new bone tissue.

Sometimes, new bone tissue forms after an accident. If you break a bone, for example, new bone tissue forms to fill the gap between the broken ends of the bone. In fact, the healed region of new bone may be stronger than the original bone!

FIGURE 9
Bone Strength
You can jump up and down or turn cartwheels without breaking bones.

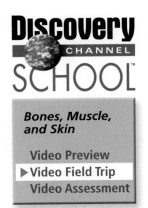

Discovery CHANNEL SCHOOL™

Bones, Muscle, and Skin

Video Preview
▶ Video Field Trip
Video Assessment

Bone Development Try this activity: Move the tip of your nose from side to side with your fingers. Notice that the tip of your nose is not stiff. That is because it contains cartilage. As an infant, much of your skeleton was cartilage. Over time, most of the cartilage was replaced with hard bone tissue.

The replacement of cartilage by bone tissue usually is complete by the time you stop growing. You've seen, however, that not all of your body's cartilage is replaced by bone. Even in adults, many joints contain cartilage that protects the ends of the bones.

Taking Care of Your Bones

Because your skeleton performs so many necessary functions, it is important to keep it healthy. **A combination of a balanced diet and regular exercise are important for a lifetime of healthy bones.**

Diet One way to help ensure healthy bones is to eat a well-balanced diet. A well-balanced diet includes enough calcium and phosphorus to keep your bones strong while they are growing. Meats, whole grains, and leafy green vegetables are all good sources of both calcium and phosphorus. Dairy products, including yogurt, are good sources of calcium.

Exercise Another way to build and maintain strong bones is to get plenty of exercise. During activities such as running, skating, or dancing, your bones support the weight of your entire body. These weight-bearing activities help your bones grow stronger and denser. To prevent injuries while exercising, be sure to wear appropriate safety equipment, such as a helmet and pads.

 **Reading Checkpoint** **What are two ways to keep your bones healthy?**

FIGURE 10
Caring for Your Bones
Exercising regularly and eating a balanced diet help to keep your bones strong and healthy.

Healthy Bone
Bone with Osteoporosis

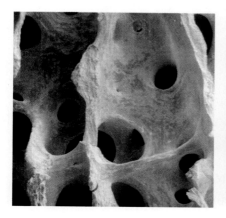
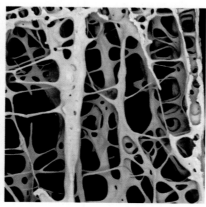

FIGURE 11
Osteoporosis
Without enough calcium in the diet, a person's bones weaken. These photos show how osteoporosis causes the bones to become less dense and more fragile than healthy bones.
Relating Cause and Effect *What can you do to prevent osteoporosis?*

Osteoporosis As people become older, their bones begin to lose some of the minerals they contain. Mineral loss can lead to **osteoporosis** (ahs tee oh puh ROH sis), a condition in which the body's bones become weak and break easily. These breaks, called fractures, can affect any bone in the body but occur most frequently in the hip, spine, and wrist. You can see the effect of osteoporosis in Figure 11. Osteoporosis is more common in women than in men. Evidence indicates that regular exercise throughout life can help prevent osteoporosis. A diet with enough calcium can also help prevent osteoporosis. If you eat enough calcium-rich foods now, during your teenage years, you may help prevent osteoporosis later in life.

Section 2 Assessment

Target Reading Skill Asking Questions Work with a partner to check the answers in your graphic organizer.

Reviewing Key Concepts

1. a. Listing What are five functions of the skeleton?
   b. Explaining How does the skeleton protect the body?
   c. Predicting How would your life be different if your backbone consisted of just one long bone?
2. a. Naming What are four types of movable joints?
   b. Comparing and Contrasting Compare immovable joints with movable joints.
   c. Classifying Which of your movable joints are ball-and-socket joints?
3. a. Describing Describe the structure of the femur.
   b. Relating Cause and Effect How does the structure of bones make them both strong and lightweight?
   c. Applying Concepts How do a well-balanced diet and weight-bearing exercise help keep bones strong?

Lab zone **At-Home Activity**

Model Joints Choose two examples of movable joints from Figure 7. Ask a family member to perform separate movements that involve one joint and then the other. Make drawings to represent the joints and bones involved in each movement. Use the drawings to explain to your family how the motions of the two joints differ.

Diagnosing Bone and Joint Injuries

Reading Preview

Key Concepts
- What are some injuries of the skeletal system, and how can they be identified?
- How can bone and joint injuries be treated?

Key Terms
- fracture • dislocation
- sprain • X-ray
- magnetic resonance imaging
- arthritis • arthroscope

Target Reading Skill
Comparing and Contrasting
When you compare and contrast things, you explain how they are alike and different. As you read, compare and contrast X-rays and MRIs by completing a table like the one below.

Procedure	X-Rays	MRI
Effect on body cells		
Types of injuries identified		

Lab zone Discover **Activity**

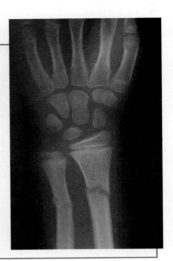

What Do X-ray Images Show?
1. Examine the photo of an X-ray image.
2. Try to identify what part of the human body the X-ray shows.
3. Locate the break in a bone.

Think It Over
Observing What types of structures are seen clearly in the X-ray? What types of structures cannot be seen?

You're walking home from school on a winter day. It's cold outside, and the ground is icy. Suddenly, you slip. As you lose your balance, you put out your arms to break your fall. The next thing you know, you're on the ground. Your hands sting, and you notice they are scraped. One wrist is starting to swell, and it hurts! If you try to move your wrist, it hurts even more. You need to get to a doctor—and fast.

Common Skeletal System Injuries

On the way to the doctor, you might be wondering, "Is my wrist broken?" Your swollen wrist could be broken, or it could be injured in some other way. **Three common skeletal system injuries are fractures, dislocations, and sprains.**

Fracture A **fracture,** or a break in a bone, can occur when you fall in such a way that all of your weight is placed on only a few bones. There are two kinds of fractures—simple and compound. In a simple fracture, the bone may be cracked or completely broken into two or more pieces. In a compound fracture, the broken ends of the bone stick out through the skin.

Dislocation A second injury of the skeletal system is a dislocation. A **dislocation** occurs when the end of a bone comes out of its joint. Sometimes a doctor can put back a dislocated bone without surgery. Other times surgery is needed.

Sprain A **sprain** occurs when ligaments are stretched too far and tear in places. If you have ever stumbled and turned an ankle, you may have felt a sharp pain. The pain probably occurred because the ligaments on the outside of your ankle stretched too far and partially tore. Sprains, especially of the ankle, are the most common joint injuries. Both sprains and fractures can cause swelling around the injured area.

 **Reading Checkpoint** What is the difference between a simple fracture and a compound fracture?

Go Online
SciLINKS NSTA

For: Links on medical technology
Visit: www.SciLinks.org
Web Code: scn-0413

Identifying Injuries

When you see the doctor, she looks at your wrist and decides she needs to look inside your wrist to determine what's wrong. **Two ways to identify injuries of the skeletal system are X-rays and magnetic resonance imaging.**

X-rays X-ray images can determine whether bones have been broken. **X-rays** are a form of energy that travels in waves, like the light that your eyes can see.

Before an X-ray image is taken, a lead apron is placed on your body to protect you from unnecessary exposure to X-rays. Photographic film is placed under the area to be viewed. Then, a machine that emits a beam of X-rays is aimed at the area. The X-rays pass through soft tissue but not through bone. The X-rays absorbed by the bone do not reach the film. After the film is developed, it shows bones as clearly defined white areas.

One limitation of X-rays is that they cannot be used directly to view injuries to soft tissues, such as muscle and internal organs. In addition, the energy in X-rays can damage your body cells. This is why you should not have unnecessary X-ray images taken.

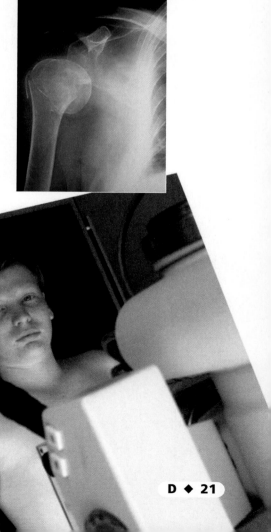

FIGURE 12
X-ray Diagnosis
X-rays can be used to determine whether or not you have broken a bone or dislocated a joint. Applying Concepts *What are some limitations of X-rays?*

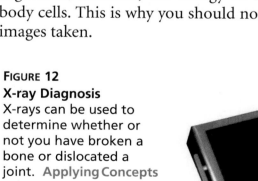

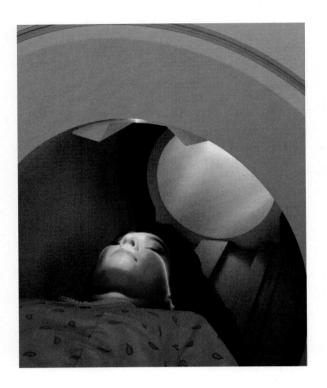

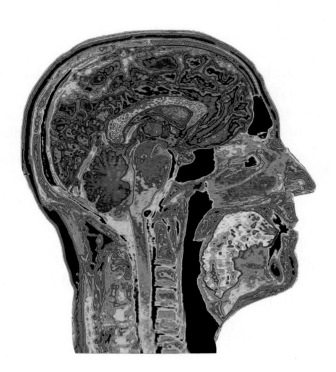

Magnetic Resonance Imaging A method for taking clear images of both the bones and soft tissues of the body is called **magnetic resonance imaging,** or MRI. An MRI scanner is a large machine that contains electromagnets. The person is placed on a platform that is inside the field of the magnet. The person is then exposed to short bursts of magnetic energy. This magnetic energy causes atoms within the body to vibrate, or resonate. A computer then analyzes the vibration patterns and produces an image of the area.

MRI images are amazingly sharp and clear. MRI can produce images of body tissues at any angle. In addition, MRI can show a clear image of muscles and other soft tissues that an X-ray image cannot show. Another advantage of MRI is that there is no evidence that it can damage cells. Because MRI machines are very expensive to buy and use, this technique is not commonly used to identify possible broken bones.

 **What is one advantage that MRI has over an X-ray?**

Treating Injuries

The doctor determines that your wrist is broken and puts a cast on it. You must wear the cast for six weeks until the bone heals. **In addition to wearing a cast, two other ways to treat skeletal system injuries include surgical procedures such as joint replacement and arthroscopy.**

Joint Replacement Not all injuries to the skeleton involve broken bones. Sometimes, the joints are injured or diseased and require treatment. This is often true for people who have arthritis. **Arthritis** is a disease of the joints that makes movement painful. When movement becomes extremely painful or impossible, the joint may need to be replaced with an artificial one made of metals or plastics. Doctors can replace knees, hips, shoulders, fingers, and wrists. During surgery, the natural joint is removed and an artificial one is cemented in its place.

Arthroscopy Joint injuries can also be treated by arthroscopic surgery. Doctors make a small incision and insert a slim, tube-shaped instrument called an **arthroscope** (AHR thruh skohp) into the joint. Attached to the arthroscope is a camera that projects the image from inside the joint onto a monitor. This allows doctors to look inside the joint to see what is wrong. After the problem is diagnosed, tiny instruments are inserted through one or more additional small incisions to make the necessary repairs. The arthroscope has helped to diagnose and repair many joint problems.

 **Reading Checkpoint**) **What is arthritis?**

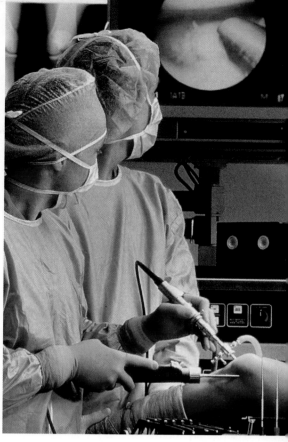

FIGURE 14
Arthroscopic Surgery
To diagnose and treat a knee injury, this surgeon has inserted an arthroscope into the patient's knee.

Section 3 Assessment

Target Reading Skill Comparing and Contrasting Use the information in your table about X-rays and MRI to help you answer Question 1 below.

Reviewing Key Concepts

1. a. Listing What are three common skeletal system injuries?
   b. Comparing and Contrasting How might each of the different skeletal system injuries be diagnosed?
   c. Applying Concepts Suppose that an X-ray of your injured wrist did not show a fracture. But, after a month, your wrist is still painful and stiff. Why might your doctor order an MRI?

2. a. Identifying What are two ways to treat bone and joint injuries surgically?
   b. Summarizing Which joints can be replaced surgically and how is it done?
   c. Making Judgments How has arthroscopic surgery improved the methods for treating skeletal injuries?

Lab zone **At-Home Activity**

Safety First List the types of exercise you and your family members do. With your family, brainstorm a list of safety gear and precautions to use for each activity in order to prevent skeletal system injuries. (For example, for bicycling, you might list wearing a helmet, stretching before riding, and avoiding busy streets and nighttime riding.) How can you put these safety measures into practice?

The Muscular System

Reading Preview

Key Concepts
• What types of muscles are found in the body?
• Why do skeletal muscles work in pairs?

Key Terms
• involuntary muscle
• voluntary muscle
• skeletal muscle
• tendon
• striated muscle
• smooth muscle
• cardiac muscle

Target Reading Skill

Previewing Visuals When you preview, you look ahead at the material to be read. Preview Figure 15. Then, in a graphic organizer like the one below, write two questions that you have about the diagram. As you read, answer your questions.

Types of Muscle

Q.	How does skeletal muscle help my body move?
A.	
Q.	

Lab zone · Discover **Activity**

How Do Muscles Work?

1. Grip a spring-type clothespin with the thumb and index finger of your writing hand. Squeeze the clothespin open and shut as quickly as possible for two minutes. Count how many times you can squeeze the clothespin before your muscles tire.
2. Rest for one minute. Then, repeat Step 1.

Think It Over
Predicting What do you think would happen if you repeated Steps 1 and 2 with your other hand? Give a reason for your prediction. Then, test your prediction.

A rabbit becomes still when it senses danger. The rabbit sits so still that it doesn't seem to move a muscle. Could you sit without moving any muscles? Saliva builds up in your mouth. You swallow. You need to breathe. Your chest expands to let air in. All of these actions involve muscles. It is impossible to sit absolutely still without muscle movement.

There are about 600 muscles in your body. Muscles have many functions. For example, they keep your heart beating, pull your mouth into a smile, and move the bones of your skeleton. The girl doing karate on the next page uses many of her muscles to move her arms, legs, hands, feet, and head. Other muscles expand and contract her chest and allow her to breathe.

Types of Muscle

Some of your body's movements, such as smiling, are easy to control. Other movements, such as the beating of your heart, are impossible to control completely. That is because some of your muscles are not under your conscious control. Those muscles are called **involuntary muscles.** Involuntary muscles are responsible for such essential activities as breathing and digesting food.

The muscles that are under your conscious control are called **voluntary muscles.** Smiling, turning a page in a book, and getting out of your chair when the bell rings are all actions controlled by voluntary muscles.

Your body has three types of muscle tissue—skeletal muscle, smooth muscle, and cardiac muscle. Some of these muscle tissues are involuntary, and some are voluntary. In Figure 15, you see a magnified view of each type of muscle in the body. Both skeletal and smooth muscles are found in many places in the body. Cardiac muscle is found only in the heart. Each muscle type performs specific functions in the body.

FIGURE 15
Types of Muscle
Your body has three types of muscle tissue: skeletal muscle, smooth muscle, and cardiac muscle. **Classifying** *Which type of muscle is found only in the heart?*

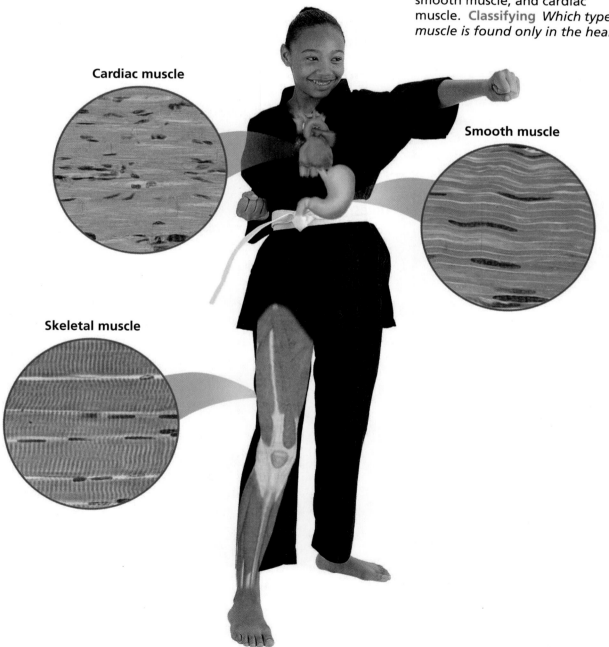

Cardiac muscle

Smooth muscle

Skeletal muscle

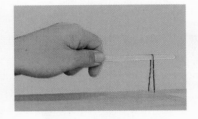

Get a Grip

Are skeletal muscles at work when you're not moving?

1. Hold a stirrer in front of you, parallel to a table top. Do not touch the table.
2. Have a partner place a hairpin on the stirrer.
3. Raise the stirrer until the "legs" of the hairpin just touch the table. The "head" of the hairpin should rest on the stirrer.
4. Hold the stirrer steady for 20 seconds. Observe what happens to the hairpin.
5. Grip the stirrer tighter and repeat Step 4. Observe.

Try This Activity

Inferring Are the skeletal muscles in your hand at work when you hold your hand still? Explain.

Skeletal Muscle Every time you walk across a room, you are using skeletal muscles. **Skeletal muscles** are attached to the bones of your skeleton and provide the force that moves your bones. At each end of a skeletal muscle is a tendon. A **tendon** is a strong connective tissue that attaches muscle to bone. Skeletal muscle cells appear banded, or striated. For this reason, skeletal muscle is sometimes called **striated** (STRY ay tid) **muscle.**

Because you have conscious control of skeletal muscles, they are classified as voluntary muscles. One characteristic of skeletal muscles is that they react very quickly. Think about what happens during a swim meet. Immediately after the starting gun sounds, a swimmer's leg muscles push the swimmer off the block into the pool. However, another characteristic of skeletal muscles is that they tire quickly. By the end of the race, the swimmer's muscles are tired and need a rest.

Smooth Muscle The inside of many internal organs, such as the stomach and blood vessels, contain **smooth muscles.** Smooth muscles are involuntary muscles. They work automatically to control certain movements inside your body, such as those involved in digestion. For example, as the smooth muscles of your stomach contract, they produce a churning action. The churning mixes the food with chemicals, and helps to digest the food.

Unlike skeletal muscles, smooth muscle cells are not striated. Smooth muscles behave differently than skeletal muscles, too. Smooth muscles react more slowly and tire more slowly.

Reading Checkpoint Where is smooth muscle found?

Cardiac Muscle The tissue called **cardiac muscle** is found only in your heart. Cardiac muscle has some characteristics in common with both smooth muscle and skeletal muscle. Like smooth muscle, cardiac muscle is involuntary. Like skeletal muscle, cardiac muscle cells are striated. However, unlike skeletal muscle, cardiac muscle does not get tired. It can contract repeatedly. You call those repeated contractions heartbeats.

Muscles at Work

Has anyone ever asked you to "make a muscle"? If so, you probably tightened your fist, bent your arm at the elbow, and made the muscles in your upper arm bulge. Like other skeletal muscles, the muscles in your arm do their work by contracting, becoming shorter and thicker. Muscle cells contract when they receive messages from the nervous system. **Because muscle cells can only contract, not extend, skeletal muscles must work in pairs. While one muscle contracts, the other muscle in the pair relaxes to its original length.**

Muscles Work in Pairs Figure 16 shows the muscle action involved in bending the arm at the elbow. First, the biceps muscle on the front of the upper arm contracts to bend the elbow, lifting the forearm and hand. As the biceps contracts, the triceps on the back of the upper arm relaxes and returns to its original length. Then, to straighten the elbow, the triceps muscle contracts. As the triceps contracts to extend the arm, the biceps relaxes and returns to its original length. Another example of muscles that work in pairs are those in your thigh that bend and straighten the knee joint.

Go Online
PHSchool.com

For: More on muscle types
Visit: PHSchool.com
Web Code: ced-4014

FIGURE 16
Muscle Pairs

Because muscles can only contract, or shorten, they must work in pairs. To bend the arm at the elbow, the biceps contracts while the triceps returns to its original length. **Interpreting Diagrams** *What happens to each muscle to straighten the arm?*

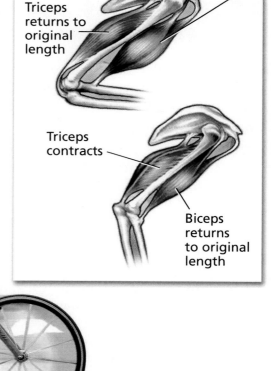

Triceps returns to original length

Biceps contracts

Triceps contracts

Biceps returns to original length

Muscular Strength and Flexibility Regular exercise is important for maintaining both muscular strength and flexibility. Exercise makes individual muscle cells grow in size. As a result, the whole muscle becomes thicker. The thicker a muscle is, the stronger the muscle is. When you warm up thoroughly before exercising, the blood flow to your muscles increases and they become more flexible. Stretching after you warm up helps prepare your muscles for the more vigorous exercise or play ahead.

Sometimes, despite taking proper precautions, muscles can become injured. A muscle strain, or pulled muscle, can occur when muscles are overworked or overstretched. Tendons can also be overstretched or partially torn. After a long period of exercise, a skeletal muscle can cramp. When a muscle cramps, the entire muscle contracts strongly and stays contracted. If you injure a muscle or tendon, it is important to follow medical instructions and to rest the injured area so it can heal.

FIGURE 17
Preventing Muscle Injuries
When you warm up before exercising, you increase the flexibility of your muscles.

✓ **Reading Checkpoint** What are two ways to prepare the muscles for exercise?

Section 4 Assessment

🎯 **Target Reading Skill** Previewing Visuals Refer to your questions and answers about Figure 15 to help you answer Question 1 below.

Reviewing Key Concepts

1. a. **Identifying** What are the three types of muscle tissue?
   b. **Comparing and Contrasting** How do voluntary and involuntary muscles differ? Give an example of each type of muscle.
   c. **Predicting** The muscles that move your fingers are attached to the bones in your fingers by tendons. Suppose one of the tendons in a person's index finger were cut. How would it affect movement in the finger?
2. a. **Identifying** Where might you find muscle pairs?
   b. **Describing** Describe how the muscles in your upper arm work together to bend and straighten your arm.
   c. **Applying Concepts** When exercising to build muscular strength, why is it important to exercise both muscles in a muscle pair equally?

Writing in Science

Comparison Paragraph Write a paragraph comparing smooth muscle tissue and skeletal muscle tissue. Include whether these muscle tissues are voluntary or involuntary, where they are found and what their functions are. In addition, describe what you might expect to see if you looked at these muscle tissues under a microscope.

A Look Beneath the Skin

Problem

What are some characteristics of skeletal muscles? How do skeletal muscles work?

Skills Focus

observing, inferring, classifying

Materials

- water
- paper towels
- scissors
- dissecting tray
- uncooked chicken wing, treated with bleach

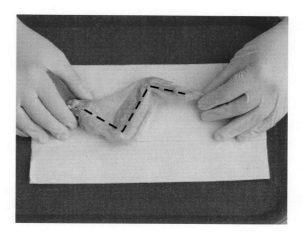

Procedure

1. Put on goggles, an apron, and protective gloves. **CAUTION:** *Wear gloves whenever you handle the chicken.*

2. Your teacher will give you a chicken wing. Rinse it well with water, dry it with paper towels, and place it in a dissecting tray.

3. Carefully extend the wing to find out how many major parts it has. Draw a diagram of the external structure. Label the upper arm, elbow, lower arm, and hand (wing tip).

4. Use scissors to remove the skin. Cut only through the skin. **CAUTION:** *Cut away from your body and your classmates.*

5. Examine the muscles, which are the bundles of pink tissue around the bones. Find the two groups of muscles in the upper arm. Hold the arm down at the shoulder, and alternately pull on each muscle group. Observe what happens.

6. Find the two groups of muscles in the lower arm. Hold down the arm at the elbow, and alternately pull on each muscle group. Then, make a diagram of the wing's muscles.

7. Find the tendons—shiny white tissue at the ends of the muscles. Notice what parts the tendons connect. Add the tendons to your diagram.

8. Remove the muscles and tendons. Find the ligaments, which are the whitish ribbon-shaped structures between bones. Add them to your diagram.

9. Dispose of the chicken parts according to your teacher's instructions. Wash your hands.

Analyze and Conclude

1. **Observing** How does a chicken wing move at the elbow? How does the motion compare to how your elbow moves? What type of joint is involved?

2. **Inferring** What happened when you pulled on one of the arm muscles? What muscle action does the pulling represent?

3. **Classifying** Categorize the muscles you observed as smooth, cardiac, or skeletal.

4. **Communicating** Why is it valuable to record your observations with accurate diagrams? Write a paragraph in which you describe what your diagrams show.

More to Explore

Use the procedures from this lab to examine an uncooked chicken thigh and leg. Compare how the chicken leg and a human leg move. *Obtain your teacher's permission before carrying out your investigation.*

The Skin

Reading Preview

Key Concepts
- What are the functions and the structures of skin?
- What habits can help keep your skin healthy?

Key Terms
- epidermis • melanin
- dermis • pore • follicle
- cancer

 Target Reading Skill

Identifying Main Ideas As you read the section titled The Body's Tough Covering, write the main idea—the biggest or most important idea—in a graphic organizer like the one below. Then, write five supporting details. The supporting details give examples of the main idea.

Main Idea

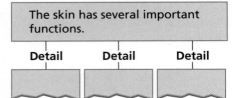

The skin has several important functions.

| Detail | Detail | Detail |

Discover **Activity**

What Can You Observe About Skin?

1. Using a hand lens, examine the skin on your hand. Look for pores and hairs on both the palm and back of your hand.
2. Place a plastic glove on your hand. After five minutes, remove the glove. Then, examine the skin on your hand with the hand lens.

Think It Over

Inferring Compare your hand before and after wearing the glove. What happened to the skin when you wore the glove? Why did this happen?

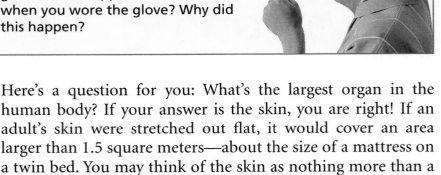

Here's a question for you: What's the largest organ in the human body? If your answer is the skin, you are right! If an adult's skin were stretched out flat, it would cover an area larger than 1.5 square meters—about the size of a mattress on a twin bed. You may think of the skin as nothing more than a covering that separates the inside of the body from the outside environment. If so, you'll be surprised to learn about the many important roles that the skin plays.

The Body's Tough Covering

The skin performs several major functions in the body. **The skin covers and protects the body from injury, infection, and water loss. The skin also helps regulate body temperature, eliminate wastes, gather information about the environment, and produce vitamin D.**

Protecting the Body The skin protects the body by forming a barrier that keeps disease-causing microorganisms and harmful substances outside the body. In addition, the skin helps keep important substances inside the body. Like plastic wrap that keeps food from drying out, the skin prevents the loss of important fluids such as water.

Maintaining Temperature Another function of the skin is to help the body maintain a steady temperature. Many blood vessels run throughout the skin. When you become too warm, these blood vessels enlarge and the amount of blood that flows through them increases. These changes allow heat to move from your body into the outside environment. In addition, sweat glands in the skin respond to excess heat by producing perspiration. As perspiration evaporates from your skin, your skin is cooled.

Eliminating Wastes Perspiration contains dissolved waste materials that come from the breakdown of chemicals during cellular processes. Thus, your skin is also helping to eliminate wastes whenever you perspire. For example, some of the wastes that come from the breakdown of proteins are eliminated in perspiration.

Gathering Information The skin also gathers information about the environment. To understand how the skin does this, place your fingertips on the skin of your arm and press down firmly. Then lightly pinch yourself. You have just tested some of the nerves in your skin. The nerves in skin provide information about such things as pressure, pain, and temperature. Pain messages are important because they warn you that something in your surroundings may have injured you.

Producing Vitamin D Lastly, some of the skin cells produce vitamin D in the presence of sunlight. Vitamin D is important for healthy bones because it helps the cells in your digestive system to absorb the calcium in your food. Your skin cells need only a few minutes of sunlight to produce all the vitamin D you need in a day.

 **Reading Checkpoint** How does your skin gather information about the environment?

FIGURE 18
Eliminating Wastes
Sweat glands in the skin produce perspiration, which leaves the body through pores. The inset photo shows beads of sweat on skin.
Relating Cause and Effect In addition to eliminating wastes, what is another important function of perspiration?

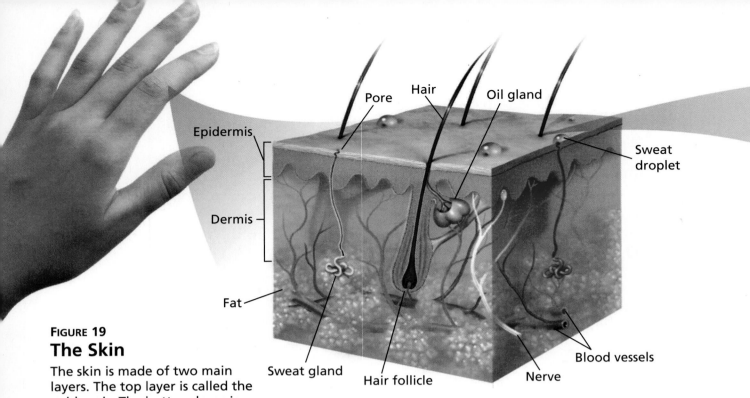

Pore Hair Oil gland

Epidermis

Sweat droplet

Dermis

Fat

Sweat gland

Hair follicle

Nerve

Blood vessels

FIGURE 19
The Skin

The skin is made of two main layers. The top layer is called the epidermis. The bottom layer is called the dermis.

Interpreting Diagrams *In which layer of the skin do you find blood vessels?*

The Epidermis

The skin is organized into two main layers, the epidermis and the dermis. The **epidermis** is the outer layer of the skin. In most places, the epidermis is thinner than the dermis. The epidermis does not have nerves or blood vessels. This is why you usually don't feel pain from very shallow scratches, and why shallow scratches do not bleed.

Epidermis Structure Like all cells, the cells in the epidermis have a life cycle. Each epidermal cell begins life deep in the epidermis, where cells divide to form new cells. The new cells mature and move upward in the epidermis as new cells form beneath them. After about two weeks, the cells die and become part of the epidermal surface layer. Under a microscope, this surface layer of dead cells resembles flat bags laid on top of one another. Cells remain in this layer for about two weeks. Then, they are shed and replaced by the dead cells below.

Epidermis Function In some ways, the cells of the epidermis are more valuable dead than alive. Most of the protection provided by the skin is due to the layer of dead cells on the surface. The thick layer of dead cells on your fingertips, for example, protects and cushions your fingertips. Also, the shedding of dead cells carries away bacteria and other substances that settle on the skin. Every time you rub your hands together, you lose thousands of dead skin cells and any bacteria on them.

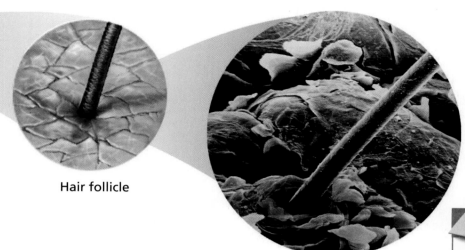

Hair follicle

Some cells in the inner layer of the epidermis help to protect the body, too. On your fingers, for example, some cells produce hard fingernails, which protect the fingertips from injury and help you scratch and pick up objects.

Other cells deep in the epidermis produce **melanin,** a pigment, or colored substance, that gives skin its color. The more melanin in your skin, the darker it is. Exposure to sunlight stimulates the skin to make more melanin. Melanin production helps to protect the skin from burning.

The Dermis

The **dermis** is the inner layer of the skin. Find the dermis in Figure 19. Notice that it is located below the epidermis and above a layer of fat. This fat layer pads the internal organs and helps keep heat in the body.

The dermis contains nerves and blood vessels. The dermis also contains sweat glands, hairs, and oil glands. Sweat glands produce perspiration, which reaches the surface through openings called **pores.** Strands of hair grow within the dermis in structures called **follicles** (FAHL ih kulz). The hair that you see above the skin's surface is made up of dead cells. Oil produced in glands around the hair follicles help to waterproof the hair. In addition, oil that reaches the surface of the skin helps to keep the skin moist.

 **Reading Checkpoint** **What is the function of pores in the skin?**

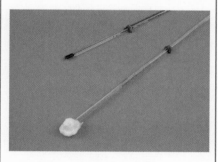

Sunscreen Ratings

The graph shows how sunscreens with different sun protection factor (SPF) ratings extend the time three people can stay in the sun without beginning to get a sunburn.

1. **Reading Graphs** What does the height of each bar in the graph represent?

2. **Interpreting Data** How long can Person B stay in the sun without sunscreen before starting to burn? With a sunscreen of SPF 4? SPF 15?

3. **Inferring** Suppose that Person C was planning to attend an all-day picnic. Which sunscreen should Person C apply? Use data to support your answer.

4. **Calculating** Which is more effective at preventing sunburn—a sunscreen with SPF 4 or one with SPF 15? How much more effective is it? Show your work.

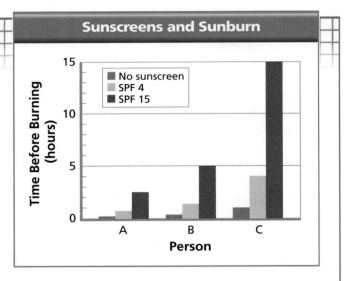

Sunscreens and Sunburn

5. **Drawing Conclusions** What does the number in the SPF rating stand for? *(Hint: Note the length of time each person can stay in the sun without sunscreen and compare this value to the length of time each can stay in the sun using SPF 4. Then, do the same for SPF 15.)*

Caring for Your Skin

Because your skin has so many vital functions, taking care of it is important. **Three simple habits can help you keep your skin healthy. Eat a healthful diet. Keep your skin clean and dry. Limit your exposure to the sun.**

Healthful Diet Your skin is always active. Eating a well-balanced diet provides the energy and raw materials needed for the growth and replacement of hair, nails, and skin cells. In addition to what you eat, a healthful diet also includes drinking plenty of water. That way, you can replace the water lost in perspiration.

Keeping Skin Clean When you wash your skin with mild soap, you get rid of dirt and harmful bacteria. Washing your skin also helps to control oiliness.

Good washing habits are particularly important during the teenage years when oil glands are more active. When glands become clogged with oil, the blackheads and whiteheads of acne can form. If acne becomes infected by skin bacteria, your doctor may prescribe an antibiotic to help control the infection.

Go Online
SciLINKS NSTA

For: Links on the skin
Visit: www.SciLinks.org
Web Code: scn-0415

Limiting Sun Exposure It is important to protect your skin from the harmful effects of the sun. Repeated exposure to sunlight can damage skin cells, and possibly lead to skin cancer. **Cancer** is a disease in which some cells in the body divide uncontrollably. In addition, repeated exposure to the sun can cause the skin to become leathery and wrinkled.

There are many things you can do to protect your skin from damage by the sun. When you are outdoors, always wear a hat, sunglasses, and use a sunscreen on exposed skin. Choose clothing made of tightly woven fabrics for the greatest protection. In addition, avoid exposure to the sun between the hours of 10 A.M. and 4 P.M. That is the time when sunlight is the strongest.

 **Reading Checkpoint** What health problems can result from repeated sun exposure?

FIGURE 20
Skin Protection
This person is wearing a hat to protect his skin from the sun.
Applying Concepts *What other behaviors can provide protection from the sun?*

Section 5 Assessment

Target Reading Skill Identifying Main Ideas Use your graphic organizer to help you answer Question 1 below.

Reviewing Key Concepts

1. **a.** Listing What are five important functions of the skin?
   b. Identifying How does the epidermis protect the body? What structure in the dermis helps to maintain body temperature?
   c. Inferring What could happen if the pores in your dermis become blocked?
2. **a.** Identifying What are three things you can do to keep your skin healthy?
   b. Explaining Why is it important to use sunscreen to protect your skin when outside?
   c. Making Judgments Do you think it is possible to wash your skin too much and damage it as a result? Why or why not?

Lab zone At-Home **Activity**

Protection From the Sun With a family member, look for products in your home that provide protection from the sun. You may also want to visit a store that sells these products. Make a list of the products and place them in categories, such as sunblocks, clothing, eye protectors, and other forms of protection. Explain to your family member why it is important to use such products.

Sun Safety

Problem

How well do different materials protect the skin from the sun?

Skills Focus

observing, predicting, interpreting data, drawing conclusions

Materials

- scissors
- photosensitive paper
- metric ruler
- white construction paper
- stapler
- pencil
- resealable plastic bag
- plastic knife
- 2 sunscreens with SPF ratings of 4 and 30
- staple remover
- 3 different fabrics

Procedure

PART 1 Sunscreen Protection

1. Read over the procedure for Part 1. Then, write a prediction about how well each of the sunscreens will protect against the sun.

2. Use scissors to cut two strips of photosensitive paper that measure 5 cm by 15 cm.

3. Divide each strip into thirds by drawing lines across the strips.

4. Cover one third of each strip with a square of white construction paper. Staple each square down.

5. Use a pencil to write the lower SPF rating on the back of the first strip. Write the other SPF rating on the back of the second strip.

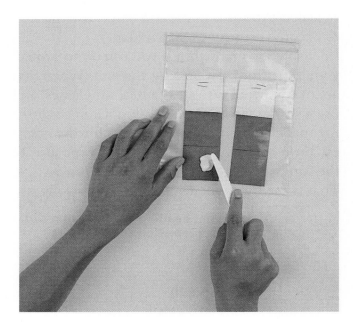

6. Place the two strips side by side in a plastic bag. Seal the bag, then staple through the white squares to hold the strips in place.

7. With a plastic knife, spread a thin layer of each sunscreen on the bag over the bottom square of its labeled strip. This is shown in the photo above. Make certain each strip has the same thickness of sunscreen. Be sure not to spread sunscreen over the middle squares.

8. Place the strips in sunlight until the color of the middle squares stops changing. Make sure the bag is sunscreen-side up when you place it in the sunlight.

9. Remove the staples from the bag, and then take out the strips. Take off the construction paper. Rinse the strips for one minute in cold water, then dry them flat.

10. Observe all the squares. Then, record your observations.

PART 2 Fabric Protection

11. Your teacher will provide three fabric pieces of different thicknesses.

12. Based on the procedure in Part 1, design an experiment to test how effective the three fabrics are in protecting against the sun. Write a prediction about which fabric you think will be most effective, next most effective, and least effective.

13. Obtain your teacher's approval before carrying out your experiment. Record all of your observations.

Analyze and Conclude

1. **Observing** Did the sunscreens protect against sun exposure? How do you know?

2. **Predicting** Which sunscreen provided more protection? Was your prediction correct? How would you predict a sunscreen with an SPF of 15 would compare to the sunscreens you tested?

3. **Interpreting Data** Did the fabrics protect against sun exposure? How do you know?

4. **Drawing Conclusions** Which of the fabrics provided the most protection? The least protection? How did your results compare with your predictions?

5. **Communicating** What advice would you give people about protecting their skin from the sun? Create a pamphlet in which you address this question by comparing the different sunscreens and fabrics you tested.

More to Explore

Design another experiment, this time to find out whether ordinary window glass protects skin against sun exposure. *Obtain your teacher's permission before carrying out your investigation.*

Study Guide

The **BIG Idea**   **Structure and Function** The human body is composed of eleven organ systems that work together to carry out life processes and maintain homeostasis.

① Body Organization and Homeostasis

Key Concepts

- The levels of organization in the body consist of cells, tissues, organs, and organ systems.
- Homeostasis is the process by which an organism's internal environment is kept stable in spite of changes in the external environment.

Key Terms

- cell • cell membrane • nucleus • cytoplasm
- tissue • muscle tissue • nervous tissue
- connective tissue • epithelial tissue • organ
- organ system • homeostasis • stress

② The Skeletal System

Key Concepts

- Your skeleton provides shape and support, enables you to move, protects your organs, produces blood cells, and stores minerals and other materials until your body needs them.
- Joints allow bones to move in different ways.
- Bones are complex living structures that undergo growth and development.
- A balanced diet and regular exercise are important for a lifetime of healthy bones.

Key Terms

skeleton
vertebrae
joint
ligament
cartilage
compact bone
spongy bone
marrow
osteoporosis

③ Diagnosing Bone and Joint Injuries

Key Concepts

- Three common skeletal system injuries are fractures, dislocations, and sprains. Two ways to identify skeletal injuries are X-rays and magnetic resonance imaging (MRI).
- Ways to treat skeletal injuries include wearing a cast, joint replacement, and arthroscopy.

Key Terms

- fracture • dislocation • sprain • X-ray
- magnetic resonance imaging • arthritis
- arthroscope

④ The Muscular System

Key Concepts

- Your body has three types of muscle tissue—skeletal, smooth, and cardiac.
- Skeletal muscles work in pairs. While one muscle contracts, the other muscle in the pair relaxes to its original length.

Key Terms

- involuntary muscle • voluntary muscle
- skeletal muscle • tendon • striated muscle
- smooth muscle • cardiac muscle

⑤ The Skin

Key Concepts

- The skin has several functions: protection, maintaining temperature, eliminating wastes, gathering information, and making vitamin D.
- The two skin layers are epidermis and dermis.
- Three simple habits can help you keep your skin healthy. Eat a healthful diet. Keep your skin clean and dry. Limit your sun exposure.

Key Terms

- epidermis • melanin • dermis • pore
- follicle • cancer

Review and Assessment

Organizing Information

Concept Mapping Copy the concept map about the types of muscles onto a separate sheet of paper. Then complete it and add a title. (For more on Concept Mapping, see the Skills Handbook.)

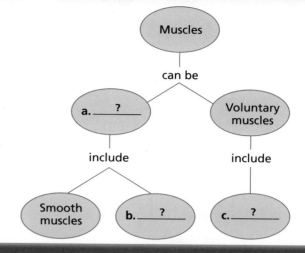

Reviewing Key Terms

Choose the letter of the best answer.

1. A group of similar cells that perform a similar function is called a(n)
   a. cell. **b.** organ.
   c. tissue. **d.** organ system.

2. A soft, connective tissue found inside some bones is
   a. cytoplasm.
   b. marrow.
   c. cartilage.
   d. osteoporosis.

3. The stretching and tearing of ligaments is
   a. a fracture.
   b. a dislocation.
   c. a sprain.
   d. osteoporosis.

4. Muscles that help the skeleton move are
   a. cardiac muscles.
   b. smooth muscles.
   c. skeletal muscles.
   d. involuntary muscles.

5. A colored substance that helps to keep the skin from burning is
   a. the dermis. **b.** the epidermis.
   c. melanin. **d.** a follicle.

If the statement is true, write *true*. If the statement is false, change the underlined word or words to make the statement true.

6. The <u>cytoplasm</u> directs the cell's activities.

7. Spongy bone is filled with <u>cartilage.</u>

8. <u>X-rays</u> produce images of soft tissues.

9. <u>Skeletal</u> muscle is called striated muscle.

10. The <u>epidermis</u> contains nerve endings and blood vessels.

Writing in Science

Descriptive Paragraph Pretend you are a writer for a science magazine for children. Write a few paragraphs that compare the characteristics of cartilage with the characteristics of bones. Be sure to explain the advantages of both types of materials.

Discovery
CHANNEL
SCHOOL™

Bones, Muscles, and Skin
Video Preview
Video Field Trip
▶ Video Assessment

Review and Assessment

Checking Concepts

11. Explain the relationship among cells, tissues, organs, and organ systems.

12. List the four kinds of movable joints. Describe the type of movement each joint allows.

13. Describe the structure of a bone.

14. How is arthroscopy used to treat injuries?

15. How does the appearance of smooth muscle differ from that of skeletal muscle?

16. Explain how skeletal muscles work in pairs.

17. How does the skin protect your body?

Thinking Critically

18. **Classifying** Identify each of the labeled parts of the cell.

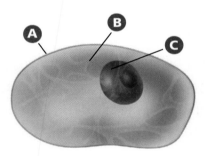

19. **Inferring** In addition to bone, cartilage, and fat, scientists classify blood as a connective tissue. Explain why.

20. **Making Generalizations** How is homeostasis important to survival?

21. **Making Judgments** A patient is admitted to the emergency room with a severe headache after a fall. What kind of image should be taken to diagnose the problem? Explain.

22. **Predicting** If smooth muscle had to be controlled consciously, what problems could you foresee in day-to-day living?

23. **Relating Cause and Effect** A person who is exposed to excessive heat may suffer from heatstroke. The first sign of heatstroke is that the person stops sweating. Why is heatstroke a life-threatening emergency?

Applying Skills

Use the graph to answer Questions 24–26.

The graph below shows the effects of the temperature of the environment on a boy's skin temperature and on the temperature inside his body.

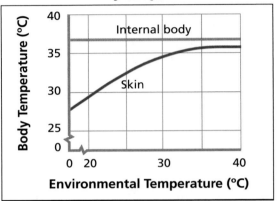

24. **Interpreting Data** As the temperature of the environment rises, what happens to the boy's internal body temperature? How does this demonstrate homeostasis?

25. **Inferring** What happens to the temperature of the boy's skin? Why is this pattern different from the pattern shown by the boy's internal body temperature?

26. **Predicting** Suppose the boy went outdoors on a chilly fall morning. Predict what would happen to his internal body temperature and his skin temperature. Explain.

Lab zone Chapter **Project**

Performance Assessment Before testing your prosthetic hand, explain to your classmates how and why you designed the hand the way you did. When you test the hand, observe how it picks up objects. How does it compare with a real human hand? How could you improve the function of your prosthetic hand?

Standardized Test Prep

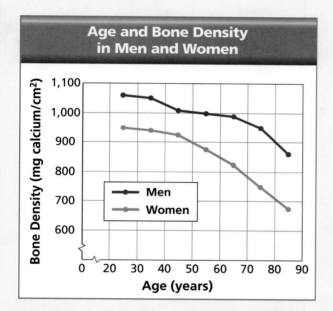
Choose the letter of the best answer.

1. Which of the following statements is true according to the graph shown at left?
   - **A** The bones of women are more dense than the bones of men.
   - **B** The bones of men contain less calcium than do the bones of women.
   - **C** The bone density of both men and women decreases as they age.
   - **D** An average 55-year-old woman has stronger bones than an average 55-year-old man.

2. A doctor cannot identify a sprained ankle by taking an X-ray because
   - **F** X-rays pass through bones.
   - **G** soft tissues block X-rays.
   - **H** X-rays pass through soft tissues.
   - **J** a sprained ankle cannot be viewed on an X-ray until the swelling decreases.

3. The muscles that you use to lift a book are
   - **A** cardiac muscles.
   - **B** smooth muscles.
   - **C** involuntary muscles.
   - **D** skeletal muscles.

4. Which of the following is *not* an important function of the skeletal system?
   - **F** It protects internal organs.
   - **G** It stores minerals until they are needed by the body.
   - **H** It allows the body to move.
   - **J** It regulates body temperature.

5. Which of the following represents the smallest level of organization in the body?
   - **A** cardiac muscle tissue
   - **B** the heart
   - **C** a muscle cell
   - **D** the circulatory system

Constructed Response

6. Compare the dermis and the epidermis layers of the skin. Discuss the following: their thickness, location, nerves, blood vessels, sweat glands, and cell life cycle.

The BIG Idea
Structure and Function

 How does the digestive system obtain nutrients for the body?

Let's eat! These baskets of vegetables offer ▶ a wide choice of tasty and healthful foods.

Lab zone™ Chapter **Project**

What's for Lunch?

When you're hungry and grab a snack, what do you choose? In this project, you'll take a close look at the foods you select each day.

Your Goal To compare your eating pattern to the recommendations in the USDA MyPyramid Plan

To complete this project successfully, you must

● keep an accurate record of everything you eat and drink for three days

● create graphs to compare your eating pattern with the recommendations of the U.S. Department of Agriculture (USDA)

● make changes in your diet, if needed, during another three-day period

Plan It! Before you begin, study this chapter to understand how foods are grouped. Then, visit the USDA Web site at www.MyPyramid.gov to get your recommended plan. Next, decide how to keep an accurate, complete food log. How will you make sure you record everything you eat and drink? How will you determine serving sizes? After your teacher approves your plan, start keeping your food log.

Food and Energy

Reading Preview

Key Concepts
- Why does your body need food?
- How do the six nutrients needed by the body help carry out essential processes?

Key Terms
- nutrient • calorie
- carbohydrate • glucose • fat
- protein • amino acid
- vitamin • mineral

 Target Reading Skill

Outlining As you read, make an outline about the six groups of nutrients needed by the body. Use the red headings for the main ideas and the blue headings for the supporting ideas.

Food and Energy
I. Why You Need Food
A. Nutrients
B.
II. Carbohydrates
A.

Lab zone · Discover **Activity**

Food Claims—Fact or Fiction?

1. Examine the list of statements at the right. Copy the list onto a separate sheet of paper.
2. Next to each statement, write *agree* or *disagree*. Give a reason for your response.
3. Discuss your responses with a small group of classmates. Compare the reasons you gave for agreeing or disagreeing with each statement.

Think It Over

Posing Questions List some other statements about nutrition that you have heard. How could you find out whether the statements are true?

Fact or Fiction?

a. Athletes need more protein in their diets than other people do.

b. The only salt that a food contains is the salt that you have added to it.

c. As part of a healthy diet, everyone should take vitamin supplements.

Imagine a Thanksgiving dinner—roast turkey on a platter, delicious stuffing, and lots of vegetables—an abundance of colors and aromas. Food is a central part of many celebrations, of times shared with friends and family. Food is also essential. Every living thing needs food to stay alive.

Why You Need Food

Foods provide your body with materials for growing and for repairing tissues. Food also provides energy for everything you do. For example, running, playing a musical instrument, reading, and even sleeping require energy. Food also helps your body maintain homeostasis. You read in Chapter 1 that the systems of the body work together to help keep the body's internal environment stable. By filling your energy needs, food enables your body to keep this balance during all your activities.

Nutrients Your body breaks down the foods you eat into nutrients. **Nutrients** (NOO tree unts) are the substances in food that provide the raw materials and energy the body needs to carry out all its essential processes. There are six groups of nutrients necessary for human health—carbohydrates, fats, proteins, vitamins, minerals, and water.

Energy When nutrients are used by the body for energy, the amount of energy they release can be measured in units called calories. One **calorie** is the amount of energy needed to raise the temperature of one gram of water by one degree Celsius. Most foods contain many thousands of calories of energy. Biologists use the term *Calorie,* with a capital *C,* to measure the energy in foods. One Calorie is the same as 1 kilocalorie (kcal) or 1,000 calories. For example, one serving of popcorn may contain 60 Calories (60 kcal), or 60,000 calories, of energy. The more Calories a food has, the more energy it contains.

You need to eat a certain number of Calories each day to meet your body's energy needs. Your daily energy requirement depends on your level of physical activity. Your needs also change as you grow and age. As an infant and child, you grew very rapidly, so you likely had very high energy needs. Your current growth and level of physical activity affect the number of Calories you need now. The more active you are, the greater your energy needs are.

 **Reading Checkpoint** How is energy in foods measured?

FIGURE 1
Burning Calories
The number of Calories you burn depends on your weight as well as your level of activity. The more active you are, the more Calories you burn.
Applying Concepts *Which activity do you think burns the most Calories per hour—playing basketball, walking, or reading?*

Playing basketball

Walking

Reading

FIGURE 2
Carbohydrates

Simple carbohydrates, or sugars, are found in fruits, milk, and some vegetables. Sugars are also added to cookies, candies, and soft drinks. Complex carbohydrates are found in rice, corn, pasta, and bread. Fruits, vegetables, nuts, and whole-grain foods also contain fiber.

Applying Concepts *Why is fiber important in the diet?*

Simple Carbohydrates

Brownie (1 square)
Total Carbohydrates 18 g
Sugars	10 g
Starches	7 g
Fiber	1 g

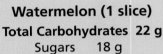

Watermelon (1 slice)
Total Carbohydrates 22 g
Sugars	18 g
Starches	3 g
Fiber	1 g

Milk (1 cup)
Total Carbohydrates 12 g
Sugars	12 g
Starches	0 g
Fiber	0 g

Carbohydrates

The nutrients called **carbohydrates** (kahr boh HY drayts), which are composed of carbon, oxygen, and hydrogen, are a major source of energy. One gram of carbohydrate provides your body with four Calories of energy. **In addition to providing energy, carbohydrates provide the raw materials to make cell parts.** Based on their chemical structure, carbohydrates are divided into simple carbohydrates and complex carbohydrates.

Simple Carbohydrates Simple carbohydrates are also known as sugars. One sugar, **glucose** (GLOO kohs), is the major source of energy for your body's cells. However, most foods do not contain large amounts of glucose. The body converts other types of sugars, such as the sugar found in fruits, into glucose. Glucose is the form of sugar the body can most easily use.

Complex Carbohydrates Complex carbohydrates are made up of many sugar molecules linked together in a chain. Starch is a complex carbohydrate found in foods from plants, such as potatoes, rice, wheat, and corn. To use starch as an energy source, your body first breaks it down into smaller, individual sugar molecules. Only then can your body release the molecules' energy.

Like starch, fiber is a complex carbohydrate found in plants. But unlike starch, fiber cannot be broken down into sugar molecules by your body. Instead, fiber passes through the body and is eliminated.

Complex Carbohydrates

Yellow Corn (1 ear)
Total Carbohydrates 19 g
  Sugars   2 g
  Starches   15 g
  Fiber   2 g

Pasta (1 cup)
Total Carbohydrates   40 g
  Sugars   1 g
  Starches   37 g
  Fiber   2 g

Wheat Bread (1 slice)
Total Carbohydrates   17 g
  Sugars   3.5 g
  Starches   12.0 g
  Fiber   1.5 g

Because your body cannot digest it, fiber is not considered a nutrient. Fiber is an important part of the diet, however, because it helps keep the digestive system functioning properly.

Nutritionists' Recommendations Nutritionists recommend that 45 to 65 percent of the Calories in a diet come from carbohydrates. It is better to eat more complex carbohydrates, such as whole grains, than simple carbohydrates. Foods made with whole grains usually contain a variety of other nutrients. Foods made with a lot of sugar, such as candy and soft drinks, have few valuable nutrients. Also, while sugars can give you a quick burst of energy, starches provide a more even, long-term energy source.

 **Reading Checkpoint** **What are two types of carbohydrates? Give an example of each.**

Fats

Like carbohydrates, **fats** are energy-containing nutrients that are composed of carbon, oxygen, and hydrogen. However, fats contain more than twice the energy of an equal amount of carbohydrates. One gram of fat provides your body with nine Calories of energy. **In addition to providing energy, fats have other important functions. Fats form part of the cell membrane, the structure that forms the boundary of a cell. Fatty tissue protects and supports your internal organs and insulates your body.**

Lab zone Skills **Activity**

Predicting
You can do a test to see which foods contain starch.

1. Put on your apron.
2. Obtain food samples from your teacher. Predict which ones contain starch. Write down your predictions.
3. Use a plastic dropper to add three drops of iodine to each food sample. **CAUTION:** *Iodine can stain skin and clothing.* Handle it carefully. If the iodine turns blue-black, starch is present.

Which foods contain starch? Were your predictions correct?

FIGURE 3

Many foods contain saturated, unsaturated, and trans fats. Unsaturated fats are considered to be more healthful than saturated fats and trans fats.
Interpreting Graphs *Which item has the most unsaturated fat—butter, tub margarine, or olive oil?*

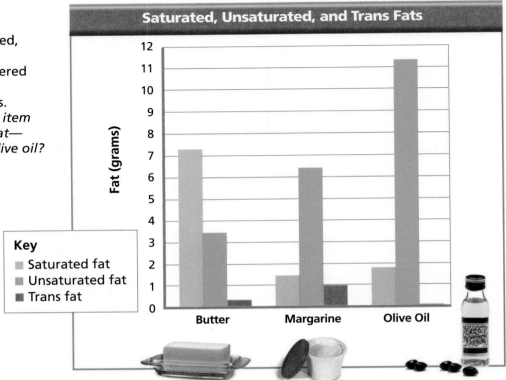

Saturated, Unsaturated, and Trans Fats

Key
- Saturated fat
- Unsaturated fat
- Trans fat

Fat (grams)

Butter   Margarine   Olive Oil

Kinds of Fats Fats may be classified as unsaturated or saturated based on their chemical structure. Unsaturated fats are usually liquid at room temperature. Most cooking oils are unsaturated fats. Saturated fats are usually solid at room temperature. Meat and dairy products contain relatively large amounts of saturated fat.

You may have heard about trans fat. Trans fats are made by adding hydrogen to vegetable oils. This allows foods like margarine and chips to stay fresh longer. Compared to unsaturated fats that are beneficial in proper amounts, saturated and trans fats are not. Cities including New York City and Philadelphia have banned the use of trans fats in restaurants.

Cholesterol Cholesterol (kuh LES tur awl) is a waxy, fatlike substance found only in animal products. Like fats, cholesterol is an important part of your body's cells. Your liver can make the cholesterol your body needs, making it an unnecessary part of the diet.

Nutritionists' Recommendations Nutritionists recommend that no more than 30 percent of the Calories eaten each day come from fats. A diet high in fat and cholesterol can lead to a buildup of fatty material in the blood vessels and cause heart disease.

 Reading Checkpoint **How can you tell the difference between most unsaturated fats and saturated fats?**

Proteins

Proteins are nutrients that contain nitrogen as well as carbon, hydrogen, and oxygen. **Proteins are needed for tissue growth and repair. They also play an important part in chemical reactions within cells.** Proteins can serve as a source of energy, but they are a less important source of energy than carbohydrates or fats. About 10 to 35 percent of your daily Calorie intake should come from proteins.

Amino Acids Proteins are made up of small units called **amino acids** (uh MEE noh), which are linked together chemically to form large protein molecules. Thousands of different proteins are built from only about 20 different amino acids. Your body can make about half of the amino acids it needs. The others, called essential amino acids, must come from the foods you eat.

Complete and Incomplete Proteins Foods from animal sources, such as meat and eggs, are sources of complete proteins because these foods contain all the essential amino acids. Proteins from plant sources, such as beans, grains, and nuts, are called incomplete proteins because they are missing one or more essential amino acid. Different plant sources lack different amino acids. Therefore, to obtain all the essential amino acids from plant sources alone, people need to eat a wide variety of plant foods.

 **Reading Checkpoint** **What are the units that make up proteins?**

Math Skills

Percentage
A percentage (%) is a ratio that compares a number to 100. For example, 30% means 30 out of 100.

Suppose that a person eats a total of 2,000 Calories in one day. Of those Calories, 300 come from protein. Follow these steps to calculate the percentage of Calories that come from protein.

1. Write the comparison as a fraction:
$$\frac{300}{2,000}$$

2. Multiply the fraction by 100% to express it as a percentage:
$$\frac{300}{2,000} \times 100\% = 15\%$$

Practice Problem Suppose that 540 Calories of the person's 2,000 Calorie total come from fats. What percentage of the Calories comes from fats?

Vitamins and Minerals

Two kinds of nutrients—vitamins and minerals—are needed by the body in very small amounts. Unlike the other nutrients, vitamins and minerals do not provide the body with energy or raw materials. Instead, they help the body carry out various processes.

Vitamins act as helper molecules in a variety of chemical reactions in the body. Vitamin K, for example, helps your blood to clot when you get a cut or a scrape. Figure 6 lists the vitamins necessary for health. The body can make a few of these vitamins. For example, your skin can make vitamin D when exposed to sunlight. Most vitamins, however, must be obtained from foods.

Fat-Soluble and Water-Soluble Vitamins Vitamins are classified as either fat-soluble or water-soluble. Fat-soluble vitamins dissolve in fat, and they are stored in fatty tissues in the body. Vitamins A, D, E, and K are all fat-soluble vitamins. Water-soluble vitamins dissolve in water and are not stored in the body. This fact makes it especially important to include sources of water-soluble vitamins—vitamin C and all of the B vitamins—in your diet every day.

FIGURE 5
Eat Your Vegetables!
Fresh vegetables are full of vitamins and are fun to pick as well.

Importance of Vitamins Although vitamins are only needed in small amounts, a lack of certain vitamins in the diet can lead to health problems. In the 1700s, sailors on long voyages survived on hard, dry biscuits, salted meat, and not much else. Because of this limited diet, many sailors developed a serious disease called scurvy. People with scurvy suffer from bleeding gums, stiff joints, and sores that do not heal. Some may even die.

A Scottish doctor, James Lind, hypothesized that scurvy was the result of the sailors' poor diet. Lind divided sailors with scurvy into groups and fed different foods to each group. The sailors who were fed citrus fruits—oranges and lemons—recovered from the disease. Lind recommended that all sailors eat citrus fruits. When Lind's recommendations were carried out, scurvy disappeared. Today scientists know that scurvy is caused by the lack of vitamin C, which is found in citrus fruits.

 **List the fat-soluble vitamins.**

FIGURE 6
Essential Vitamins
Both fat-soluble vitamins and water-soluble vitamins are necessary to maintain health.
Interpreting Tables *What foods provide a supply of both vitamins E and K?*

Fat-Soluble Vitamins		
Vitamin	Sources	Function
A	Dairy products; eggs; liver; yellow, orange, and dark green vegetables; fruits	Maintains healthy skin, bones, teeth, and hair; aids vision in dim light
D	Fortified dairy products; fish; eggs; liver; made by skin cells in presence of sunlight	Maintains bones and teeth; helps in the use of calcium and phosphorus
E	Vegetable oils; margarine; green, leafy vegetables; whole-grain foods; seeds; nuts	Aids in maintenance of red blood cells
K	Green, leafy vegetables; milk; liver; made by bacteria in the intestines	Aids in blood clotting

Water-Soluble Vitamins		
Vitamin	Sources	Function
B1 (thiamin)	Pork; liver; whole-grain foods; legumes; nuts	Needed for breakdown of carbohydrates
B2 (riboflavin)	Dairy products; eggs; whole-grain breads and cereals; green, leafy vegetables	Needed for normal growth
B3 (niacin)	Many protein-rich foods; milk; eggs; meat; fish; whole-grain foods; nuts; peanut butter	Needed for release of energy
B6 (pyridoxine)	Green, leafy vegetables; meats; fish; legumes; fruits; whole-grain foods	Helps in the breakdown of proteins, fats, and carbohydrates
B12	Meats; fish; poultry; dairy products; eggs	Maintains healthy nervous system; needed for red blood cell formation
Biotin	Liver; meat; fish; eggs; legumes; bananas; melons	Aids in the release of energy
Folic acid	Green, leafy vegetables; legumes; seeds; liver	Needed for red blood cell formation
Pantothenic acid	Liver; meats; fish; eggs; whole-grain foods	Needed for the release of energy
C	Citrus fruits; tomatoes; potatoes; dark green vegetables; mangoes	Needed to form connective tissue and fight infection

FIGURE 7
Eating a variety of foods each day provides your body with the minerals it needs. *Interpreting Tables Which minerals play a role in regulating water levels in the body?*

Essential Minerals		
Mineral	**Sources**	**Function**
Calcium	Milk; cheese; dark green, leafy vegetables; tofu; legumes	Helps build bones and teeth; aids in blood clotting; muscle and nerve function
Chlorine	Table salt; soy sauce	Helps maintain water balance
Fluorine	Fluoridated drinking water; fish	Helps form bones and teeth
Iodine	Seafood, iodized salt	Helps in the release of energy
Iron	Red meats; seafood; green, leafy vegetables; legumes; dried fruits	Needed for red blood cell function
Magnesium	Green, leafy vegetables; legumes; nuts; whole-grain foods	Aids in muscle and nerve function; helps in the release of energy
Phosphorus	Meat; poultry; eggs; fish; dairy products	Helps produce healthy bones and teeth; helps in the release of energy
Potassium	Grains; fruits; vegetables; meat; fish	Helps maintain water balance; muscle and nerve function
Sodium	Table salt; soy sauce	Helps maintain water balance; nerve function

◄ Source of calcium

◄ Source of potassium

Source of sodium ►

Importance of Minerals Nutrients that are not made by living things are called **minerals.** Minerals are present in soil and are absorbed by plants through their roots. You obtain minerals by eating plant foods or animals that have eaten plants. Figure 7 lists some minerals you need. You probably know that calcium is needed for strong bones and teeth. Iron is needed for the proper functioning of red blood cells.

Both vitamins and minerals are needed by your body in small amounts to carry out chemical processes. If you eat a wide variety of foods, you probably will get enough vitamins and minerals. Most people who eat a balanced diet do not need to take vitamin or mineral supplements.

Reading Checkpoint What are minerals?

Water

Imagine that a boat is sinking. The people on board are getting into a lifeboat. They have room for only one of these items: a bag of fruit, a can of meat, a loaf of bread, or a jug of water. Which item should they choose?

You might be surprised to learn that the lifeboat passengers should choose the water. Although people can probably survive for weeks without food, they will die within days without fresh water. Water is the most abundant substance in the body. It accounts for about 65 percent of the average person's body weight.

Water is the most important nutrient because the body's vital processes—including chemical reactions such as the breakdown of nutrients—take place in water. Water makes up most of the body's fluids, including blood. Nutrients and other important substances are carried throughout the body dissolved in the watery part of the blood. Your body also needs water to produce perspiration, which helps regulate body temperature and remove wastes.

Under normal conditions, you need to take in about 2 liters of water every day. You can do this by drinking water and other beverages and by eating foods with lots of water, such as fruits and vegetables. If the weather is hot or you are exercising, you need to drink additional water to replace the water that you lose in sweat.

FIGURE 8
Water—An Essential Nutrient
All living things need water. Without regular water intake, an organism would not be able to carry out the processes that keep it alive.

Section 1 Assessment

🔄 **Target Reading Skill** Outlining Use the information in your outline about nutrients to help you answer the questions below.

Reviewing Key Concepts

1. a. Identifying Name two ways in which foods are used by the body.
   b. Defining What is a calorie? How does it relate to the amount of energy in foods?
   c. Inferring Why do young children and active teenagers have high energy needs?
2. a. Listing List the six nutrients that are needed by the body.
   b. Summarizing For each nutrient you listed, briefly describe the role it plays in the body.
   c. Applying Concepts Why is it especially important that vegetarians eat a varied diet?

Math Practice

3. Percentage Suppose that a person eats 2,500 Calories in one day. Of those Calories, 1,200 are from carbohydrates, 875 are from fat, and the rest are from protein. What percentages of the person's Calories are from carbohydrates, from fats, and from proteins?

Raisin' the Raisin Question

Problem

Raisins are a good source of the mineral iron. Which raisin bran cereal contains the most raisins?

Skills Focus

measuring, calculating, controlling variables

Materials

- balance
- paper towels
- beaker (250 mL)
- raisin bran cereals (several brands)

Procedure

1. Use a balance to find the mass of a clean 250-mL beaker. Record the mass in a data table like the one below.

2. Fill the beaker to the top with one of the brands of raisin bran cereal, but do not pack down the cereal. **CAUTION:** *Do not put any cereal in your mouth.* Write the brand name in the data table. Measure and record the mass of the beaker plus cereal. Subtract the mass of the empty beaker to get the mass of the cereal alone. Record the result.

3. Pour the cereal onto a paper towel. Separate the raisins from the bran and place the raisins back in the beaker. Measure and record the mass of the beaker plus raisins. Subtract the mass of the empty beaker to get the mass of the raisins alone. Record the result.

4. Repeat Steps 1–3 with each of the other brands of cereal.

Analyze and Conclude

1. **Measuring** Why did you first measure the mass of an empty beaker and then the mass of the beaker plus cereal?

2. **Calculating** Calculate the percentage mass of raisins in each cereal as follows:

$$\% \text{ Mass of raisins} = \frac{\text{Mass of raisins}}{\text{Mass of cereal}} \times 100\%$$

Record the results in your data table.

3. **Interpreting Data** Based on your observations, which brand of cereal had the greatest percentage of raisins by mass?

4. **Controlling Variables** Was it important that all of the cereal samples were collected in the same-size beaker? Why or why not?

5. **Communicating** Based on your results, write a paragraph that could be printed on a box of raisin bran cereal that would help consumers understand that this brand is the best source of iron.

Design an Experiment

In this investigation, you examined a *sample* of cereal rather than the contents of the entire box. Scientists often use samples because it is a more practical way to make observations. Redesign this experiment to improve upon the sampling technique and increase the accuracy of your results. *Obtain your teacher's permission before carrying out your investigation.*

Data Table						
Cereal Brand	Mass (g)					Percentage Mass of Raisins (%)
	Empty Beaker	Beaker plus Cereal	Cereal	Beaker plus Raisins	Raisins	

Healthy Eating

Reading Preview

Key Concepts
- How can food pyramids help you plan a healthy diet?
- What kind of information is included on food labels?

Key Terms
- Percent Daily Value
- Dietary Reference Intakes (DRIs)

Target Reading Skill
Asking Questions Before you read, preview the red headings. In a graphic organizer like the one below, ask a *what* or *how* question for each heading. As you read, write answers to your questions.

Healthy Eating

Question	Answer
What is a food pyramid?	A food pyramid classifies . . .

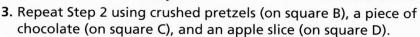

Lab zone Discover **Activity**

Do Snack Foods Contain Fat?
1. Cut four small squares from a brown paper bag. Label them A, B, C, and D.
2. Rub some crushed potato chips on square A. **CAUTION:** *Do not eat any of the foods in this activity.*
3. Repeat Step 2 using crushed pretzels (on square B), a piece of chocolate (on square C), and an apple slice (on square D).
4. Remove any food. Allow the paper squares to dry.
5. Note which squares have spots of oil on them.

Think It Over
Classifying If a food contains fat, it will leave oily spots on the paper. What does this tell you about the foods you tested?

What does healthy eating mean to you? Eating more fresh fruits and vegetables? Not skipping breakfast? Cutting down on soft drinks and chips? You have just learned about the six types of nutrients—carbohydrates, fats, proteins, vitamins, minerals, and water—that are part of a healthy diet. You may now be wondering how you can use this information to make healthy choices in your diet.

With so many foods available, it may seem more difficult, not easier, to establish a healthy diet. Luckily, nutritionists have developed dietary guidelines and food labels as a way to help.

FIGURE 9
Healthy Food Choices
Fruits and vegetables are essential parts of a healthy diet. Some people enjoy picking these foods right off the plant.

Guidelines for a Healthy Diet

In 2005, the United States Department of Agriculture (USDA) introduced a new set of guidelines to promote healthy eating and physical activity. Unlike past plans, these new guidelines tie a person's level of physical activity directly to a nutritional plan. **The USDA guidelines provide a personalized way to help people make healthy food choices based on their age, sex, and amount of physical activity.**

Go **Online**
active art

For: Reading a Food Pyramid activity
Visit: PHSchool.com
Web Code: cep-4022

FIGURE 10
Reading a Food Pyramid
This food pyramid recommends the proportion of foods from each group that make up a healthy diet.

Stay Active
Daily physical activity is an important part to staying healthy.

Know Your Food Groups
The pyramid is divided into six colored bands, representing the five food groups, plus oils.

Know Your Calorie Needs
Depending on physical activity, a 13-year-old girl needs 1600–2200 Calories per day. A 13-year-old boy needs 1800–2400 Calories per day.

Balance Your Diet
The proportions of each food group you need daily are shown by the width of each band.

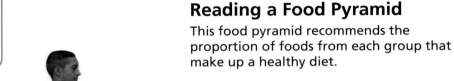

GRAINS	VEGETABLES	FRUITS	OILS	MILK	MEAT & BEANS
Make half the grains you eat whole grains.	Vary your vegetables. Include dark green and orange veggies more often.	Eat a variety of fruits. Limit juices and canned fruits with added sugar.	Limit solid fats. Choose oils from plant sources most often.	Get plenty of calcium-rich foods. Eat mostly low-fat dairy products.	Vary your protein sources. Choose lean meats and poultry. Eat more fish, beans, and nuts.

For a 2,000-Calorie diet, you need to eat the amounts shown below from each food group every day. To find the amounts that are right for you, go to **MyPyramid.gov**.

GRAINS	VEGETABLES	FRUITS	OILS	MILK	MEAT & BEANS
6 ounces	2½ cups	2 cups	6 teaspoons	3 cups	5½ ounces

Understanding a MyPyramid Plan One part of the USDA guidelines is a set of diagrams called the "MyPyramid Plans." In contrast to the older, single plan, the MyPyramid plans differ from one person to another. Look at Figure 10. It shows the basic parts of a food pyramid diagram. You can see that the pyramid is divided into six colored bands. Each band represents one of five food groups, plus oils. The differing widths of the bands tell you what proportion of your diet should come from each food group. Grains, vegetables, and milk (or milk products) should be eaten in greater amounts than protein-rich foods or oils.

Limiting Sugars and Fats Are you surprised that sugar-rich foods, such as candy bars, cookies, and soft drinks, are not even included in the pyramid? That's because added sugars contribute extra Calories to your diet but relatively few nutrients. Similarly, foods heavy in hidden oils—such as fried foods, cakes, and potato chips—pack many more Calories than they supply in nutrients. The USDA recommends that people limit their intake of added sugars and extra fats. So, ice cream may be a tasty treat, but it should be eaten less often compared to drinking low-fat milk.

Getting MyPyramid Information You can get more information about the USDA dietary guidelines by visiting its Web site on the Internet. The site contains details about the different foods in each group, suggestions for how to plan menus, Calorie counts based on physical activity, and other facts that can help you and your family make healthy food choices. The site is a helpful tool for designing your own MyPyramid Plan.

 **Reading Checkpoint** Which three food groups should make up the largest part of a healthy diet?

Food and Digestion

Video Preview
▶ Video Field Trip
Video Assessment

Lab zone Skills **Activity**

Graphing
You can graph the nutrient content in a meal. The meal of chicken, beans, rice, and salad has about 27 g of protein, 25 g of carbohydrates, and 4 g of fat. Use this information to draw a bar graph showing protein, carbohydrate, and fat content for this meal.

FIGURE 11
Healthy Eating
A food pyramid can help you plan healthy meals. Classifying *Which of the food groups in the USDA guidelines are contained in this meal of chicken, beans, rice, and salad?*

Food Labels

After a long day, you and your friends stop into a store on your way home from school. What snack should you buy? How can you make a wise choice? One thing you can do is to read the information provided on food labels. **Food labels allow you to evaluate a single food as well as to compare the nutritional value of two different foods.**

How to Read a Food Label Figure 12 shows a food label that might appear on a box of cereal. Refer to that label as you read about some of the important nutritional information it contains.

❶ Serving Size This information tells you the size of a single serving and the number of servings in the container. The information on the rest of the label is based on serving size. If you eat twice the serving size, then you'll consume twice the number of Calories.

❷ Calories This information tells you how much energy you get from one serving of this food, including how many Calories come from fat.

❸ Percent Daily Value The **Percent Daily Value** shows you how the nutritional content of one serving fits into the recommended diet for a person who consumes 2,000 Calories a day. For example, one serving of this cereal contains 12% of the total amount of sodium a person should consume in one day. You might eat more or less than 2,000 Calories a day. But, you can still use this percentage as a general guide.

❹ Ingredients The ingredients are listed in order by weight, starting with the main ingredient. The list can alert you to substances that have been added to a food to improve its flavor or color, or to keep it from spoiling. In addition, reading ingredients lists can help you avoid substances that make you ill.

Using Food Labels Food labels can help you make healthful food choices. Suppose you are shopping for breakfast cereals. By reading the labels, you might find that one cereal contains little fat and a high percentage of the Daily Values for complex carbohydrates and several vitamins. Another cereal might have fewer complex carbohydrates and vitamins, and contain significant amounts of fat. You can see that the first cereal would be a better choice as a regular breakfast food.

FIGURE 12
Food Label
By law, specific nutritional information must be listed on food labels.
Calculating *How many servings of this product would you have to eat to get 90% of the Daily Value for iron?*

Nutrition Facts

Serving Size	1 cup (30g)
Servings Per Container	About 10

Amount Per Serving

Calories 110	Calories from Fat 15

	% Daily Value*
Total Fat 2g	3%
Saturated Fat 0g	0%
Trans Fat 0g	0%
Cholesterol 0mg	0%
Sodium 280mg	12%
Total Carbohydrate 22g	7%
Dietary Fiber 3g	12%
Sugars 1g	
Protein 3g	

Vitamin A	10%	•	Vitamin C	20%
Calcium	4%	•	Iron	45%

* Percent Daily Values are based on a 2,000 Calorie diet. Your daily values may be higher or lower depending on your caloric needs:

		Calories	2,000	2,500
Total Fat	Less than		65g	80g
Sat. Fat	Less than		20g	25g
Cholesterol	Less than		300mg	300mg
Sodium	Less than		2,400mg	2,400mg
Total Carbohydrate			300g	375g
Fiber			25g	30g

Calories per gram:
Fat 9 • Carbohydrate 4 • Protein 4

Ingredients: Whole grain oats, sugar, salt, milled corn, oat fi... almonds...

Dietary Reference Intakes Food labels can also help you monitor the nutrients in your diet. Guidelines that show the amounts of nutrients that are needed every day are known as **Dietary Reference Intakes (DRIs).** For example, the DRIs for vitamins recommend that people your age get 45 milligrams of vitamin C every day.

DRIs also show how the Calories that people eat each day should be split among carbohydrates, fats, and proteins. The Percent Daily Values listed on food labels can help you make sure that you are meeting the DRIs for different nutrients.

 **What are Dietary Reference Intakes?**

FIGURE 13
Reading Food Labels
Food labels allow you to compare the nutritional content of similar kinds of foods.

Section 2 Assessment

Target Reading Skill Asking Questions Work with a partner to check the answers in your graphic organizer.

Reviewing Key Concepts

1. a. Identifying Into what groups are foods classified in the USDA food pyramid plans?
  b. Interpreting Diagrams What do the differing widths of the bands in a food pyramid tell you about the food groups?
  c. Applying Concepts Why might a runner be able to eat more servings from some of the food groups than a less active person could?
2. a. Reviewing What are three kinds of information contained on food labels?
  b. Explaining How can food labels help a person make healthy food choices?

  c. Calculating Use Figure 12 to calculate the following: (1) the total number of Calories in 3 servings, (2) the number of servings needed to get 50 percent of the day's Daily Value for Vitamin C, and (3) the number of servings needed to get all the dietary fiber needed for the day.

Lab zone At-Home **Activity**

Menu Planning Work with a family member to plan menus for three days that meet the guidelines of the U.S. Department of Agriculture. Follow the recommended number of servings for each group. Remember to write down fats, such as butter or margarine, that may be used to add flavor to dishes. Include all snack items as well.

The Digestive Process Begins

Reading Preview

Key Concepts
- What functions are carried out in the digestive system?
- What roles do the mouth, esophagus, and stomach play in digestion?

Key Terms
- digestion • absorption
- saliva • enzyme • epiglottis
- esophagus • mucus
- peristalsis • stomach

Target Reading Skill
Using Prior Knowledge Before you read, look at the section headings and visuals to see what this section is about. Then write what you know about the digestive system in a graphic organizer like the one below. As you read, continue to write in what you learn.

What You Know
1. Food is digested in the stomach.
2.

What You Learned
1.
2.

Lab zone Discover Activity

How Can You Speed Up Digestion?
1. Obtain two plastic jars with lids. Fill the jars with equal amounts of water at the same temperature.
2. Place a whole sugar cube into one jar. Place a crushed sugar cube into the other jar.
3. Fasten the lids on the jars. Holding one jar in each hand, shake the two jars gently and for equal amounts of time.
4. Place the jars on a flat surface. Observe whether the whole cube or the crushed cube dissolves faster.

Think It Over
Predicting Use the results of this activity to predict which would take longer to digest: a large piece of food or one that has been cut up into many small pieces. Explain your answer.

In 1822, a man named Alexis St. Martin was wounded in the stomach. Dr. William Beaumont saved St. Martin's life. The wound, however, left an opening in St. Martin's stomach that never healed completely. Beaumont realized that by looking through the opening in St. Martin's abdomen, he could observe what was happening inside the stomach.

Beaumont observed that food changed chemically inside the stomach. He hypothesized that chemical reactions in the stomach broke down foods into smaller particles. Beaumont removed liquid from St. Martin's stomach and analyzed it. The stomach liquid contained an acid that played a role in the breakdown of foods into simpler substances.

Functions of the Digestive System

Beaumont's observations helped scientists understand the role of the stomach in the digestive system. **The digestive system has three main functions. First, it breaks down food into molecules the body can use. Then, the molecules are absorbed into the blood and carried throughout the body. Finally, wastes are eliminated from the body.** Figure 14 shows the organs of the digestive system, which is about 9 meters long from beginning to end.

Digestion The process by which your body breaks down food into small nutrient molecules is called **digestion.** There are two kinds of digestion—mechanical and chemical. In mechanical digestion, foods are physically broken down into smaller pieces. Mechanical digestion occurs when you bite into a sandwich and chew it into small pieces.

In chemical digestion, chemicals produced by the body break foods into their smaller chemical building blocks. For example, the starch in bread is broken down into individual sugar molecules.

Absorption and Elimination After your food is digested, the molecules are ready to be transported throughout your body. **Absorption** (ab SAWRP shun) is the process by which nutrient molecules pass through the wall of your digestive system into your blood. Materials that are not absorbed, such as fiber, are eliminated from the body as wastes.

For: Links on digestion
Visit: www.SciLinks.org
Web Code: scn-0423

Reading Checkpoint **What is chemical digestion?**

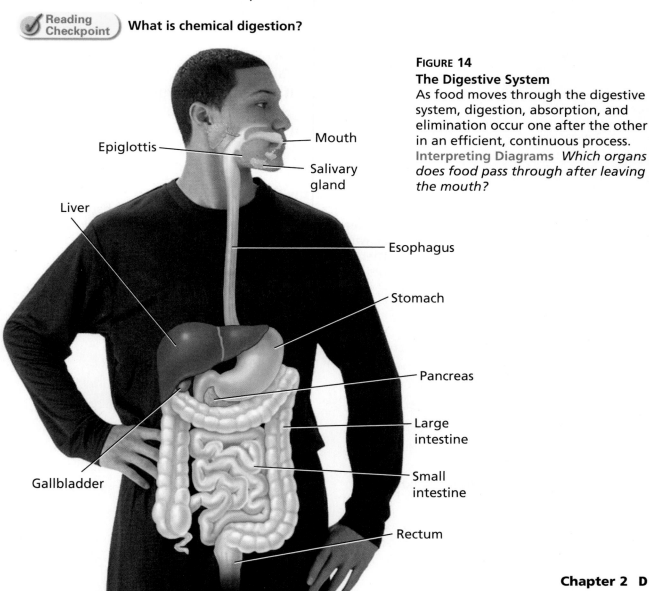

FIGURE 14
The Digestive System
As food moves through the digestive system, digestion, absorption, and elimination occur one after the other in an efficient, continuous process.
Interpreting Diagrams *Which organs does food pass through after leaving the mouth?*

Epiglottis
Mouth
Salivary gland
Liver
Esophagus
Stomach
Pancreas
Large intestine
Small intestine
Gallbladder
Rectum

The Mouth

Have you ever walked past a bakery or restaurant and noticed your mouth watering? Smelling or even just thinking about food when you're hungry is enough to start your mouth watering. This response isn't accidental. When your mouth waters, your body is preparing for the delicious meal it expects. **Both mechanical and chemical digestion begin in the mouth.** The fluid released when your mouth waters is **saliva** (suh LY vuh). Saliva plays an important role in both kinds of digestion.

Mechanical Digestion in the Mouth Your teeth carry out the first stage of mechanical digestion. Your center teeth, or incisors (in SY zurz), cut the food into bite-sized pieces. On either side of the incisors there are sharp, pointy teeth called canines (KAY nynz). These teeth tear and slash the food into smaller pieces. Behind the canines are the premolars and molars, which crush and grind the food. As the teeth do their work, saliva moistens the pieces of food into one slippery mass.

Chemical Digestion in the Mouth As mechanical digestion begins, so does chemical digestion. If you take a bite of a cracker and suck on it, the cracker begins to taste sweet. It tastes sweet because a chemical in the saliva has broken down the starch molecules in the cracker into sugar molecules.

FIGURE 15

Digestion in the Mouth
Mechanical digestion begins in the mouth, where the teeth cut and tear food into smaller pieces. Salivary glands release enzymes that begin chemical digestion. Observing *Which teeth are best suited for biting into a juicy apple?*

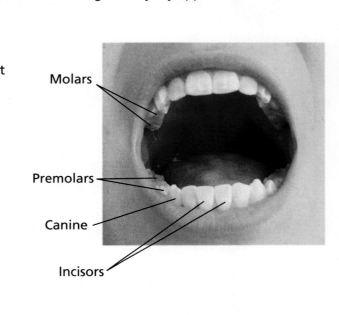

Salivary duct

Tongue

Tooth

Salivary glands

Molars

Premolars

Canine

Incisors

FIGURE 16
How Enzymes Work
The shape of an enzyme molecule is specific to
the shape of the food molecule it breaks down.
Here, an enzyme breaks down a starch into sugars.

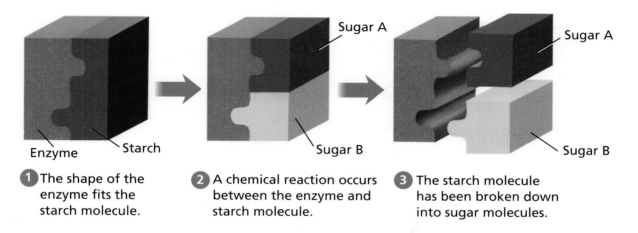

Sugar A

Sugar A

Enzyme   Starch

Sugar B

Sugar B

1 The shape of the enzyme fits the starch molecule.

2 A chemical reaction occurs between the enzyme and starch molecule.

3 The starch molecule has been broken down into sugar molecules.

The chemical in saliva that digests starch is an enzyme. **Enzymes** are proteins that speed up chemical reactions in the body. Your body produces many different enzymes. Each enzyme has a specific chemical shape. Its shape enables it to take part in only one kind of chemical reaction. An example of enzyme action is shown in Figure 16.

The Esophagus

If you've ever choked on food, your food may have "gone down the wrong way." That's because there are two openings at the back of your mouth. One opening leads to your windpipe, which carries air into your lungs. As you swallow, a flap of tissue called the **epiglottis** (ep uh GLAHT is) seals off your windpipe, preventing the food from entering. The food goes into the **esophagus** (ih SAHF uh gus), a muscular tube that connects the mouth to the stomach. The esophagus is lined with **mucus,** a thick, slippery substance produced by the body. Mucus makes food easier to swallow and move along.

Food remains in the esophagus for only about 10 seconds. **After food enters the esophagus, contractions of smooth muscles push the food toward the stomach.** These involuntary waves of muscle contraction are called **peristalsis** (pehr ih STAWL sis). Peristalsis also occurs in the stomach and farther down the digestive system. These muscular waves keep food moving in one direction.

 **Reading Checkpoint** How is food prevented from entering the windpipe?

Protein Digestion

A scientist performed an experiment to determine the amount of time needed to digest protein. He placed small pieces of hard-boiled egg white (a protein) in a test tube containing hydrochloric acid, water, and the enzyme pepsin. He measured the rate at which the egg white was digested over a 24-hour period. His data are recorded in the graph.

1. **Reading Graphs** What do the values on the *y*-axis represent?

2. **Interpreting Data** After about how many hours would you estimate that half of the protein was digested?

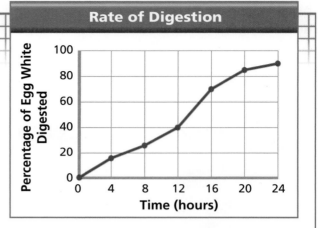

Rate of Digestion

3. **Interpreting Data** How much digestion occurred in 16 hours?

4. **Drawing Conclusions** During which 4-hour period did the most digestion take place?

The Stomach

When food leaves the esophagus, it enters the **stomach,** a J-shaped, muscular pouch located in the abdomen. As you eat, your stomach expands to hold all of the food that you swallow. **Most mechanical digestion and some chemical digestion occur in the stomach.**

Mechanical Digestion in the Stomach The process of mechanical digestion occurs as three strong layers of smooth muscle contract to produce a churning motion. This action mixes the food with fluids in somewhat the same way that clothes and soapy water are mixed in a washing machine.

Chemical Digestion in the Stomach Chemical digestion occurs as the churning food makes contact with digestive juice, a fluid produced by cells in the lining of the stomach. Digestive juice contains the enzyme pepsin. Pepsin chemically digests the proteins in your food, breaking them down into short chains of amino acids.

Digestive juice also contains hydrochloric acid, a very strong acid. Without this strong acid, your stomach could not function properly. First, pepsin works best in an acid environment. Second, the acid kills many bacteria that you swallow with your food.

Why doesn't stomach acid burn a hole in your stomach? The reason is that cells in the stomach lining produce a thick coating of mucus, which protects the stomach lining. Also, the cells that line the stomach are quickly replaced as they are damaged or worn out.

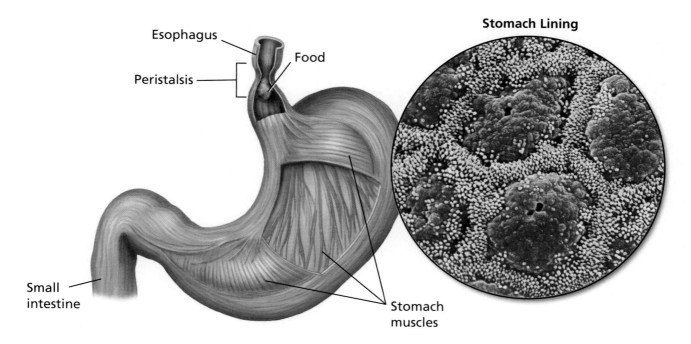

Esophagus

Food

Peristalsis

Small intestine

Stomach muscles

Stomach Lining

Food remains in the stomach until all of the solid material has been broken down into liquid form. A few hours after you finish eating, the stomach completes mechanical digestion of the food. By that time, most of the proteins have been chemically digested into shorter chains of amino acids. The food, now a thick liquid, is released into the next part of the digestive system. That is where final chemical digestion and absorption will take place.

 **Reading Checkpoint** What is pepsin?

FIGURE 17
The Stomach
The stomach has three layers of muscle that help to break down foods mechanically. The inset photo shows a microscopic view of the stomach lining. The yellow dots are mucus.
Relating Cause and Effect *What role does mucus play inside the stomach?*

Section 3 Assessment

Target Reading Skill Using Prior Knowledge Review your graphic organizer and revise it based on what you just learned in the section.

Reviewing Key Concepts

1. **a.** Listing What are the functions of the digestive system?
   b. Comparing and Contrasting Distinguish between mechanical and chemical digestion.
   c. Inferring Why must mechanical digestion start before chemical digestion?
2. **a.** Reviewing What key chemicals do the mouth and stomach contain?
   b. Describing How do pepsin and hydrochloric acid work together to digest food in the stomach?
   c. Predicting What could happen if your stomach didn't produce enough mucus? Explain.

Lab zone **At-Home Activity**

First Aid for Choking Explain to your family what happens when people choke on food. With your family, find out how to recognize when a person is choking and what to do to help the person. Learn about the Heimlich maneuver and how it is used to help someone who is choking.

As the Stomach Churns

Problem

What conditions are needed for the digestion of proteins in the stomach?

Skills Focus

interpreting data, controlling variables, drawing conclusions

Materials

- test-tube rack
- pepsin
- water
- 4 strips blue litmus paper
- cubes of boiled egg white
- 10-mL plastic graduated cylinder
- 4 test tubes with stoppers
- marking pencil
- diluted hydrochloric acid
- plastic stirrers

Procedure

1. In this lab, you will investigate how acidic conditions affect protein digestion. Read over the entire lab to see what materials you will be testing. Write a prediction stating which conditions you think will speed up protein digestion. Then, copy the data table into your notebook.

2. Label four test tubes A, B, C, and D, and place them in a test-tube rack.

3. In this lab, the protein you will test is boiled egg white, which has been cut into cubes about 1 cm on each side. Add 3 cubes to each test tube. Note and record the size and overall appearance of the cubes in each test tube. **CAUTION:** *Do not put any egg white into your mouth.*

4. Use a graduated cylinder to add 10 mL of the enzyme pepsin to test tube A. Observe the egg white cubes to determine whether an immediate reaction takes place. Record your observations under Day 1 in your data table. If no changes occur, write "no immediate reaction."

5. Use a clean graduated cylinder to add 5 mL of pepsin to test tube B. Then rinse out the graduated cylinder and add 5 mL of water to test tube B. Observe whether or not an immediate reaction takes place.

6. Use a clean graduated cylinder to add 10 mL of hydrochloric acid to test tube C. Observe whether or not an immediate reaction takes place. **CAUTION:** *Hydrochloric acid can burn skin and clothing. Avoid direct contact with it. Wash any splashes or spills with plenty of water, and notify your teacher.*

Data Table				
Test Tube	Egg White Appearance		Litmus Color	
	Day 1	Day 2	Day 1	Day 2
A				
B				
C				
D				

7. Use a clean graduated cylinder to add 5 mL of pepsin to test tube D. Then, rinse the graduated cylinder and add 5 mL of hydrochloric acid to test tube D. Observe whether or not an immediate reaction takes place. Record your observations.

8. Obtain four strips of blue litmus paper. (Blue litmus paper turns pink in the presence of an acid.) Dip a clean plastic stirrer into the solution in each test tube, and then touch the stirrer to a piece of litmus paper. Observe what happens to the litmus paper. Record your observations.

9. Insert stoppers in the four test tubes and store the test tube rack as directed by your teacher.

10. The next day, examine the contents of each test tube. Note any changes in the size and overall appearance of the egg white cubes. Then, test each solution with litmus paper. Record your observations in your data table.

Analyze and Conclude

1. **Interpreting Data** Which materials were the best at digesting the egg white? What observations enabled you to determine this?

2. **Inferring** Is the chemical digestion of protein in food a fast or a slow reaction? Explain.

3. **Controlling Variables** Why was it important that the cubes of egg white all be about the same size?

4. **Drawing Conclusions** What did this lab show about the ability of pepsin to digest protein?

5. **Communicating** Write a paragraph in which you describe the purpose of test tube A and test tube C as they relate to the steps you followed in the procedure.

Design an Experiment

Design a way to test whether protein digestion is affected by the size of the food pieces. Write down your hypothesis and the procedure you will follow. *Obtain your teacher's permission before carrying out your investigation.*

Final Digestion and Absorption

Reading Preview

Key Concepts
- What digestive processes occur in the small intestine, and how are other digestive organs involved?
- What role does the large intestine play in digestion?

Key Terms
- small intestine • liver • bile
- gallbladder • pancreas
- villus • large intestine
- rectum • anus

Target Reading Skill

Identifying Main Ideas As you read the section titled The Small Intestine, write the main idea in a graphic organizer like the one below. Then, write three supporting details that further explain the main idea.

Main Idea

Chemical digestion takes place in the . . .

Detail	Detail	Detail

Discover **Activity**

Which Surface Is Larger?

1. Work with a partner to carry out this investigation.
2. Begin by placing your hand palm-side down on a table. Keep your thumb and fingers tightly together. Lay string along the outline of your hand. Have your partner help you determine how long a string you need to outline your hand.
3. Use a metric ruler to measure the length of that string.

Think It Over

Predicting How long would you expect your hand outline to be if you spread out your thumb and fingers? Use string to test your prediction. Compare the two string lengths.

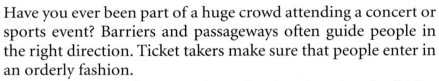

Have you ever been part of a huge crowd attending a concert or sports event? Barriers and passageways often guide people in the right direction. Ticket takers make sure that people enter in an orderly fashion.

In some ways, the stomach can be thought of as the "ticket taker" of the digestive system. Once the food has been changed into a thick liquid, the stomach releases a little of the liquid at a time into the next part of the digestive system. This slow, smooth passage of food through the digestive system ensures that digestion and absorption can take place efficiently.

The Small Intestine

After the thick liquid leaves the stomach, it enters the small intestine. The **small intestine** is the part of the digestive system where most chemical digestion takes place. You may wonder how the small intestine got its name. After all, at about 6 meters—longer than some full-sized cars—it makes up two thirds of the length of the digestive system. The small intestine was named for its small diameter. It is from 2 to 3 centimeters wide, about half the diameter of the large intestine.

When food reaches the small intestine, it has already been mechanically digested into a thick liquid. But chemical digestion has just begun. Starches and proteins have been partially broken down, but fats haven't been digested at all. **Almost all chemical digestion and absorption of nutrients takes place in the small intestine.** As the liquid moves into the small intestine, it mixes with enzymes and secretions that are produced by the small intestine, the liver, and the pancreas. The liver and the pancreas deliver their substances to the small intestine through small tubes.

The Liver As you can see in Figure 18, the liver is located in the upper right portion of the abdomen. It is the largest organ inside the body. The liver is like an extremely busy chemical factory and plays a role in many body processes. For example, it breaks down medicines, and it helps eliminate nitrogen from the body. **The role of the liver in the digestive system is to produce bile.**

Bile is a substance that breaks up fat particles. Bile flows from the liver into the **gallbladder,** the organ that stores bile. After you eat, bile passes through a tube from the gallbladder into the small intestine.

Bile is not an enzyme. It does not chemically digest foods. It does, however, physically break up large fat particles into smaller fat droplets. You can compare the action of bile on fats with the action of soap on a greasy frying pan. Soap physically breaks up the grease into small droplets that can mix with the soapy water and be washed away. Bile mixes with the fats in food to form small fat droplets. The droplets can then be chemically broken down by enzymes produced in the pancreas.

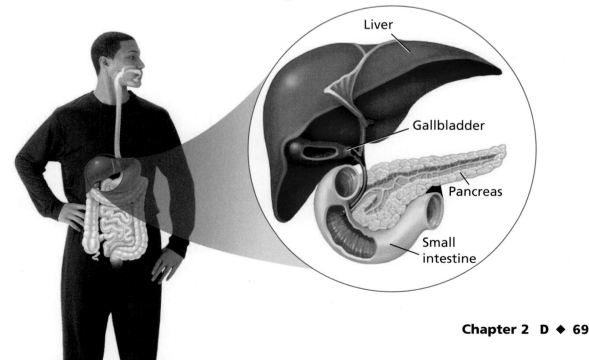

FIGURE 18
The Liver and Pancreas
Substances produced by the liver and pancreas aid in digestion.
Predicting *How would digestion be affected if the tube leading from the gallbladder to the small intestine became blocked?*

Liver

Gallbladder

Pancreas

Small intestine

For: More on the digestive system
Visit: PHSchool.com
Web Code: ced-4024

FIGURE 19
The Small Intestine
Tiny finger-shaped projections called villi line the inside of the small intestine. Blood vessels in the villi are covered by a single layer of cells.
Relating Cause and Effect How does the structure of the villi help them carry out their function?

The Pancreas The **pancreas** is a triangular organ that lies between the stomach and the first part of the small intestine. Like the liver, the pancreas plays a role in many body processes. **As part of the digestive system, the pancreas produces enzymes that flow into the small intestine and help break down starches, proteins, and fats.**

Digestive enzymes do not break down all food substances. Recall that the fiber in food isn't broken down. Instead, fiber thickens the liquid material in the intestine. This thickening makes it easier for peristalsis to push the material forward.

Absorption in the Small Intestine After chemical digestion takes place, the small nutrient molecules are ready to be absorbed by the body. The structure of the small intestine makes it well suited for absorption. The inner surface, or lining, of the small intestine looks bumpy. Millions of tiny finger-shaped structures called **villi** (VIL eye) (singular *villus*) cover the surface. The villi absorb nutrient molecules. Notice in Figure 19 that tiny blood vessels run through the center of each villus. Nutrient molecules pass from cells on the surface of a villus into blood vessels. The blood carries the nutrients throughout the body for use by body cells.

Villi greatly increase the surface area of the small intestine. If all the villi were laid out flat, the total surface area of the small intestine would be about as large as a tennis court. This increased surface enables digested food to be absorbed much faster than if the walls of the small intestine were smooth.

Reading Checkpoint **How does the pancreas aid in digestion?**

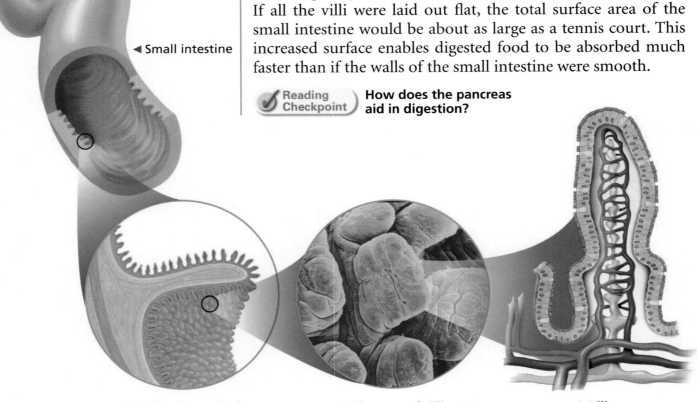

◄ Small intestine

▲ Fold in the wall of the small intestine

▲ Close-up of villi

▲ Villus

The Large Intestine

By the time material reaches the end of the small intestine, most nutrients have been absorbed. The remaining material moves from the small intestine into the large intestine. The **large intestine** is the last section of the digestive system. It is about 1.5 meters long—about as long as the average bathtub. It runs up the right-hand side of the abdomen, across the upper abdomen, and then down the left-hand side. The large intestine contains bacteria that feed on the material passing through. These bacteria normally do not cause disease. In fact, they are helpful because they make certain vitamins, including vitamin K.

The material entering the large intestine contains water and undigested food. **As the material moves through the large intestine, water is absorbed into the bloodstream. The remaining material is readied for elimination from the body.**

The large intestine ends in a short tube called the **rectum.** Here, waste material is compressed into a solid form. This waste material is eliminated from the body through the **anus,** a muscular opening at the end of the rectum.

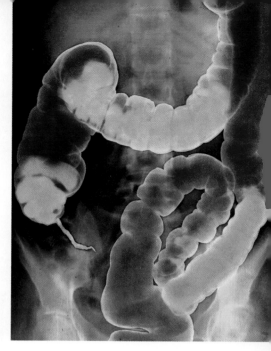

FIGURE 20
The Large Intestine
As material passes through the large intestine, most of the water is absorbed by the body. The remaining material will be eliminated from the body.

 **Reading Checkpoint** What role do bacteria play in the large intestine?

Section 4 Assessment

Target Reading Skill
Identifying Main Ideas Use your graphic organizer to help you answer Question 1 below.

Reviewing Key Concepts
1. **a. Reviewing** What two digestive processes occur in the small intestine?
   b. Explaining Explain how bile produced by the liver and enzymes produced in the pancreas function in the small intestine.
   c. Relating Cause and Effect Some people are allergic to a protein in wheat. When these people eat foods made with wheat, a reaction destroys the villi in the small intestine. What problems would you expect these people to experience?
2. **a. Identifying** Which key nutrient is absorbed in the large intestine?

   b. Describing What happens as food moves through the large intestine?
   c. Applying Concepts Diarrhea is a condition in which waste material that is eliminated contains too much water. How might diarrhea upset homeostasis in the body? How could a person reduce the effects of diarrhea on the body?

Writing in Science

Sequence of Events Describe the journey of a bacon, lettuce, and tomato sandwich through a person's digestive system, starting in the mouth and ending with absorption. Include where digestion of fats, carbohydrates, and proteins take place. Use words like *first*, *next*, and *finally* in your writing.

Study Guide

Structure and Function The digestive system breaks food down into small nutrient molecules that are then absorbed into the blood and carried throughout the body.

1 Food and Energy

Key Concepts

- Foods provide the body with raw materials and energy.
- Carbohydrates provide energy as well as the raw materials to make cell parts.
- In addition to providing energy, fats form part of the cell membrane. Fatty tissue also protects and supports internal organs and insulates the body.
- Proteins are needed for tissue growth and repair. They also play an important part in chemical reactions within cells.
- Vitamins and minerals are needed in small amounts to carry out chemical processes.
- Water is the most important nutrient because the body's vital processes take place in water.

Key Terms

- nutrient • calorie • carbohydrate • glucose
- fat • protein • amino acid • vitamin
- mineral

2 Healthy Eating

Key Concepts

- The USDA guidelines help people make healthy food choices based on their age, sex, and amount of physical activity.
- Food labels allow you to evaluate a single food as well as to compare the nutritional value of two different foods.

Key Terms

Percent Daily Value
Dietary Reference Intakes (DRIs)

3 The Digestive Process Begins

Key Concepts

- The digestive system breaks down food into molecules the body can use. Then, the molecules are absorbed into the blood and carried throughout the body. Finally, wastes are eliminated.
- Both mechanical and chemical digestion begin in the mouth.
- In the esophagus, contractions of smooth muscles push the food toward the stomach.
- Most mechanical digestion and some chemical digestion occur in the stomach.

Key Terms

- digestion • absorption • saliva • enzyme
- epiglottis • esophagus • mucus • peristalsis
- stomach

4 Final Digestion and Absorption

Key Concepts

- Almost all chemical digestion and absorption of nutrients takes place in the small intestine.
- The liver produces bile, which breaks up fats.
- The pancreas produces enzymes that help break down starches, proteins, and fats.
- In the large intestine, water is absorbed into the bloodstream. The remaining material is readied for elimination.

Key Terms

- small intestine • liver • bile • gallbladder
- pancreas • villus • large intestine • rectum
- anus

Review and Assessment

Go Online
PHSchool.com
For: Self-Assessment
Visit: PHSchool.com
Web Code: cea-4020

Organizing Information

Sequencing Copy the flowchart about digestion onto a separate sheet of paper. Then, complete it and add a title. (For more on Sequencing, see the Skills Handbook.)

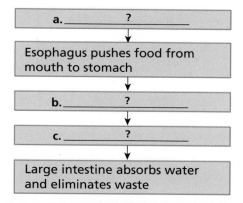

a. ?

↓

Esophagus pushes food from mouth to stomach

↓

b. ?

↓

c. ?

↓

Large intestine absorbs water and eliminates waste

Reviewing Key Terms

Choose the letter of the best answer.

1. The building blocks of proteins are
   a. vitamins.
   b. minerals.
   c. amino acids.
   d. fats.

2. Dietary Reference Intakes (DRIs) are guidelines that show the
   a. Calories in a specific food.
   b. nutrients in a specific food.
   c. proportions of different food groups in a healthy diet.
   d. amounts of nutrients needed every day.

3. The enzyme in saliva chemically breaks down
   a. fats.
   b. proteins.
   c. glucose.
   d. starches.

4. Most mechanical digestion takes place in the
   a. liver.
   b. esophagus.
   c. stomach.
   d. small intestine.

5. Bile is produced by the
   a. liver.
   b. pancreas.
   c. small intestine.
   d. large intestine.

If the statement is true, write *true*. If it is false, change the underlined word or words to make the statement true.

6. Proteins that come from animal sources are <u>incomplete</u> proteins.

7. <u>Vitamins</u> are nutrients that are not made by living things.

8. To determine which of two cereals supplies more iron, check the <u>Percent Daily Value</u> on the food label.

9. <u>Absorption</u> moves food through the digestive system.

10. Most materials are absorbed into the bloodstream in the <u>large</u> intestine.

Writing in Science

Information Sheet You are a nutritionist assigned to work with a family trying to eat a more healthful diet. Write an instruction sheet outlining what kinds of foods they should eat. Provide some examples of each kind of food.

Discovery CHANNEL SCHOOL

Food and Digestion

Video Preview
Video Field Trip
▶ Video Assessment

Review and Assessment

Checking Concepts

11. How does a person's level of physical activity affect his or her daily energy needs?

12. Why is fiber necessary in a person's diet?

13. Why do the USDA MyPyramid plans differ from one person to another?

14. Describe the function of the epiglottis.

15. Explain the role of peristalsis.

16. What is the function of the pancreas in the digestive process?

17. What is the function of villi?

Thinking Critically

18. Applying Concepts Before winter, animals that hibernate often prepare by eating foods high in fat. How is this behavior helpful?

19. Predicting Suppose a medicine killed all the bacteria in your body. How might this affect vitamin production in your body?

20. Inferring Why is it important for people to chew their food thoroughly before swallowing?

21. Relating Cause and Effect How does the condition illustrated in the diagram below affect the esophagus?

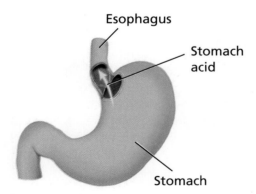

Esophagus

Stomach acid

Stomach

22. Comparing and Contrasting The digestive system is sometimes said to be "an assembly line in reverse." Identify some similarities and some differences between your digestive system and an assembly line.

Math Practice

23. Percentage Your aunt eats 250 Calories of protein and 1,800 Calories total for the day. Did she get enough protein on that particular day? Show your calculations.

Applying Skills

Use the table to answer Questions 24–27.

Comparing Nutrient Data

Food (1 cup)	Calcium (% Daily Value)	Calories	Calories From Fat
Chocolate milk	30	230	80
Low-fat milk	35	110	20
Plain yogurt	35	110	35

24. Classifying To which group in a food pyramid do the foods in the chart belong? How does the body benefit from calcium in the diet?

25. Interpreting Data How many cups of low-fat milk provide 100% of the day's Daily Value for calcium?

26. Calculating Which of the foods meet the recommendation that no more than 30 percent of a food's Calories come from fat? Explain.

27. Making Judgments Which of the foods would be the most healthful choice for an afterschool snack? Explain your reasoning.

Lab zone Chapter Project

Performance Assessment Write a summary of what you've learned from keeping a food log. How close were your eating patterns to those recommended in your USDA MyPyramid Plan? How successful were you in making changes in your diet to match the MyPyramid Plan?

Standardized Test Prep

Choose the letter of the best answer.

1. Which of the following parts of the digestive system is *best* paired with its function?
   A esophagus—digests carbohydrates
   B stomach—digests fats
   C small intestine—absorbs water
   D liver—produces bile

2. A food label on a cereal box gives you the following information: a serving size equals one cup and there are 110 Calories per serving. You measure the amount of cereal you plan to eat and find that it measures 1 1/2 cups. How many Calories will you consume?
   F 110 Calories
   G 165 Calories
   H 220 Calories
   J 1,100 Calories

Use the table below and your knowledge of science to answer Questions 3 and 4.

Length of Time Food Stays in Organ	
Organ	**Time**
Mouth	Less than 1 minute
Esophagus	Less than 1 minute
Stomach	1–3 hours
Small Intestine	1–6 hours
Large Intestine	12–36 hours

3. If a meal is eaten at noon, what is happening to the food at 1 P.M.?
   A Saliva is breaking down starch into sugar.
   B Proteins are being digested into short chains of amino acids.
   C Fats are being digested.
   D Digested food is being absorbed into the blood.

4. For food eaten at noon, absorption cannot have begun by
   F 1 P.M.
   G 7 P.M.
   H 9 P.M.
   J noon the next day.

5. Which of the following organs is *not* just a digestive organ?
   A stomach
   B liver
   C small intestine
   D large intestine

Constructed Response

6. Compare the processes of mechanical and chemical digestion. How are they similar? How are they different? In what parts of the digestive system do the two processes take place? How do the processes occur?

Chapter 3

Circulation

The BIG Idea
Structure and Function

 Q What are the major functions of the circulatory system?

Blood cells travel in blood vessels ▶
to all parts of the body.

Lab zone™ Chapter **Project**

Travels of a Red Blood Cell

Every day, you travel from home to school and back home again. Your travel path makes a loop, or circuit, ending where it began. In this chapter, you'll learn how your blood also travels in circuits. In this project, you'll create a display to show how blood circulates throughout the body.

Your Goal To design and construct a display showing a complete journey of a red blood cell through the human body

Your display must
- show a red blood cell that leaves from the heart and returns to the same place
- show where the exchange of oxygen and carbon dioxide takes place
- provide written descriptions of the circuits made by the red blood cell
- be designed following the safety guidelines in Appendix A

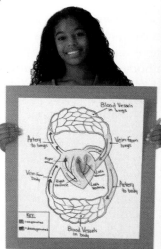

Plan It! Preview the chapter and find diagrams that show the heart, red blood cells, and the pathway of blood throughout the body. Then discuss the kinds of displays you could use, including a three-dimensional model, posters, a series of drawings, a flip book, or a video animation. Write down any content questions you'll need to answer.

The Body's Transport System

Reading Preview

Key Concepts
- What are the functions of the cardiovascular system?
- What is the structure and function of the heart?
- What path does blood take through the cardiovascular system?

Key Terms
- cardiovascular system • heart
- atrium • ventricle • valve
- pacemaker • artery
- capillary • vein • aorta

Target Reading Skill
Sequencing As you read, make a cycle diagram like the one below that shows the path that blood follows as it circulates throughout the body. Write each step of the pathway in a separate circle.

Pathway of Blood

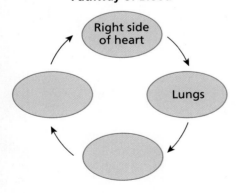

Discover **Activity**

How Hard Does Your Heart Work?

1. Every minute, your heart beats about 75 to 85 times. With each beat, it pumps about 60 milliliters of blood. Can you work as hard and fast as your heart does?

2. Cover a table or desk with newspapers. Place two large plastic containers side by side on the newspapers. Fill one with 2.5 liters of water, which is about the volume of blood that your heart pumps in 30 seconds. Leave the other container empty.

3. With a plastic cup that holds about 60 milliliters, transfer water as quickly as possible into the empty container, trying not to spill any. **CAUTION:** *Wipe up spills on the floor immediately.* Have a partner time you for 30 seconds. As you work, count how many transfers you make in 30 seconds.

4. Multiply your results by 2 to find the number of transfers in 1 minute.

Think It Over
Inferring Compare your performance with the number of times your heart beats every minute. What do your results tell you about the strength and speed of a heartbeat?

Late at night, a truck rolls through the darkness. Loaded with fresh fruits and vegetables, the truck is headed for a city supermarket. The driver steers off the interstate and onto a smaller highway. Finally, after driving through narrow city streets, the truck reaches its destination. As dawn breaks, store workers unload the cargo. At the same time, a garbage truck removes yesterday's trash and drives off down the road.

The Cardiovascular System

Like the roads that link all parts of the country, your body has a "highway" network, called the cardiovascular system, that links all parts of your body. The **cardiovascular system,** also called the circulatory system, consists of the heart, blood vessels, and blood. **The cardiovascular system carries needed substances to cells and carries waste products away from cells. In addition, blood contains cells that fight disease.**

Delivering Needed Materials Most substances that need to get from one part of the body to another are carried by blood. For example, blood carries oxygen from your lungs to your other body cells. Blood also transports the glucose your cells use to produce energy.

Removing Waste Products The cardiovascular system picks up wastes from cells. For example, when cells break down glucose, they produce carbon dioxide as a waste product. The carbon dioxide passes from the cells into the blood. The cardiovascular system then carries carbon dioxide to the lungs, where it is exhaled.

Fighting Disease The cardiovascular system also transports cells that attack disease-causing microorganisms. This process can help keep you from becoming sick. If you do get sick, these disease-fighting blood cells will kill the microorganisms and help you get well.

Reading Checkpoint How does the cardiovascular system help fight disease?

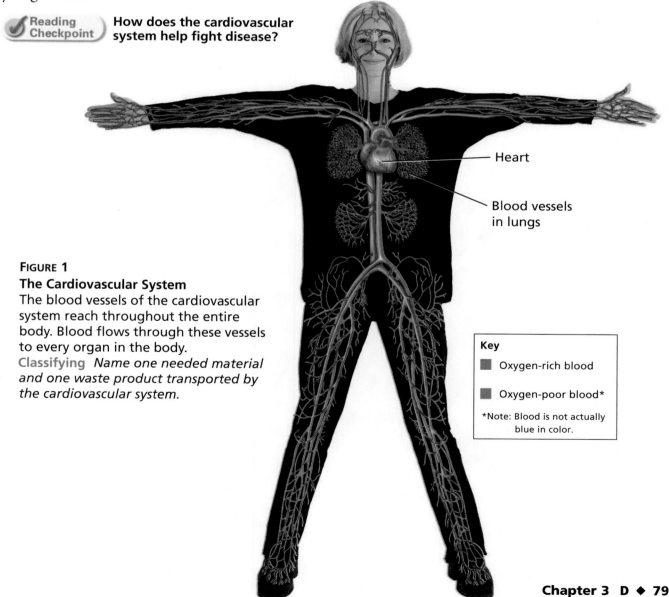

FIGURE 1
The Cardiovascular System
The blood vessels of the cardiovascular system reach throughout the entire body. Blood flows through these vessels to every organ in the body.
Classifying *Name one needed material and one waste product transported by the cardiovascular system.*

Heart

Blood vessels in lungs

Key

■ Oxygen-rich blood

■ Oxygen-poor blood*

*Note: Blood is not actually blue in color.

The Heart

Without the heart, blood wouldn't go anywhere. The **heart** is a hollow, muscular organ that pumps blood throughout the body. Your heart, which is about the size of your fist, is located in the center of your chest. The heart lies behind the sternum (breastbone) and inside the rib cage. These bones protect the heart from injury.

Each time the heart beats, it pushes blood through the blood vessels of the cardiovascular system. The heart is made of cardiac muscle, which can contract over and over without getting tired. Figure 2 shows the structure of the heart.

Go Online
active art

For: The Heart activity
Visit: PHSchool.com
Web Code: cep-4031

FIGURE 2
The Heart

Every second of your life, your heart pumps blood through your body. In a year, the heart pumps enough blood to fill more than 30 competition-size swimming pools.

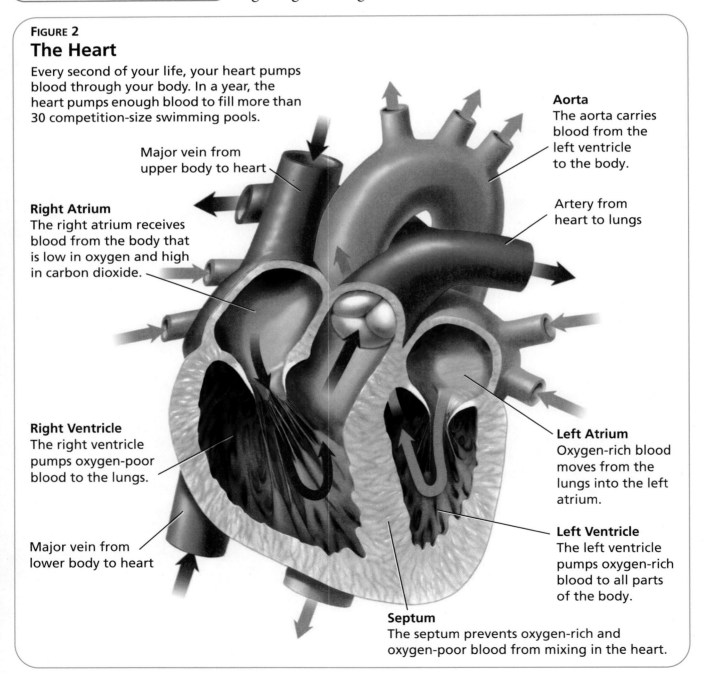

Major vein from upper body to heart

Aorta
The aorta carries blood from the left ventricle to the body.

Right Atrium
The right atrium receives blood from the body that is low in oxygen and high in carbon dioxide.

Artery from heart to lungs

Right Ventricle
The right ventricle pumps oxygen-poor blood to the lungs.

Left Atrium
Oxygen-rich blood moves from the lungs into the left atrium.

Major vein from lower body to heart

Left Ventricle
The left ventricle pumps oxygen-rich blood to all parts of the body.

Septum
The septum prevents oxygen-rich and oxygen-poor blood from mixing in the heart.

The Heart's Structure Notice in Figure 2 that the heart has a right side and a left side. **The right side of the heart is completely separated from the left side by a wall of tissue called the septum. Each side has two compartments, or chambers— an upper chamber and a lower chamber.** Each of the two upper chambers, called an **atrium** (AY tree um) (plural *atria*), receives blood that comes into the heart.

Each lower chamber, called a **ventricle,** pumps blood out of the heart. The atria are separated from the ventricles by valves. A **valve** is a flap of tissue that prevents blood from flowing backward. Valves are also located between the ventricles and the large blood vessels that carry blood away from the heart.

How the Heart Works The action of the heart has two main phases. In one phase, the heart muscle relaxes and the heart fills with blood. In the other phase, the heart muscle contracts and pumps blood forward. A heartbeat, which sounds something like *lub-dup*, can be heard during the pumping phase.

When the heart muscle relaxes, blood flows into the chambers. Then, the atria contract. This muscle contraction squeezes blood out of the atria, through the valves, and into the ventricles. Next, the ventricles contract. This contraction closes the valves between the atria and ventricles, making the *lub* sound and squeezing blood into large blood vessels. As the valves between the ventricles and the blood vessels snap shut, they make the *dup* sound. All of this happens in less than a second.

The Force of the Ventricles When muscle cells in the ventricles contract, they exert a force on the blood. A force is a push or a pull. The force exerted by the ventricles pushes blood out of your heart and into arteries.

The contraction of the left ventricle exerts much more force than the contraction of the right ventricle. The right ventricle pumps blood only to the lungs. In contrast, the left ventricle pumps blood throughout the body.

FIGURE 3
Open and Closed Heart Valves
As blood flows out of the heart and toward the lungs, it passes through a valve like the one in the photograph. **Applying Concepts** *What is the function of a closed heart valve?*

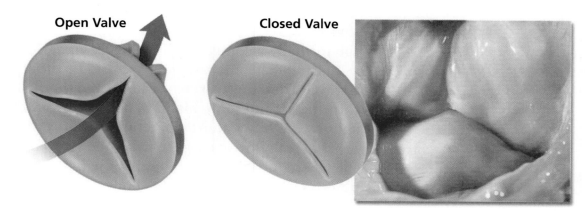

Open Valve   **Closed Valve**

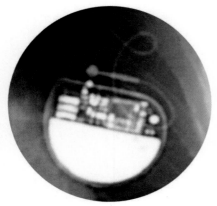

FIGURE 4
An Artificial Pacemaker
This pacemaker has been implanted beneath a patient's skin and connected with wires to the heart. The pacemaker will regulate the patient's heartbeat.

Regulation of Heartbeat A group of heart cells called the **pacemaker** sends out signals that make the heart muscle contract. The pacemaker is located in the right atrium of the heart.

The pacemaker constantly receives messages about the body's oxygen needs. It then adjusts the heart rate to match. For example, your heart beats much faster when you are exercising than when you are sitting quietly. When you exercise, the entire process from the beginning of one heartbeat to the beginning of the next can take less than half a second. Your muscles need more oxygen during exercise. Your rapid heartbeat supplies blood that carries the oxygen throughout your body.

In some people, the pacemaker becomes damaged as a result of disease or an accident. Damage to the pacemaker often results in an irregular or slow heartbeat. In the 1950s, doctors and engineers developed an artificial, battery-operated pacemaker. Modern artificial pacemakers are implanted beneath the skin and are connected by wires to the heart. Tiny electrical impulses travel from the battery through the wires, and make the heart contract.

 **Reading Checkpoint** **What is the function of the heart's pacemaker?**

Two Loops

After leaving the heart, blood travels in blood vessels through the body. Your body has three kinds of blood vessels—arteries, capillaries, and veins. **Arteries** are blood vessels that carry blood away from the heart. From the arteries, blood flows into tiny, narrow vessels called **capillaries.** In the capillaries, substances are exchanged between the blood and body cells. From capillaries, blood flows into **veins,** blood vessels that carry blood back to the heart.

Pattern of Blood Flow The overall pattern of blood flow through the body is something like a figure eight. The heart is at the center where the two loops cross. **In the first loop, blood travels from the heart to the lungs and then back to the heart. In the second loop, blood is pumped from the heart throughout the body and then returns again to the heart.** The heart is really two pumps, one on the right and one on the left. The right side pumps blood to the lungs, and the left side pumps blood to the rest of the body.

Blood travels in only one direction. If you were a drop of blood, you could start at any point and eventually return to the same point. The entire trip would take less than a minute. As you read about the path that blood takes through the cardiovascular system, trace the path in Figure 5.

Loop One: To the Lungs and Back When blood from the body flows into the right atrium, it contains little oxygen but a lot of carbon dioxide. This oxygen-poor blood is dark red. The blood then flows from the right atrium into the right ventricle. Then, the ventricle pumps the oxygen-poor blood into the arteries that lead to the lungs.

As blood flows through the lungs, large blood vessels branch into smaller ones. Eventually, blood flows through tiny capillaries that are in close contact with the air that comes into the lungs. The air in the lungs has more oxygen than the blood in the capillaries. Therefore, oxygen moves from the lungs into the blood. For the same reason, carbon dioxide moves in the opposite direction—from the blood into the lungs. As the blood leaves the lungs, it is now rich in oxygen and contains little carbon dioxide. This blood, which is bright red, flows to the left side of the heart and will be pumped through the second loop.

Circulation

Video Preview
▶ Video Field Trip
Video Assessment

FIGURE 5
Direction of Blood Flow
Blood circulates through the body in two loops, with the heart at the center. Loop one goes from the heart to the lungs and back. Loop two circulates blood throughout the rest of the body.
Interpreting Diagrams *Where does the blood that enters the left atrium come from?*

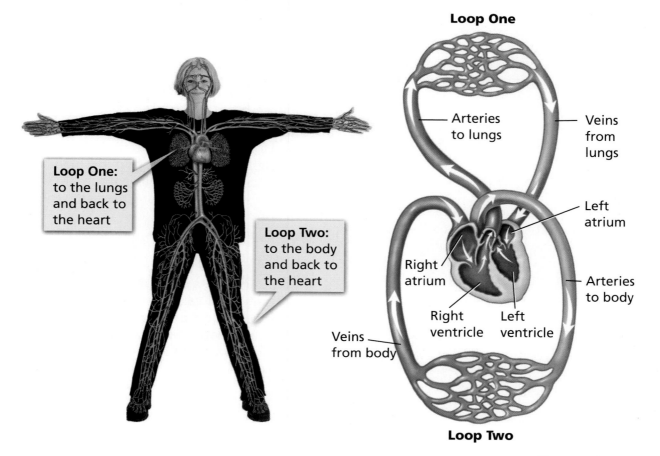

Loop Two: To the Body and Back The second loop begins as the left atrium fills with oxygen-rich blood coming from the lungs. The blood then moves into the left ventricle. From the left ventricle, the blood is pumped into the **aorta** (ay AWR tuh), the largest artery in the body.

Eventually, after passing through branching arteries, blood flows through tiny capillaries in different parts of your body, such as your brain, liver, and legs. These vessels are in close contact with body cells. Oxygen moves out of the blood and into the body cells. At the same time, carbon dioxide passes from the body cells into the blood. This blood, which is low in oxygen, then flows back to the right atrium of the heart through veins, completing the second loop.

FIGURE 6
Getting Blood to Body Cells
In loop two, oxygen-rich blood is pumped throughout the body. The oxygen moves out of the blood and into the body cells in this swimmer's arms and legs.

 **Reading Checkpoint** **What is the largest artery in the body?**

Section 1 Assessment

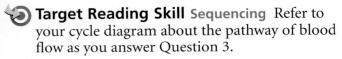

Target Reading Skill **Sequencing** Refer to your cycle diagram about the pathway of blood flow as you answer Question 3.

Reviewing Key Concepts

1. a. **Reviewing** What three functions does the cardiovascular system perform?
   b. **Comparing and Contrasting** Distinguish between substances that the cardiovascular system transports to cells and substances that it transports away from cells.

2. a. **Listing** Name the four chambers of the heart. What structures in the heart separate one chamber from another?
   b. **Summarizing** What function does the heart perform?
   c. **Predicting** What would happen if the valve between the right atrium and right ventricle did not work properly?

3. a. **Identifying** Where does blood returning from the body enter the heart?
   b. **Sequencing** Where does the blood move next?
   c. **Interpreting Diagrams** Review Figure 5. How does the blood in the artery leaving the right ventricle differ from the blood in the artery leaving the left ventricle? To where does the artery leaving the right ventricle carry blood?

Writing in Science

Comparison Paragraph Write a paragraph comparing the cardiovascular system in the body to a system of roads, telephone lines, or any other "network" you can think of. How are the two systems alike? How do they differ?

A Closer Look at Blood Vessels

Reading Preview

Key Concepts
- What are the structures and functions of arteries?
- What are the structures and functions of capillaries and veins?
- What causes blood pressure?

Key Terms
- coronary artery • pulse
- diffusion • blood pressure

Target Reading Skill

Comparing and Contrasting As you read, compare and contrast the three kinds of blood vessels by completing a table like the one below.

Comparing Blood Vessels

Blood Vessel	Function	Structure of Wall
Artery	Carries blood away from heart	
Capillary		
Vein		

Discover Activity

How Does Pressure Affect Blood Flow?

1. Spread newspapers over a table or desktop. Then, fill a plastic squeeze bottle with water.
2. Hold the bottle over a dishpan. Squeeze the bottle with one hand. Observe how far the water travels. **CAUTION:** *Wipe up spills on the floor to prevent anyone from slipping.*
3. Now, grasp the bottle with both hands and squeeze again. Observe how far the water travels this time.

Think It Over

Inferring Blood is pushed through arteries with much more force than it is pushed through veins. Which part of the activity models an artery? Which part models a vein? Which organ in the body provides the pushing force for blood transport?

Like corridors in a large building, blood vessels run through all of the tissues of your body. Although some blood vessels are as wide as your thumb, most of them are much finer than a human hair. If all the arteries, capillaries, and veins in your body were hooked together end to end, they would stretch a distance of almost 100,000 kilometers. That's long enough to wrap around Earth twice—with a lot left over!

FIGURE 7
Blood Vessels
Thousands of kilometers of blood vessels throughout your body transport the liquid vital to your survival—blood. This model shows the major arteries and veins in the arm.

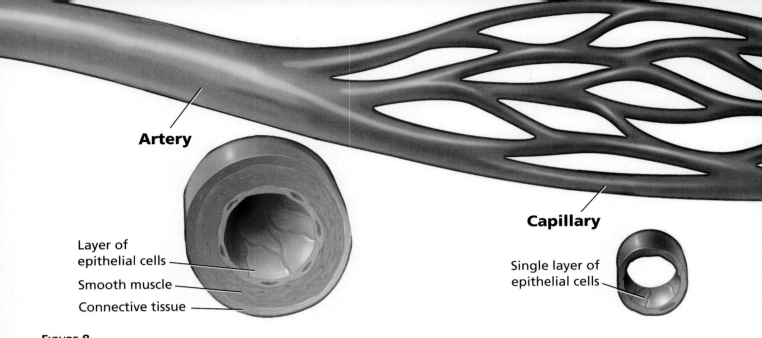

Artery

Layer of
epithelial cells
Smooth muscle
Connective tissue

Capillary

Single layer of
epithelial cells

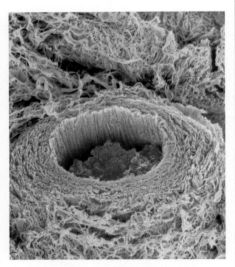

▲ The artery wall appears as a
thick pink band surrounding a
clump of red blood cells.

Arteries

When blood leaves the heart, it travels through arteries. The right ventricle pumps blood into the arteries that go to the lungs. The left ventricle pumps blood into the aorta. Smaller arteries branch off the aorta. The first branches, called the **coronary arteries,** carry blood to the heart itself. Other branches carry blood to the brain, intestines, and other organs. Each artery branches into smaller and smaller arteries.

Artery Structure **The walls of arteries are generally very thick. In fact, artery walls consist of three cell layers.** The innermost layer, which is made up of epithelial cells, is smooth. This smooth surface enables blood to flow freely. The middle layer consists mostly of muscle tissue. The outer wall is made up of flexible connective tissue. Because of this layered structure, arteries have both strength and flexibility. Arteries are able to withstand the enormous pressure of blood as it is pumped by the heart and to expand and relax between heart beats.

Pulse If you lightly touch the inside of your wrist, you can feel the artery in your wrist rise and fall repeatedly. This **pulse** is caused by the alternating expansion and relaxation of the artery wall. Every time the heart's ventricles contract, they send a spurt of blood out through all the arteries in your body. As this spurt travels through the arteries, it pushes the artery walls and makes them expand. After the spurt passes, the artery walls relax and become narrower again.

When you count the number of times an artery pulses beneath your fingers, you are counting heartbeats. By taking your pulse rate, you can determine how fast your heart is beating.

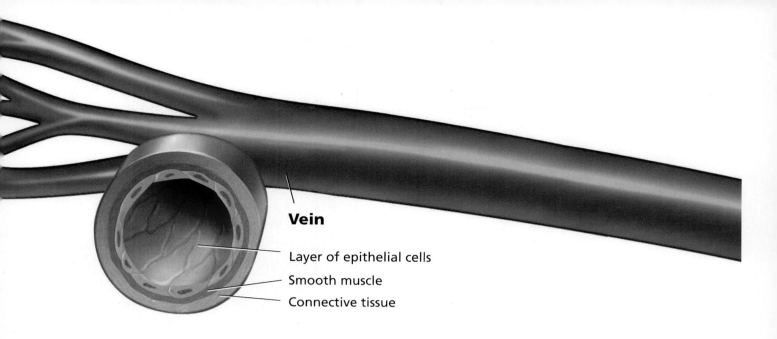

Vein

Layer of epithelial cells

Smooth muscle

Connective tissue

Regulating Blood Flow The layer of muscle in an artery acts as a control gate, adjusting the amount of blood sent to different organs. When the muscle contracts, the opening in the artery becomes smaller. When the muscle relaxes, the opening becomes larger. For example, after you eat, your stomach and intestines need a greater blood supply for digestion. The arteries leading to those organs open wider, and more blood flows through them. In contrast, when you are running, your stomach and intestines need less blood than the muscles in your legs. The arteries leading to the digestive organs become narrower, decreasing the blood flow to these organs.

 **What causes your pulse?**

Capillaries

Eventually, blood flows from small arteries into the tiny capillaries. **In the capillaries, materials are exchanged between the blood and the body's cells. Capillary walls are only one cell thick.** Thus, materials can pass easily through them. Materials such as oxygen and glucose pass from the blood, through the capillary walls, to the cells. Cellular waste products travel in the opposite direction—from cells, through the capillary walls, and into the blood.

One way that materials are exchanged between the blood and body cells is by diffusion. **Diffusion** is the process by which molecules move from an area of higher concentration to an area of lower concentration. For example, glucose is more highly concentrated in the blood than it is in the body cells. Therefore, glucose diffuses from the blood into the body cells.

Math Skills

Calculating a Rate
A rate is the speed at which something happens. When you calculate a rate, you compare the number of events with the time period in which they occur. Here's how to calculate the pulse rate of a person whose heart beats 142 times in 2 minutes.

1. Write the comparison as a fraction.

$$\frac{142 \text{ heartbeats}}{2 \text{ minutes}}$$

2. Divide the numerator and the denominator by 2.

$$\frac{142 \div 2}{2 \div 2} = \frac{71}{1}$$

The person's pulse rate is 71 heartbeats per minute.

Practice Problem Calculate your pulse rate if your heart beats 170 times in 2.5 minutes.

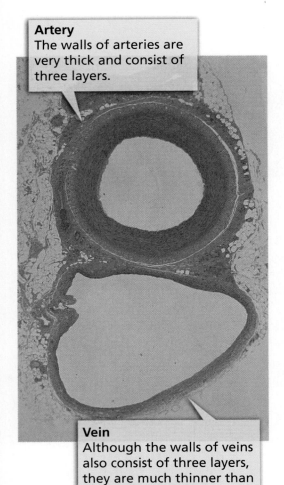

Artery
The walls of arteries are very thick and consist of three layers.

Vein
Although the walls of veins also consist of three layers, they are much thinner than the walls of arteries.

FIGURE 9
Artery and Vein
In this photo, you can compare the wall of an artery (top) with the wall of a vein (bottom).
Comparing and Contrasting
Where is the pushing force of the heart greater—in arteries or in veins?

Veins

After blood moves through capillaries, it enters larger blood vessels called veins, which carry blood back to the heart. The walls of veins, like those of arteries, have three layers, with muscle in the middle layer. However, the walls of veins are generally much thinner than those of arteries.

By the time blood flows into veins, the pushing force of the heart has much less effect than it did in the arteries. Several factors help move blood through veins. First, because many veins are located near skeletal muscles, the contraction of the muscles helps push the blood along. For example, as you run or walk, the skeletal muscles in your legs contract and squeeze the veins in your legs. Second, larger veins in your body have valves in them that prevent blood from flowing backward. Third, breathing movements, which exert a squeezing pressure against veins in the chest, also force blood toward the heart.

 **Reading Checkpoint** How do skeletal muscles help move blood in veins?

Blood Pressure

Suppose that you are washing a car. You attach the hose to the faucet and turn on the faucet. The water flows out in a slow, steady stream. Then, while your back is turned, your little brother turns the faucet on all the way. Suddenly, the water spurts out rapidly, and the hose almost jumps out of your hand.

As water flows through a hose, it pushes against the walls of the hose, creating pressure on the walls. Pressure is the force that something exerts over a given area. When your brother turned on the faucet all the way, the additional water flow increased the pressure exerted on the inside of the hose. The extra pressure made the water spurt out of the nozzle faster.

What Causes Blood Pressure? Blood traveling through blood vessels behaves in a manner similar to that of water moving through a hose. Blood exerts a force, called **blood pressure,** against the walls of blood vessels. **Blood pressure is caused by the force with which the ventricles contract.** In general, as blood moves away from the heart, blood pressure decreases. This change happens because the farther away from the ventricle the blood moves, the lower its force is. Blood flowing through the arteries exerts the highest pressure. Blood pressure in arteries farther from the heart is much lower.

Measuring Blood Pressure Blood pressure can be measured with an instrument called a sphygmomanometer (sfig moh muh NAHM uh tur). A cuff is wrapped around the upper arm. Air is pumped into the cuff until the blood flow through the artery is stopped. As the pressure is released, the examiner listens to the pulse and records two numbers. Blood pressure is expressed in millimeters of mercury. The first number is a measure of the blood pressure while the heart's ventricles contract and pump blood into the arteries. The second number, which is lower, measures the blood pressure while the ventricles relax. The two numbers are expressed as a fraction: the contraction pressure over the relaxation pressure.

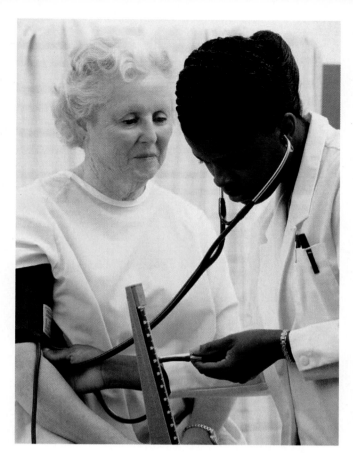

FIGURE 10
Measuring Blood Pressure
Blood pressure can be measured with a sphygmomanometer. A typical blood pressure reading for a healthy person is 120/80 or lower.

Section 2 Assessment

Target Reading Skill Comparing and Contrasting Use the information in your table about blood vessels to help you answer the questions below.

Reviewing Key Concepts

1. a. **Identifying** In which direction do arteries carry blood?
   b. **Explaining** How does the structure of arteries enable them to withstand high pressure?
   c. **Applying Concepts** Arteries adjust the amount of blood flowing to different parts of the body, depending on where blood is needed. Use this fact to explain why you should not exercise vigorously shortly after you eat.
2. a. **Reviewing** What is the function of capillaries in the body?
   b. **Summarizing** Summarize the factors that enable blood in your leg veins to return to the heart in spite of the downward pull of gravity.

3. a. **Defining** What is blood pressure?
   b. **Relating Cause and Effect** Why is blood pressure lower in leg veins than in the aorta?
   c. **Predicting** How might having low blood pressure affect your body?

Math Practice

Before a run, you take your pulse rate for 30 seconds and count 29 beats. Immediately after the run, you count 63 beats in 30 seconds. After resting for 15 minutes, you count 31 beats in 30 seconds.

4. **Calculating a Rate** What was your pulse rate per minute before the run?
5. **Calculating a Rate** What was your pulse rate immediately after the run? After resting for 15 minutes?

Heart Beat, Health Beat

Problem

How does physical activity affect your pulse rate?

Skills Focus

graphing, interpreting data, drawing conclusions

Materials

- graph paper
- watch with second hand or heart rate monitor

Procedure

1. Predict how your pulse rate will change as you go from resting to being active, then back to resting again. Then, copy the data table into your notebook.

2. Locate your pulse by placing the index and middle finger of one hand on your other wrist at the base of your thumb. Move the two fingers slightly until you feel your pulse. If you are using a heart rate monitor, see your teacher for instructions.

3. Work with a partner for the rest of this lab. Begin by determining your resting pulse rate. Count the number of beats in your pulse for exactly 1 minute while your partner times you. Record your resting pulse rate in your data table. **CAUTION:** *Do not complete the rest of this lab if there is any medical reason why you should avoid physical activities.*

4. Walk in place for 1 minute while your partner times you. Stop and immediately take your pulse for 1 minute. Record the number in your data table.

5. Run in place for 1 minute. Take your pulse again, and record the result.

6. Sit down right away, and have your partner time you as you rest for 1 minute. Then, take your pulse rate again.

7. Have your partner time you as you rest for 3 more minutes. Then take your pulse rate again and record it.

Analyze and Conclude

1. **Graphing** Use the data you obtained to create a bar graph of your pulse rate under the different conditions you tested.

2. **Interpreting Data** What happens to the pulse rate when the physical activity has stopped?

3. **Inferring** What can you infer about the heartbeat when the pulse rate increases?

4. **Drawing Conclusions** What conclusion can you draw about the relationship between physical activity and a person's pulse rate?

5. **Communicating** How could you improve the accuracy of your pulse measurements? Write a paragraph in which you discuss this question in relation to the steps you followed in your procedure.

Design an Experiment

Design an experiment to determine whether the resting pulse rates of adults, teens, and young children differ. *Obtain your teacher's permission before carrying out your investigation.*

Data Table	
Activity	Pulse Rate
Resting	
Walking	
Running	
Resting after exercise (1 min)	
Resting after exercise (3+ min)	

For: Data sharing
Visit: PHSchool.com
Web Code: ced-4032

Blood and Lymph

Reading Preview

Key Concepts
- What are the components of blood?
- What determines the type of blood that a person can receive in a transfusion?
- What are the structures and functions of the lymphatic system?

Key Terms
- plasma • red blood cell
- hemoglobin
- white blood cell • platelet
- lymphatic system • lymph
- lymph node

Target Reading Skill
Identifying Main Ideas As you read the section titled Blood, write the main idea in a graphic organizer like the one below. Then, write four supporting details that give examples of the main idea.

Main Idea

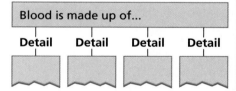

Blood is made up of...			
Detail	Detail	Detail	Detail

Lab zone **Discover Activity**

What Kinds of Cells Are in Blood?
1. Obtain a microscope slide of human blood. Look at the slide under the microscope, first under low power and then under high power.
2. Look carefully at the different kinds of cells that you see.
3. Make several drawings of each kind of cell. Use red pencil for the red blood cells.

Think It Over
Observing How many kinds of cells did you see? How do they differ from one another?

While riding your bike through the neighborhood, you take a tumble and scrape your knee. Your knee begins to sting, and you notice blood oozing from the wound. You go inside to clean the wound. As you do, you wonder, "Just what is blood?"

Blood

Blood may seem like just a plain red liquid, but it is actually a complex tissue that has several parts. **Blood is made up of four components: plasma, red blood cells, white blood cells, and platelets.** About 45 percent of the volume of blood is cells. The rest is plasma.

Plasma Most of the materials transported in the blood travel in the plasma. **Plasma** is the liquid part of the blood. Water makes up 90 percent of plasma. The other 10 percent is dissolved materials. Plasma carries nutrients, such as glucose, fats, vitamins, and minerals. Plasma also carries chemical messengers that direct body activities such as the uptake of glucose by your cells. In addition, many wastes produced by cell processes are carried away by plasma.

Protein molecules give plasma its yellow color. There are three groups of plasma proteins. One group helps to regulate the amount of water in blood. The second group, which is produced by white blood cells, helps fight disease. The third group of proteins interacts with platelets to form blood clots.

Red Blood Cells Without red blood cells, your body could not use the oxygen that you breathe in. **Red blood cells** take up oxygen in the lungs and deliver it to cells elsewhere in the body. Red blood cells, like most blood cells, are produced in bone marrow. Under a microscope, these cells look like disks with pinched-in centers. Because of their pinched shape, red blood cells are thin in the middle and can bend and twist easily. This flexibility enables them to squeeze through narrow capillaries.

A red blood cell is made mostly of **hemoglobin** (HEE muh gloh bin), which is an iron-containing protein that binds chemically to oxygen molecules. When hemoglobin combines with oxygen, the cells become bright red. Without oxygen, the cells are dark red. Thus, blood leaving the heart through the aorta is bright red, whereas blood returning from the body to the heart through veins is dark red. Hemoglobin picks up oxygen in the lungs and releases it as blood travels through capillaries in the rest of the body. Hemoglobin also picks up some of the carbon dioxide produced by cells. However, most of the carbon dioxide is carried by plasma. The blood carries the carbon dioxide to the lungs, where it is released from the body.

Mature red blood cells have no nuclei. Without a nucleus, a red blood cell cannot reproduce or repair itself. Mature red blood cells live only about 120 days. Every second, about 2 million red blood cells in your body die. Fortunately, your bone marrow produces new red blood cells at the same rate.

Reading Checkpoint **What is hemoglobin?**

White Blood Cells Like red blood cells, white blood cells are produced in bone marrow. **White blood cells** are the body's disease fighters. Some white blood cells recognize disease-causing organisms, such as bacteria, and alert the body that it has been invaded. Other white blood cells produce chemicals to fight the invaders. Still others surround and kill the organisms.

White blood cells are different from red blood cells in several important ways. There are fewer of them—only about one white blood cell for every 500 to 1,000 red blood cells. White blood cells are also larger than red blood cells. In addition, white blood cells contain nuclei. Most white blood cells can live for months or even years.

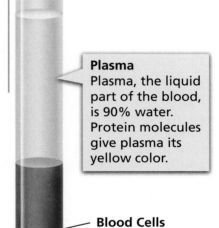

Plasma
Plasma, the liquid part of the blood, is 90% water. Protein molecules give plasma its yellow color.

— **Blood Cells**

FIGURE 11
Parts of Blood
Blood consists of liquid plasma and three kinds of cells—red blood cells, white blood cells, and platelets.
Observing *Describe the shape of a red blood cell.*

Red Blood Cells
Oxygen is carried throughout your body by red blood cells. Your blood contains more red blood cells than any other kind of cell.

White Blood Cells
By finding and destroying disease-causing organisms, white blood cells fight disease.

Platelets
When you cut yourself, platelets help form the blood clot that stops the bleeding. Platelets aren't really whole cells. Instead, they are small pieces of cells and do not have nuclei.

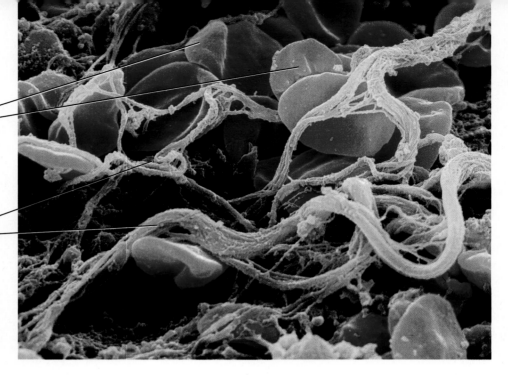

Red blood cells

Fibrin

FIGURE 12
Formation of a Blood Clot
When you cut your skin, a blood clot forms. The blood clot consists of blood cells trapped in a fiber net.
Relating Cause and Effect How is this net of fibers produced?

Platelets When you scraped your knee, blood oozed out of the wound. After a short time, however, a blood clot formed, stopping the blood flow. **Platelets** (PLAYT lits) are cell fragments that play an important part in forming blood clots.

When a blood vessel is cut, platelets collect and stick to the vessel at the site of the wound. The platelets release chemicals that start a chain reaction. This series of reactions eventually produces a protein called fibrin (FY brin). Fibrin gets its name from the fact that it weaves a net of tiny fibers across the cut in the blood vessel. Look at Figure 12 to see how the fiber net traps the blood cells. As more and more platelets and blood cells become trapped in the net, a blood clot forms. A scab is a dried blood clot on the skin surface.

 **What is the role of platelets?**

Blood Types

If a person loses a lot of blood—either from a wound or during surgery—he or she may be given a blood transfusion. A blood transfusion is the transfer of blood from one person to another. Most early attempts at blood transfusion failed, but no one knew why until the early 1900s. At that time, Karl Landsteiner, an Austrian American physician, tried mixing blood samples from pairs of people. Sometimes the two blood samples blended smoothly. In other cases, however, the red blood cells clumped together. This clumping accounted for the failure of many blood transfusions. If clumping occurs within the body, it clogs the capillaries and may lead to death.

Marker Molecules Landsteiner went on to discover that there are four major types of blood—A, B, AB, and O. Blood types are determined by proteins known as marker molecules that are on the red blood cells. If your blood type is A, you have the A marker. If your blood type is B, you have the B marker. People with type AB blood have both A and B markers. People with type O blood have neither A nor B markers.

Your plasma contains clumping proteins that recognize red blood cells with "foreign" markers (not yours) and make those cells clump together. For example, if you have blood type A, your blood contains clumping proteins that act against cells with B markers. So, if you receive a transfusion of type B blood, your clumping proteins will make the "foreign" type B cells clump together.

Safe Transfusions Landsteiner's work led to a better understanding of transfusions. **The marker molecules on your red blood cells determine your blood type and the type of blood that you can safely receive in transfusions.** A person with type A blood can receive transfusions of either type A or type O blood. Neither of these two blood types has B markers. Thus they would not be recognized as foreign by the clumping proteins in type A blood. A person with type AB blood can receive all blood types in transfusion because type AB blood has no clumping proteins. Figure 13 shows which transfusions are safe for each blood type.

If you ever receive a transfusion, your blood type will be checked first. Then, donated blood that you can safely receive will be found. This process is called cross matching. You may have heard a doctor on a television show give the order to "type and cross." The doctor wants to find out what blood type the patient has and then cross match it with donated blood.

Go Online
SciLINKS™ NSTA

For: Links on blood
Visit: www.SciLinks.org
Web Code: scn-0433

FIGURE 13
Blood Types and Their Markers
The chemical markers on a person's red blood cells determine the types of blood he or she can safely receive in a transfusion.
Interpreting Tables *What types of blood can be given safely to a person with blood type AB?*

Blood Types and Their Markers				
Blood Type Characteristic	**Blood Type A**	**Blood Type B**	**Blood Type AB**	**Blood Type O**
Marker Molecules on Red Blood Cells				
Clumping Proteins	anti-B	anti-A	no clumping proteins	anti-A and anti-B
Blood Types That Can Be Safely Received in a Transfusion	A and O	B and O	A, B, AB, and O	O

Blood Type Distribution

The circle graph shows the percentage of each blood type found in the U.S. population.

1. **Reading Graphs** What does each wedge of the graph represent?

2. **Interpreting Data** Rank the four major blood types—A, B, AB, and O—from least common to most common. What is the percentage of each type?

3. **Calculating** According to the graph, what percentage of the population is Rh positive? What percentage is Rh negative?

4. **Predicting** What type of blood can someone who is B negative (blood type B and Rh negative) receive? What percentage of the population does that represent?

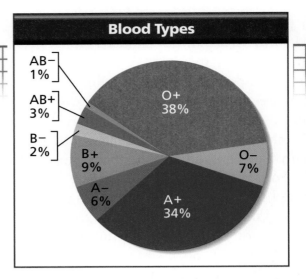

Blood Types

- AB− 1%
- AB+ 3%
- B− 2%
- B+ 9%
- A− 6%
- A+ 34%
- O+ 38%
- O− 7%

5. **Creating Data Tables** Use the data to make a table of the eight possible blood types. Include columns for the A, B, AB, and O blood types and Rh factor (positive or negative), and a row for percentage of the population.

Rh Factor Landsteiner also discovered the presence of another protein on red blood cells, which he called Rh factor. About 85 percent of the people he tested had this protein, and about 15 percent lacked it. Like the A, B, AB, and O blood types, the presence of Rh factor is determined by a marker on the red blood cell. If your blood type is Rh positive, you have the Rh marker. If your blood type is Rh negative, you lack the marker on your cells. If you are Rh negative and ever received Rh positive blood, you would develop Rh clumping proteins in your plasma. This situation is potentially dangerous.

 **Reading Checkpoint** Where is the Rh marker found?

The Lymphatic System

As blood travels through the capillaries in the cardiovascular system, some of the fluid leaks out. It moves through the walls of capillaries and into surrounding tissues. This fluid carries materials that the cells in the tissues need.

After bathing the cells, this fluid moves into your body's drainage system, called the **lymphatic system** (lim FAT ik). **The lymphatic system is a network of veinlike vessels that returns the fluid to the bloodstream.** The lymphatic system acts something like rain gutters after a rainstorm, carrying the excess fluid away.

Lymph Once the fluid is inside the lymphatic system, it is called **lymph.** Lymph consists of water and dissolved materials such as glucose. It also contains some white blood cells that have left the capillaries.

The lymphatic system has no pump, so lymph moves slowly. Lymphatic vessels, which are part of the cardiovascular system, connect to large veins in the chest. Lymph empties into these veins, and the fluid once again becomes part of blood plasma.

Lymph Nodes As lymph flows through the lymphatic system, it passes through small knobs of tissue called lymph nodes. The **lymph nodes** filter lymph, trapping bacteria and other disease-causing microorganisms in the fluid. When the body is fighting an infection, the lymph nodes enlarge. If you've ever had "swollen glands" when you've been sick, you've actually had swollen lymph nodes.

 **What is lymph?**

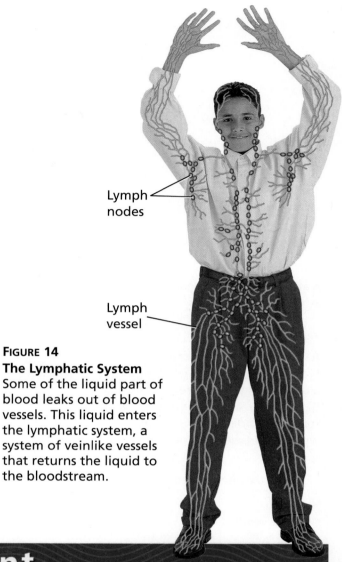

Lymph nodes

Lymph vessel

FIGURE 14
The Lymphatic System
Some of the liquid part of blood leaks out of blood vessels. This liquid enters the lymphatic system, a system of veinlike vessels that returns the liquid to the bloodstream.

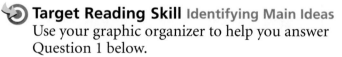
Section 3 Assessment

Target Reading Skill Identifying Main Ideas Use your graphic organizer to help you answer Question 1 below.

Reviewing Key Concepts

1. a. **Listing** Name the four components of blood. Identify whether each is a cell, a part of a cell, or a liquid.
   b. **Summarizing** Briefly describe what happens to stop the bleeding when you cut yourself.
   c. **Relating Cause and Effect** People with the disorder hemophilia do not produce the protein fibrin. Explain why hemophilia is a serious disorder.
2. a. **Reviewing** What is a marker molecule?
   b. **Explaining** Explain why a person with type O blood cannot receive a transfusion of type A blood.

   c. **Predicting** Can a person with type AB, Rh negative blood safely receive a transfusion of type O, Rh negative blood? Explain.
3. a. **Identifying** Where does lymph come from?
   b. **Sequencing** What happens to lymph after it travels through the lymphatic system?

Lab zone At-Home **Activity**

What's Your Blood Type? If possible, find out your blood type. Explain to family members the types of blood you can receive and to whom you can donate blood. Create a chart to help with your explanation.

Cardiovascular Health

Reading Preview

Key Concepts
- What are some diseases of the cardiovascular system?
- What behaviors can help maintain cardiovascular health?

Key Terms
- atherosclerosis • heart attack
- hypertension

 **Target Reading Skill**

Asking Questions Before you read, preview the red headings. In a graphic organizer like the one below, ask a *what* or *how* question for each heading. As you read, write the answers to your questions.

Cardiovascular Health

Question	Answer
What are some cardiovascular diseases?	Cardiovascular diseases include...

Discover **Activity**

Which Foods Are "Heart Healthy"?

1. Your teacher will give you an assortment of foods. If they have nutrition labels, read the information.

2. Sort the foods into three groups. In one group, put those foods that you think are good for your cardiovascular system. In the second group, put foods that you think might damage your cardiovascular system if eaten often. Place foods you aren't sure about in the third group.

Think It Over
Forming Operational Definitions How did you define a "heart-healthy" food?

Shortly after sunrise, when most people are just waking up, a team of rowers is already out on the river. Rhythmically, with perfectly coordinated movement, the rowers pull on the oars, making the boat glide swiftly through the water. Despite the chilly morning air, sweat glistens on the rowers' faces and arms. Inside their chests, their hearts are pounding, delivering blood to the arm and chest muscles that power the oars.

FIGURE 15
Exercising for Health
Strenuous exercise, such as rowing, requires a healthy cardiovascular system. In turn, exercise keeps the cardiovascular system healthy.

Healthy, unblocked artery

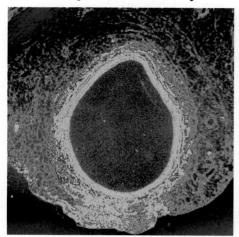

Partially blocked artery

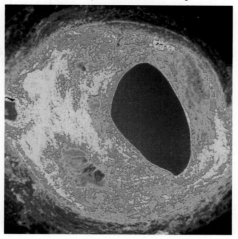

FIGURE 16
Effect of Atherosclerosis
The artery on the right shows atherosclerosis, which is caused by deposits of fat on the artery walls.
Relating Cause and Effect *What kind of diet can lead to atherosclerosis?*

Cardiovascular Diseases

Rowers cannot perform at their peaks unless their cardiovascular systems are in excellent condition. But cardiovascular health is important for all people, not just for athletes. Cardiovascular disease is the leading cause of death in the United States today. **Diseases of the cardiovascular system include atherosclerosis and hypertension.**

Atherosclerosis Compare the photos of the two arteries in Figure 16. The one on the left is a healthy artery. It has a large space in the center through which blood can flow easily. The artery on the right, in contrast, has a smaller space in the middle. This artery exhibits **atherosclerosis** (ath uh roh skluh ROH sis), a condition in which an artery wall thickens as a result of the buildup of fatty materials. One of these fatty materials is cholesterol, a waxy substance. Atherosclerosis results in a reduced flow of blood in the affected artery.

Atherosclerosis can develop in the coronary arteries, which supply the heart muscle. When that happens, the heart muscle receives less blood and therefore less oxygen. This condition may lead to a heart attack. A **heart attack** occurs when blood flow to part of the heart muscle is blocked. Cells die in the part of the heart that does not receive blood and oxygen. This permanently damages the heart.

Treatment for mild atherosclerosis usually includes a low-fat diet and a moderate exercise program. In addition, medications that lower the levels of cholesterol and fats in the blood may be prescribed. People with severe atherosclerosis may need to undergo surgery or other procedures to unclog the blocked arteries.

Lab zone **Try This Activity**

Blocking the Flow

Use this activity to model how fatty deposits affect the flow of blood through an artery.

1. Put a funnel in the mouth of a plastic jar. The funnel will represent an artery.

2. Slowly pour 100 mL of water into the funnel. Have your partner time how many seconds it takes for all the water to flow through the funnel. Then, discard the water.

3. Use a plastic knife to spread a small amount of paste along the bottom of the funnel's neck. Then, with a toothpick, carve out a hole in the paste so that the funnel is partly, but not completely, clogged.

4. Repeat Steps 1 and 2.

Predicting If the funnels were arteries, which one—blocked or unblocked—would do a better job of supplying blood to tissues? Explain.

For: Links on cardiovascular problems
Visit: www.SciLinks.org
Web Code: scn-0434

Hypertension High blood pressure, or **hypertension** (hy pur TEN shun), is a disorder in which a person's blood pressure is consistently higher than normal—usually defined as greater than 140/90.

Hypertension makes the heart work harder to pump blood throughout the body. It also may damage the walls of the blood vessels. Over time, both the heart and arteries can be severely harmed by hypertension. Because people with hypertension often have no obvious symptoms to warn them of the danger until damage is severe, hypertension is sometimes called the "silent killer."

• Tech & Design in History •

Advances in Cardiovascular Medicine

Scientists today have an in-depth understanding of how the cardiovascular system works and how to treat cardiovascular problems. This timeline describes some of the advances in cardiovascular medicine.

1958
Artificial Pacemaker
Electrical engineer Earl Baaken developed an external pacemaker to correct irregular heartbeats. A small electric generator connected to the pacemaker generated electric pulses that regulated heart rate. The first pacemakers had a fixed rate of 70 to 75 pulses per minute.

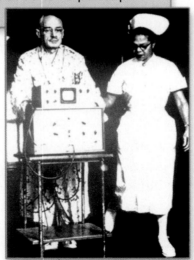

1930s–1940s
Blood Banks
Charles Drew demonstrated that emergency blood transfusions could be done with plasma if whole blood was not available. During World War II, Drew established blood banks for storing donated blood. His work helped save millions of lives on and off the battlefield.

1961
Heart Valve Replacement
The first successful artificial heart valve was inserted into a patient's heart by surgeons Albert Starr and M. L. Edwards in Oregon. The valve was a rubberlike ball inside a stainless steel cage.

| 1930 | 1940 | 1950 | 1960 |

Hypertension and atherosclerosis are closely related. As the arteries narrow, blood pressure increases. For mild hypertension, regular exercise and careful food choices may be enough to lower blood pressure. People with hypertension may need to limit their intake of sodium, which can increase blood pressure. Sodium is found in table salt and in processed foods such as soups and packaged snack foods. For many people who have hypertension, however, medications are needed to reduce their blood pressure.

Reading Checkpoint **Why is hypertension called the "silent killer"?**

Writing in Science

Research and Write Choose one of the scientists whose work is described in the timeline. Imagine that you are on a committee that has chosen this scientist to receive an award. Write the speech you would give at the award ceremony, explaining the scientist's contributions.

1967
First Heart Transplant
Christiaan Barnard, a South African surgeon, performed the first transplant of a human heart. Louis Washkansky, the man who received the heart, lived for only 18 days after the transplant. But Barnard's work paved the way for future successes in transplanting hearts and other organs.

1977
Angioplasty
The first coronary balloon angioplasty was performed by Andreas Gruentzig and a team of surgeons in San Francisco. A balloon is inserted into the coronary artery and inflated, thus opening the artery. In 2001, more than two million angioplasties were performed worldwide.

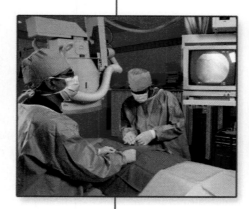

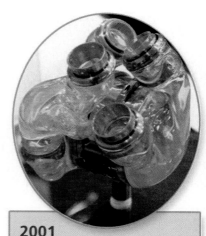

2001
Replacement Heart
The first replacement heart was implanted by a team of surgeons in Louisville, Kentucky. Unlike the first artificial heart, the Jarvik-7, the replacement heart has its own internal batteries. The patient does not have to be "plugged in" to an external power source. The first patient to receive the replacement heart lived for more than 500 days.

1970   **1980**   **1990**   **2000**

Keeping Healthy

Few young people have heart attacks, but signs of atherosclerosis can be found in some people as young as 18 to 20 years old. You can establish habits now that will lessen your risk of developing atherosclerosis and hypertension. **To help maintain cardiovascular health, people should exercise regularly; eat a balanced diet that is low in saturated fats and trans fats, cholesterol, and sodium; and avoid smoking.**

Exercise and Diet Do you participate in sports, ride a bike, swim, dance, or climb stairs instead of taking the elevator? Every time you do one of those activities, you are helping to strengthen your heart muscle and prevent atherosclerosis.

Foods that are high in cholesterol, saturated fats, and trans fats can lead to atherosclerosis. Foods such as red meats, eggs, and cheese are high in cholesterol. But because they also contain substances that your body needs, a smart approach might be to eat them only in small quantities. Foods that are high in saturated fat include butter, whole milk, and ice cream. Foods high in trans fat include margarine, potato chips, and doughnuts.

Avoid Smoking Smokers are more than twice as likely to have a heart attack as are nonsmokers. Every year, about 180,000 people in the United States who were smokers die from cardiovascular disease. If smokers quit, however, their risk of death from cardiovascular disease decreases.

 **Reading Checkpoint** What are some foods that are high in cholesterol?

FIGURE 17
Eating for Health
Eating foods that are low in fat can help keep your cardiovascular system healthy.
Applying Concepts What are some heart-healthy low-fat foods?

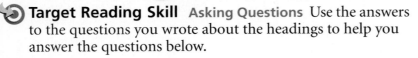

Section 4 Assessment

Target Reading Skill Asking Questions Use the answers to the questions you wrote about the headings to help you answer the questions below.

Reviewing Key Concepts

1. **a. Defining** What is atherosclerosis? What is hypertension?
   b. Relating Cause and Effect How do these two diseases affect the heart?
2. **a. Listing** List three things you can do to help your cardiovascular system stay healthy.
   b. Explaining Why it is important to exercise?
   c. Inferring Coronary heart disease is less common in some countries than in the United States. What factors might account for this difference?

Lab zone At-Home Activity

Heart-Healthy Activities With your family, discuss things you all can do to maintain heart health. Make a list of activities that you can enjoy together. You might also work with your family to cook and serve a "heart-healthy" meal. List the foods you would serve at the meal.

Do You Know Your A-B-O's?

Problem

Which blood types can safely receive transfusions of type A blood? Which can receive type O blood?

Skills Focus

interpreting data, drawing conclusions

Materials

- 4 paper cups
- 8 plastic petri dishes
- marking pen
- 4 plastic droppers
- white paper
- toothpicks
- four model "blood" types

Procedure

1. Write down your ideas about why type O blood might be in higher demand than other blood types. Then, make two copies of the data table in your notebook.

2. Label four paper cups A, B, AB, and O. Fill each cup about one-third full with the model "blood" supplied by your teacher. Place one clean plastic dropper into each cup. Use each dropper to transfer only that one type of blood.

3. Label the side of each of four petri dishes with a blood type: A, B, AB, or O. Place the petri dishes on a sheet of white paper.

Data Table			
Donor: Type _____			
Potential Receiver	Original Color	Final Color of Mixture	Safe or Unsafe?
A			
B			
AB			
O			

4. Use the plastic droppers to place 10 drops of each type of blood in its labeled petri dish. Each sample represents the blood of a potential receiver of a blood transfusion. Record the original color of each sample in your data table as yellow, blue, green, or colorless.

5. Label your first data table Donor: Type A. To test whether each potential receiver can safely receive type A blood, add 10 drops of type A blood to each sample. Stir each mixture with a separate, clean toothpick.

6. Record the final color of each mixture in the data table. If the color stayed the same, write "safe" in the last column. If the color of the mixture changed, write "unsafe."

7. Label your second data table Donor: Type O. Obtain four clean petri dishes, and repeat Steps 3 through 6 to determine who could safely receive type O blood.

Analyze and Conclude

1. **Interpreting Data** Which blood types can safely receive a transfusion of type A blood? Type O blood?

2. **Inferring** Use what you know about marker molecules to explain why some transfusions of type A blood are safe while others are unsafe.

3. **Drawing Conclusions** If some blood types are not available, how might type O blood be useful?

4. **Communicating** Write a paragraph in which you discuss why it is important for hospitals to have an adequate supply of different types of blood.

More to Explore

Repeat this activity to find out which blood types can safely receive donations of type B and type AB blood.

Heart-Lung Machines

What if you were too tired to make it through the day? What if walking up stairs left you out of breath and dizzy? These are symptoms that a person with a damaged heart may experience. A severely damaged heart may require surgery. While the heart is being repaired, blood must continue to circulate through the body around the heart. One way to bypass the heart during surgery is by using a heart-lung machine.

Repairing a Damaged Heart

A heart-lung machine takes over the functions of the heart and the lungs when the heart is stopped during heart surgery. Surgeons insert one tube into the right atrium and a second tube into the aorta. Oxygen-poor blood flows into the heart-lung machine from the right atrium. Within the machine, carbon dioxide is removed, oxygen is added, the blood is filtered, and the blood temperature is regulated. The filtered, oxygen-rich blood is then pumped through the second tube into the aorta, without flowing through the patient's heart. Once the surgical procedure is completed, doctors disconnect the machine and restart the heart.

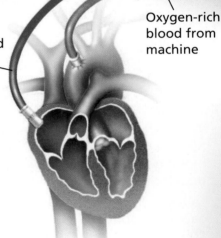

Oxygen-poor blood to machine

Oxygen-rich blood from machine

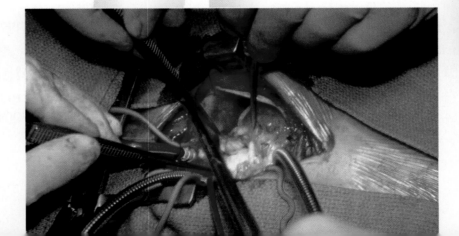

Heart-lung machine in use for open heart surgery ▶

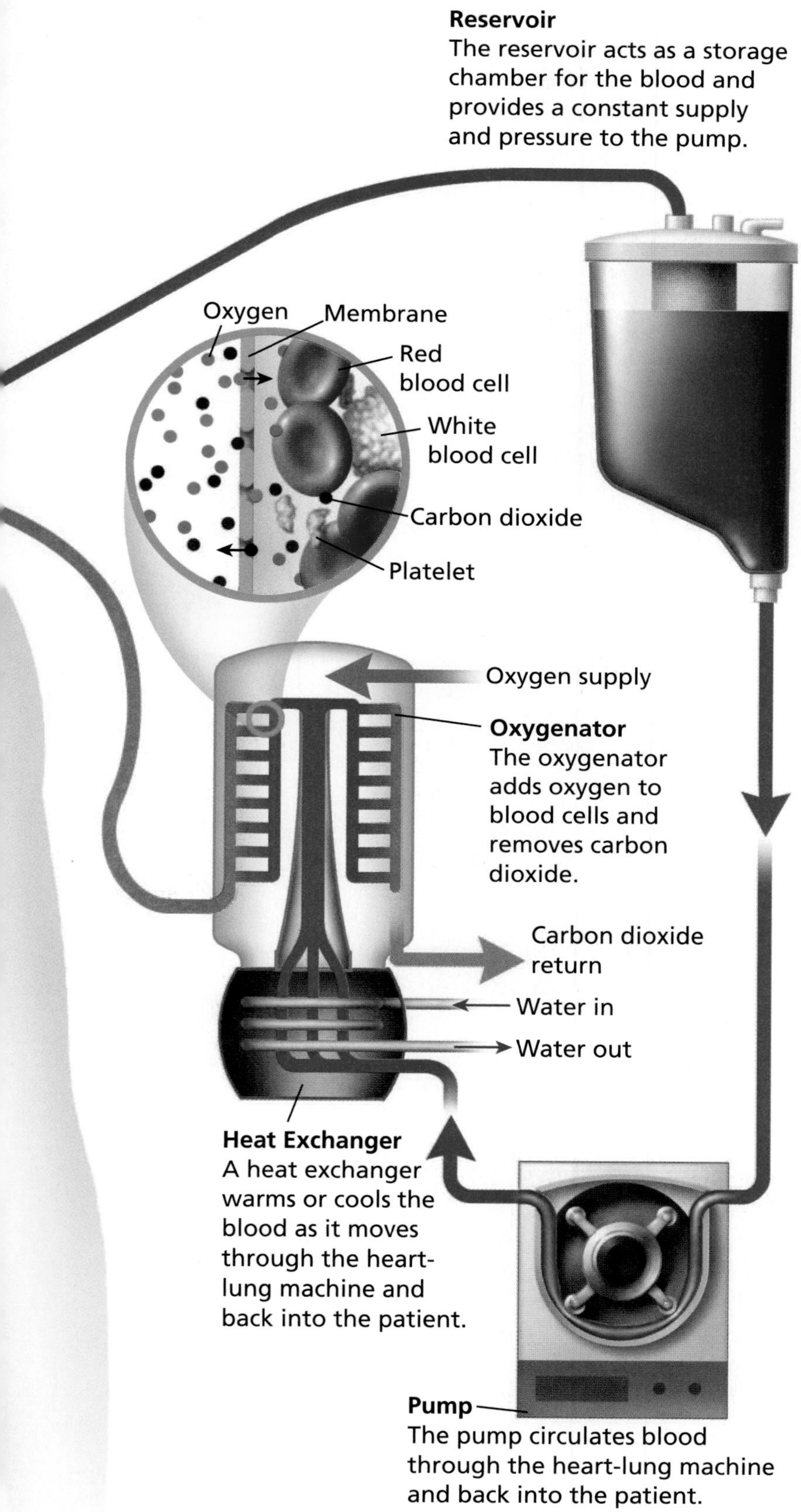

Reservoir
The reservoir acts as a storage chamber for the blood and provides a constant supply and pressure to the pump.

Oxygen Membrane
Red blood cell
White blood cell
Carbon dioxide
Platelet

Oxygen supply

Oxygenator
The oxygenator adds oxygen to blood cells and removes carbon dioxide.

Carbon dioxide return
Water in
Water out

Heat Exchanger
A heat exchanger warms or cools the blood as it moves through the heart-lung machine and back into the patient.

Pump
The pump circulates blood through the heart-lung machine and back into the patient.

Missing a Beat?

Heart valve repair and replacement, heart transplants, and coronary bypass surgery are a few of the surgeries that may use a heart-lung machine. Heart-lung machines have been credited with saving nearly one million lives around the world each year.

However, like all technologies, heart-lung machines pose certain risks. Use of the heart-lung machine has been associated with an increased risk of bleeding, stroke, kidney and lung problems, and memory loss. As with any surgical procedure, patients must consider the trade-offs.

Weigh the Impact

1. **Identify the Need**
   What is the purpose of a heart-lung machine?

2. **Research**
   Research to find out the success rate of bypass surgery using a heart-lung machine. Then research steps that patients might take to prevent the need for bypass surgery.

3. **Write**
   Write a paragraph on steps patients might take to prevent the need for bypass surgery. Use your research and notes.

Go Online
PHSchool.com

For: More on heart-lung machines
Visit: PHSchool.com
Web Code: ceh-4030

Chapter 3

Study Guide

The **BIG Idea** **Structure and Function** The circulatory system moves blood through the body, transports food, and enables the exchange of gases.

① The Body's Transport System

Key Concepts

- The cardiovascular system carries needed substances to cells and carries waste products away from cells. In addition, blood contains cells that fight disease.

- When the heart beats, it pushes blood through the blood vessels of the cardiovascular system.

- The right side of the heart is completely separated from the left side by a wall of tissue called the septum. Each side has two compartments, or chambers—an upper chamber and a lower chamber.

- Blood circulates in two loops. In the first loop, blood travels from the heart to the lungs and back to the heart. In the second loop, blood is pumped from the heart throughout the body and then returns to the heart.

Key Terms

- cardiovascular system • heart • atrium
- ventricle • valve • pacemaker • artery
- capillary • vein • aorta

② A Closer Look at Blood Vessels

Key Concepts

- When blood leaves the heart, it travels through arteries. Artery walls are thick and consist of three cell layers.

- In the capillaries, materials are exchanged between the blood and the body's cells. Capillary walls are only one cell thick.

- After blood moves through capillaries, it enters larger blood vessels called veins, which carry blood back to the heart. The walls of veins have three layers, with muscle in the middle layer.

- Blood pressure is caused by the force with which the ventricles contract.

Key Terms

coronary artery	diffusion
pulse	blood pressure

③ Blood and Lymph

Key Concepts

- Blood is made up of four components: plasma, red blood cells, white blood cells, and platelets.

- The marker molecules on your red blood cells determine your blood type and the type of blood that you can safely receive in transfusions.

- The lymphatic system is a network of vein-like vessels that returns the fluid to the bloodstream.

Key Terms

- plasma • red blood cell • hemoglobin
- white blood cell • platelet
- lymphatic system • lymph • lymph node

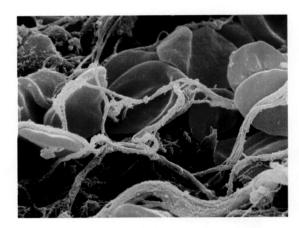

④ Cardiovascular Health

Key Concepts

- Diseases of the cardiovascular system include atherosclerosis and hypertension.

- To help maintain cardiovascular health, people should exercise regularly; eat a balanced diet that is low in saturated fats and trans fats, cholesterol, and sodium; and avoid smoking.

Key Terms

atherosclerosis	hypertension
heart attack	

Review and Assessment

Go Online
PHSchool.com
For: Self-Assessment
Visit: PHSchool.com
Web Code: cea-4030

Organizing Information

Comparing and Contrasting Copy the compare/contrast table about the two loops of the circulatory system onto a sheet of paper. Then complete it and add a title. (For more on Comparing and Contrasting, see the Skills Handbook.)

Loop	Side of heart where loop starts	Where blood flows to	Where blood returns to
Loop One	a. _____?_____	Lungs	b. _____?_____
Loop Two	Left side	c. _____?_____	d. _____?_____

Reviewing Key Terms

Choose the letter of the best answer.

1. The heart's upper chambers are called
   a. ventricles.
   b. atria.
   c. valves.
   d. arteries.

2. Nutrients are exchanged between the blood and body cells in the
   a. capillaries.
   b. veins.
   c. aorta.
   d. arteries.

3. The alternating expansion and relaxation of the artery that you feel in your wrist is your
   a. pulse.
   b. coronary artery.
   c. blood pressure.
   d. plasma.

4. Blood components that help the body to control bleeding are
   a. platelets.
   b. red blood cells.
   c. white blood cells.
   d. hemoglobin.

5. Cholesterol is a waxy substance associated with
   a. lymph nodes.
   b. white blood cells.
   c. atherosclerosis.
   d. plasma.

If the statement is true, write *true*. If it is false, change the underlined word or words to make the statement true.

6. The two lower chambers of the heart are called <u>atria</u>.

7. The <u>veins</u> are the narrowest blood vessels in the body.

8. <u>White blood cells</u> contain hemoglobin.

9. The <u>lymphatic system</u> is involved in returning fluid to the bloodstream.

10. Elevated blood pressure is called <u>atherosclerosis</u>.

Writing in Science

Letter Write a letter to a friend describing what you do to stay active. For example, do you participate in team sports, jog, or take long walks with your dog? Include in your letter additional ways you can be even more active.

Discovery CHANNEL SCHOOL™

Circulation
Video Preview
Video Field Trip
▶ Video Assessment

Review and Assessment

Checking Concepts

11. A red blood cell is moving through an artery in your leg. Describe the path that the blood cell will follow back to your heart. Identify the chamber of the heart to which it will return.

12. Contrast the forces with which the right and left ventricles contract. How does this relate to each ventricle's function?

13. How is a capillary's structure adapted to its function?

14. What is the function of hemoglobin?

15. What is lymph? How does lymph return to the cardiovascular system?

16. Give two reasons why food choices are important to cardiovascular health.

Thinking Critically

17. **Predicting** Some babies are born with an opening between the left and right ventricles of the heart. How would this heart defect affect the ability of the cardiovascular system to deliver oxygen to body cells?

18. **Classifying** Which two chambers of the heart shown below are the ventricles? Through which chamber does oxygen-poor blood enter the heart from the body?

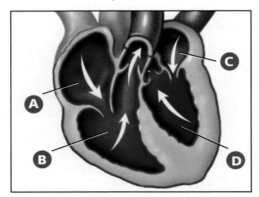

19. **Relating Cause and Effect** People who do not have enough iron in their diets sometimes develop a condition in which their blood cannot carry a normal amount of oxygen. Explain why this is so.

20. **Making Generalizations** Why is atherosclerosis sometimes called a "lifestyle disease"?

Math Practice

21. **Calculating a Rate** The veterinarian listens to your cat's heart and counts 30 beats in 15 seconds. What is your cat's heart rate?

Applying Skills

Use the graph to answer Questions 22–25.

The graph below shows how average blood pressure changes as men and women grow older.

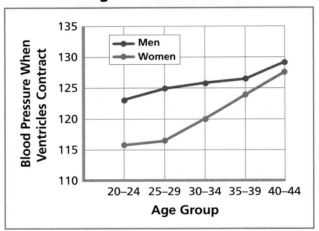

22. **Reading Graphs** What is plotted on each axis?

23. **Interpreting Data** At age 20, who is likely to have higher blood pressure—men or women?

24. **Drawing Conclusions** In general, what happens to blood pressure as people age?

25. **Predicting** Do you think that there is some age at which both men and women have about the same blood pressure? Use the graph lines to explain your prediction.

Lab zone Chapter **Project**

Performance Assessment You should now be ready to present your display. First show it to a small group of classmates to make sure it is clear and accurate. When you present your display, be ready to answer questions.

Standardized Test Prep

Choose the letter of the best answer.

1. The most important function of the cardiovascular system is to
   - **A** transport needed materials to body cells and remove wastes.
   - **B** provide structural support for the lungs.
   - **C** generate blood pressure so the arteries and veins do not collapse.
   - **D** produce blood and lymph.

2. The correct sequence for the path of blood through the body is
   - **F** heart—lungs—other body parts.
   - **G** heart—lungs—heart—other body parts.
   - **H** lungs—other body parts—heart.
   - **J** heart—other body parts—lungs—heart.

3. Which of the following is true about blood in the aorta?
   - **A** The blood is going to the lungs.
   - **B** The blood is oxygen-rich.
   - **C** The blood is dark red in color.
   - **D** The blood is going to the heart.

Use the table below and your knowledge of science to answer Questions 4 and 5.

Blood Types		
Blood Type	**Marker Molecules**	**Clumping Proteins**
A	A	anti-B
B	B	anti-A
AB	A and B	none
O	none	anti-A and anti-B

4. A person who has type O blood can safely receive blood from a person with
   - **F** type O blood.
   - **G** type A blood.
   - **H** type AB blood.
   - **J** type B blood.

5. A person who has type O blood can safely donate blood to a person with
   - **A** type AB blood.
   - **B** type O blood.
   - **C** types A, B, AB, or O blood.
   - **D** type A or type B blood.

Constructed Response

6. Explain what blood pressure is and what causes it. How is blood pressure measured and what is the significance of the two numbers in a blood pressure reading? Why can high blood pressure be dangerous?

Respiration and Excretion

The BIG Idea
Structure and Function

 What are the major functions of the respiratory and excretory systems?

Playing the pan flute requires ▶ strong, healthy lungs.

Lab zone™ Chapter **Project**

Get the Message Out

Imagine that you're part of a team of writers and designers who create advertisements. You've just been given the job of creating antismoking ads for different age groups. As you read this chapter and learn about the respiratory system, you can use your knowledge in your ad campaign.

Your Goal To design three different antismoking ads: one telling young children about the dangers of smoking, the second one discouraging teenagers from trying cigarettes, and the third encouraging adult smokers to quit

To complete this project successfully, each ad must

- accurately communicate at least three health risks associated with smoking
- address at least two pressures that influence people to start or continue smoking
- use images and words in convincing ways that gear your message to each audience

Plan It! Brainstorm a list of reasons why people smoke. Consider the possible influences of family and friends as well as that of ads, movies, videos, and television. Also, decide which types of ads you will produce, such as magazine ads or billboards. After your teacher approves your plan, begin to design your ads.

The Respiratory System

Reading Preview

Key Concepts
- What are the functions of the respiratory system?
- What structures does air pass through as it travels to the lungs?
- What happens during gas exchange and breathing?

Key Terms
- respiration • cilia • pharynx
- trachea • bronchi • lungs
- alveoli • diaphragm • larynx
- vocal cords

Target Reading Skill
Sequencing As you read, make a flowchart that shows the path of air in the respiratory system. Write each step of the process in a separate box in the order in which it occurs.

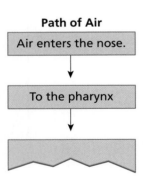

Path of Air

Air enters the nose.

↓

To the pharynx

↓

Discover Activity

How Big Can You Blow Up a Balloon?

1. Take a normal breath, then blow as much air as possible into a balloon. Twist the end and hold it closed. Have your partner measure around the balloon at its widest point.
2. Let the air out of the balloon. Repeat Step 1 and calculate the average of the two measurements.
3. Compare your results with those of your classmates. The bigger the circumference, the greater the volume of air exhaled.

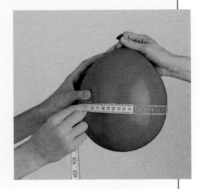

Think It Over
Inferring What factors might affect the volume of air a person can exhale?

Jerry, the main character in Doris Lessing's story "Through the Tunnel," is on vacation at the seaside. Day after day, he watches some older boys dive into deep water on one side of a huge rock. The boys mysteriously reappear on the other side. Jerry figures out that there must be an underwater tunnel in the rock. He finds the tunnel beneath the water and decides to swim through it. Once inside, though, he is terrified. The walls are slimy, and rocks scrape his body. He can barely see where he is going. But worst of all, Jerry has to hold his breath for far longer than ever before. The author describes Jerry this way: "His head was swelling, his lungs were cracking."

Hold your breath!

Respiratory System Functions

No one can go for very long without breathing. Your body cells need oxygen, and they get that oxygen from the air you breathe. **The respiratory system moves oxygen from the outside environment into the body. It also removes carbon dioxide and water from the body.**

Taking in Oxygen The oxygen your body needs comes from the atmosphere—the mixture of gases that blankets Earth. Your body doesn't use most of the other gases in the air you breathe in. When you exhale, most of the air goes back into the atmosphere.

Oxygen is needed for the energy-releasing chemical reactions that take place inside your cells. Like a fire, which cannot burn without oxygen, your cells cannot "burn" enough fuel to keep you alive without oxygen. The process in which oxygen and glucose undergo a complex series of chemical reactions inside cells is called **respiration.** Respiration, which is also called cellular respiration, is different from breathing. Breathing refers to the movement of air into and out of the lungs. Respiration, on the other hand, refers to the chemical reactions inside cells. As a result of respiration, your cells release the energy that fuels growth and other cell processes.

Removing Carbon Dioxide and Water In addition to the release of energy, respiration produces carbon dioxide and water. Your respiratory system eliminates the carbon dioxide and some of the water through your lungs.

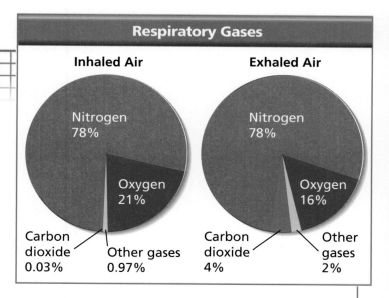

Respiratory Gases

Math ▶ Analyzing Data

The Air You Breathe

The air you breathe in contains several different gases, shown in the circle graph on the left. The air you breathe out contains the same gases, but in the amounts shown in the circle graph on the right.

1. **Reading Graphs** What does each wedge in the graphs represent?

2. **Interpreting Data** Based on the data, which gas is used by the body? Explain.

3. **Drawing Conclusions** Compare the percentage of carbon dioxide in inhaled air with the percentage in exhaled air. How can you account for the difference?

4. **Inferring** Explain why the percentage of nitrogen is the same in both inhaled air and exhaled air.

FIGURE 1
Fueling Your Cells

Oxygen from the air and glucose from digested food are both carried to cells by the blood. During respiration, oxygen reacts with glucose to release energy.

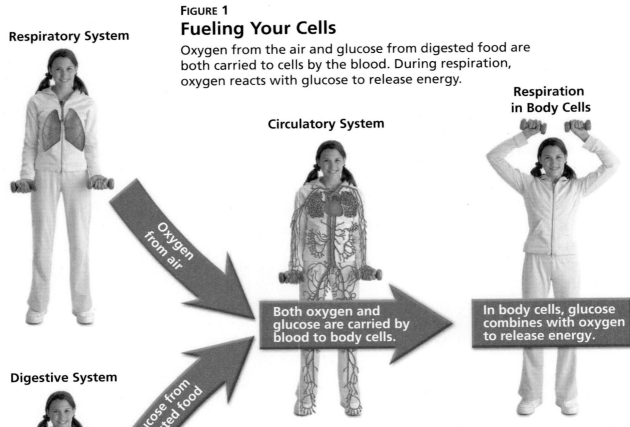

Respiratory System

Digestive System

Circulatory System

Respiration in Body Cells

Oxygen from air

Glucose from digested food

Both oxygen and glucose are carried by blood to body cells.

In body cells, glucose combines with oxygen to release energy.

Systems Working Together The respiratory system is just one of the body systems that makes respiration possible. As you can see in Figure 1, respiration could not take place without the digestive and circulatory systems as well. Your respiratory system brings oxygen into your lungs. Meanwhile, your digestive system absorbs glucose from the food you eat. Then, your circulatory system carries both the oxygen and the glucose to your cells, where respiration occurs.

The Path of Air

If you look toward a window on a bright day, you may see tiny particles dancing in the air. These particles include such things as floating grains of dust, plant pollen, and ash from fires. Though you can't see them, air also contains microorganisms. Some of these microorganisms can cause diseases in humans. When you breathe in, all these materials enter your body along with the air.

However, most of these materials never reach your lungs. On its way to the lungs, air passes through a series of structures that filter and trap particles. These organs also warm and moisten the air. **As air travels from the outside environment to the lungs, it passes through the following structures: nose, pharynx, trachea, and bronchi.** It takes air only a few seconds to complete the route from the nose to the lungs.

The Nose Air enters the body through the nose and then moves into spaces called the nasal cavities. Some of the cells lining the nasal cavities produce mucus. This sticky material moistens the air and keeps the lining from drying out. Mucus also traps particles such as dust.

The cells that line the nasal cavities have **cilia** (SIL ee uh), tiny hairlike extensions that can move together in a sweeping motion. The cilia sweep the mucus into the throat, where you swallow it. Stomach acid destroys the mucus, along with everything trapped in it.

Some particles and bacteria can irritate the lining of your nose or throat, causing you to sneeze. The powerful force of a sneeze shoots the particles out of your nose and into the air.

The Pharynx Next, air enters the **pharynx** (FAR ingks), or throat. The pharynx is the only part of the respiratory system that is shared with another system—the digestive system. Both the nose and the mouth connect to the pharynx.

Reading Checkpoint **What is the role of cilia?**

FIGURE 2
The Respiratory System
On its path from outside the body into the lungs, air passes through several structures that clean, warm, and moisten it. Once in the lungs, the oxygen in the air can enter your bloodstream.
Classifying *Which part of the respiratory system is also part of the digestive system?*

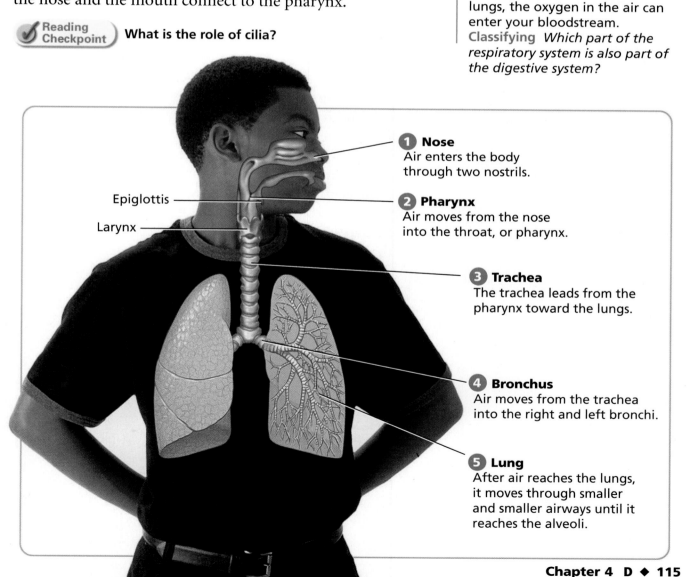

Epiglottis

Larynx

1 Nose
Air enters the body through two nostrils.

2 Pharynx
Air moves from the nose into the throat, or pharynx.

3 Trachea
The trachea leads from the pharynx toward the lungs.

4 Bronchus
Air moves from the trachea into the right and left bronchi.

5 Lung
After air reaches the lungs, it moves through smaller and smaller airways until it reaches the alveoli.

Try This Activity

Lab zone Try This **Activity**

What Do You Exhale?
Learn whether carbon dioxide is present in exhaled air.

1. Label two test tubes *A* and *B*.
2. Fill each test tube with 10 mL of water and a few drops of bromthymol blue solution. Bromthymol blue solution turns green or yellow in the presence of carbon dioxide.
3. Using a straw, gently blow air into the liquid in test tube A for a few seconds. **CAUTION:** *Do not suck the solution back through the straw.*
4. Compare the solutions in the test tubes.

Predicting Suppose you had exercised immediately before you blew into the straw. Predict how this would have affected the results.

The Trachea From the pharynx, air moves into the **trachea** (TRAY kee uh), or windpipe. You can feel your trachea if you gently run your fingers down the center of your neck. The trachea feels like a tube with a series of ridges. The firm ridges are rings of cartilage that strengthen the trachea and keep it open.

The trachea, like the nose, is lined with cilia and mucus. The cilia in the trachea sweep upward, moving mucus toward the pharynx, where it is swallowed. The trachea's cilia and mucus continue the cleaning and moistening of air that began in the nose. If particles irritate the lining of the trachea, you cough. A cough, like a sneeze, sends the particles into the air.

Normally, only air—not food—enters the trachea. If food does enter the trachea, the food can block the opening and prevent air from getting to the lungs. When that happens, a person chokes. Fortunately, food rarely gets into the trachea. The epiglottis, a small flap of tissue that folds over the trachea, seals off the trachea while you swallow.

The Bronchi and Lungs Air moves from the trachea to the **bronchi** (BRAHNG ky) (singular *bronchus*), the passages that direct air into the lungs. The **lungs** are the main organs of the respiratory system. The left bronchus leads into the left lung, and the right bronchus leads into the right lung. Inside the lungs, each bronchus divides into smaller and smaller tubes in a pattern that resembles the branches of a tree.

At the end of the smallest tubes are structures that look like bunches of grapes. The "grapes" are **alveoli** (al VEE uh ly) (singular *alveolus*), tiny sacs of lung tissue specialized for the movement of gases between air and blood. Notice in Figure 3 that each alveolus is surrounded by a network of capillaries. It is here that the blood picks up its cargo of oxygen from the air.

Reading Checkpoint **How is food prevented from entering the trachea?**

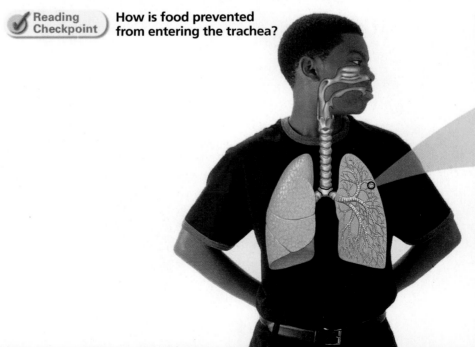

Gas Exchange

Because the walls of both the alveoli and the capillaries are very thin, certain materials can pass through them easily. **After air enters an alveolus, oxygen passes through the wall of the alveolus and then through the capillary wall into the blood. Carbon dioxide and water pass from the blood into the alveoli. This whole process is known as gas exchange.**

How Gas Exchange Occurs Imagine that you are a drop of blood beginning your journey through a capillary that wraps around an alveolus. When you begin that journey, you are carrying a lot of carbon dioxide and little oxygen. As you move through the capillary, oxygen gradually attaches to the hemoglobin in your red blood cells. At the same time, you are getting rid of carbon dioxide. At the end of your journey around the alveolus, you are rich in oxygen and poor in carbon dioxide.

FIGURE 3
Gas Exchange in the Alveoli

Alveoli are hollow air sacs surrounded by capillaries. As blood flows through the capillaries, oxygen moves from the alveoli into the blood. At the same time, carbon dioxide moves from the blood into the alveoli.
Interpreting Diagrams *How is the structure of the alveoli important for gas exchange?*

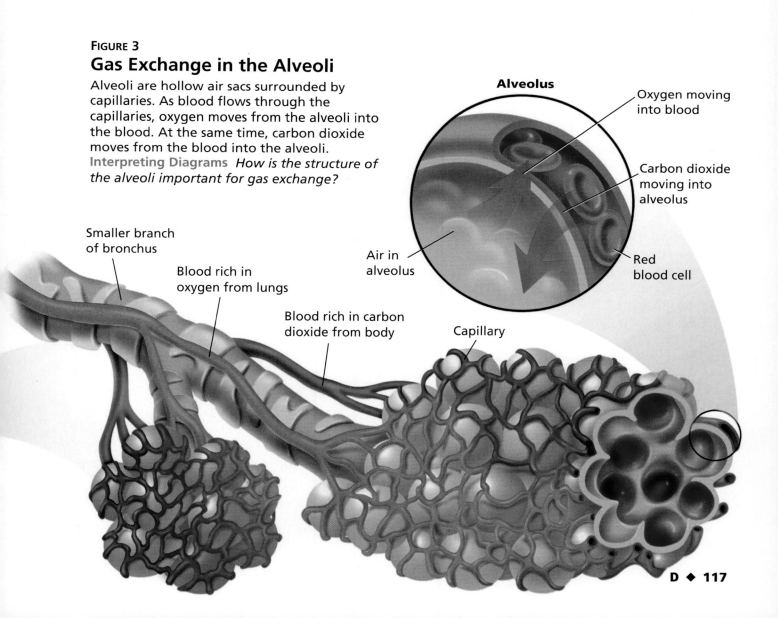

Alveolus

Oxygen moving into blood

Carbon dioxide moving into alveolus

Air in alveolus

Red blood cell

Smaller branch of bronchus

Blood rich in oxygen from lungs

Blood rich in carbon dioxide from body

Capillary

FIGURE 4
Oxygen for Activities
The huge surface area of the alveoli supplies the oxygen these trombone players need to march and play.

Surface Area

Surface area refers to the total area of all of the surfaces of a three-dimensional object. Consider a cube, which has six equal sides. Each side measures 2 cm by 2 cm.

1. To find the surface area of the cube, first calculate the area of one of the six sides:
   Area = length × width
   $$= 2 \text{ cm} \times 2 \text{ cm} = 4 \text{ cm}^2$$
   Each side has an area of 4 cm^2.

2. Next, add the areas of the six sides together to find the total surface area:
   $$4 \text{ cm}^2 + 4 \text{ cm}^2 + 4 \text{ cm}^2 + 4 \text{ cm}^2 + 4 \text{ cm}^2 + 4 \text{ cm}^2 = 24 \text{ cm}^2$$
   The surface area of the cube is 24 cm^2.

Practice Problem Calculate the surface area of a cube whose side measures 3 cm.

Surface Area for Gas Exchange Your lungs can absorb a large amount of oxygen because of the large surface area of the alveoli. An adult's lungs contain about 300 million alveoli. If you opened the alveoli and spread them out on a flat surface, you would have a surface area of about 70 square meters.

The huge surface area of the alveoli enables the lungs to absorb a large amount of oxygen. The lungs can, therefore, supply the oxygen that people need—even when they are performing strenuous activities. When you play a wind instrument or a fast-paced game of basketball, you have your alveoli to thank.

Your lungs are not the only organs that provide a large surface area in a relatively small space. Recall from Chapter 2 that the small intestine contains numerous, tiny villi that increase the surface available to absorb food molecules.

Reading Checkpoint What gases are exchanged across the alveoli?

How You Breathe

In an average day, you may breathe more than 20,000 times. The rate at which you breathe depends on your body's need for oxygen. The more oxygen you need, the faster you breathe.

Muscles for Breathing Breathing, like other body movements, is controlled by muscles. Figure 5 shows the structure of the chest, including the muscles that enable you to breathe. Notice that the lungs are surrounded by the ribs, which have muscles attached to them. At the base of the lungs is the **diaphragm** (DY uh fram), a large, dome-shaped muscle that plays an important role in breathing.

The Process of Breathing When you breathe, the actions of your rib muscles and diaphragm expand or contract your chest. As a result, air flows in or out.

Here's what happens when you inhale, or breathe in. The rib muscles contract, lifting the chest wall upward and outward. At the same time, the diaphragm contracts and moves downward. The combined action of these muscles makes the chest cavity larger. The same amount of air now occupies a larger space, causing the pressure of the air inside your lungs to decrease. This change means that the pressure of air inside the chest cavity is lower than the pressure of the atmosphere pushing on the body. Because of this difference in air pressure, air rushes into your chest, in the same way that air is sucked into a vacuum cleaner.

When you exhale, or breathe out, the rib muscles and diaphragm relax. This reduces the size of the chest cavity. This decrease in size squeezes air out of the lungs, the way squeezing a container of ketchup pushes ketchup out of the opening.

 **Reading Checkpoint** What muscles cause the chest to expand during breathing?

FIGURE 5

The Breathing Process

When you inhale, the diaphragm moves downward and pressure in the lungs decreases, causing air to flow in. When you exhale, the diaphragm moves upward and the pressure in the lungs increases, pushing the air out.

Interpreting Diagrams *How does the movement of the diaphragm affect the size of the chest cavity?*

Go Online
active art

For: The Breathing Process activity
Visit: PHSchool.com
Web Code: cep-4041

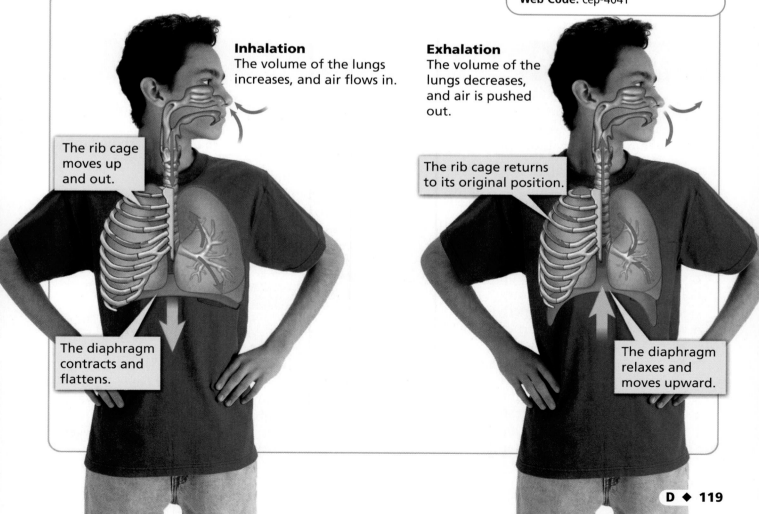

Inhalation
The volume of the lungs increases, and air flows in.

Exhalation
The volume of the lungs decreases, and air is pushed out.

The rib cage moves up and out.

The rib cage returns to its original position.

The diaphragm contracts and flattens.

The diaphragm relaxes and moves upward.

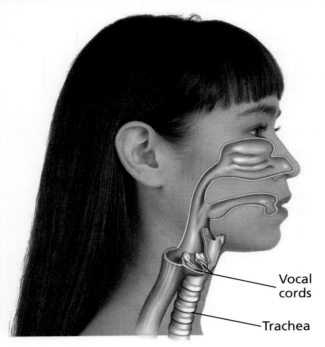

Vocal cords

Trachea

FIGURE 6
The Vocal Cords
Air moving over the vocal cords causes them to vibrate and produce sound.
Interpreting Diagrams *Where are the vocal cords located?*

Relating Breathing and Speaking The air that moves out of your lungs as you breathe also helps you speak. The **larynx** (LAR ingks), or voice box, is located in the top part of the trachea, underneath the epiglottis. Place your fingers on your Adam's apple, which sticks out from the front of your neck. You can feel some of the cartilage that makes up the larynx. Two **vocal cords,** folds of connective tissue that produce your voice, stretch across the opening of the larynx.

If you've ever let air out of a balloon while stretching its neck, you've heard the squeaking sound that the air makes. The neck of the balloon is something like your vocal cords. If you look at Figure 6 you can see that the vocal cords have a slitlike opening between them. When you speak, muscles make the vocal cords contract, narrowing the opening. Air from the lungs rushes through this opening. The movement of the vocal cords makes the air molecules vibrate, or move rapidly back and forth. This vibration creates a sound—your voice.

Section 1 Assessment

Target Reading Skill Sequencing With a partner, review your flowchart about the path of air. Add any necessary information.

Reviewing Key Concepts

1. a. Listing What are the functions of the respiratory system?
   b. Comparing and Contrasting Explain the difference between respiration and breathing.
   c. Predicting How might respiration in your body cells be affected if your respiratory system did not work properly?
2. a. Identifying Name the structures of the respiratory system.
   b. Sequencing Describe the path that a molecule of oxygen takes as it moves from the air outside your body into the alveoli.
   c. Relating Cause and Effect In a healthy person, how do coughing and sneezing protect the respiratory system?

3. a. Reviewing What three substances are exchanged in the alveoli?
   b. Explaining What happens to the carbon dioxide in the blood when it flows through the capillaries in the alveoli?
   c. Applying Concepts How would gas exchange be affected at the top of a tall mountain, where air pressure is lower and there is less oxygen than at lower elevations? Explain.

Math **Practice**

4. Surface Area A cube measures 4 cm × 4 cm on a side. Find its surface area.
5. Surface Area Suppose you cut up the cube into eight smaller cubes, each 2 cm × 2 cm on a side. If the larger cube represents a lung, and the smaller cubes represent alveoli, which would provide a larger surface area for oxygen exchange?

A Breath of Fresh Air

Problem

What causes your body to inhale and exhale air?

Skills Focus

making models, observing, drawing conclusions

Materials

- small balloon
- large balloon
- scissors
- transparent plastic bottle with narrow neck

Procedure

1. In your notebook, explain how you think air gets into the lungs during the breathing process.

2. Cut off and discard the bottom of a small plastic bottle. Trim the cut edge so there are no rough spots.

3. Stretch a small balloon; then blow it up a few times to stretch it further. Insert the round end of the balloon through the mouth of the bottle. Then, with a partner holding the bottle, stretch the neck of the balloon and pull it over the mouth of the bottle.

4. Stretch a large balloon; then blow it up a few times to stretch it further. Cut off and discard the balloon's neck.

5. Have a partner hold the bottle while you stretch the remaining part of the balloon over the bottom opening of the bottle, as shown in the photo.

6. Use one hand to hold the bottle firmly. With the knuckles of your other hand, push upward on the large balloon, causing it to form a dome. Remove your knuckles from the balloon, letting the balloon flatten. Repeat this procedure a few times. Observe what happens to the small balloon. Record your observations in your notebook.

Analyze and Conclude

1. **Making Models** Make a diagram of the completed model in your notebook. Add labels to show which parts of your model represent the chest cavity, diaphragm, lungs, and trachea.

2. **Observing** In this model, what is the position of the "diaphragm" just after you have made the model "exhale"? What do the lungs look like just after you have exhaled?

3. **Drawing Conclusions** In this model, how does the "diaphragm" move? How do these movements of the "diaphragm" affect the "lungs"?

4. **Communicating** Write a paragraph describing how this model shows that pressure changes are responsible for breathing.

More to Explore

How could you improve on this model to show more closely what happens in the chest cavity during the process of breathing? *Obtain your teacher's permission before carrying out your investigation.*

Smoking and Your Health

Reading Preview

Key Concepts
- What harmful chemicals are found in tobacco smoke?
- How can tobacco smoke affect a person's health over time?

Key Terms
- tar • carbon monoxide
- nicotine • addiction
- bronchitis • emphysema

🎯 Target Reading Skill
Relating Cause and Effect As you read, identify the effects of smoking on the body. Write the information in a graphic organizer like the one below.

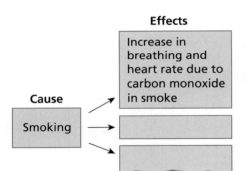

Effects

Cause

Smoking → Increase in breathing and heart rate due to carbon monoxide in smoke

Discover Activity

What Are the Dangers of Smoking?

The graph shows the rate of lung cancer deaths in the United States from 1930 to 2000.

1. What was the rate of lung cancer deaths for males in 1930? For females?
2. What was the rate of lung cancer deaths for males in 1990? For females?
3. Did males or females show a faster rate of increase in the number of lung cancer deaths? How can you tell?
4. Cigarette smoking increased until 1965 but then decreased between 1965 and 1990. How does the trend in smoking compare with the rate of lung cancer deaths?

Think It Over

Predicting Do you think that the rate of lung cancer deaths is likely to increase, decrease, or remain the same by 2010? Explain.

Whoosh! Millions of tiny but dangerous aliens are invading the respiratory system. The aliens are pulled into the mouth with an inhaled breath. The cilia trap some aliens, and others get stuck in mucus. But thousands of the invaders get past these defenses and enter the lungs. The aliens then land on the surface of the alveoli!

The "aliens" are not tiny creatures from space. They are the substances found in cigarette smoke. In this section you will learn how tobacco smoke damages the respiratory system.

A heavy smoker may smoke two packs of cigarettes in a day.

Chemicals in Tobacco Smoke

With each puff, a smoker inhales more than 4,000 different chemicals. **Some of the most deadly chemicals in tobacco smoke are tar, carbon monoxide, and nicotine.**

Tar The dark, sticky substance that forms when tobacco burns is called **tar.** When someone inhales tobacco smoke, some tar settles on cilia that line the trachea, bronchi, and smaller airways. Tar makes cilia clump together so they can't function to prevent harmful materials from getting into the lungs. Tar also contains chemicals that have been shown to cause cancer.

Carbon Monoxide When substances—including tobacco—are burned, a colorless, odorless gas called **carbon monoxide** is produced. Carbon monoxide is dangerous because its molecules bind to hemoglobin in red blood cells. When carbon monoxide binds to hemoglobin, it takes the place of some of the oxygen that the red blood cells normally carry. The carbon monoxide molecules are something like cars that are parked in spaces reserved for other cars.

When carbon monoxide binds to hemoglobin, red blood cells carry less than their normal load of oxygen throughout the body. To make up for the decrease in oxygen, the breathing rate increases and the heart beats faster. Smokers' blood may contain too little oxygen to meet their bodies' needs.

Nicotine Another dangerous chemical found in tobacco is **nicotine.** Nicotine is a stimulant drug that increases the activities of the nervous system and heart. It makes the heart beat faster and increases blood pressure. Over time, nicotine produces an **addiction,** or physical dependence. Smokers feel an intense craving for a cigarette if they go without one. Addiction to nicotine is one reason why smokers have difficulty quitting.

 **Reading Checkpoint** How does the tar in cigarettes affect the body?

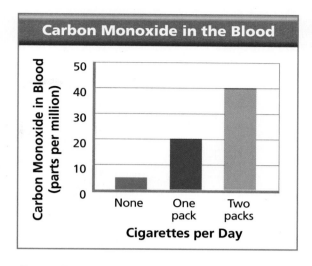

Carbon Monoxide in the Blood

FIGURE 7
Carbon Monoxide in the Blood
The more cigarettes a person smokes, the more carbon monoxide he or she inhales.
Relating Cause and Effect *How does carbon monoxide deprive the body of oxygen?*

SURGEON GENERAL'S WARNING: Cigarette Smoke Contains Carbon Monoxide.

SURGEON GENERAL'S WARNING: Smoking Causes Lung Cancer, Heart Disease, Emphysema, and May Complicate Pregnancy.

SURGEON GENERAL'S WARNING: Smoking By Pregnant Women May Result in Fetal Injury, Premature Birth, and Low Birth Weight.

Lung of a nonsmoker

Health Problems and Smoking

Tobacco smoke causes health problems in several ways. For example, because the cilia can't sweep away mucus, many smokers have a frequent cough. The mucus buildup also limits the space for airflow, thus decreasing oxygen intake. Because they are not getting enough oxygen, long-term or heavy smokers may be short of breath during even light exercise.

You probably know that smoking damages the respiratory system, but did you know that it strains the circulatory system as well? The respiratory and circulatory systems work together to get oxygen to body cells. If either system is damaged, the other one must work harder. Serious health problems can result from long-term smoking. **Over time, smokers can develop chronic bronchitis, emphysema, lung cancer, and atherosclerosis.** Every year in the United States, more than 400,000 people die from smoking-related illnesses. That's one out of every five deaths. Tobacco smoke is the most important preventable cause of major illness and death.

Chronic Bronchitis Bronchitis (brahng KY tis) is an irritation of the breathing passages in which the small passages become narrower than normal and may be clogged with mucus. People with bronchitis have difficulty breathing. If the irritation continues over a long time, it is called chronic bronchitis. Chronic bronchitis can cause permanent damage to the breathing passages. It is often accompanied by infection with disease-causing microorganisms. Chronic bronchitis is five to ten times more common in heavy smokers than in nonsmokers.

Lab zone Skills **Activity**

Calculating

Heavy smokers may smoke two packs of cigarettes every day. Find out what one pack of cigarettes costs. Then, use that price to calculate how much a person would spend on cigarettes if he or she smoked two packs a day for 30 years.

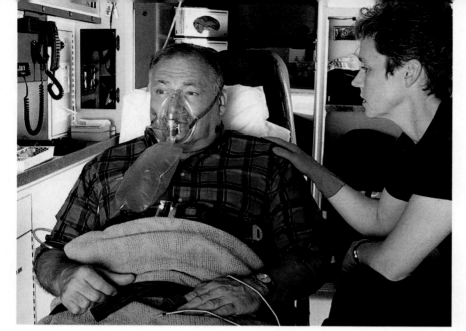

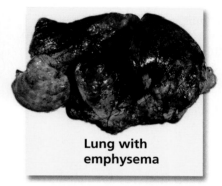

FIGURE 9
Effects of Smoking on the Lungs
Over time, smoking damages the lungs and leads to serious health problems. Comparing and Contrasting *Compare the lungs of a person with emphysema and a person with lung cancer to the lung of a nonsmoker shown in Figure 8.*

Lung with emphysema

Lung with cancer

Emphysema The chemicals in tobacco smoke damage lung tissue as well as breathing passages. **Emphysema** (em fuh SEE muh) is a serious disease that destroys lung tissue and causes breathing difficulties. People with emphysema do not get enough oxygen and cannot adequately eliminate carbon dioxide. Therefore, they are always short of breath. Some people with emphysema even have trouble blowing out a match. Unfortunately, the damage caused by emphysema is permanent, even if a person stops smoking.

Lung Cancer About 140,000 Americans die each year from lung cancer caused by smoking. Cigarette smoke contains more than 50 different chemicals that cause cancer, including the chemicals in tar. Cancerous growths, or tumors, take away space in the lungs that are used for gas exchange. Unfortunately, lung cancer is rarely detected early, when treatment would be most effective.

Atherosclerosis The chemicals in tobacco smoke also harm the circulatory system. Some of the chemicals get into the blood and are absorbed by the blood vessels. The chemicals then irritate the walls of the blood vessels. This irritation contributes to the buildup of fatty material on the blood vessel walls that causes atherosclerosis. Atherosclerosis can lead to heart attacks. Compared to nonsmokers, smokers are more than twice as likely to have heart attacks.

 **Reading Checkpoint** **How does emphysema affect a person's lungs?**

FIGURE 10
Passive Smoking
Billboards like this one increase people's awareness that nonsmokers can also suffer from the effects of tobacco smoke.

For: Links on respiratory disorders
Visit: www.SciLinks.org
Web Code: scn-0442

Passive Smoking Smokers are not the only people to suffer from the effects of tobacco smoke. In passive smoking, people involuntarily inhale the smoke from other people's cigarettes, cigars, or pipes. This smoke contains the same harmful chemicals that smokers inhale. Each year, passive smoking is associated with the development of bronchitis and other respiratory problems, such as asthma, in about 300,000 young children in the United States.

Section 2 Assessment

Target Reading Skill Relating Cause and Effect Refer to your graphic organizer about the effects of smoking on the body to help you answer the questions below.

Reviewing Key Concepts

1. a. Listing What are three harmful substances in tobacco smoke?
  b. Relating Cause and Effect How does each of the harmful substances directly affect the body?
  c. Developing Hypotheses Why might nicotine-containing products, such as chewing gums or skin patches, help a person who is trying to quit smoking?

2. a. Reviewing Identify four health problems that can develop in smokers over time.
  b. Describing How does smoking contribute to atherosclerosis?
  c. Inferring What effect would it have on the circulatory system if a person quit smoking?

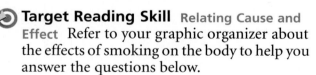

Warning Labels With a family member, make a list of the warning statements found on cigarette labels. What chemicals found in tobacco smoke and health problems do the labels identify? Summarize the information you find to share with the class.

The Excretory System

Reading Preview

Key Concepts
- What are the structures and functions of the excretory system?
- How do the kidneys filter wastes from the blood?
- How does excretion contribute to homeostasis?

Key Terms
- excretion • urea • kidney
- urine • ureter
- urinary bladder • urethra
- nephron

Target Reading Skill

Previewing Visuals Before you read, preview Figure 11. Then, write two questions that you have about the diagram in a graphic organizer like the one below. As you read, answer your questions.

How the Kidneys Filter Wastes

Q.	Where are nephrons located?
A.	
Q.	

Lab zone Discover **Activity**

How Does Filtering a Liquid Change the Liquid?

1. Your teacher will give you 50 mL of a liquid in a small container. Pour a small amount of sand into the liquid.
2. Use a glucose test strip to determine whether glucose is present in the liquid.
3. Put filter paper in a funnel. Then, put the funnel into the mouth of a second container. Slowly pour the liquid through the funnel into the second container.
4. Look for any solid material on the filter paper. Remove the funnel, and carefully examine the liquid that passed through the filter.
5. Test the liquid again to see whether it contains glucose.

Think It Over

Observing Which substances passed through the filter, and which did not? How might a filtering device be useful in the body?

The human body faces a challenge that is a bit like trying to keep your room clean. Magazines, notebook paper, and CD wrappers tend to pile up in your room. You use all of these things, but sooner or later you must clean your room if you don't want to be buried in trash. Something similar happens in your body. As your cells use nutrients in respiration and other processes, wastes are created. Different organs in the body have roles for the removal of these wastes. The removal process is known as **excretion.**

If wastes were not removed from your body, they would pile up and make you sick. Excretion helps keep the body's internal environment stable and free of harmful materials. **The excretory system is the system in the body that collects wastes produced by cells and removes the wastes from the body.**

The Excretory System

Two wastes that your body must eliminate are excess water and urea. **Urea** (yoo REE uh) is a chemical that comes from the breakdown of proteins. **The structures of the excretory system that eliminate urea, water, and other wastes include the kidneys, ureters, urinary bladder, and urethra.**

Your two **kidneys,** which are the major organs of the excretory system, remove urea and other wastes from the blood. The kidneys act like filters. They remove wastes but keep materials that the body needs. The wastes are eliminated in **urine**, a watery fluid that contains urea and other wastes. Urine flows from the kidneys through two narrow tubes called **ureters** (yoo REE turz). The ureters carry urine to the **urinary bladder,** a sacklike muscular organ that stores urine. Urine leaves the body through a small tube called the **urethra** (yoo REE thruh).

 **Reading Checkpoint** What is the role of the ureters?

Filtration of Wastes

The kidneys are champion filters. Each of your kidneys contains about a million **nephrons,** tiny filtering factories that remove wastes from blood and produce urine. **The nephrons filter wastes in stages. First, both wastes and needed materials, such as glucose, are filtered out of the blood. Then, much of the needed material is returned to the blood, and the wastes are eliminated from the body.** Follow this process in Figure 11.

Filtering Out Wastes During the first stage of waste removal, blood enters the kidneys. Here, the blood flows through smaller and smaller arteries. Eventually it reaches a cluster of capillaries in a nephron. The capillaries are surrounded by a thin-walled, hollow capsule that is connected to a tube. In the capillary cluster, urea, glucose, and some water move out of the blood and into the capsule. Blood cells and most protein molecules do not move into the capsule. Instead, they remain in the capillaries.

Formation of Urine Urine forms from the filtered material in the capsule. This material flows through the long, twisting tube. As the liquid moves through the tube, many of the substances are returned to the blood. Normally, all the glucose, most of the water, and small amounts of other materials pass back into the blood in the capillaries that surround the tube. In contrast, urea and other wastes remain in the tube.

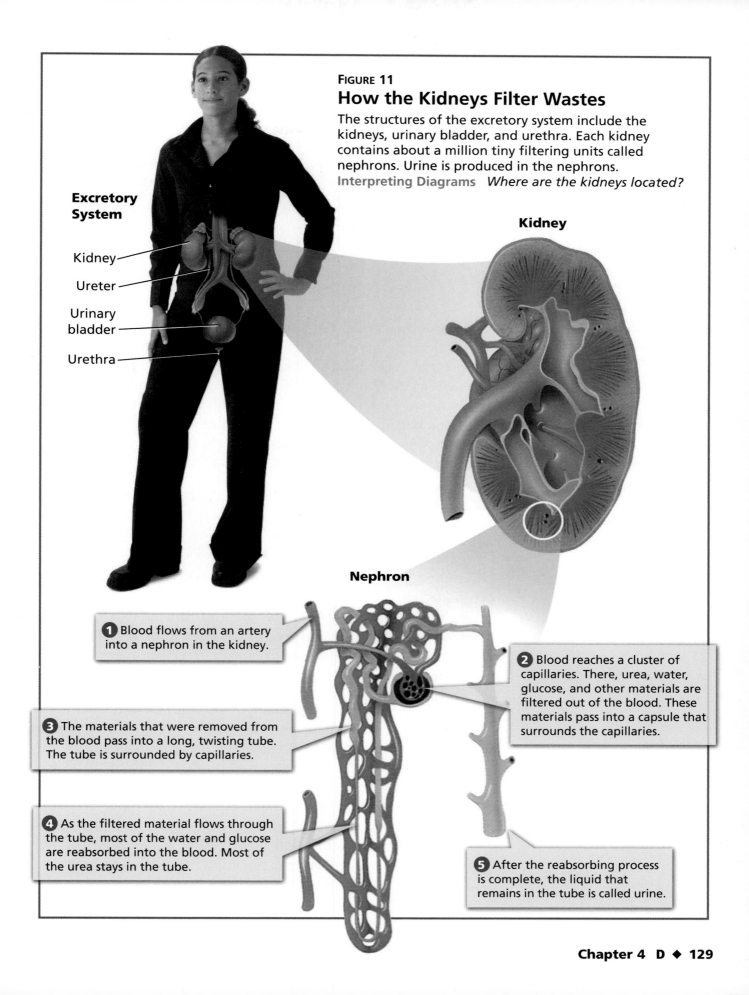

FIGURE 11

How the Kidneys Filter Wastes

The structures of the excretory system include the kidneys, urinary bladder, and urethra. Each kidney contains about a million tiny filtering units called nephrons. Urine is produced in the nephrons.
Interpreting Diagrams *Where are the kidneys located?*

Excretory System

Kidney

Ureter

Urinary bladder

Urethra

Kidney

Nephron

1 Blood flows from an artery into a nephron in the kidney.

2 Blood reaches a cluster of capillaries. There, urea, water, glucose, and other materials are filtered out of the blood. These materials pass into a capsule that surrounds the capillaries.

3 The materials that were removed from the blood pass into a long, twisting tube. The tube is surrounded by capillaries.

4 As the filtered material flows through the tube, most of the water and glucose are reabsorbed into the blood. Most of the urea stays in the tube.

5 After the reabsorbing process is complete, the liquid that remains in the tube is called urine.

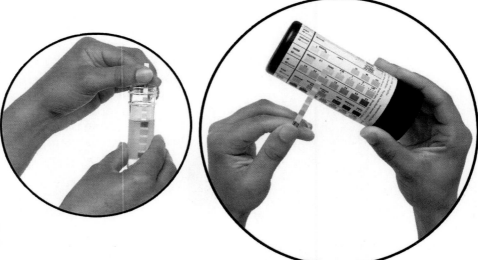

FIGURE 12
Analyzing Urine
Lab technicians can analyze urine by using a dipstick that changes color in the presence of glucose and other substances. The technician dips the dipstick into a urine sample and compares the results to a color chart.
Applying Concepts What are two substances for which urine can be tested?

Analyzing Urine for Signs of Disease When people go to a doctor for a medical checkup, they usually have their urine analyzed. A chemical analysis of urine can be useful in detecting some medical problems. Normally, urine contains almost no glucose or protein. If glucose is present in urine, it may indicate that a person has diabetes, a condition in which body cells cannot absorb enough glucose from the blood. Protein in urine can be a sign that the kidneys are not functioning properly.

 **Reading Checkpoint** **What could it mean if there is glucose in the urine?**

Excretion and Homeostasis

Eliminating wastes, such as urea, excess water, and carbon dioxide, is important for maintaining homeostasis. **Excretion maintains homeostasis by keeping the body's internal environment stable and free of harmful levels of chemicals. In addition to the kidneys, organs of excretion that maintain homeostasis include the lungs, skin, and liver.**

Kidneys As the kidneys filter blood, they help to maintain homeostasis by regulating the amount of water in your body. Remember that as urine is being formed, water passes from the tube back into the bloodstream. The exact amount of water that is reabsorbed depends on conditions both outside and within the body. For example, suppose that it's a hot day. You've been sweating a lot, and you haven't had much to drink. In that situation, almost all of the water in the tube will be reabsorbed, and you will excrete only a small amount of urine. If, however, the day is cool and you've drunk a lot of water, less water will be reabsorbed. Your body will produce a larger volume of urine.

Go Online
SciLINKS NSTA

For: Links on organs of excretion
Visit: www.SciLinks.org
Web Code: scn-0443

Lungs and Skin Most of the wastes produced by the body are removed through the kidneys. However, the lungs and skin remove some wastes from the body as well. When you exhale, carbon dioxide and some water are removed from the body by the lungs. Sweat glands in the skin also serve an excretory function because water and urea are excreted in perspiration.

Liver Have you ever torn apart a large pizza box so that it could fit into a wastebasket? If so, then you understand that some wastes need to be broken down before they can be excreted. The liver performs this function. For example, urea, which comes from the breakdown of proteins, is produced by the liver. The liver also converts part of the hemoglobin molecule from old red blood cells into substances such as bile. Because the liver produces a usable material from old red blood cells, you can think of the liver as a recycling facility.

FIGURE 13
Excretion Through the Lungs
Your lungs function as excretory organs. When you exhale on a cold morning, you can see the water in your breath.

 **Reading Checkpoint** What substances are excreted in perspiration?

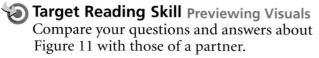

Section 3 Assessment

🎯 **Target Reading Skill** Previewing Visuals Compare your questions and answers about Figure 11 with those of a partner.

Reviewing Key Concepts

1. a. Reviewing What is the role of the excretory system in the body?
  b. Sequencing Name the structures of the excretory system in order of their roles in producing and eliminating urine. Describe the function of each structure.
2. a. Reviewing What are the two main stages of waste removal by the kidneys?
  b. Describing What happens as wastes are filtered in a nephron?
  c. Relating Cause and Effect Why is protein in the urine a sign that something could be wrong with the kidneys?

3. a. Identifying What is the role of excretion in maintaining homeostasis?
  b. Explaining How do the kidneys help maintain homeostasis?
  c. Predicting On a long bus trip, a traveler does not drink any water for several hours. How will the volume of urine she produces that day compare to the volume on a day when she drinks several glasses of water? Explain.

Writing in Science

Explanation Write a paragraph explaining how wastes are filtered in the kidneys. To help you with your writing, first make two lists—one that includes materials removed from the blood in the kidneys and one that includes materials returned to the blood.

Clues About Health

Problem

How can you test urine for the presence of glucose and protein?

Skills Focus

observing, interpreting data, drawing conclusions

Materials

- 6 test tubes
- test-tube rack
- 6 plastic droppers
- water
- glucose solution
- protein solution
- marking pencil
- white paper towels
- 6 glucose test strips
- Biuret solution
- 3 simulated urine samples

Procedure

PART 1 Testing for Glucose

1. Label six test tubes as follows: *W* for water, *G* for glucose, *P* for protein, and *A, B,* and *C* for three patients' "urine samples." Place the test tubes in a test-tube rack.

2. Label six glucose test strips with the same letters: *W, G, P, A, B,* and *C.*

3. Copy the data table into your notebook.

4. Fill each test tube about $\frac{3}{4}$ full with the solution that corresponds to its label.

5. Place glucose test strip W on a clean, dry section of a paper towel. Then, use a clean plastic dropper to place 2 drops of the water from test tube W on the test strip. Record the resulting color of the test strip in your data table. If no color change occurs, write "no reaction."

6. Use the procedure in Step 5 to test each of the other five solutions with the correctly labeled glucose test strip. Record the color of each test strip in the data table.

PART 2 Testing for Protein

7. Obtain a dropper bottle containing Biuret solution. Record the original color of the solution in your notebook.

8. Carefully add 30 drops of Biuret solution to test tube W. **CAUTION:** *Biuret solution can harm skin and damage clothing. Handle it with care.* Gently swirl the test tube to mix the two solutions together. Hold the test tube against a white paper towel to help you detect any color change. Observe the color of the final mixture, and record that color in your data table.

9. Repeat Step 8 for each of the other test tubes.

Data Table						
	Test Tube					
Test for	W (water)	G (glucose)	P (protein)	A (Patient A)	B (Patient B)	C (Patient C)
Glucose						
Protein						

Analyze and Conclude

1. **Observing** What color reaction occurred when you used the glucose test strip on sample W? On sample G?

2. **Interpreting Data** What do the changes in color you observed in Part 1 indicate? Explain.

3. **Observing** What happened when you added Biuret solution to test tube W? To test tube P?

4. **Interpreting Data** What do the changes in color of the Biuret solution you observed in Part II indicate? Explain.

5. **Drawing Conclusions** Which of the three patients' urine samples tested normal? How do you know?

6. **Drawing Conclusions** Which urine sample(s) indicated that diabetes might be present? How do you know?

7. **Drawing Conclusions** Which urine sample(s) indicated that kidney disease might be present? How do you know?

8. **Communicating** Do you think a doctor should draw conclusions about the presence of a disease based on a single urine sample? Write a paragraph in which you discuss this question based on what you know about gathering data in experiments.

More to Explore

Propose a way to determine whether a patient with glucose in the urine could reduce the level through changes in diet.

Study Guide

① The Respiratory System

Key Concepts

- The respiratory system moves oxygen from the outside environment into the body. It also removes carbon dioxide and water from the body.

- As air travels from the outside environment to the lungs, it passes through the following structures: nose, pharynx, trachea, and bronchi.

- After air enters an alveolus, oxygen passes through the wall of the alveolus and then through the capillary wall into the blood. Carbon dioxide and water pass from the blood into the alveoli. This whole process is known as gas exchange.

- When you breathe, the actions of your rib muscles and diaphragm expand or contract your chest, causing air to flow in or out.

Key Terms
- respiration • cilia • pharynx • trachea
- bronchi • lungs • alveoli • diaphragm
- larynx • vocal cords

② Smoking and Your Health

Key Concepts

- Some of the most deadly chemicals in tobacco smoke are tar, carbon monoxide, and nicotine.

- Over time, smokers can develop chronic bronchitis, emphysema, lung cancer, and atherosclerosis.

Key Terms
- tar • carbon monoxide • nicotine
- addiction • bronchitis • emphysema

③ The Excretory System

Key Concepts

- The excretory system is the system in the body that collects wastes produced by cells and removes the wastes from the body.

- The structures of the excretory system that eliminate urea, water, and other wastes include the kidneys, ureters, the urinary bladder, and the urethra.

- The nephrons filter wastes in stages. First, both wastes and needed materials, such as glucose, are filtered from the blood into a nephron. Then, much of the needed material is returned to the blood, and the wastes are eliminated from the body.

- Excretion maintains homeostasis by keeping the body's internal environment stable and free of harmful levels of chemicals. In addition to the kidneys, organs of excretion that maintain homeostasis include the lungs, skin, and liver.

Key Terms

excretion	ureter
urea	urinary bladder
kidney	urethra
urine	nephron

SURGEON GENERAL'S WARNING: Cigarette Smoke Contains Carbon Monoxide.

SURGEON GENERAL'S WARNING: Smoking Causes Lung Cancer, Heart Disease, Emphysema, and May Complicate Pregnancy.

SURGEON GENERAL'S WARNING: Smoking By Pregnant Women May Result in Fetal Injury, Premature Birth, and Low Birth Weight.

Review and Assessment

Organizing Information

Sequencing Copy the flowchart about excretion onto a separate sheet of paper. Then, fill in the empty spaces and add a title. (For more on Sequencing, see the Skills Handbook.)

```
┌─────────────────────────────────┐
│ Blood flows into the nephron's   │
│ capillary cluster.               │
└─────────────────────────────────┘
              ↓
┌─────────────────────────────────┐
│ a. _____ ?_____  │
└─────────────────────────────────┘
              ↓
┌─────────────────────────────────┐
│ b. _____ ?_____  │
└─────────────────────────────────┘
              ↓
┌─────────────────────────────────┐
│ c. _____ ?_____  │
└─────────────────────────────────┘
              ↓
┌─────────────────────────────────┐
│ d. _____ ?_____  │
└─────────────────────────────────┘
```

Reviewing Key Terms

Choose the letter of the best answer.

1. The process in which glucose and oxygen react in cells to release energy is called
   a. excretion.
   b. respiration.
   c. bronchitis.
   d. emphysema.

2. The trachea divides into two tubes called
   a. bronchi.
   b. alveoli.
   c. ureters.
   d. vocal cords.

3. Your voice is produced by the
   a. pharynx.   b. larynx.
   c. trachea.   d. alveoli.

4. A colorless, odorless gas produced by burning tobacco is
   a. carbon monoxide.
   b. tar.
   c. nicotine.
   d. urea.

5. The filtration of wastes takes place inside the kidneys in the
   a. ureters.
   b. urethra.
   c. urinary bladder.
   d. nephrons.

If the statement is true, write *true*. If it is false, change the underlined word or words to make the statement true.

6. Dust particles trapped in mucus are swept away by tiny, hairlike <u>alveoli</u>.

7. Clusters of air sacs in the lungs are <u>bronchi</u>.

8. <u>Tar</u> is a chemical in tobacco smoke that makes the heart beat faster.

9. Urine leaves the body through the <u>ureter</u>.

10. Urine is stored in the <u>urethra</u>.

Writing in Science

Informational Brochure Pretend you are a doctor advising high-altitude climbers. Develop an informational brochure that focuses on the effects that high altitude has on the human body. Be sure to include one method climbers can use to become used to the higher altitudes.

Discovery CHANNEL SCHOOL™

Respiration and Excretion
Video Preview
Video Field Trip
▶ Video Assessment

Review and Assessment

Checking Concepts

11. Explain the difference between breathing and respiration.

12. Explain how the alveoli provide a large surface area for gas exchange in the lungs.

13. Describe how the diaphragm and rib muscles work together to control inhaling and exhaling.

14. Describe what happens when carbon monoxide enters the body. How does this affect the body?

15. Explain two ways in which the kidneys help to maintain homeostasis in the body.

Thinking Critically

16. **Comparing and Contrasting** How is respiration similar to the burning of fuel? How is it different?

17. **Relating Cause and Effect** What process is shown in the diagram below? What role do changes in pressure play in this process?

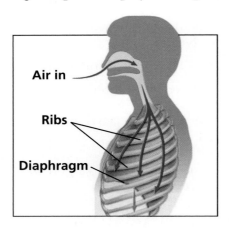

Air in

Ribs

Diaphragm

18. **Applying Concepts** Explain how babies can develop smoking-related respiratory problems.

19. **Making Judgments** Do you think that drugstores, which sell medicines, should also sell cigarettes and other tobacco products? Why or why not?

20. **Predicting** If the walls of the capillary cluster in a nephron were damaged or broken, what substance might you expect to find in urine that is not normally present? Explain.

Math Practice

21. **Surface Area** Which has a greater surface area, a cube that is 2 cm × 2 cm on a side, or eight cubes that are each 1 cm × 1 cm on a side? Show your work.

Applying Skills

Use your knowledge of the excretory system and the information in the data table below to answer Questions 22–25.

Average Daily Water Loss in Humans (mL)

Source	Normal Weather	Hot Weather	Extended Heavy Exercise
Lungs	350	250	650
Urine	1,400	1,200	500
Sweat	450	1,750	5,350
Digestive waste	200	200	200

22. **Interpreting Data** Identify the major source of water loss during normal weather and the major source of water loss during hot weather.

23. **Drawing Conclusions** How do the data for normal weather and hot weather show that the body is maintaining homeostasis?

24. **Calculating** What is the total amount of water lost on a hot-weather day? What is the total amount of water lost during extended heavy exercise?

25. **Inferring** Use the data to explain why it is important to drink a lot of water when you are exercising heavily.

Lab zone Chapter **Project**

Performance Assessment Your three anti-smoking ads should be ready for display. Be prepared to explain why you chose the message you did for each group of viewers. What health risks do each of your ads identify? Why do you think your ads would be effective?

Standardized Test Prep

Choose the letter of the best answer.

1. Which of the following organs functions as both a respiratory organ and an excretory organ?
   A the liver
   B the lungs
   C the skin
   D the kidneys

2. The correct sequence of organs through which air travels when it is breathed into the body is
   F pharynx, nose, trachea, bronchi.
   G nose, trachea, pharynx, bronchi.
   H nose, pharynx, bronchi, trachea.
   J nose, pharynx, trachea, bronchi.

The graph below shows the percentage of total lung function in people who have never smoked and in smokers from ages 25–75. Use the graph to answer Questions 3 and 4.

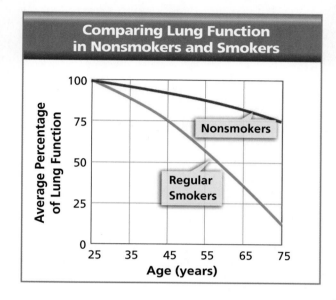

3. At approximately what age do the lungs of a smoker have the same capacity as the lungs of a 75-year-old who has never smoked?
   A 25
   B 45
   C 65
   D 75

4. What general conclusion about lung function and smoking could you draw from this graph?
   F Smoking does not affect lung function.
   G People who smoke are more likely to have greater lung function than those who have never smoked.
   H By the age of 50, a smoker will likely have 50 percent lung function.
   J Smoking significantly reduces the lung function of smokers compared to people who have never smoked.

Constructed Response

5. What is respiration? Explain where this process occurs and what body systems are involved in making respiration possible.

Chapter
5

Fighting Disease

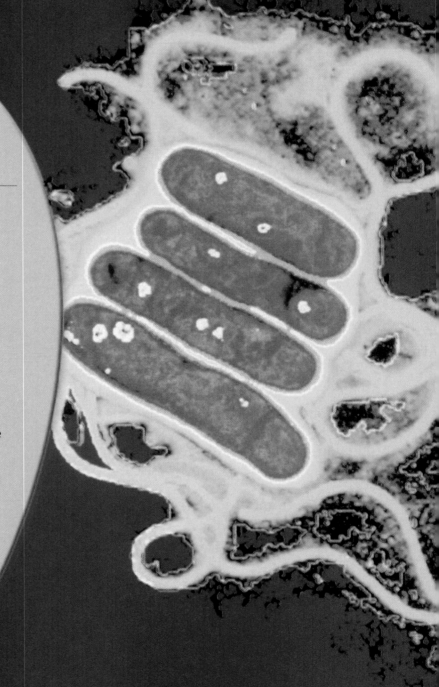

The BIG Idea
Personal Health

 How does the human body fight disease?

These rod-shaped bacteria *(Legionella)* ▶ cause **Legionnaires'** disease.

Discovery
CHANNEL
SCHOOL™

Fighting Disease

▶ **Video Preview**
Video Field Trip
Video Assessment

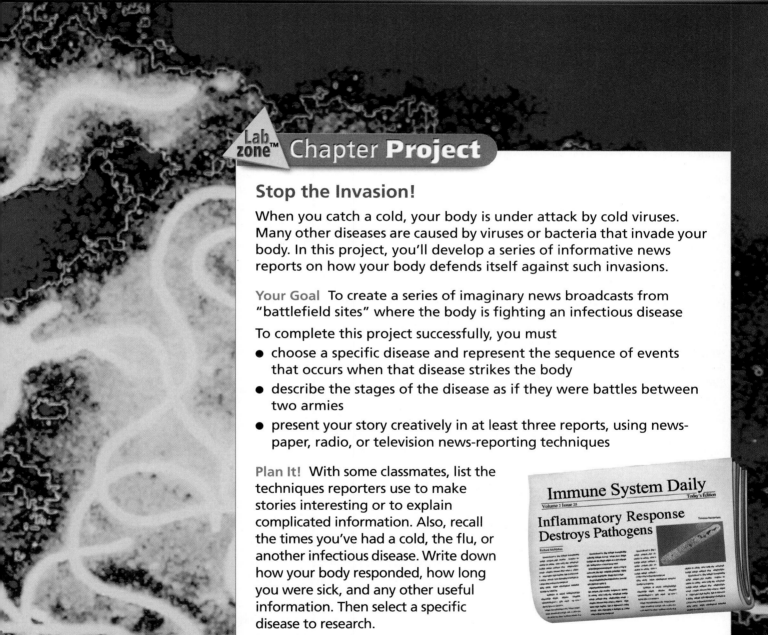

Lab zone™ Chapter **Project**

Stop the Invasion!

When you catch a cold, your body is under attack by cold viruses. Many other diseases are caused by viruses or bacteria that invade your body. In this project, you'll develop a series of informative news reports on how your body defends itself against such invasions.

Your Goal To create a series of imaginary news broadcasts from "battlefield sites" where the body is fighting an infectious disease

To complete this project successfully, you must

● choose a specific disease and represent the sequence of events that occurs when that disease strikes the body

● describe the stages of the disease as if they were battles between two armies

● present your story creatively in at least three reports, using newspaper, radio, or television news-reporting techniques

Plan It! With some classmates, list the techniques reporters use to make stories interesting or to explain complicated information. Also, recall the times you've had a cold, the flu, or another infectious disease. Write down how your body responded, how long you were sick, and any other useful information. Then select a specific disease to research.

Immune System Daily
Volume 7 Issue 25   Today's Edition

Inflammatory Response Destroys Pathogens

Richard McMahan

Infectious Disease

Reading Preview

Key Concepts
- What is the relationship between pathogens and infectious disease?
- What kinds of pathogens cause infectious diseases in humans?
- What are four ways that pathogens can spread?

Key Terms
- pathogen
- infectious disease
- toxin

Target Reading Skill

Using Prior Knowledge Before you read, look at the section headings and visuals to see what this section is about. Then write what you know about infectious diseases in a graphic organizer like the one below. As you read, continue to write in what you learn.

What You Know
1. Bacteria and viruses can cause disease.
2.

What You Learned
1.
2.

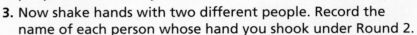

Discover Activity

How Does a Disease Spread?

1. On a sheet of paper, write three headings: Round 1, Round 2, and Round 3.
2. Everyone in the class should shake hands with two people. Under Round 1, record the names of the people whose hand you shook.
3. Now shake hands with two different people. Record the name of each person whose hand you shook under Round 2.
4. Repeat Step 3. Under Round 3, record the names of the people whose hand you shook.

Think It Over

Calculating Suppose you had a disease that was spread by shaking hands. Everyone whose hand you shook has caught the disease and so has anyone who later shook hands with those people. Calculate how many people you "infected."

Before the twentieth century, surgery was a risky business. Even if people lived through an operation, they were not out of danger. After the operation, many patients' wounds became infected, and the patients often died. No one knew what caused these infections.

In the 1860s, a British surgeon named Joseph Lister hypothesized that microorganisms caused the infections. Before performing an operation, Lister washed his hands and surgical instruments with carbolic acid, a chemical that kills microorganisms. After the surgery, he covered the patient's wounds with bandages dipped in carbolic acid. Lister's results were dramatic. Before he used his new method, about 45 percent of his surgical patients died from infection. With Lister's new techniques, only 15 percent died.

Understanding Infectious Disease

Like the infections that Lister observed after surgery, many illnesses, such as ear infections and food poisoning, are caused by living things that are too small to see without a microscope. Organisms that cause disease are called **pathogens.**

Diseases that are caused by pathogens are called infectious diseases. An **infectious disease** is a disease that is caused by the presence of a living thing within the body. **When you have an infectious disease, pathogens have gotten inside your body and caused harm.** Pathogens make you sick by damaging individual cells, even though you may feel pain throughout your body. For example, when you have strep throat, pathogens have damaged cells in your throat.

Before Lister's time, people believed that things like evil spirits or swamp air led to sickness. Several scientists in the late 1800s contributed to the understanding of infectious diseases. In the 1860s, the French scientist Louis Pasteur showed that microorganisms cause certain kinds of diseases. Pasteur also showed that killing the microorganisms could prevent the spread of those diseases. In the 1870s and 1880s, the German physician Robert Koch demonstrated that each infectious disease is caused by a specific kind of pathogen. In other words, one kind of pathogen causes pneumonia, another kind causes chickenpox, and still another kind causes rabies.

 **What causes infectious disease?**

For: More on infectious disease
Visit: PHSchool.com
Web Code: ced-4051

FIGURE 1
Preventing Infections
The illustration on the left shows how Lister used a carbolic steam sprayer to spread a mist of carbolic acid. The photo on the right shows a modern operating room.
Comparing and Contrasting
Identify some ways in which present-day surgery differs from surgery in Lister's time.

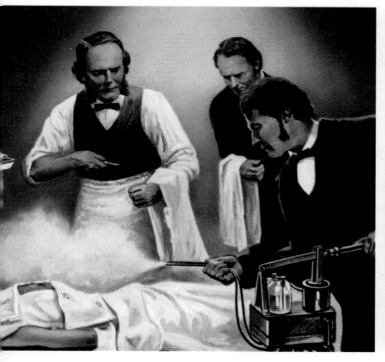
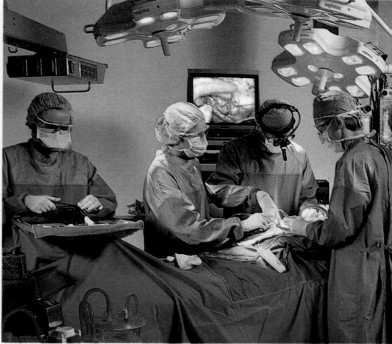

FIGURE 2
Pathogens
Most infectious diseases are caused by microscopic organisms.

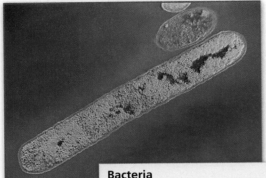

Bacteria
This rod-shaped bacterium causes tetanus, a disease that harms the nervous system.

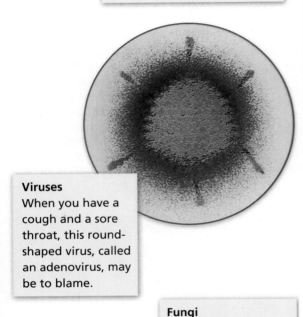

Viruses
When you have a cough and a sore throat, this round-shaped virus, called an adenovirus, may be to blame.

Fungi
This fungus causes ringworm, a disease that makes a round, ring-shaped skin rash.

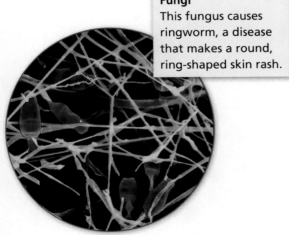

Kinds of Pathogens

You share Earth with many kinds of organisms. Most of these organisms are harmless, but some can make you sick. Some diseases are caused by multicelled animals, such as worms. However, most pathogens can be seen only with a microscope. **The four major groups of human pathogens are bacteria, viruses, fungi, and protists.** Look at Figure 2 to see some examples of pathogens.

Bacteria Bacteria are one-celled microorganisms. They cause a wide variety of diseases, including ear infections, food poisoning, and strep throat.

Some bacterial pathogens damage body cells directly. Strep throat is caused by streptococcus bacteria that invade cells in your throat. Other bacterial pathogens damage cells indirectly by producing a poison, or **toxin.** For example, if the bacteria that cause tetanus get into a wound, they produce a toxin that damages the nervous system. Tetanus is also called lockjaw because the nerve damage can lock the jaw muscles.

Viruses Viruses are tiny particles, much smaller than bacteria. Viruses cannot reproduce unless they are inside living cells. The cells are damaged or destroyed in the process, releasing new viruses to infect other cells. Both colds and flu are caused by viruses that invade cells in the respiratory system. There are more than 200 kinds of cold viruses, each of which can give you a sore throat and runny nose.

Fungi Fungi, which include molds and yeasts, also cause some infectious diseases. Fungi grow best in warm, dark, and moist areas. Two examples of fungal diseases are athlete's foot and ringworm.

Protists Protists are also a cause of disease. Malaria, an infection of the blood that is common in tropical areas, is one disease caused by protists. Other diseases caused by protists are African sleeping sickness and amebic dysentery.

 **Reading Checkpoint** **What is required in order for viruses to reproduce?**

How Pathogens Are Spread

Like all living things, pathogens need food and a place to live and reproduce. Unfortunately, your body may be the right place to meet a pathogen's needs. You can become infected by a pathogen in several ways. **Pathogens can spread through contact with either an infected person; soil, food, or water; a contaminated object; or an infected animal.**

Infected People Pathogens often pass from one person to another through direct physical contact, such as kissing and shaking hands. For example, if you kiss someone who has an open cold sore, cold-sore viruses may get into your body.

Diseases are also spread through indirect contact with an infected person. For example, when a person with a cold or the flu sneezes, pathogens shoot into the air. Other people may catch a cold or the flu if they inhale these pathogens.

Soil, Food, and Water Some pathogens occur naturally in the environment. The bacteria that cause botulism, a severe form of food poisoning, live in soil. Botulism bacteria can produce toxins in foods that have been improperly canned.

Some pathogens can contaminate food and water. If people then eat the food or drink the water, they may become sick. Some pathogens that cause severe diarrhea are spread through contaminated food and water. Cholera and dysentery are two deadly diseases that spread through food or water.

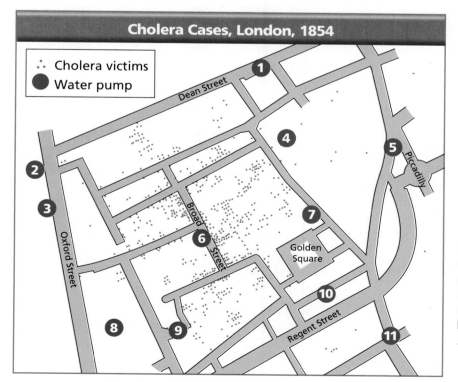

Cholera Cases, London, 1854

∴ Cholera victims
● Water pump

Dean Street
Oxford Street
Broad Street
Piccadilly
Golden Square
Regent Street

FIGURE 3
Cholera is a deadly disease caused by cholera bacteria. The map shows the location of cholera cases in the 1854 epidemic in London, England.
Inferring *How are cholera bacteria spread?*

FIGURE 4
Deer Ticks and Lyme Disease
The tiny deer tick may carry the bacteria that cause Lyme disease, a serious condition that can damage the joints.
Problem Solving How might people reduce their risk of catching Lyme disease?

Contaminated Objects Some pathogens can survive for a time outside a person's body. People can come into contact with pathogens by using objects, such as towels or silverware, that have been handled by an infected person. Colds and flu can be spread in this way. Tetanus bacteria can enter the body if a person steps on a contaminated object.

Infected Animals If an animal that is infected with certain pathogens bites a person, it can pass the pathogens to the person. People can get rabies, a serious disease that affects the nervous system, from the bite of an infected animal, such as a dog or a raccoon. Lyme disease and Rocky Mountain spotted fever are both spread by tick bites. For example, if a deer tick that is carrying Lyme disease bacteria bites a person, the person may get Lyme disease. The protist that causes malaria is transferred by the bites of mosquitoes that live in tropical regions.

 **Reading Checkpoint** **Name a disease that can be spread by an animal bite.**

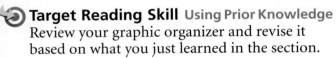

Section 1 Assessment

Target Reading Skill Using Prior Knowledge Review your graphic organizer and revise it based on what you just learned in the section.

Reviewing Key Concepts

1. **a. Defining** What is a pathogen?
   b. Explaining How do pathogens cause infectious disease?
   c. Relating Cause and Effect How did Pasteur and Koch contribute to the understanding of the causes of infectious disease?
2. **a. Identifying** Name four kinds of pathogens that cause disease in humans.
   b. Explaining In what two ways do bacteria cause disease?
   c. Comparing and Contrasting Compare and contrast bacteria and viruses—both in terms of their size and how they cause disease.

3. **a. Listing** What are four ways that pathogens can infect humans?
   b. Describing How are pathogens spread by contaminated objects?
   c. Applying Concepts If you have a cold, what steps can you take to keep from spreading it to other people? Explain.

Writing in Science

Speech Write a short speech that Joseph Lister might have delivered to other surgeons to convince them to use his surgical techniques. In the speech, Lister should explain why his techniques were so successful.

The Body's Defenses

Reading Preview

Key Concepts
- How does the body's first line of defense guard against pathogens?
- What happens during the inflammatory response?
- How does the immune system respond to pathogens?
- How does HIV affect the immune system and how does it spread?

Key Terms
- inflammatory response
- phagocyte • immune response
- lymphocyte • T cell
- antigen • B cell • antibody
- AIDS • HIV

Target Reading Skill

Building Vocabulary After you read this section, reread the paragraphs that contain definitions of Key Terms. Use all the information you have learned to write a definition of each Key Term in your own words.

Lab zone Discover Activity

Which Pieces Fit Together?

1. Your teacher will give you a piece of paper with one jagged edge.
2. One student in the class has a piece of paper with a jagged edge that matches yours, like two pieces of a jigsaw puzzle. Find the student whose paper matches yours and fit the two edges together.

Think It Over

Inferring Imagine that one piece of paper in each matching pair is a pathogen. The other is a cell in your body that defends your body against the invading pathogen. How many kinds of invaders can each defender cell recognize?

Your eyes are glued to the video screen. Enemy troops have gotten through an opening in the wall. Your soldiers have held back most of the invaders. However, some enemy soldiers are breaking through the defense lines. You need your backup defenders. They can zap invaders with their more powerful weapons. If your soldiers can fight off the enemy until the backup team arrives, you can save your fortress.

Video games create fantasy wars, but in your body, real battles happen all the time. In your body, the "enemies" are invading pathogens. You are hardly ever aware of these battles. The body's disease-fighting system is so effective that most people get sick only occasionally. By eliminating pathogens that can harm your cells, your body maintains homeostasis.

The fight is on. ▶

Barriers That Keep Pathogens Out

Your body has three lines of defense against pathogens. The first line consists of barriers that keep most pathogens from getting into the body. You do not wear a sign that says "Pathogens Keep Out," but that doesn't matter. **In the first line of defense, the surfaces of the skin, breathing passages, mouth, and stomach function as barriers to pathogens. These barriers trap and kill most pathogens with which you come into contact.**

Skin When pathogens land on the skin, they are exposed to destructive chemicals in oil and sweat. Even if these chemicals don't kill them, the pathogens may fall off with dead skin cells. If the pathogens manage to stay on the skin, they must get through the tightly packed dead cells that form a barrier on top of living skin cells. Most pathogens get through the skin only when it is cut. Scabs form over cuts so rapidly that the period in which pathogens can enter the body in this way is very short.

Breathing Passages Pathogens can also enter the body when you inhale. The nose, pharynx, trachea, and bronchi, however, contain mucus and cilia. Together, the mucus and cilia trap and remove most of the pathogens that enter the respiratory system. In addition, irritation by pathogens may make you sneeze or cough. Both actions force the pathogens out of your body.

Mouth and Stomach Some pathogens are found in foods, even if the foods are handled safely. The saliva in your mouth contains destructive chemicals, and your stomach produces acid. Most pathogens that you swallow are destroyed by saliva or stomach acid.

✔ **Reading Checkpoint** How do your breathing passages help keep pathogens out of your body?

FIGURE 5
Barriers to Pathogens
The surfaces of your skin and breathing passages are the first line of defense for keeping pathogens out of your body.
Relating Cause and Effect How can washing your hands help prevent infection?

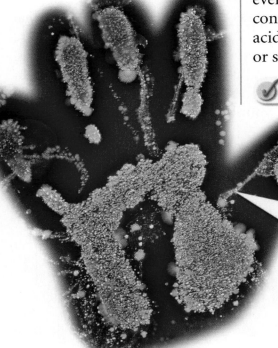

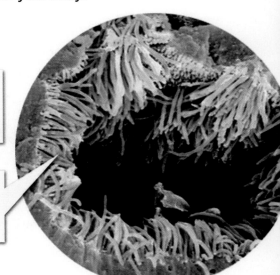

Skin
The dots in this photo are colonies of bacteria living on a person's hand.

Breathing Passages
Cilia that line the trachea help keep pathogens out of the lungs.

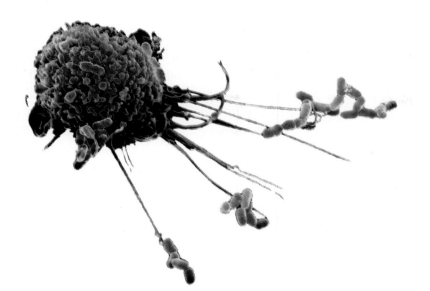

FIGURE 6
Phagocytes Destroy Pathogens
Caught! A phagocyte (shown in red) is a white blood cell that engulfs and destroys bacteria (shown in green). As phagocytes do their job, the body shows visible signs of inflammation, which include redness and swelling.

The Inflammatory Response

In spite of barriers, pathogens sometimes get into your body and begin to damage cells. When body cells are damaged, they release chemicals that trigger the **inflammatory response,** which is the body's second line of defense. **In the inflammatory response, fluid and white blood cells leak from blood vessels into nearby tissues. The white blood cells then fight the pathogens.** Because the inflammatory response is the same regardless of the pathogen, it is called the body's general defense.

White Blood Cells All white blood cells are disease fighters. However, there are different types of white blood cells, each with its own particular function. The type involved in the inflammatory response are the phagocytes. A **phagocyte** (FAG uh syt) is a white blood cell that engulfs pathogens and destroys them by breaking them down.

Inflammation During the inflammatory response, blood vessels widen in the area affected by the pathogens. This enlargement increases blood flow to the area. As a result, more disease-fighting white blood cells are delivered to the area. The enlarged blood vessels, and the fluid that leaks out of them, make the affected area red and swollen. If you touch the swollen area, it will feel slightly warmer than normal.

Fever In some cases, chemicals produced during the inflammatory response cause a fever. Although fever makes you feel bad, it actually helps your body fight the infection. Some pathogens do not grow and reproduce well at higher temperatures.

 **Reading Checkpoint** **What role do white blood cells play in the inflammatory response?**

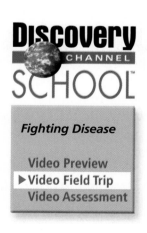

Discovery CHANNEL SCHOOL

Fighting Disease

Video Preview
▶ Video Field Trip
Video Assessment

The Immune System

If a pathogen infection is severe enough to cause a fever, it triggers the body's third line of defense—the **immune response.** The immune response is controlled by the immune system, the body's disease-fighting system. **The cells of the immune system can distinguish between different kinds of pathogens. The immune system cells react to each kind of pathogen with a defense targeted specifically at that pathogen.**

The white blood cells that distinguish between different kinds of pathogens are called **lymphocytes** (LIM fuh syts). There are two major kinds of lymphocytes—T lymphocytes and B lymphocytes, which are also called T cells and B cells. In Figure 7, you can see how T cells and B cells work together to destroy flu viruses.

T Cells A major function of **T cells** is to identify pathogens and distinguish one kind of pathogen from another. You have tens of millions of T cells circulating in your blood. Each kind of T cell recognizes a different kind of pathogen. What T cells actually recognize are marker molecules, called antigens, found on each pathogen. **Antigens** are molecules that the immune system recognizes either as part of your body or as coming from outside your body.

You can think of antigens as something like the uniforms that athletes wear. When you watch a track meet, you can look at the runners' uniforms to tell which school each runner comes from. Like athletes from different schools, each different pathogen has its own kind of antigen. Antigens differ from one another because each kind of antigen has a different chemical structure. T cells distinguish one chemical structure from another.

B Cells The lymphocytes called **B cells** produce proteins that help destroy pathogens. These proteins are called **antibodies.** Each kind of B cell produces only one kind of antibody, and each kind of antibody has a different structure. Antigen and antibody molecules fit together like pieces of a puzzle. An antigen on a flu virus will only bind to one kind of antibody—the antibody that acts against that flu virus.

When antibodies bind to the antigens on a pathogen, they mark the pathogen for destruction. Some antibodies make pathogens clump together. Others keep pathogens from attaching to the body cells that they might damage. Still other antibodies make it easier for phagocytes to destroy the pathogens.

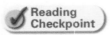 **Reading Checkpoint** What is the function of an antibody?

Lab zone Try This **Activity**

Stuck Together

In this activity, you will model one way in which an antibody prevents a pathogen from infecting a body cell.

1. Use a large ball to represent a body cell, and a smaller ball to represent a pathogen.

2. Press a lump of modeling clay onto the small ball. Then use the clay to stick the two balls together. This model shows how a pathogen attaches itself to a body cell.

3. Pull the two balls apart, keeping the clay on the small ball (the pathogen).

4. Put strips of tape over the clay, so that the clay is completely covered. The tape represents an antibody.

5. Now try to reattach the small ball to the larger one.

Making Models Use the model to explain how antibodies prevent pathogens from attaching to body cells.

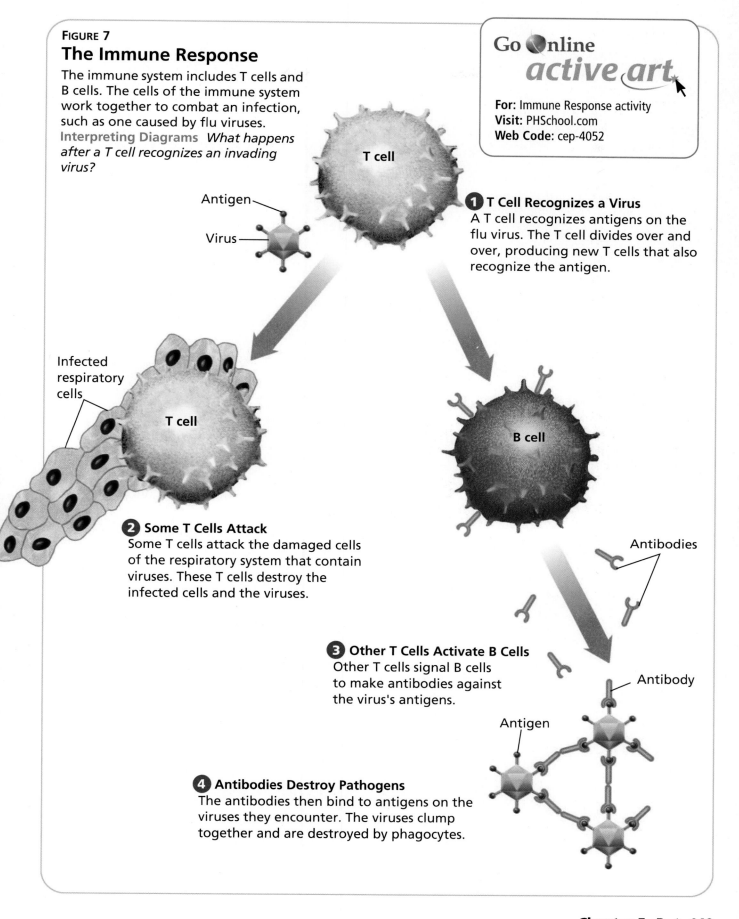

FIGURE 7
The Immune Response

The immune system includes T cells and B cells. The cells of the immune system work together to combat an infection, such as one caused by flu viruses. **Interpreting Diagrams** *What happens after a T cell recognizes an invading virus?*

Go Online
active art

For: Immune Response activity
Visit: PHSchool.com
Web Code: cep-4052

Antigen

Virus

T cell

1 T Cell Recognizes a Virus
A T cell recognizes antigens on the flu virus. The T cell divides over and over, producing new T cells that also recognize the antigen.

Infected respiratory cells

T cell

B cell

Antibodies

2 Some T Cells Attack
Some T cells attack the damaged cells of the respiratory system that contain viruses. These T cells destroy the infected cells and the viruses.

3 Other T Cells Activate B Cells
Other T cells signal B cells to make antibodies against the virus's antigens.

Antibody

Antigen

4 Antibodies Destroy Pathogens
The antibodies then bind to antigens on the viruses they encounter. The viruses clump together and are destroyed by phagocytes.

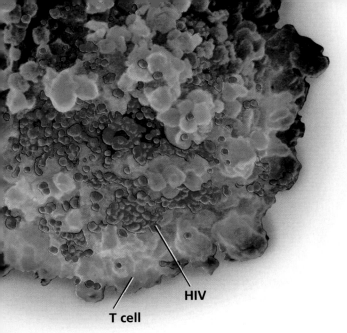

HIV

T cell

FIGURE 8
**Human Immunodeficiency Virus
(HIV)**
The tiny red particles are HIV viruses
emerging from a T cell. The viruses
multiply inside the T cell and
eventually cause the cell to die.
Relating Cause and Effect
*Why does the destruction of T cells
interfere with the body's ability
to fight disease?*

AIDS

Acquired immunodeficiency syndrome, or **AIDS,** is a disease caused by a virus that attacks the immune system. The virus that causes AIDS is called the human immunodeficiency virus, or **HIV.**

How HIV Affects the Body **HIV is the only kind of virus known to attack the human immune system directly and destroy T cells.** Once it invades the body, HIV enters T cells and reproduces inside them. People can be infected with HIV—that is, have the virus living in their T cells—for years before they become sick. More than 40 million people in the world, including more than 3 million children under 15, are infected with HIV.

Eventually, HIV begins to destroy the T cells it has infected. As the viruses destroy T cells, the body loses its ability to fight disease. Most persons infected with HIV eventually develop the symptoms of AIDS.

Because their immune systems no longer function properly, people with AIDS become sick with diseases not normally found in people with healthy immune systems. Many people survive attack after attack of such diseases. But eventually their immune systems fail, ending in death. At this time, there is no cure for AIDS. However, new drug treatments allow many people with AIDS to survive much longer than those in the past.

How HIV Is Spread Like all other viruses, HIV can only reproduce inside cells. However, the virus can survive for a short time outside the human body in body fluids, such as blood and the fluids produced by the male and female reproductive systems.

HIV can spread from one person to another only if body fluids from an infected person come in contact with those of an uninfected person. Sexual contact is one way in which this can happen. HIV may also pass from an infected woman to her baby during pregnancy or childbirth or through breast milk. In addition, infected blood can spread HIV. For example, if an infected drug user shares a needle, the next person who uses the needle may also become infected. Before 1985, HIV was sometimes transmitted through blood transfusions. Since 1985, however, all donated blood in the United States has been tested for signs of HIV. If blood is identified as infected, it is not used in transfusions.

FIGURE 9
How HIV Is Not Spread
You cannot get HIV, the virus that causes AIDS, by hugging someone infected with the virus.

How HIV Is Not Spread It is important to know the many ways in which HIV is *not* spread. HIV does not live on skin, so you cannot be infected by hugging or shaking hands with an infected person. You can't get infected by using a toilet seat after it has been used by someone with HIV. HIV is also not spread when you bump into someone while playing sports.

 **Reading Checkpoint** **What disease is caused by HIV?**

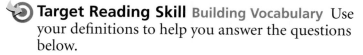

Section 2 Assessment

🔄 **Target Reading Skill** Building Vocabulary Use your definitions to help you answer the questions below.

Reviewing Key Concepts

1. a. Listing Name four barriers that prevent pathogens from getting into the body.
   b. Explaining Briefly describe how each barrier prevents infections.
   c. Predicting What could happen if you got a cut that did not heal?

2. a. Reviewing What triggers the inflammatory response?
   b. Describing How does the inflammatory response defend against invading pathogens?
   c. Relating Cause and Effect Why is the presence of large numbers of white blood cells in a wound a sign of infection?

3. a. Identifying Identify the cells that are part of the immune system.
   b. Sequencing Outline the steps involved in the immune response.

4. a. Reviewing Where in the body does HIV reproduce?
   b. Summarizing What are three ways that HIV can be passed from one person to another?

Writing in Science

Explanation An antigen and antibody can be compared to a lock and key. Write a paragraph in which you explain how the lock-and-key model is a good way to describe the relationship between an antigen and antibody.

Skills Lab

The Skin as a Barrier

Problem

How does the skin act as a barrier to pathogens?

Skills Focus

observing, making models, controlling variables

Materials

- 4 sealable plastic bags
- 4 fresh apples
- rotting apple
- cotton swabs
- marking pen
- paper towels
- toothpick
- rubbing alcohol

Procedure

1. Read over the entire procedure to see how you will treat each of four fresh apples. Write a prediction in your notebook about the change(s) you expect to see in each apple. Then, copy the data table into your notebook.

2. Label four plastic bags *1, 2, 3,* and *4.*

3. Wash your hands with soap and water. Then, gently wash four fresh apples with water and dry them carefully with paper towels. Place one apple into plastic bag 1, and seal the bag.

4. Insert a toothpick tip into a rotting apple and withdraw it. Lightly draw the tip of the toothpick down the side of the second apple without breaking the skin. Repeat these actions three more times, touching the toothpick to different parts of the apple without breaking the skin. Insert the apple into plastic bag 2, and seal the bag.

5. Insert the toothpick tip into the rotting apple and withdraw it. Use the tip to make a long, thin scratch down the side of the third apple. Be sure to pierce the apple's skin. Repeat these actions three more times, making additional scratches on different parts of the apple. Insert the apple into plastic bag 3, and seal the bag.

6. Repeat Step 5 with the fourth apple. However, before you place the apple into the bag, dip a cotton swab in rubbing alcohol, and swab the scratches. Then, place the apple into plastic bag 4, and seal the bag. **CAUTION:** *Alcohol and its vapors are flammable. Work where there are no sparks, exposed flames, or other heat sources.*

Data Table				
Date	Apple 1 (no contact with decay)	Apple 2 (contact with decay, unbroken skin)	Apple 3 (contact with decay, scratched, untreated)	Apple 4 (contact with decay, scratched, treated with alcohol)

7. Store the four bags in a warm, dark place. Wash your hands thoroughly with soap and water.

8. Every day for one week, remove the apples from their storage place and observe them without opening the bags. Record your observations, and return the bags to their storage location. At the end of the activity, dispose of the unopened bags as directed by your teacher.

Analyze and Conclude

1. **Observing** How did the appearance of the four apples compare?

2. **Inferring** Explain the differences you observed in Question 1.

3. **Making Models** In this experiment, what condition in the human body is each of the four fresh apples supposed to model?

4. **Controlling Variables** What is the purpose of Apple 1 in this experiment? Explain.

5. **Making Models** What is the role of the rotting apple in this experiment?

6. **Communicating** Write a paragraph in which you explain how this investigation shows why routine cuts and scrapes should be cleaned and bandaged.

Design an Experiment

Using apples as you did in this activity, design an experiment to model how washing hands can prevent the spread of disease. *Obtain your teacher's permission before carrying out your investigation.*

Preventing Infectious Disease

Reading Preview

Key Concepts
- How does the body acquire active immunity?
- How does passive immunity occur?

Key Terms
- immunity • active immunity
- vaccination • vaccine
- antibiotic • passive immunity

Target Reading Skill
Comparing and Contrasting
As you read, compare and contrast active immunity and passive immunity in a Venn diagram like the one below. Write the similarities in the space where the circles overlap and the differences on the left and right sides.

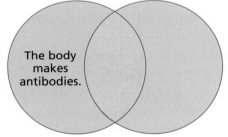

Active Immunity   Passive Immunity

The body makes antibodies.

Lab zone Discover **Activity**

What Substances Can Kill Pathogens?

1. Your teacher will give you a variety of products, such as disinfectant cleansers and mouthwashes, that claim to kill pathogens. Read the labels to learn the pathogens that each product is supposed to destroy.
2. Also note the ingredients in each product that act against pathogens. These are labeled "active ingredients."

Think It Over
Designing Experiments How could you determine which of two different cleansers is more effective at killing bacteria? Design an experiment to find out. Do not perform the experiment without obtaining your teacher's approval.

Ask an adult if he or she remembers having the chickenpox. Chances are, the response will be, "Wow, did I itch!" But someone who has had chickenpox can be pretty sure of never getting that disease again. As people recover from some diseases, they develop immunity to the diseases. **Immunity** is the body's ability to destroy pathogens before they can cause disease. There are two basic types of immunity—active and passive.

Active Immunity

Someone who has been sick with chickenpox was invaded by chickenpox viruses. The immune system responded to the virus antigens by producing antibodies. The next time chickenpox viruses invade the body, a healthy immune system will produce antibodies so quickly that the person will not become sick with chickenpox. This reaction is called **active immunity** because the body has produced the antibodies that fight the disease pathogens. **A person acquires active immunity when their own immune system produces antibodies in response to the presence of a pathogen.** Active immunity can result from either getting the disease or being vaccinated.

The Immune Response When someone gets a disease such as chickenpox, active immunity is produced by the immune system as part of the immune response. Remember that during the immune response, T cells and B cells help destroy the pathogens. After the person recovers, some T cells and B cells keep the "memory" of the pathogen's antigen. If that kind of pathogen enters the body again, these memory cells recognize the antigen. The memory cells start the immune response so quickly that the person usually does not get sick. Active immunity often lasts for many years, and sometimes it lasts for life.

Vaccination A second way to gain active immunity is by being vaccinated. **Vaccination** (vac suh NAY shun), or immunization, is the process by which harmless antigens are deliberately introduced into a person's body to produce active immunity. Vaccinations are given by injection, by mouth, or through a nasal spray. Vaccinations can prevent polio, chickenpox, and other diseases.

The substance that is used in a vaccination is called a vaccine. A **vaccine** (vak SEEN) usually consists of pathogens that have been weakened or killed but can still trigger the immune system to go into action. The T cells and B cells still recognize and respond to the antigens of the weakened or dead pathogen. When you receive a vaccination with weakened pathogens, you usually do not get sick. However, your immune system responds by producing memory cells and active immunity to the disease.

FIGURE 10
Vaccination
Follow the steps below to see how vaccinations work. Classifying *Why do vaccinations produce active immunity?*

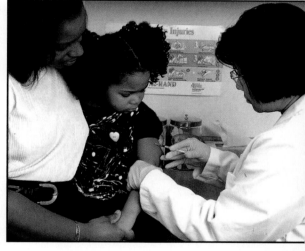

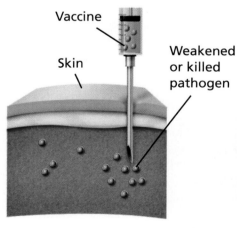

❶ A person receives an injection with weakened or killed pathogens.

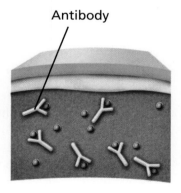

❷ The immune system produces antibodies against the disease. It also produces memory cells.

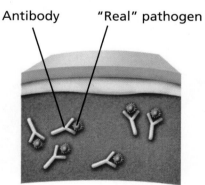

❸ If the "real" pathogen invades later, memory cells help to produce antibodies that disable the pathogen.

For: More on disease prevention
Visit: PHSchool.com
Web Code: ced-4053

When You Do Get Sick You develop immunity to certain diseases either because you have had the diseases or because you have been vaccinated against them. However, no one is immune to all diseases.

Unfortunately, you probably will become sick from time to time. Sometimes, when you become sick, medications can help you get better. If you have a disease that is caused by bacteria, you may be given an antibiotic. An **antibiotic** (an tih by AHT ik) is a chemical that kills bacteria or slows their growth without harming body cells. Unfortunately, there are no medications that are effective against viral illnesses, including the common cold. The best way to deal with most viral diseases is to get plenty of rest.

Science and **History**

Fighting Infectious Disease

From ancient times, people have practiced methods for preventing disease and caring for sick people. About 200 years ago, people began to learn much more about the causes of infectious diseases and how to protect against them.

1796 Edward Jenner
Edward Jenner, a country doctor in England, successfully vaccinated a child against smallpox, a deadly viral disease. Jenner used material from the sore of a person with cowpox, a mild but similar disorder. Although Jenner's procedure was successful, he did not understand why it worked.

1868 Louis Pasteur
In France, Louis Pasteur showed that microorganisms were the cause of disease in silkworms. Pasteur reasoned that he could control the spread of disease by killing microorganisms. He also proposed that infectious disease in humans are caused by microorganisms.

1854 Florence Nightingale
As an English nurse caring for British soldiers during the Crimean War, Florence Nightingale insisted that army hospitals be kept clean. By doing this, she saved many soldiers' lives. She is considered to be the founder of the modern nursing profession.

1800	1840	1880

Although some medicines don't kill pathogens, they may help you feel more comfortable while you get better. Many of these are over-the-counter medications—drugs that can be purchased without a doctor's prescription. Such medications may reduce fever, clear your nose so you can breathe more easily, or stop a cough. Be sure you understand and follow the instructions for all types of medications.

While you recover, be sure to get plenty of rest. Drink plenty of fluids. Unless your stomach is upset, try to eat well-balanced meals. And if you don't start to feel better in a short time, you should see a doctor.

Reading Checkpoint **What is an antibiotic?**

Writing in Science

Research and Write Learn more about the work of one of these scientists. Then, imagine that a new hospital is going to be dedicated to that person and that you have been chosen to deliver the dedication speech. Write a speech that praises the person's contributions to fighting disease.

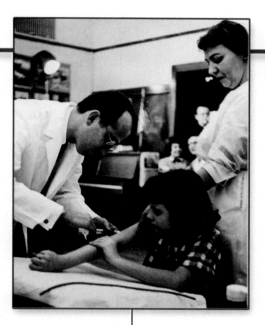

1928 Alexander Fleming
In Britain, Alexander Fleming observed that bacteria growing on laboratory plates were killed when various kinds of fungi grew on the same plate. He discovered that one fungus produced a substance that killed bacteria—penicillin.

1952 Jonas Salk
In 1952, there were more than 57,000 cases of polio, making it one of the most dreaded diseases known at the time. That same year, Jonas Salk, a professor at a medical university in the United States, showed that people injected with killed polio viruses did not get the disease, but produced antibodies against it.

1985 Mathilde Krim
Mathilde Krim, an American biomedical researcher, founded The American Foundation for AIDS Research, or AmFAR. Krim recognized that AIDS was a serious threat to public health and has dedicated her life to supporting AIDS research.

1920   **1960**   **2000**

Passive Immunity

Some diseases, such as rabies, are so uncommon that people rarely receive vaccinations against them. However, if a person is bitten by an animal that might have rabies, the person is usually given injections that contain antibodies to the rabies antigen. The protection that the person acquires this way is an example of passive immunity. **Passive immunity** results when antibodies are given to a person—the person's immune system does not make them. **A person acquires passive immunity when the antibodies that fight the pathogen come from a source other than the person's body.** Unlike active immunity, which is long-lasting, passive immunity usually lasts no more than a few months.

A baby acquires passive immunity to some diseases before birth. This immunity results from antibodies that are passed from the mother's blood into the baby's blood during pregnancy. After birth, these antibodies protect the baby for a few months. By then, the baby's own immune system has begun to function fairly efficiently.

FIGURE 11
Passive Immunity
This baby has acquired passive immunity from her mother.
Relating Cause and Effect *How do babies acquire passive immunity?*

Reading Checkpoint **What is one disease for which you can acquire passive immunity?**

Section 3 Assessment

Target Reading Skill Comparing and Contrasting Use the information in your Venn diagram about active immunity and passive immunity to help you answer the questions below.

Reviewing Key Concepts

1. a. **Defining** What is active immunity?
   b. **Explaining** What are two ways in which active immunity can be acquired?
   c. **Applying Concepts** After receiving certain vaccinations, some children may develop mild symptoms of the disease. Explain why.
2. a. **Reviewing** What is passive immunity?
   b. **Describing** How is passive immunity acquired?
   c. **Inferring** Why does passive immunity usually not last for very long?

Lab zone At-Home **Activity**

Vaccination History With a family member, make a list of all the vaccinations you have received. For each, note when you received the vaccination. Then, with your family member, learn about one of the diseases against which you were vaccinated. What kind of pathogen causes the disease? What are the symptoms of the disease? Is the disease still common in the United States?

Noninfectious Disease

Reading Preview

Key Concepts
- What causes allergies?
- How does diabetes affect the body?
- What are the effects of cancer on the body?

Key Terms
- noninfectious disease
- allergy • allergen
- histamine • asthma • insulin
- diabetes • tumor • carcinogen

Target Reading Skill

Asking Questions Before you read, preview the red headings. In a graphic organizer like the one below, ask a *what* or *how* question for each heading. As you read, answer your questions.

Noninfectious Disease

Question	Answer
What is an allergy?	An allergy is a disorder in which . . .

Lab zone Discover **Activity**

What Happens When Airflow Is Restricted?

1. Asthma is a disorder in which breathing passages become narrower than normal. This activity will help you understand how this condition affects breathing. **CAUTION:** *Do not perform this activity if you have a medical condition that affects your breathing.* Begin by breathing normally, first through your nose and then through your mouth. Observe how deeply you breathe.

2. Put one end of a drinking straw in your mouth. Then, gently pinch your nostrils shut so that you cannot breathe through your nose.

3. With your nostrils pinched closed, breathe by inhaling air through the straw. Continue breathing this way for thirty seconds.

Think It Over

Observing Compare your normal breathing pattern to that when breathing through the straw. Which way were you able to take deeper breaths? Did you ever feel short of breath?

Americans are living longer today than ever before. A person who was born in 2000 can expect to live about 77 years. In contrast, a person born in 1950 could expect to live only about 68 years, and a person born in 1900 only about 50 years.

Progress against infectious disease is one reason why life spans have increased. However, as infectious diseases have become less common, noninfectious diseases have grown more common. **Noninfectious diseases** are diseases that are not caused by pathogens in the body. Unlike infectious diseases, noninfectious diseases cannot be transmitted from person to person. One noninfectious disease, cardiovascular disease, is the leading cause of death in the United States. Allergies, diabetes, and cancer are other noninfectious diseases.

◄ People live longer today than ever before.

Lab zone Skills Activity

Drawing Conclusions

Two weeks ago, after you ate strawberry shortcake with whipped cream, you broke out in an itchy rash. The ingredients in the dessert were strawberries, sugar, flour, butter, eggs, vanilla, baking powder, salt, and cream. Last night, you ate a strawberry tart with whipped cream and again broke out in a rash. The ingredients were strawberries, sugar, cornstarch, milk, eggs, flour, shortening, salt, and vanilla.

You think that you may be allergic to strawberries. Do you have enough evidence to support this conclusion? If so, why? If not, what additional evidence do you need?

Allergies

Spring has arrived. Flowers are in bloom, and the songs of birds fill the air. Unfortunately, for some people, sneezing is another sound that fills the air. People who sneeze and cough in the spring may not have colds. Instead, they may be suffering from allergies to plant pollen. An **allergy** is a disorder in which the immune system is overly sensitive to a foreign substance—something not normally found in the body. **An allergy develops in response to various foreign substances that set off a series of reactions in the body.**

Allergens Any substance that causes an allergy is called an **allergen.** In addition to different kinds of pollen, allergens include dust, molds, some foods, and even some medicines. If you are lucky, you have no allergies at all. However, the bodies of many people react to one or more allergens.

Allergens may get into your body when you inhale them, eat them in food, or touch them with your skin. When lymphocytes encounter an allergen, they produce antibodies to that allergen. These antibodies, unlike the ones made during the immune response, signal cells in the body to release a substance called histamine. **Histamine** (HIS tuh meen) is a chemical that is responsible for the symptoms of an allergy, such as sneezing and watery eyes. Drugs that interfere with the action of histamine, called antihistamines, may lessen this reaction. However, if you have an allergy, the best strategy is to try to avoid the substance to which you are allergic.

FIGURE 12
Allergens
Some people have allergic reactions to plant pollen, dust mites, or cats.

Dust Mite ▲

◄ Pollen

◄ Cat

Asthma Some allergic reactions can create a condition called asthma. **Asthma** (AZ muh) is a disorder in which the respiratory passages narrow significantly. This narrowing causes the person to wheeze and become short of breath. Asthma attacks may be brought on by factors other than allergies, such as stress and exercise.

 **Reading Checkpoint** **What is asthma?**

 **Go Online**
SciLINKS NSTA

For: Links on noninfectious disease
Visit: www.SciLinks.org
Web Code: scn-0454

Diabetes

The pancreas is an organ with many different functions. One function is to produce a chemical called insulin. **Insulin** (IN suh lin) enables body cells to take in glucose from the blood and use it for energy. In the condition known as **diabetes** (dy uh BEE tis), either the pancreas fails to produce enough insulin or the body's cells fail to properly use insulin. **As a result, a person with diabetes has high levels of glucose in the blood and may even excrete glucose in the urine. The person's body cells, however, do not have enough glucose.**

Effects of Diabetes If untreated, people with diabetes may lose weight, feel weak, and be hungry all the time. These symptoms occur because body cells are unable to take in the glucose they need. In addition, diabetics may urinate frequently and feel thirsty as the kidneys work to eliminate the excess glucose from the body. The long-term effects of diabetes are serious and can include blindness, kidney failure, and heart disease.

Forms of Diabetes There are two main forms of diabetes. Type I diabetes usually begins in childhood or early adulthood. In Type I diabetes, the pancreas produces little or no insulin. People with this condition must get insulin injections.

Type II diabetes usually develops during adulthood. In this condition, either the pancreas does not make enough insulin, or body cells do not respond normally to insulin. People with Type II diabetes may be able to control their symptoms through proper diet, weight control, and exercise.

 **Reading Checkpoint** **What are two symptoms of diabetes?**

FIGURE 13
Glucose Testing
Many people with diabetes must test their blood frequently to determine the level of glucose in their blood.
Relating Cause and Effect *What accounts for the high level of glucose in the blood of diabetics?*

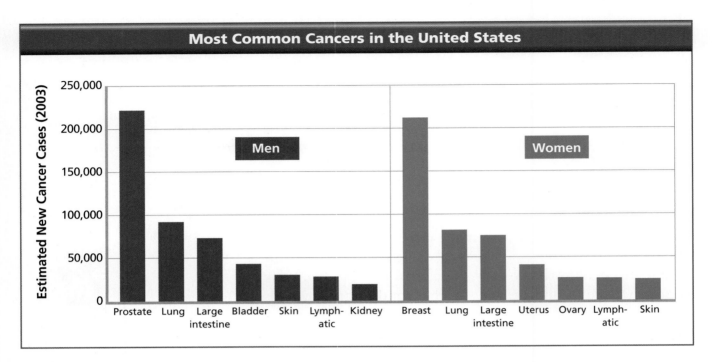

Most Common Cancers in the United States

Men

Women

Estimated New Cancer Cases (2003)

250,000
200,000
150,000
100,000
50,000
0

Prostate | Lung | Large intestine | Bladder | Skin | Lymph-atic | Kidney

Breast | Lung | Large intestine | Uterus | Ovary | Lymph-atic | Skin

FIGURE 14
The graph shows the leading types of cancer that affect men and women in the United States.
Reading Graphs *Do more women or men develop lung cancer each year?*

Cancer

Under normal conditions, the body produces new cells at about the same rate that other cells die. In a condition known as cancer, however, the situation is quite different. **Cancer is a disease in which cells multiply uncontrollably, over and over, destroying healthy tissue in the process.**

How Cancer Develops As cells divide over and over, they often form abnormal tissue masses called **tumors**. Not all tumors are cancerous. Cancerous tumors invade and destroy the healthy tissue around them. Cancer cells can break away from a tumor and invade blood or lymph vessels. The blood or lymph carries the cancer cells to other parts of the body, where they may begin to divide and form new tumors. Unless stopped by treatment, cancer progresses through the body.

Causes of Cancer Different factors may work together in causing cells to become cancerous. One such factor is the characteristics that people inherit from their parents. Because of their inherited characteristics, some people are more likely than others to develop certain kinds of cancer. For example, if you are female, and your mother or grandmother has breast cancer, you have an increased chance of developing breast cancer.

Some substances or factors in the environment, called **carcinogens** (kahr SIN uh junz), can cause cancer. The tar in cigarette smoke is an example of a carcinogen. Ultraviolet light, which is part of sunlight, can also be a carcinogen.

Cancer Treatment Surgery, drugs, and radiation are all used to treat cancer. If cancer is detected before it has spread, doctors may remove the cancerous tumors through surgery. After surgery, radiation or drugs may be used to make sure all the cancer cells have been killed.

Radiation treatment uses high-energy waves to kill cancer cells. When these rays are aimed at tumors, the intense energy damages and kills cancer cells more than it damages normal cells. Drug therapy is the use of chemicals to destroy cancer cells. Many of these chemicals, however, destroy some normal cells as well.

Cancer Prevention As with other diseases, the best way to fight cancer is to prevent it. People can reduce their risk of cancer by avoiding carcinogens, such as those found in tobacco. Even chewing tobacco and snuff contain carcinogens, which can cause mouth cancers. A low-fat diet that includes plenty of fruits and vegetables can help prevent cancers of the digestive system.

People can also increase their chance of surviving cancer by having regular medical checkups. The earlier cancer is detected, the more likely it can be treated successfully.

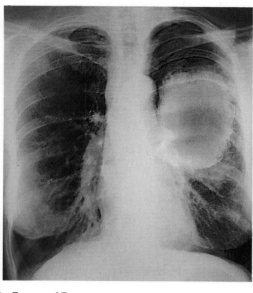

FIGURE 15
Lung Tumor
The large orange mass in the X-ray is a cancerous tumor in the lung.

 **Reading Checkpoint** What is a carcinogen?

Section 4 Assessment

Target Reading Skill Asking Questions Use the answers to the questions you wrote about the headings to help you answer the questions below.

Reviewing Key Concepts

1. a. **Defining** What is an allergy?
   b. **Describing** Describe how the body reacts to the presence of an allergen.
   c. **Inferring** You and your friends go to a movie. When you enter the theater, you start to sneeze and your throat feels scratchy. Explain what you think is happening.
2. a. **Identifying** What is the function of insulin in the body?
   b. **Explaining** How does diabetes affect the level of glucose in the blood and in body cells?

3. a. **Reviewing** What is a cancerous tumor?
   b. **Relating Cause and Effect** Describe how cancerous tumors harm the body.
   c. **Applying Concepts** Why do doctors look for cancerous tumors in the lymphatic system when someone is diagnosed with cancer?

Lab zone **At-Home Activity**

Family History of Allergies Explain to your family what allergies are and how allergens affect the body. Make a list of any substances to which your family members are allergic. Use this list to determine whether certain allergies occur frequently in your family.

Causes of Death, Then and Now

Problem

How do the leading causes of death today compare with those in 1900?

Skills Focus

graphing, interpreting data, drawing conclusions

Materials ✂

- colored pencils
- ruler
- calculator (optional)
- protractor
- compass

Procedure

1. The data table on the next page shows the leading causes of death in the United States in 1900 and today. Examine the data and note that one cause of death—accidents—is not a disease. The other causes are labeled either "I," indicating an infectious disease, or "NI," indicating a noninfectious disease.

PART 1 Comparing Specific Causes of Death

2. Look at the following causes of death in the data table: (a) pneumonia and influenza, (b) heart disease, (c) accidents, and (d) cancer. Construct a bar graph that compares the numbers of deaths from each of those causes in 1900 and today. Label the horizontal axis *"Causes of Death."* Label the vertical axis *"Deaths per 100,000 People."* Draw two bars side by side for each cause of death. Use a key to show which bars refer to 1900 and which refer to today.

PART 2 Comparing Infectious and Noninfectious Causes of Death

3. In this part of the lab, you will make two circle graphs showing three categories: infectious diseases, noninfectious diseases, and "other." You may want to review the information on creating circle graphs on page 262 of the Skills Handbook.

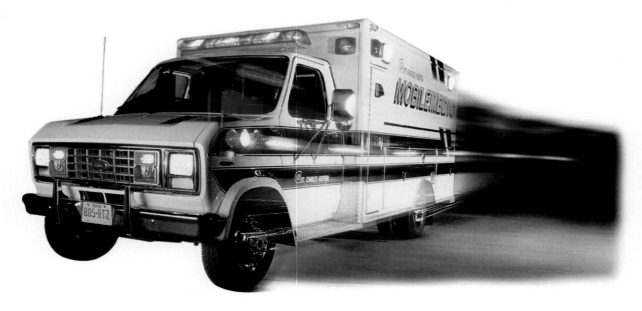

Ten Leading Causes of Death in the United States, 1900 and Today

1900		Today	
Cause of Death	**Deaths Per 100,000**	**Cause of Death**	**Deaths Per 100,000**
Pneumonia, influenza (I)*	215	Heart disease (NI)	246
Tuberculosis (I)	185	Cancer (NI)	194
Diarrhea (I)	140	Stroke (NI)	57
Heart disease (NI)	130	Lung disease (NI)	43
Stroke (NI)	110	Accidents	34
Kidney disease (NI)	85	Diabetes (NI)	25
Accidents	75	Pneumonia, influenza (I)	22
Cancer (NI)	65	Alzheimer's disease (NI)	19
Senility (NI)	55	Kidney disease (NI)	14
Diphtheria (I)	40	Septicemia (I)	11
Total	**1,100**	**Total**	**665**

* (I) indicates an infectious disease. (NI) indicates a noninfectious disease.

4. Start by grouping the data from 1900 into the three categories—infectious diseases, noninfectious diseases, and other causes. Calculate the total number of deaths for each category. Then find the size of the "pie slice" (the number of degrees) for each category, and construct your circle graph. To find the size of the infectious disease slice for 1900, for example, use the following formula:

$$\frac{\text{Number of deaths from infectious diseases}}{\text{1,100 deaths total}} = \frac{x}{360°}$$

5. Calculate the percentage represented by each category using this formula:

$$\frac{\text{Numbers of degrees in a slice}}{360°} \times 100 = \blacksquare\%$$

6. Repeat Steps 4 and 5 using the data from today to make the second circle graph. What part of the formula in Step 4 do you need to change?

Analyze and Conclude

1. **Observing** What information did you learn from examining the data table in Step 1?

2. **Graphing** According to your bar graph, which cause of death showed the greatest increase between 1900 and today? The greatest decrease?

3. **Interpreting Data** In your circle graphs, which category decreased the most from 1900 to today? Which increased the most?

4. **Drawing Conclusions** Suggest an explanation for the change in the number of deaths due to infectious diseases from 1900 to today.

5. **Communicating** In a paragraph, explain how graphs help you identify patterns and other information in data that you might otherwise overlook.

More to Explore

Write a question related to the data table that you have not yet answered. Then create a graph or work with the data in other ways to answer your question.

Cancer and the Environment

Reading Preview

Key Concepts
- How can people's environments affect their risk of cancer?
- What are three carcinogens found in the environment?

Target Reading Skill
Relating Cause and Effect
As you read, identify environmental carcinogens and the types of cancer they cause. Write the information in a graphic organizer like the one below.

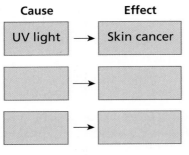

Cause		Effect
UV light	→	Skin cancer
	→	
	→	

Lab zone Discover **Activity**

What Does Sunlight Do to the Beads?
1. Your teacher will give you beads that change color under certain conditions. Thread five beads on a pipe cleaner. Observe what the beads look like.
2. Wrap the pipe cleaner around your wrist. Go outdoors for 1 minute. Observe what happens to the beads.

Think It Over
Developing Hypotheses The ultraviolet light in sunlight causes the reaction you observed. Form a hypothesis about how you might prevent the beads from reacting as they did. How can you test your hypothesis?

You are trapped in a place that is dark, tight, and so warm that you can hardly breathe. You climb upwards, carefully feeling for footholds as you inch along. The surfaces are so warm that your knees feel hot as they scrape against the walls. Grimy dirt falls on your face, and you blink to keep it out of your eyes. This story sounds like a nightmare. But it was real life for the children who worked as chimney sweeps in the 1700s.

In 1775, about one million people lived in London, England. Their homes were heated by coal fires. Because burning coal produces lots of black soot, the soot had to be cleaned out of the chimneys regularly. Chimney sweeps did this job by crawling into the chimneys and scraping the soot off the walls.

1770s
Making Observations
Percival Pott notices that chimney sweeps have a high rate of skin cancer.

1775
Developing a Hypothesis
Pott hypothesizes that something in soot causes skin cancer.

1775
Testing the Hypothesis
Pott recommends that chimney sweeps bathe frequently, thus removing the cancer-causing soot.

Linking Cancer to the Environment

Because chimney sweeps had to be small and thin enough to fit inside a chimney, most chimney sweeps were children. The chimney sweeps were a type of indentured servant. The master would teach them the trade in exchange for housing. At the end of a hard day, chimney sweeps were covered with soot, but few washed it off. The chimney sweeps often slept in their soot sacks and bathed infrequently.

A Link Between Soot and Cancer Percivall Pott, a London doctor, saw many chimney sweeps at his medical clinic. Pott noticed that the chimney sweeps often had soot ground deeply into their skin. He also observed that a high number of chimney sweeps developed skin cancer. Pott hypothesized that something in soot caused cancer. He recommended frequent bathing to reduce the risk of skin cancer. Many years later, scientists identified the carcinogens in soot. They are the same substances that make up the tar in cigarette smoke.

Carcinogens in the Environment Percivall Pott was one of the first scientists to recognize the connection between the environment and cancer. **The environment may contain carcinogens. To reduce the risk of cancer, carcinogens need to be removed or people need to be protected from them.**

Pott's work led to efforts to control environmental carcinogens. In the United States, the Environmental Protection Agency (EPA) is in charge of enforcing environmental laws. The EPA identifies environmental carcinogens and develops strategies for protecting people from them.

 Reading Checkpoint **How could chimney sweeps reduce their risk of skin cancer?**

FIGURE 16
Soot and Skin Cancer
Percivall Pott hypothesized that there was a connection between soot and skin cancer in chimney sweeps. **Drawing Conclusions** *What additional evidence supported Pott's hypothesis?*

1892
Collecting Data
Later evidence shows that chimney sweeps who bathe regularly develop skin cancer at a lower rate than sweeps who rarely bathe.

Early 1900s
Confirming the Hypothesis
Certain substances in soot are found to cause skin cancer in laboratory animals.

Skin Cancer

The graph shows the frequency of skin cancer in the United States from 1998 to 2003.

1. **Reading Graphs** What variable is being plotted on the *y*-axis?

2. **Interpreting Data** How many cases of skin cancer were estimated for women in 1998? In 2003?

3. **Calculating** Using the data from Question 2, calculate the increase in the number of skin cancer cases among women.

4. **Calculating** What was the difference in the number of skin cancer cases for men and women in 1999?

5. **Predicting** Based on these graphs, do you think the number of skin cancers will increase, decrease, or remain the same in the next five years? Explain your answer.

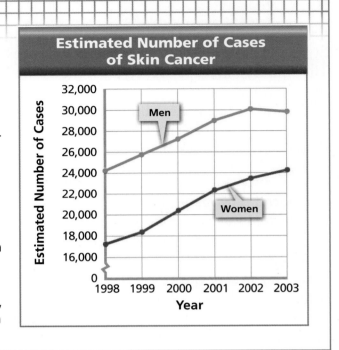

Estimated Number of Cases of Skin Cancer

Environmental Carcinogens Today

Scientists have identified many carcinogens found in the environment. **Three important environmental carcinogens are ultraviolet light, vinyl chloride, and arsenic.**

Ultraviolet Light Skin cancer can result from overexposure to sunlight. Ultraviolet light is the part of sunlight that causes cancer. Fortunately, as sunlight arrives on Earth from the sun, much of the ultraviolet light is absorbed before it can reach Earth's surface. Ozone, a gas present high in Earth's atmosphere, absorbs most of the ultraviolet light.

In the 1970s and 1980s, scientists noticed that ozone levels in the upper atmosphere were decreasing. This decrease in ozone means that more ultraviolet light can reach Earth's surface. At the same time, new cases of skin cancer have increased markedly. Although the causes of the increase in skin cancer are complicated, many scientists say that it is linked to the loss of ozone in the atmosphere.

Vinyl Chloride Vinyl chloride is a manufactured material that exists as a colorless gas at normal temperatures. Most vinyl chloride is used to make polyvinyl chloride, or PVC. PVC is used in a wide variety of plastic products, including pipes, coatings for wires, packaging, upholstery, housewares, and car parts.

Go Online
SCi*LINKS* NSTA

For: Links on cancer
Visit: www.SciLinks.org
Web Code: scn-0455

People can be exposed to vinyl chloride by breathing in the vapors. Repeatedly inhaling the vapors over long periods can result in cancers of the liver, brain, or lungs. For example, people who work in the manufacturing of vinyl chloride have an increased risk of liver cancer. In spite of the potential hazards, production of vinyl chloride continues because it is used in so many everyday products.

Arsenic Arsenic is a substance that occurs naturally in soil and rock. At one time, it was widely used in pesticides. Since the 1970s, however, it has been used more and more as a wood preservative. Wood treated with CCA, a chemical that contains arsenic, is called pressure-treated wood. Pressure-treated wood is resistant to rotting and decay. Pressure-treated wood is used for utility poles and building lumber.

Arsenic has long been recognized as poisonous and is lethal if consumed in large doses. More recently, arsenic has been reported to increase the risk of cancers of the liver, bladder, kidneys, and lungs. In 2002, the EPA announced that CCA in wood products for home use would be eliminated by 2004.

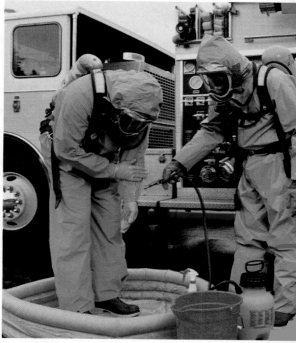

FIGURE 17
Making the Environment Safer
People who clean up environmental carcinogens must wear protective suits to prevent touching or inhaling these substances.

 **Reading Checkpoint** **What kinds of cancers might result from inhaling vinyl chloride?**

Section 5 **Assessment**

Target Reading Skill Relating Cause and Effect Refer to your graphic organizer about environmental carcinogens to help you answer Question 2.

Reviewing Key Concepts

1. a. Reviewing What did Percivall Pott observe about the relationship between skin cancer and soot?
   b. Developing Hypotheses In your own words, write a possible hypothesis that explains Pott's observations about chimney sweeps.
   c. Designing Experiments How could you use methods similar to those used by Pott and others to study the relationship between skin cancer and another carcinogen?

2. a. Listing Name three carcinogens found in the environment.
   b. Relating Cause and Effect What is the relationship between ultraviolet light, ozone, and skin cancer?
   c. Predicting If ozone levels in the atmosphere continue to decrease, what could happen to the number of skin cancer cases? Explain.

Lab zone **At-Home Activity**

Warning Labels With a family member, read the labels on various products around your home. Do any of the products contain cancer warnings? Work with your family to identify ways to protect yourselves from exposure to carcinogens contained in common everyday products.

The BIG Idea **Personal Health** The human body has three lines of defense against fighting disease—barriers, the inflammatory response, and the immune response.

1 Infectious Disease

Key Concepts

- When you have an infectious disease, pathogens have gotten inside your body and caused harm.
- The four major groups of human pathogens are bacteria, viruses, fungi, and protists.
- Pathogens can spread through contact with either an infected person; soil, food, or water; a contaminated object; or an infected animal.

Key Terms

pathogen
infectious disease
toxin

2 The Body's Defenses

Key Concepts

- The surfaces of the skin, breathing passages, mouth, and stomach function as barriers to pathogens. These barriers trap and kill most pathogens with which you come into contact.
- In the inflammatory response, fluid and white blood cells leak from blood vessels into nearby tissues. The white blood cells then fight the pathogens.
- The cells of the immune system can distinguish between different kinds of pathogens. The immune system cells react to each kind of pathogen with a defense targeted specifically at that pathogen.
- HIV is the only kind of virus known to attack the human immune system directly and destroy T cells. HIV can spread from one person to another only if body fluids from an infected person come in contact with those of an uninfected person.

Key Terms

- inflammatory response • phagocyte
- immune response • lymphocyte • T cell
- antigen • B cell • antibody • AIDS • HIV

3 Preventing Infectious Disease

Key Concepts

- A person acquires active immunity when their own immune system produces antibodies in response to the presence of a pathogen.
- A person acquires passive immunity when the antibodies that fight the pathogen come from a source other than the person's body.

Key Terms

- immunity • active immunity • vaccination
- vaccine • antibiotic • passive immunity

4 Noninfectious Disease

Key Concepts

- An allergy develops in response to various foreign substances that set off a series of reactions in the body.
- A diabetic has high levels of glucose in the blood and excretes glucose in the urine. The person's body cells do not have enough glucose.
- Cancer is a disease in which cells multiply uncontrollably and destroy healthy tissue.

Key Terms

- noninfectious disease • allergy • allergen
- histamine • asthma • insulin • diabetes
- tumor • carcinogen

5 Cancer and the Environment

Key Concepts

- To reduce the risk of cancer, environmental carcinogens need to be removed or people need to be protected from them.
- Three important environmental carcinogens are ultraviolet light, vinyl chloride, and arsenic.

Review and Assessment

Organizing Information

Sequencing Copy the flowchart showing what happens after strep bacteria begin to multiply in the throat. Then complete it and add a title. (For more on Sequencing, see the Skills Handbook.)

> T cell recognizes bacterial antigen.
>
> ↓
>
> a. _____ ?
>
> ↓
>
> b. _____ ?
>
> ↓
>
> c. _____ ?
>
> ↓
>
> d. _____ ?

Reviewing Key Terms

Choose the letter of the best answer.

1. Some bacteria produce poisons called
   a. histamines.   b. toxins.
   c. phagocytes.   d. pathogens.

2. Antibodies are produced by
   a. phagocytes.   b. B cells.
   c. T cells.   d. pathogens.

3. A chemical that kills bacteria or slows their growth without harming body cells is called a(n)
   a. pathogen.
   b. antibiotic.
   c. allergen.
   d. histamine.

4. High levels of glucose in the blood may be a sign of
   a. an allergy.
   b. AIDS.
   c. cancer.
   d. diabetes.

5. A carcinogen causes
   a. cancer.
   b. AIDS.
   c. an infectious disease.
   d. an allergy.

If the statement is true, write _true._ If it is false, change the underlined word or words to make the statement true.

6. Bacteria, viruses, fungi, and protists are the major human <u>phagocytes</u>.

7. A <u>T cell</u> engulfs pathogens and destroys them.

8. Vaccination produces <u>active immunity.</u>

9. During an allergic reaction, cells in the body release the chemical <u>insulin</u>.

10. A <u>tumor</u> is a mass of abnormal tissue.

Writing in Science

Newspaper Article Suppose you are a reporter who is able to travel inside the human body and document how the body fights a virus. Write an article on the battle between the virus and the human immune system, describing the different ways the body fights pathogens.

Discovery CHANNEL SCHOOL

Fighting Disease

Video Preview
Video Field Trip
▶ Video Assessment

The Nervous System

The **BIG Idea**
Structure and Function

 Which organs and other structures enable the nervous system to function?

Without your nervous system, a sport like windsurfing would be impossible!

The Nervous System

▶ Video Preview
Video Field Trip
Video Assessment

Lab zone™ Chapter **Project**

Tricks and Illusions

Things aren't always what they seem. For example, an optical illusion is a picture or other visual effect that tricks you into seeing something incorrectly. In this project, you'll investigate how your senses some- times can be fooled by illusions.

Your Goal To set up a science fair booth to demonstrate how different people respond to one or more illusions

To complete this project, you must

● try out a variety of illusions, includ- ing some that involve the senses of hearing or touch as well as sight

● select one or more illusions and set up an experiment to monitor people's responses to the illusions

● learn why the illusions fool the senses

● follow the safety guidelines in Appendix A

Plan It! In a small group, discuss optical illusions or other illusions that you know about. Look in books to learn about others. Try them out. Which illusions would make an interesting experiment? How could you set up such an experiment at a science fair?

FIGURE 2
Structure of a Neuron
A neuron has one axon and many dendrites that extend from the cell body.

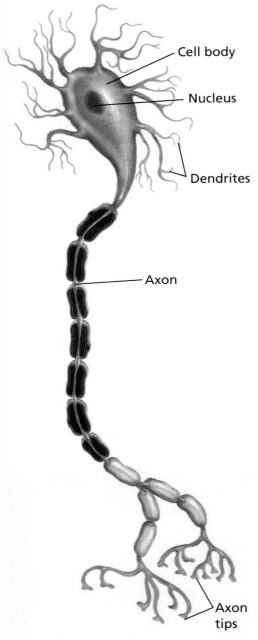

Cell body

Nucleus

Dendrites

Axon

Axon tips

Go Online
PHSchool.com

For: More on nerve impulses
Visit: PHSchool.com
Web Code: ced-4061

The Neuron

Your nervous system includes various organs, tissues, and cells. For example, your brain is an organ, and the nerves running throughout your body are tissues. The cells that carry information through your nervous system are called **neurons** (NOO rahnz), or nerve cells. The message that a neuron carries is called a **nerve impulse.**

The Structure of a Neuron The structure of a neuron enables it to carry nerve impulses. **A neuron has a large cell body that contains the nucleus, threadlike extensions called dendrites, and an axon.** The **dendrites** carry impulses toward the neuron's cell body. The **axon** carries impulses away from the cell body. Nerve impulses begin in a dendrite, move toward the cell body, and then move down the axon. A neuron can have many dendrites, but it has only one axon. An axon, however, can have more than one tip, so the impulse can go to more than one other cell.

Axons and dendrites are sometimes called nerve fibers. Nerve fibers are often arranged in parallel bundles covered with connective tissue, something like a package of uncooked spaghetti wrapped in cellophane. A bundle of nerve fibers is called a **nerve.**

Kinds of Neurons **Three kinds of neurons are found in the body—sensory neurons, interneurons, and motor neurons.** Figure 3 shows how these three kinds of neurons work together.

A **sensory neuron** picks up stimuli from the internal or external environment and converts each stimulus into a nerve impulse. The impulse travels along the sensory neuron until it reaches an interneuron, usually in the brain or spinal cord. An **interneuron** is a neuron that carries nerve impulses from one neuron to another. Some interneurons pass impulses from sensory neurons to motor neurons. A **motor neuron** sends an impulse to a muscle or gland, and the muscle or gland reacts in response.

 **Reading Checkpoint** **What is the function of an axon?**

How a Nerve Impulse Travels

Every day of your life, billions of nerve impulses travel through your nervous system. Each of those nerve impulses begins in the dendrites of a neuron. The impulse moves rapidly toward the neuron's cell body and then down the axon until it reaches the axon tip. A nerve impulse travels along the neuron in the form of electrical and chemical signals. Nerve impulses can travel as fast as 120 meters per second!

FIGURE 3
The Path of a Nerve Impulse

When you hear your phone ring, you pick it up to answer it. Many sensory neurons, interneurons, and motor neurons are involved in this action.

Interpreting Diagrams *To where does the impulse pass from the sensory neurons?*

Receptors in ear

1 Sensory Neuron
Nerve impulses begin when receptors pick up stimuli from the environment. Receptors in the ear pick up the sound of the phone ringing. The receptors trigger nerve impulses in sensory neurons.

2 Interneuron
From the sensory neurons, the nerve impulse passes to interneurons in the brain. Your brain interprets the impulses from many interneurons and makes you realize that the phone is ringing. Your brain also decides that you should answer the phone.

Muscle in hand

3 Motor Neuron
Impulses then travel along thousands of motor neurons. The motor neurons send the impulses to muscles. The muscles carry out the response, and you reach for the phone.

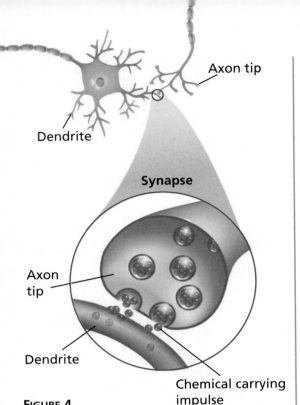

Axon tip

Dendrite

Synapse

Axon tip

Dendrite

Chemical carrying impulse

FIGURE 4
The Synapse
When a nerve impulse reaches the tip of an axon, chemicals are released into the gap at the synapse. The chemicals carry the nerve impulse across the gap.

The Synapse What happens when a nerve impulse reaches the axon tip at the end of a neuron? At that point, the impulse can pass to the next structure. Sometimes the structure is the dendrite of another neuron. Other times, the structure is a muscle or a cell in another organ, such as a sweat gland. The junction where one neuron can transfer an impulse to another structure is called a **synapse** (SIN aps).

How an Impulse is Transferred Figure 4 shows a synapse between the axon tip of one neuron and the dendrite of another neuron. Notice that a small gap separates these two structures. **For a nerve impulse to be carried along at a synapse, it must cross the gap between the axon and the next structure. The axon tips release chemicals that carry the impulse across the gap.**

You can think of the gap at a synapse as a river, and an axon as a road that leads up to the riverbank. The nerve impulse is like a car traveling on the road. To get to the other side, the car has to cross the river. The car gets on a ferry boat, which carries it across the river. The chemicals that the axon tips release are like the ferry, carrying the nerve impulse across the gap.

Section 1 Assessment

Target Reading Skill Previewing Visuals Refer to your questions and answers about Figure 3 to help you answer Question 2 below.

Reviewing Key Concepts

1. a. Listing What are three functions of the nervous system?
   b. Describing Give an example of a stimulus and describe how the nervous system produces a response.
   c. Predicting Your heart rate is controlled by involuntary actions of the nervous system. What would life be like if your heartbeat were under voluntary control?

2. a. Identifying Identify the three kinds of neurons that are found in the nervous system.
   b. Explaining How do the three kinds of neurons interact to carry nerve impulses?

   c. Comparing and Contrasting How do sensory neurons and motor neurons differ?

3. a. Reviewing What is a synapse?
   b. Sequencing Outline the steps by which a nerve impulse reaches and then crosses the gap at a synapse.

Lab zone At-Home **Activity**

Pass the Salt, Please During dinner, ask a family member to pass the salt and pepper to you. Observe what your family member then does. Explain that the words you spoke were a stimulus and that the family member's reaction was a response. Discuss other examples of stimuli and responses with your family.

Ready or Not!

Problem

Do people's reaction times vary at different times of the day?

Skills Focus

developing hypotheses, controlling variables, drawing conclusions

Material

• meter stick

Procedure

PART 1 Observing a Response to a Stimulus

1. Have your partner hold a meter stick with the zero end about 50 cm above a table.

2. Get ready to catch the meter stick by positioning the top of your thumb and forefinger just at the zero position, as shown in the photograph.

3. Your partner should drop the meter stick without any warning. Using your thumb and forefinger only (no other part of your hand), catch the meter stick as soon as you can. Record the distance in centimeters that the meter stick fell. This distance is a measure of your reaction time.

PART 2 Designing Your Experiment

4. With your partner, discuss how you can use the activity from Part 1 to find out whether people's reaction times vary at different times of day. Consider the questions below. Then, write up your experimental plan.
   • What hypothesis will you test?
   • What variables do you need to control?
   • How many people will you test? How many times will you test each person?

5. Submit your plan for your teacher's review. Make any changes your teacher recommends. Create a data table to record your results. Then, perform your experiment.

Analyze and Conclude

1. **Inferring** In this lab, what is the stimulus? What is the response? Is the response voluntary or involuntary? Explain.

2. **Developing Hypotheses** What hypothesis did you test in Part 2?

3. **Controlling Variables** In Part 2, why was it important to control all variables except the time of day?

4. **Drawing Conclusions** Based on your results in Part 2, do people's reaction times vary at different times of the day? Explain.

5. **Communicating** Write a paragraph to explain why you can use the distance on the meter stick as a measure of reaction time.

More to Explore

Do you think people can do arithmetic problems more quickly and accurately at certain times of the day? Design an experiment to investigate this question. *Obtain your teacher's permission before carrying out your investigation.*

Divisions of the Nervous System

Reading Preview

Key Concepts
- What are the structures and functions of the central nervous system?
- What are the structures and functions of the peripheral nervous system?
- What is a reflex?
- What are two ways in which the nervous system can be injured?

Key Terms
- central nervous system
- peripheral nervous system
- brain • spinal cord
- cerebrum • cerebellum
- brain stem
- somatic nervous system
- autonomic nervous system
- reflex • concussion

Target Reading Skill

Building Vocabulary After you read this section, reread the paragraphs that contain definitions of Key Terms. Use all the information you have learned to write a definition of each Key Term in your own words.

Lab zone Discover **Activity**

How Does Your Knee React?

1. Sit on a table or counter so that your legs dangle freely. Make sure that your partner is not directly in front of your legs.

2. Have your partner use the side of his or her hand to tap one of your knees gently just below the kneecap. Observe what happens to your leg. Note whether you have any control over your reaction.

3. Change places with your partner. Repeat Steps 1 and 2.

Think It Over
Inferring When might it be an advantage for your body to react very quickly and without your conscious control?

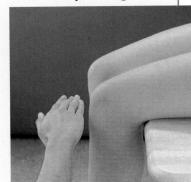

You are standing at a busy street corner, waiting to cross the street. A traffic cop blows his whistle and waves his arms energetically. For the heavy traffic to move smoothly, there needs to be a traffic cop and responsive drivers. The traffic cop coordinates the movements of the drivers, and they maneuver the cars safely through the intersection.

Similarly, your nervous system has two divisions that work together. The **central nervous system** consists of the brain and spinal cord. The **peripheral nervous system** (puh RIF uh rul) includes all the nerves located outside of the central nervous system. The central nervous system is like a traffic cop. The peripheral nervous system is like the drivers and pedestrians.

The traffic cop keeps everybody moving.

Central Nervous System

You can see the central and peripheral nervous systems in Figure 5. **The central nervous system is the control center of the body. It includes the brain and spinal cord.** All information about what is happening in the world inside or outside your body is brought to the central nervous system. The **brain,** located in the skull, is the part of the central nervous system that controls most functions in the body. The **spinal cord** is the thick column of nervous tissue that links the brain to most of the nerves in the peripheral nervous system.

Most impulses from the peripheral nervous system travel through the spinal cord to get to the brain. Your brain then directs a response. The response usually travels from the brain, through the spinal cord, and then to the peripheral nervous system.

For example, here is what happens when you reach under the sofa to find a lost quarter. Your fingers move over the floor, searching for the quarter. When your fingers finally touch the quarter, the stimulus of the touch triggers nerve impulses in sensory neurons in your fingers. These impulses travel through nerves of the peripheral nervous system to your spinal cord. Then the impulses race up to your brain. Your brain interprets the impulses, telling you that you've found the quarter. Your brain starts nerve impulses that move down the spinal cord. From the spinal cord, the impulses travel through motor neurons in your arm and hand. The impulses in the motor neurons cause your fingers to grasp the quarter.

 **Reading Checkpoint** What are the parts of the central nervous system?

Go Online
active art

For: Nervous System activity
Visit: PHSchool.com
Web Code: cep-4062

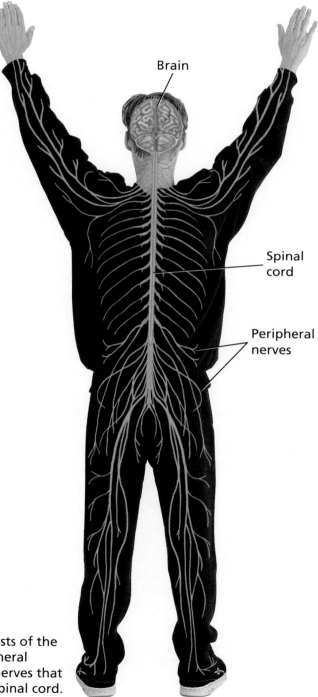

Brain

Spinal cord

Peripheral nerves

FIGURE 5
The Nervous System
The central nervous system consists of the brain and spinal cord. The peripheral nervous system includes all the nerves that branch out from the brain and spinal cord.

The Brain and Spinal Cord

Your brain contains about 100 billion neurons, all of which are interneurons. Each of those neurons may receive messages from up to 10,000 other neurons and may send messages to about 1,000 more! Three layers of connective tissue cover the brain. The space between the middle layer and innermost layer is filled with a watery fluid. The skull, the layers of connective tissue, and the fluid all help protect the brain from injury.

There are three main regions of the brain that receive and process information. These are the cerebrum, the cerebellum, and the brain stem. Find each in Figure 6.

Cerebrum The largest part of the brain is called the cerebrum. The **cerebrum** (suh REE brum) interprets input from the senses, controls movement, and carries out complex mental processes such as learning and remembering. Because of your cerebrum, you can locate your favorite comic strip in the newspaper, read it, and laugh at its funny characters.

The cerebrum is divided into a right and a left half. The right half sends impulses to skeletal muscles on the left side of the body. In contrast, the left half controls the right side of the body. When you reach with your right hand for a pencil, the messages that tell you to do so come from the left half of the cerebrum. In addition, each half of the cerebrum controls slightly different kinds of mental activity. The right half is usually associated with creativity and artistic ability. The left half is usually associated with mathematical skills and logical thinking.

As you can see in Figure 6, certain areas of the cerebrum are associated with smell, touch, taste, hearing, and vision. Other areas control movement, speech, written language, and abstract thought.

Cerebellum and Brain Stem The second largest part of your brain is called the cerebellum. The **cerebellum** (sehr uh BEL um) coordinates the actions of your muscles and helps you keep your balance. When you walk, the impulses that tell your feet to move start in your cerebrum. However, your cerebellum gives you the muscular coordination and sense of balance that keep you from falling down.

The **brain stem,** which lies between the cerebellum and spinal cord, controls your body's involuntary actions—those that occur automatically. For example, neurons in the brain stem regulate your breathing and help control your heartbeat.

 **Reading Checkpoint** What actions does the brain stem control?

FIGURE 6

The Brain

Each of the three main parts of the human brain—the cerebrum, cerebellum, and brain stem—carries out specific functions.
Interpreting Diagrams *What are three functions of the cerebrum?*

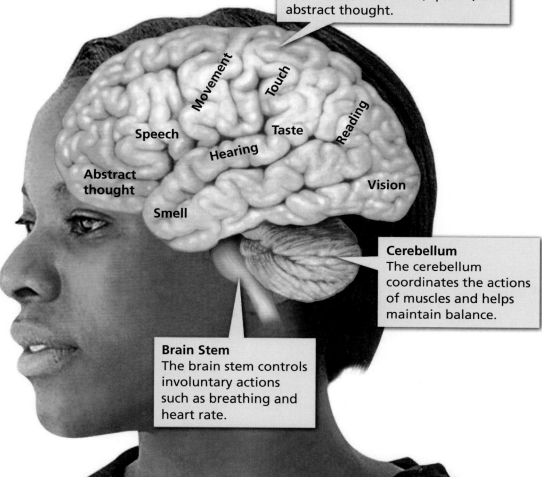

Cerebrum
The cerebrum is the largest part of the brain. Different areas of the cerebrum control such functions as movement, the senses, speech, and abstract thought.

Movement

Touch

Speech

Taste

Reading

Hearing

Abstract thought

Vision

Smell

Cerebellum
The cerebellum coordinates the actions of muscles and helps maintain balance.

Brain Stem
The brain stem controls involuntary actions such as breathing and heart rate.

Top View of Cerebrum

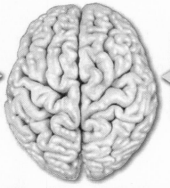

Left Half
The left half of the cerebrum is associated with mathematical and logical thinking.

Right Half
The right half of the cerebrum is associated with creativity and artistic ability.

The Spinal Cord Run your fingers down the center of your back to feel the bones of the vertebral column. The vertebral column surrounds and protects the spinal cord. **The spinal cord is the link between your brain and the peripheral nervous system.** The layers of connective tissue that surround and protect the brain also cover the spinal cord. In addition, like the brain, the spinal cord is further protected by a watery fluid.

Peripheral Nervous System

The second division of the nervous system is the peripheral nervous system. **The peripheral nervous system consists of a network of nerves that branch out from the central nervous system and connect it to the rest of the body. The peripheral nervous system is involved in both involuntary and voluntary actions.**

A total of 43 pairs of nerves make up the peripheral nervous system. Twelve pairs originate in the brain. The other 31 pairs—the spinal nerves—begin in the spinal cord. One nerve in each pair goes to the left side of the body, and the other goes to the right. As you can see in Figure 7, spinal nerves leave the spinal cord through spaces between the vertebrae.

How Spinal Nerves Function A spinal nerve is like a two-lane highway. Impulses travel on a spinal nerve in two directions—both to and from the central nervous system. Each spinal nerve contains axons of both sensory and motor neurons. The sensory neurons carry impulses from the body to the central nervous system. The motor neurons carry impulses in the opposite direction—from the central nervous system to the body.

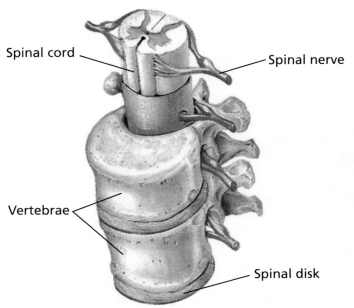

FIGURE 7
The Spinal Nerves
The spinal nerves, which connect to the spinal cord, emerge from spaces between the vertebrae. Each spinal nerve consists of both sensory and motor neurons.

Spinal cord

Spinal nerve

Vertebrae

Spinal disk

FIGURE 8
Somatic and Autonomic Nervous Systems
The somatic nervous system controls voluntary actions. The autonomic nervous system controls involuntary actions. *Classifying* *Which system helps regulate the artist's heartbeat?*

Actions Controlled by the Somatic Nervous System
• Hands shape the clay.
• Foot turns the wheel.
• Mouth smiles.

Actions Controlled by the Autonomic Nervous System
• Heartbeat is regulated.
• Breathing rate is kept steady.
• Body temperature remains constant.

Somatic and Autonomic Systems The nerves of the peripheral nervous system can be divided into two groups, the somatic (soh MAT ik) and autonomic (awt uh NAHM ik) nervous systems. The nerves of the **somatic nervous system** control voluntary actions such as using a fork or tying your shoes. In contrast, nerves of the **autonomic nervous system** control involuntary actions. For example, the autonomic nervous system regulates the contractions of the smooth muscles that adjust the diameter of blood vessels.

 **Reading Checkpoint** **What kinds of actions are controlled by the autonomic nervous system?**

Reflexes

Imagine that you are watching an adventure movie. The movie is so thrilling that you don't notice a fly circling above your head. When the fly zooms right in front of your eyes, however, your eyelids immediately blink shut. You didn't decide to close your eyes. The blink, which is a **reflex,** is a response that happened automatically. **A reflex is an automatic response that occurs very rapidly and without conscious control. Reflexes help to protect the body.** If you did the Discover activity for this section, you observed another reflex.

Lab zone Try This Activity

You Blinked!

Can you make yourself *not* blink? To answer this question, try the following activity.

1. Put on safety goggles.
2. Have your partner stand across from you and gently toss ten cotton balls toward your goggles. Your partner should not give you any warning before tossing the cotton balls.
3. Count the number of times you blink and the number of times you are able to keep from blinking.

Interpreting Data Compare the two numbers. Why is blinking considered a reflex?

A Reflex Pathway As you have learned, the contraction of skeletal muscles is usually controlled by the brain. However, in some reflex actions, skeletal muscles contract with the involvement of the spinal cord only—not the brain.

Figure 9 shows the reflex action that occurs when you touch a sharp object. When your finger touches the object, sensory neurons send impulses to the spinal cord. The impulses may then pass to interneurons in the spinal cord. From there the impulses pass directly to motor neurons in your arm and hand. The muscles then contract, and your hand jerks up and away from the sharp object. By removing your hand quickly, this reflex protects you from getting badly cut.

Signaling the Brain At the same time that some nerve impulses make your arm muscles contract, other nerve impulses travel up your spinal cord to your brain. When these impulses reach your brain, your brain interprets them. You then feel a sharp pain in your finger.

It takes longer for the pain impulses to get to the brain and be interpreted than it does for the reflex action to occur. By the time you feel the pain, you have already moved your hand away.

Reading Checkpoint What is an example of a reflex?

FIGURE 9
A Reflex Action
If you touch a sharp object, your hand immediately jerks away. This action, which is known as a reflex, happens automatically. Follow the numbered steps to understand how a reflex happens.
Sequencing *Do you pull your hand away before or after you feel the pain? Explain.*

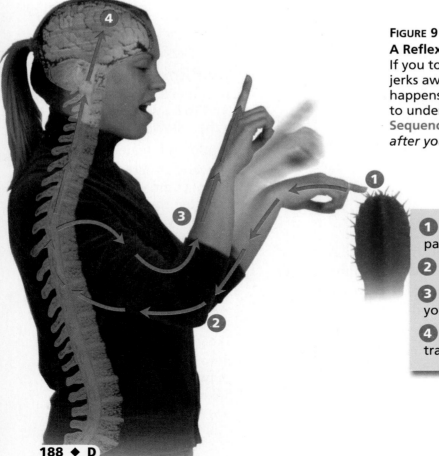

1 Sensory neurons in your fingertip detect a pain stimulus.

2 Nerve impulses travel to your spinal cord.

3 Nerve impulses return to motor neurons in your hand, and you pull your hand away.

4 As you pull your hand away, nerve impulses travel to your brain. You feel the pain.

Nervous System Injuries

The nervous system can suffer injuries that interfere with its functioning. **Concussions and spinal cord injuries are two ways in which the central nervous system can be damaged.**

Concussions A **concussion** is a bruiselike injury of the brain. A concussion occurs when the soft tissue of the brain collides against the skull. Concussions can happen when you bump your head in a hard fall, an automobile accident, or a contact sport such as football.

With most concussions, you may have a headache for a short time, but the injured tissue heals by itself. However, with more serious concussions, you may lose consciousness, experience confusion, or feel drowsy after the injury. To decrease your chances of getting a brain injury, wear a helmet during activities in which you risk bumping your head.

Spinal Cord Injuries Spinal cord injuries occur when the spinal cord is cut or crushed. As a result, axons in the injured region are damaged, so impulses cannot pass through them. This type of injury usually results in paralysis, which is the loss of movement in some part of the body. Car crashes are the most common cause of spinal cord injuries.

FIGURE 10
Protecting the Nervous System
You can help protect yourself from a spinal cord injury by wearing a seatbelt when you travel in a car.

 **Reading Checkpoint** What is paralysis?

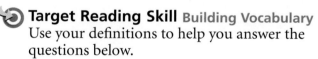

Section 2 Assessment

Target Reading Skill Building Vocabulary Use your definitions to help you answer the questions below.

Reviewing Key Concepts

1. a. Listing What two structures are part of the central nervous system?
   b. Describing Describe the functions of the three main regions of the brain.
   c. Relating Cause and Effect What symptoms might indicate that a person's cerebellum has been injured?
2. a. Identifying What are the two groups of nerves into which the peripheral nervous system is divided?
   b. Comparing and Contrasting How do the functions of the two groups of peripheral nerves differ?

3. a. Defining What is a reflex?
   b. Sequencing Trace the pathway of a reflex in the nervous system.
   c. Inferring How do reflexes help protect the body from injury?
4. a. Reviewing What is a concussion?
   b. Applying Concepts How can you reduce your risk of concussion?

Writing in Science

Comparison Paragraph Write a paragraph in which you compare the functions of the left and right halves of the cerebrum. Discuss what kinds of mental activities each half controls as well as which side of the body it controls.

Should People Be Required to Wear Bicycle Helmets?

Bicycling is an enjoyable activity. Unfortunately, many bicyclists are injured while riding. Each year, more than 500,000 people in the United States are treated in hospitals for bicycling injuries. Many of those people suffer head injuries. Head injuries can affect everything your brain does—thinking, remembering, seeing, and being able to move.

Depending on the age group and geographic location, helmet use ranges from less than 10 percent to about 80 percent of bicyclists. What is the best way to get bicyclists to protect themselves from head injury?

The Issues

Should Laws Require the Use of Bicycle Helmets?

Experts estimate that bicycle helmets could reduce the risk of bicycle-related head injuries by as much as 85 percent. Today, about 19 states have passed laws requiring bicycle riders to wear helmets. Most of these statewide laws, however, apply only to children.

Some supporters of helmet laws want to see the laws extended to all riders. They claim that laws are the most effective way to increase helmet use.

What Are the Drawbacks of Helmet Laws?

Opponents of helmet laws believe it is up to the individual to decide whether or not to wear a helmet. They say it is not the role of government to stop people from taking risks. They argue that, rather than making people pay fines if they don't wear bicycle helmets, governments should educate people about the benefits of helmets. Car drivers should also be educated about safe driving procedures near bicycles.

Are There Alternatives to Helmet Laws?

Instead of laws requiring people to wear helmets, some communities and organizations have set up educational programs that teach about the advantages of helmets. Effective programs teach about the dangers of head injuries and the protection that helmets provide. Effective education programs, though, can be expensive. They also need to reach a wide audience, including children, teens, and adults.

You Decide

1. **Identify the Problem**
   In your own words, explain the issues concerning laws requiring people to wear bicycle helmets.

2. **Analyze the Options**
   List two different plans for increasing helmet use by bicycle riders. List at least one advantage and one drawback of each plan.

3. **Find a Solution**
   You are a member of the city government hoping to increase helmet use. Write a speech outlining your position for either a helmet law or an alternative plan. Support your position.

For: More on bicycle helmets
Visit: PHSchool.com
Web Code: ceh-4060

3 The Senses

Reading Preview

Key Concepts
- How do your eyes enable you to see?
- How do you hear and maintain your sense of balance?
- How do your senses of smell and taste work together?
- How is your skin related to your sense of touch?

Key Terms
- cornea • pupil • iris • lens
- retina • nearsightedness
- farsightedness • eardrum
- cochlea • semicircular canal

🔄 Target Reading Skill

Outlining As you read, make an outline about the senses. Use the red headings for the main ideas and the blue headings for the supporting ideas.

The Senses
I. Vision
A. How light enters your eye
B.
C.

Lab zone Discover Activity

What's in the Bag?

1. Your teacher will give you a paper bag that contains several objects. Your challenge is to use only your sense of touch to identify each object. You will not look inside the bag.

2. Put your hand in the bag and carefully touch each object. Observe the shape of each object. Note whether its surface is rough or smooth. Also note other characteristics, such as its size, what it seems to be made of, and whether it can be bent.

3. After you have finished touching each object, write your observations on a sheet of paper. Then, write your inference about what each object is.

Think It Over

Observing What could you determine about each object without looking at it? What could you not determine?

You waited in line to get on the ride, and now it's about to begin. You grip the wheel as the bumper cars jerk into motion. The next thing you know, you are zipping around crazily and bumping into cars driven by your friends.

You can thrill to the motion of amusement park rides because of your senses. The sense organs pick up information about your environment, change the information into nerve impulses, and send the impulses to your brain. Your brain then interprets the information. Your senses and brain working together enable you to respond to things in your environment, such as the other bumper cars around you.

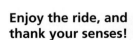

Enjoy the ride, and thank your senses!

Pupil in Bright Light

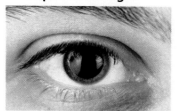

Pupil in Dim Light

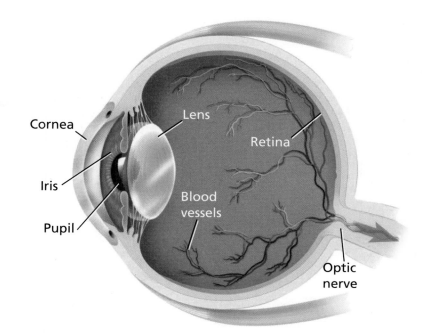

Cornea

Lens

Retina

Iris

Blood vessels

Pupil

Optic nerve

Vision

Your eyes are the sense organs that enable you to see the objects in your environment. They let you see this textbook in front of you, the window across the room, and the world outside the window. **Your eyes respond to the stimulus of light. They convert that stimulus into impulses that your brain interprets, enabling you to see.**

How Light Enters Your Eye When rays of light strike the eye, they pass through the structures shown in Figure 11. First, the light strikes the **cornea** (KAWR nee uh), the clear tissue that covers the front of the eye. The light then passes through a fluid-filled chamber behind the cornea and reaches the pupil. The **pupil** is the opening through which light enters the eye.

You may have noticed that people's pupils change size when they go from a dark room into bright sunshine. In bright light, the pupil becomes smaller. In dim light, the pupil becomes larger. The size of the pupil is adjusted by muscles in the iris. The **iris** is a circular structure that surrounds the pupil and regulates the amount of light entering the eye. The iris also gives the eye its color. If you have brown eyes, it is actually your irises that are brown.

How Light Is Focused Light that passes through the pupil strikes the lens. The **lens** is a flexible structure that focuses light. The lens of your eye functions something like the lens of a camera, which focuses light on photographic film. Because of the way in which the lens of the eye bends the light rays, the image it produces is upside down and reversed. Muscles that attach to the lens adjust its shape, producing an image that is in focus.

FIGURE 11
The Eye
The eye is a complex organ that allows you to sense light. The pupil is the opening through which light enters the eye. In bright light, the pupil becomes smaller. In dim light, the pupil enlarges and allows more light to enter the eye.
Interpreting Diagrams What structure adjusts the size of the pupil?

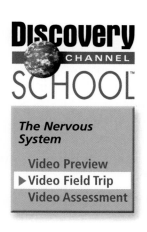

DISCOVERY
CHANNEL
SCHOOL™

The Nervous System
Video Preview
▶Video Field Trip
Video Assessment

FIGURE 12
How You See

Light coming from an object enters your eye and is focused by the lens. The light produces an upside-down image on your retina. Receptors in your retina then send impulses to your cerebrum, which turns the image right-side up.
Comparing and Contrasting Which receptors work best in dim light?

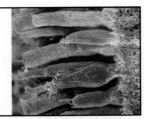

Rods and Cones
Receptors in the retina include rods (shown in green) and cones (shown in blue).

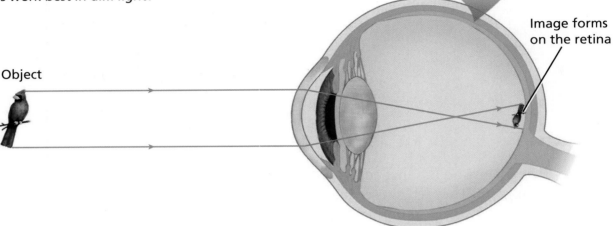

Object

Image forms on the retina

Lab zone **Try This Activity**

Working Together

Discover how your two eyes work together.

1. With your arms fully extended, hold a drinking straw in one hand and a pipe cleaner in the other.

2. With both eyes open, try to insert the pipe cleaner into the straw.

3. Now close your right eye. Try to insert the pipe cleaner into the straw.

4. Repeat Step 3 with your left eye closed.

Inferring How does closing one eye affect your ability to judge distances?

How You See an Image After passing through the lens, the focused light rays pass through a transparent, jellylike fluid. Then the light rays strike the **retina** (RET 'n uh), the layer of receptor cells that lines the back of the eye. The retina contains about 130 million receptor cells that respond to light. There are two types of receptors: rods and cones. Rod cells work best in dim light and enable you to see black, white, and shades of gray. In contrast, cone cells work best in bright light and enable you to see colors. This difference between rods and cones explains why you see colors best in bright light, but you see only shadowy gray images in dim light.

When light strikes the rods and cones, nerve impulses travel to the cerebrum through the optic nerves. One optic nerve comes from the left eye and the other one comes from the right eye. In the cerebrum, two things happen. The brain turns the reversed image right-side up, and it also combines the images from each eye to produce a single image.

Correcting Nearsightedness A lens—whether it is in your eye or in eyeglasses—is a curved, transparent object that bends light rays as they pass through it. If the lens of the eye does not focus light properly on the retina, vision problems result. The lenses in eyeglasses can help correct vision problems.

FIGURE 13
Correcting Vision Problems

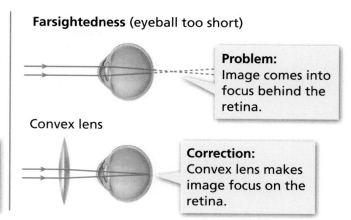

Nearsightedness (eyeball too long)

Concave lens

Problem:
Image comes into focus in front of the retina.

Correction:
Concave lens makes image focus on the retina.

Farsightedness (eyeball too short)

Convex lens

Problem:
Image comes into focus behind the retina.

Correction:
Convex lens makes image focus on the retina.

People with **nearsightedness** can see nearby objects clearly. However, they have trouble seeing objects far away. Nearsightedness results when the eyeball is too long. Because of the extra length that light must travel to reach the retina, distant objects do not focus sharply on the retina. Instead, the lens of the eye makes the image come into focus at a point in front of the retina, as shown in Figure 13.

To correct nearsightedness, eyeglasses with concave lenses are worn. A concave lens is thicker at the edges than it is in the center. When light rays pass through a concave lens, they are bent away from the center of the lens. The concave lenses in glasses make light rays spread out before they reach the lens of the eye. After the rays pass through the lens of the eye, they focus on the retina rather than in front of it.

Correcting Farsightedness People with **farsightedness** can see distant objects clearly. Nearby objects, however, look blurry. The eyeballs of people with farsightedness are too short. Because of this, the lens of the eye bends light from nearby objects so that the image does not focus properly on the retina. If light could pass through the retina, the image would come into sharp focus at a point behind the retina, as shown in Figure 13.

Convex lenses are used to help correct farsightedness. A convex lens is thicker in the middle than at the edges. The convex lens makes the light rays bend toward each other before they reach the eye. Then the lens of the eye bends the rays even more. This bending makes the image focus exactly on the retina.

 **Reading Checkpoint** **What type of lens corrects nearsightedness?**

Hearing and Balance

What wakes you up in the morning? Maybe an alarm clock buzzes, or perhaps your parent calls you. On a summer morning, you might hear birds singing. Whatever wakes you up, there's a good chance that it's a sound of some sort. **Your ears are the sense organs that respond to the stimulus of sound. The ears convert the sound to nerve impulses that your brain interprets.** So when you hear an alarm clock or another morning sound, your brain tells you that it's time to wake up.

How Sound Is Produced Sound is produced by vibrations. The material that is vibrating, or moving rapidly back and forth, may be almost anything—a guitar string, an insect's wings, or a stereo speaker.

The vibrations move outward from the source of the sound, something like ripples moving out from a stone dropped in water. The vibrations cause particles, such as the gas molecules that make up air, to vibrate. In this way, sound is carried. When you hear a friend's voice, for example, sound has traveled from your friend's larynx to your ears. In addition to being able to travel through gases such as those in air, sound waves can also travel through liquids, such as water, and solids, such as wood.

Math ▸ Analyzing Data

Sound Intensity

Sound intensity, or loudness, is measured in units called decibels. The threshold of hearing for the human ear is 0 decibels. For every 10-decibel increase, the sound intensity increases ten times. Thus, a 20-decibel sound is ten times more intense than a 10-decibel sound, not twice as intense. A 30-decibel sound is 100 times more intense than a 10-decibel sound. Sound levels for several sound sources are shown in the bar graph.

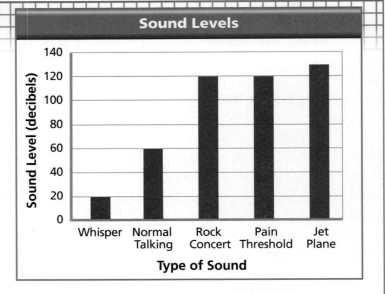

1. **Reading Graphs** What unit of measure is represented on the *y*-axis? What is represented on the *x*-axis?

2. **Interpreting Data** What is the sound intensity in decibels of a whisper? Normal talking? A rock concert?

3. **Calculating** How much more intense is normal talking than a whisper? Explain.

4. **Predicting** Based on the graph, what types of sound could be painful if you were exposed to them?

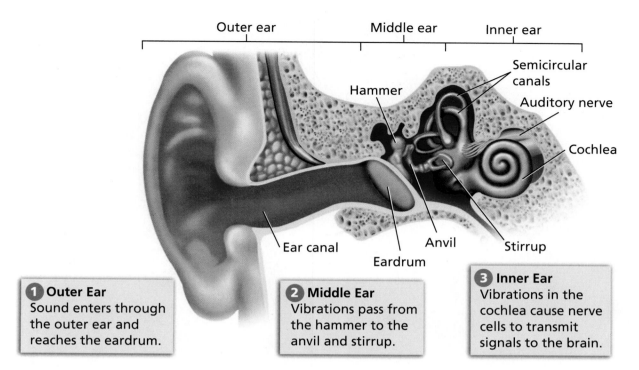

Outer ear Middle ear Inner ear

Hammer

Semicircular canals

Auditory nerve

Cochlea

Ear canal

Anvil

Stirrup

Eardrum

1 Outer Ear
Sound enters through the outer ear and reaches the eardrum.

2 Middle Ear
Vibrations pass from the hammer to the anvil and stirrup.

3 Inner Ear
Vibrations in the cochlea cause nerve cells to transmit signals to the brain.

FIGURE 14
The Ear
Sound waves enter the outer ear and make structures in the middle ear vibrate. When the vibrations reach the inner ear, nerve impulses travel to the cerebrum through the auditory nerve. **Predicting** *What would happen if the bones of the middle ear were stuck together and could not move?*

The Outer Ear The ear is structured to receive sound vibrations. The three regions of the ear—the outer ear, middle ear, and inner ear—are shown in Figure 14. The visible part of the outer ear is shaped like a funnel. This funnel-like shape enables the outer ear to gather sound waves. The sound vibrations then travel down the ear canal, which is also part of the outer ear.

The Middle Ear At the end of the ear canal, sound vibrations reach the eardrum. The **eardrum,** which separates the outer ear from the middle ear, is a membrane that vibrates when sound strikes it. Your eardrum vibrates in much the same way that a drum vibrates when it is struck. Vibrations from the eardrum pass to the middle ear, which contains the three smallest bones in the body—the hammer, anvil, and stirrup. These bones are named for their shapes. The vibrating eardrum makes the hammer vibrate. The hammer passes the vibrations to the anvil, and the anvil passes them to the stirrup.

The Inner Ear The stirrup vibrates against a thin membrane that covers the opening of the inner ear. The membrane channels the vibrations into the fluid in the cochlea. The **cochlea** (KAHK le uh) is a snail-shaped tube that is lined with receptor cells that respond to sound. When the fluid in the cochlea vibrates, it stimulates these receptors. Sensory neurons then send nerve impulses to the cerebrum through the auditory nerve. These impulses are interpreted as sounds that you hear.

Go Online
SCiLINKS NSTA

For: Links on the senses
Visit: www.SciLinks.org
Web Code: scn-0463

Semicircular canals

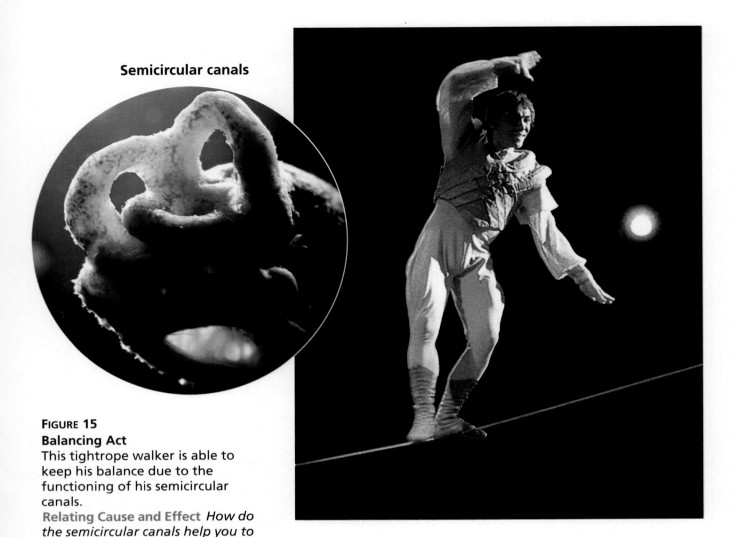

FIGURE 15
Balancing Act
This tightrope walker is able to keep his balance due to the functioning of his semicircular canals.
Relating Cause and Effect *How do the semicircular canals help you to maintain balance?*

The Inner Ear and Balance Structures in your inner ear control your sense of balance. Above the cochlea in your inner ear are the **semicircular canals,** which are the structures in the ear that are responsible for your sense of balance. You can see how these structures got their name if you look at Figure 15. These canals, as well as the two tiny sacs located behind them, are full of fluid. The canals and sacs are also lined with tiny cells that have hairlike extensions.

When your head moves, the fluid in the semicircular canals is set in motion. The moving fluid makes the cells' hairlike extensions bend. This bending produces nerve impulses in sensory neurons. The impulses travel to the cerebellum. The cerebellum then analyzes the impulses to determine the way your head is moving and the position of your body. If the cerebellum senses that you are losing your balance, it sends impulses to muscles that help you restore your balance.

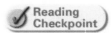 **Reading Checkpoint** Where in the ear are the semicircular canals located?

Smell and Taste

You walk into the house and smell the aroma of freshly baked cookies. You bite into one and taste its rich chocolate flavor. When you smelled the cookies, receptors in your nose reacted to chemicals carried by the air from the cookies to your nose. When you took a bite of a cookie, taste buds on your tongue responded to chemicals in the food. These food chemicals were dissolved in saliva, which came in contact with your taste buds.

The senses of smell and taste work closely together. Both depend on chemicals in food or in the air. The chemicals trigger responses in receptors in the nose and mouth. Nerve impulses then travel to the brain, where they are interpreted as smells or tastes.

The nose can distinguish at least 50 basic odors. In contrast, there are only five main taste sensations—sweet, sour, salty, bitter, and a meatlike taste called *umami*. When you eat, however, you experience a much wider variety of tastes. The flavor of food is influenced by both smell and taste. When you have a cold, foods may not taste as good as they usually do. That is because a stuffy nose decreases your ability to smell food.

 **Reading Checkpoint** What basic tastes can the tongue detect?

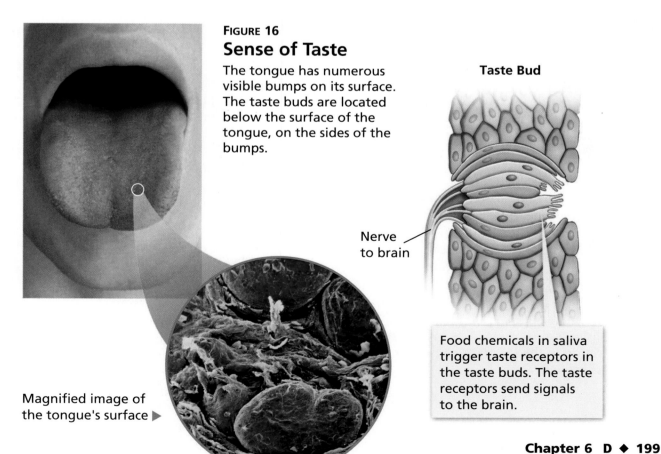

FIGURE 16
Sense of Taste
The tongue has numerous visible bumps on its surface. The taste buds are located below the surface of the tongue, on the sides of the bumps.

Taste Bud

Nerve to brain

Food chemicals in saliva trigger taste receptors in the taste buds. The taste receptors send signals to the brain.

Magnified image of the tongue's surface ▶

Lab zone Skills Activity

Designing Experiments
Can people tell one food from another if they can taste the foods but not smell them? Design an experiment to find out. Use these foods: a peeled pear, a peeled apple, and a peeled raw potato. Be sure to control all variables except the one you are testing. Write your hypothesis and a description of your procedure. Obtain your teacher's approval before carrying out your experiment.

Touch

Unlike vision, hearing, balance, smell, and taste, the sense of touch is not found in one specific place. Instead, the sense of touch is found in all areas of your skin. Your skin is your largest sense organ! **Your skin contains different kinds of touch receptors that respond to a number of stimuli.** Some of these receptors respond to light touch and others to heavy pressure. Still other receptors pick up sensations of pain and temperature change.

The receptors that respond to light touch are in the upper part of the dermis. They tell you when something brushes against your skin. These receptors also let you feel the textures of objects, such as smooth glass and rough sandpaper. Receptors deeper in the dermis pick up the feeling of pressure. Press down hard on the top of your desk, for example, and you will feel pressure in your fingertips.

The dermis also contains receptors that respond to temperature and pain. Pain is unpleasant, but it can be one of the body's most important feelings because it alerts the body to possible danger. Have you ever stepped into a bathtub of very hot water and then immediately pulled your foot out? If so, you can appreciate how pain can trigger an important response in your body.

FIGURE 17
Reading by Touch
People who are blind use their sense of touch to read. To do this, they run their fingers over words written in Braille. Braille uses raised dots to represent letters and numbers. Here, a teacher shows a blind child how to read Braille.

Section 3 Assessment

Target Reading Skill Outlining Use the information in your outline about the senses to help you answer the questions below.

Reviewing Key Concepts

1. a. Listing What are the parts of the eye?
   b. Sequencing Describe the process by which the eye produces an image. Begin at the point at which light is focused by the lens.
   c. Inferring If nearby objects seem blurry, what type of vision problem might you have? How can it be corrected?

2. a. Identifying What are the three regions of the ear?
   b. Describing Describe the location and function of the eardrum and the cochlea.
   c. Relating Cause and Effect Why may an infection of the inner ear cause you to lose your balance?

3. a. Reviewing What two senses work together to influence the flavor of food?
   b. Comparing and Contrasting How are the senses of taste and smell similar? How are they different?

4. a. Identifying What kinds of touch receptors are found in the skin?
   b. Applying Concepts What happens in the dermis when you accidentally touch a hot stove?

Writing in Science

Cause-and-Effect Paragraph Write a description of how you feel after an amusement park ride. Explain how your feeling is related to the structure and function of the semicircular canals. Be sure to include a topic sentence and three to four supporting points.

Alcohol and Other Drugs

Reading Preview

Key Concepts
- What are the immediate and long-term effects of drug abuse?
- What are some commonly abused drugs and how does each affect the body?
- How does alcohol abuse harm the body?

Key Terms
- drug • drug abuse
- tolerance • addiction
- withdrawal • depressant
- stimulant • anabolic steroid
- alcoholism

Target Reading Skill
Relating Cause and Effect As you read, identify commonly abused drugs and how they affect the body. Write the information in a graphic organizer like the one below.

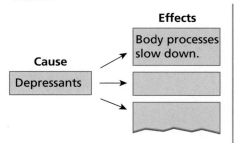

Effects

Cause

Body processes slow down.

Depressants

Lab zone Discover **Activity**

How Can You Best Say No?

1. In this activity, you will use marbles to represent drugs. Your teacher will divide the class into groups of three students. In each group, your teacher will appoint two students to try to convince the other person to take the "drugs."
2. Depending on your role, you should think of arguments to get the person to accept the marbles or arguments against accepting them. After everyone has had a chance to think of arguments, begin the discussion.
3. After a while, students in each group should exchange roles.

Think It Over
Inferring What role does peer pressure play in whether or not a person decides to abuse drugs?

Drugs! You probably hear and see that word in a lot of places. Drugstores sell drugs to relieve headaches, soothe upset stomachs, and stop coughs. Radio and television programs and magazine articles explore drug-related problems. Your school probably has a program to educate students about drugs. When people talk about drugs, what do they mean? To a scientist, a **drug** is any chemical taken into the body that causes changes in a person's body or behavior. Many drugs affect the functioning of the central nervous system.

Drug Abuse

The deliberate misuse of drugs for purposes other than medical ones is called **drug abuse.** Even medicines can be abused drugs if they are used in a way for which they were not intended. Many abused drugs, however, such as cocaine and heroin, are illegal under any circumstances. The use of these drugs is against the law because their effects on the body are almost always dangerous.

Effects of Abused Drugs Abused drugs start to affect the body shortly after they are taken. **Most commonly abused drugs, such as marijuana, alcohol, and cocaine, are especially dangerous because of their immediate effects on the brain and other parts of the nervous system. In addition, long-term drug abuse can lead to addiction and other health and social problems.**

Different drugs have different effects. Some drugs cause nausea and a fast, irregular heartbeat. Others can cause sleepiness. Drug abusers may also experience headaches, dizziness, and trembling. Alcohol can cause confusion, poor muscle coordination, and blurred vision. These effects are especially dangerous in situations in which an alert mind is essential, such as driving a car.

Most abused drugs can alter, or change, a person's mood and feelings. Because of this effect, these drugs are often called mood-altering drugs. For example, the mood of a person under the influence of marijuana may change from calm to anxious. Alcohol can sometimes make a person angry and even violent. Mood-altering drugs also affect patterns of thinking and the way in which the brain interprets information from the senses.

Tolerance If a person takes a drug regularly, the body may develop a tolerance to the drug. **Tolerance is a state in which a drug user needs larger and larger amounts of the drug to produce the same effect on the body.** Tolerance can cause people to take a very large amount of a drug, or an overdose. People who take an overdose may become unconscious or even die.

FIGURE 18
Drug Abuse
Drug abuse can have serious consequences. However, there are ways to tell if someone is abusing drugs and ways to help that person. *Interpreting Diagrams What are two ways you can help if someone you know is abusing drugs?*

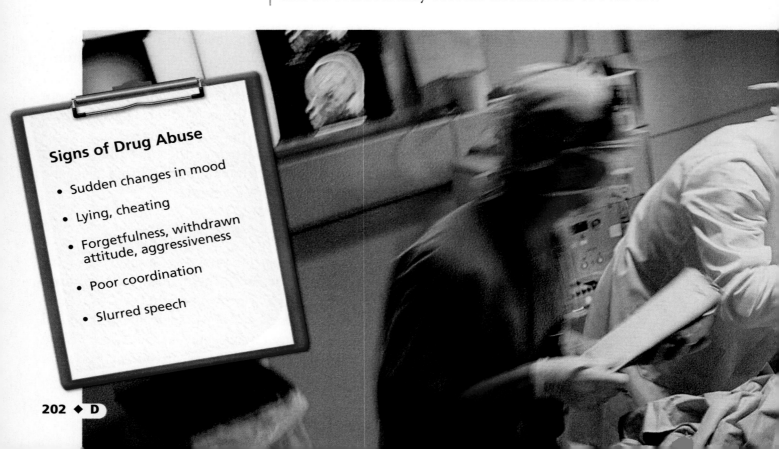

Signs of Drug Abuse

- Sudden changes in mood
- Lying, cheating
- Forgetfulness, withdrawn attitude, aggressiveness
- Poor coordination
- Slurred speech

Addiction For many commonly abused drugs, repeated use can result in addiction. In **addiction,** the body becomes physically dependent on the drug. If a drug addict misses a few doses of the drug, the body reacts to the lack of the drug. The person may experience headaches, dizziness, fever, vomiting, body aches, and muscle cramps. The person is experiencing **withdrawal,** a period of adjustment that occurs when a person stops taking a drug on which the body is dependent.

Some drugs may also cause a person to become emotionally dependent on them. The person becomes accustomed to the feelings and moods produced by the drug. Therefore, the person has a strong desire to continue using the drug.

Other Effects of Drug Abuse Drugs can also affect a person's health indirectly. Some drug users sometimes share needles. When a person uses a needle to inject a drug, some of the person's blood remains in the needle after it is withdrawn. If the person has HIV or another pathogen in the blood, the next person to use the needle may become infected with the pathogen.

The abuse of drugs also has serious legal and social effects. A person who is caught using or selling an illegal drug may have to pay a fine or go to jail. Drug abuse can also make a person unable to get along with others. Drug abusers often have a hard time doing well in school or holding a job.

 **Reading Checkpoint** **What is withdrawal?**

Lab zone Skills **Activity**

Communicating
Plan a 30-second television commercial aimed at teenagers to help them avoid the pressure to try drugs. Your commercial should reveal some harmful effects of drugs and give strategies for avoiding drugs. Create several storyboards to show what the commercial will look like. Then, write a script for your commercial.

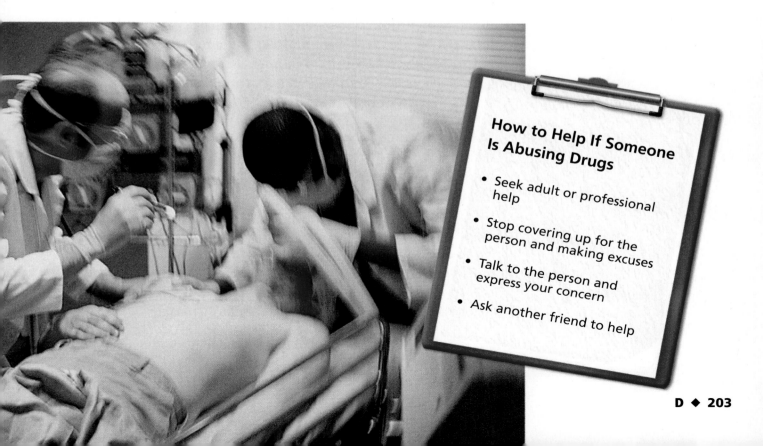

How to Help If Someone Is Abusing Drugs

- Seek adult or professional help
- Stop covering up for the person and making excuses
- Talk to the person and express your concern
- Ask another friend to help

Kinds of Abused Drugs

There are many kinds of drugs, with a wide range of effects on the body. Some are legitimate medicines that a doctor prescribes to help the body fight disease and injury. However, many kinds of drugs are frequently abused. **Commonly abused drugs include depressants, stimulants, inhalants, hallucinogens, anabolic steroids, and alcohol. Many drugs affect the central nervous system, while others affect the overall chemical balance in the body.** Figure 20 lists and describes the characteristics of some commonly abused drugs.

Depressants Notice in Figure 20 that some drugs are classified as depressants. **Depressants** are drugs that slow down the activity of the central nervous system. When people take depressants, their muscles relax and they may become sleepy. They may take longer than normal to respond to stimuli. For example, depressants may prevent people from reacting quickly to the danger of a car rushing toward them. Alcohol and narcotics, such as heroin, are depressants.

Stimulants In contrast to depressants, **stimulants** speed up body processes. They make the heart beat faster and make the breathing rate increase. Cocaine and nicotine are stimulants, as are amphetamines (am FET uh meenz). Amphetamines are prescription drugs that are sometimes sold illegally.

Inhalants and Hallucinogens Some substances, called inhalants, produce mood-altering effects when they are inhaled, or breathed in. Inhalants include paint thinner, nail polish remover, and some kinds of cleaning fluids. Hallucinogens, such as LSD and mescaline, can make people see or hear things that do not really exist.

Steroids Some athletes try to improve their performance by taking drugs known as steroids. **Anabolic steroids** (an uh BAH lik STEER oydz) are synthetic chemicals that are similar to hormones produced in the body.

Anabolic steroids may increase muscle size and strength. However, steroids can cause mood changes that lead to violence. In addition, steroid abuse can cause serious health problems, such as heart damage, liver damage, and increased blood pressure. Steroid use is especially dangerous for teenagers, whose growing bodies can be permanently damaged.

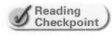 **Reading Checkpoint** What kinds of drugs are classified as stimulants?

FIGURE 19
Making a Statement About Drug Abuse
Many teens are becoming active in antidrug campaigns.

FIGURE 20
Abused drugs can have many serious effects on the body. Interpreting Tables *What are the long-term effects of using inhalants?*

Some Effects of Commonly Abused Drugs				
Drug Type	Short-Term Effects	Long-Term Effects	Addiction?	Emotional Dependence?
Marijuana (including hashish)	Unclear thinking, loss of coordination, increased heart rate	Difficulty with concentration and memory; respiratory disease and lung cancer	Probably not	Yes
Nicotine (in cigarettes, cigars, chewing tobacco)	Stimulant; nausea, loss of appetite, headache	Heart and lung disease, difficulty breathing, heavy coughing	Yes, strongly so	Yes
Alcohol	Depressant; decreased alertness, poor reflexes, nausea, emotional depression	Liver and brain damage, inadequate nutrition	Yes	Yes
Inhalants (glue, nail polish remover, paint thinner)	Sleepiness, nausea, headaches, emotional depression	Damage to liver, kidneys, and brain; hallucinations	No	Yes
Cocaine (including crack)	Stimulant; nervousness, disturbed sleep, loss of appetite	Mental illness, damage to lining of nose, irregular heartbeat, heart or breathing failure, liver damage	Yes	Yes, strongly so
Amphetamines	Stimulant; restlessness, rapid speech, dizziness	Restlessness, irritability, irregular heartbeat, liver damage	Possible	Yes
Hallucinogens (LSD, mescaline, PCP)	Hallucinations, anxiety, panic; thoughts and actions not connected to reality	Mental illness; fearfulness; behavioral changes, including violence	No	Yes
Barbiturates (Phenobarbital, Nembutal, Seconal)	Depressant; decreased alertness, slowed thought processes, poor muscle coordination	Sleepiness, irritability, confusion	Yes	Yes
Tranquilizers (Valium, Xanax)	Depressant; blurred vision, sleepiness, unclear speech, headache, skin rash	Blood and liver disease	Yes	Yes
Narcotics (opium, codeine, morphine, heroin)	Depressant; sleepiness, nausea, hallucinations	Convulsion, coma, death	Yes, very rapid development	Yes, strongly so
Anabolic steroids	Mood swings	Heart, liver, and kidney damage; hypertension; overgrowth of skull and facial bones	No	Yes

Alcohol

Alcohol is a drug found in many beverages, including beer, wine, cocktails, and hard liquor. Alcohol is a powerful depressant. In all states, it is illegal for people under the age of 21 to buy or possess alcohol. In spite of this fact, alcohol is the most commonly abused legal drug in people aged 12 to 17.

How Alcohol Affects the Body Alcohol is absorbed by the digestive system quickly. If a person drinks alcohol on an empty stomach, the alcohol enters the blood and gets to the brain and other organs almost immediately. If alcohol is drunk with a meal, it takes longer to get into the blood.

The chart in Figure 21 describes what alcohol does to the body. The more alcohol in the blood, the more serious the effects. The amount of alcohol in the blood is usually expressed as blood alcohol concentration, or BAC. A BAC value of 0.1 percent means that one tenth of one percent of the fluid in the blood is alcohol. In some states, if car drivers have a BAC of 0.08 percent or more, they are legally drunk. In other states, drivers with a BAC of 0.1 are considered legally drunk.

Alcohol produces serious negative effects, including loss of normal judgment, at a BAC of less than 0.08 percent. This loss of judgment can have serious consequences. People who have been drinking may not realize that they cannot drive a car safely. About every two minutes, a person in the United States is injured in a car crash related to alcohol.

FIGURE 21
Alcohol's Effects
Alcohol affects every system of the body. It also impacts a person's thought processes, judgment, and reaction time. In the bottom photo, a police officer tests the blood alcohol concentration of a driver suspected of drinking.

Short-Term Effects of Alcohol	
Body System	**Effect**
Cardiovascular system	First, heartbeat rate and blood pressure increase. Later, they may decrease.
Digestive system	Alcohol is absorbed directly from the stomach and small intestine, which allows it to enter the bloodstream quickly.
Excretory system	The kidneys produce more urine, causing the drinker to excrete more water than usual.
Nervous system	Vision blurs. Speech becomes unclear. Control of behavior is reduced. Judgment becomes poor.
Skin	Blood flow to the skin increases, causing rapid loss of body heat.

Long-Term Alcohol Abuse Many adults drink occasionally and in moderation, without serious safety or health problems. However, heavy drinking, especially over a long period, can result in significant health problems. **Alcohol abuse can cause the destruction of cells in the brain and liver, and can lead to addiction and emotional dependence.** Damage to the brain can cause mental disturbances, such as hallucinations and loss of consciousness. The liver, which breaks down alcohol for elimination from the body, can become so scarred that it does not function properly. In addition, long-term alcohol abuse can increase the risk of getting certain kinds of cancer.

Abuse of alcohol can result in **alcoholism,** a disease in which a person is both physically addicted to and emotionally dependent on alcohol. To give up alcohol, as with any addictive drug, alcoholics must go through withdrawal. To give up drinking, alcoholics need both medical and emotional help. Medical professionals, psychologists, and organizations such as Alcoholics Anonymous can help a person stop drinking.

Healthy Liver

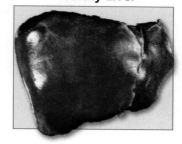

Alcohol-damaged Liver

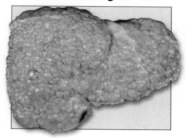

 **What organs are affected by alcohol abuse?**

FIGURE 22
Alcohol's Effect on the Liver
Long-term alcohol abuse can cause serious damage to the liver. **Relating Cause and Effect** *What other effects can alcohol abuse have on the body?*

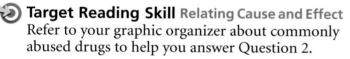

Section 4 Assessment

Target Reading Skill Relating Cause and Effect Refer to your graphic organizer about commonly abused drugs to help you answer Question 2.

Reviewing Key Concepts

1. **a. Defining** In your own words, explain what a drug is. What is drug abuse?
   b. Explaining How can the repeated use of some drugs lead to addiction and emotional dependence?
   c. Applying Concepts What reasons would you give someone to not try drugs in the first place?
2. **a. Listing** Name two commonly abused depressants and two commonly abused stimulants.
   b. Comparing and Contrasting Contrast the effects that depressants and stimulants have on the body.
   c. Inferring Why might a person's risk of a heart attack increase with the use of stimulants?
3. **a. Reviewing** What type of drug is alcohol?
   b. Explaining What immediate effects does alcohol have on the body?
   c. Relating Cause and Effect Based on alcohol's effect on the nervous system, explain why drinking and driving is extremely dangerous.

Lab zone **At-Home Activity**

Medicine Labels Collect several medicine bottles and read the warning labels. Make a list of the kinds of warnings you find. Discuss these warnings with a family member. Why do you think medicines provide warnings?

With Caffeine or Without?

Problem

What body changes does caffeine produce in blackworms (Lumbriculus)?

Skills Focus

observing, controlling variables, drawing conclusions

Materials

- blackworms
- plastic dropper
- adrenaline solution
- stereomicroscope
- paraffin specimen trough
- noncarbonated spring water
- beverages with and without caffeine
- stopwatch or clock with second hand

Procedure

PART 1 Observing the Effects of a Known Stimulant

1. Copy the data table into your notebook. Use a dropper to remove one worm and a drop or two of water from the blackworm population provided by your teacher.

2. Place the worm and the water in the trough of the paraffin block. Use the dropper or the corner of a paper towel to remove any excess water that does not fit in the trough. Let the blackworm adjust for a few minutes.

3. Place the paraffin block under the stereomicroscope. Select the smallest amount of light and the lowest possible power to view the blackworm.

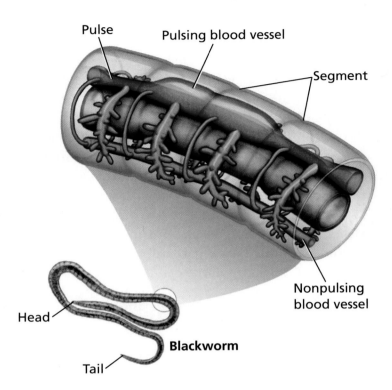

Pulse
Pulsing blood vessel
Segment
Nonpulsing blood vessel
Head
Blackworm
Tail

4. Look through the stereomicroscope and locate a segment near the middle of the worm. Count the number of times blood pulses through this segment for 30 seconds. Multiply this number by two to get the pulse in beats per minute. Record the pulse in your data table.

Data Table	
Condition	Pulse Rate
No adrenaline	
With adrenaline	
Beverage without caffeine	
Beverage with caffeine	

5. Remove the block from the stereomicroscope. Use the dropper to add 1 drop of adrenaline solution to the trough. (Adrenaline is a substance produced by the human body that acts as a stimulant.) Let the worm sit in the adrenaline solution for 5 minutes.

6. Place the paraffin block under the stereomicroscope. Again locate a segment near the middle of the worm. Count the number of pulses through this segment for 30 seconds. Multiply this number by two to get the pulse in beats per minute. Record the blackworm's pulse with adrenaline.

PART 2 Testing the Effects of Caffeine

7. Using the procedures you followed in Part 1, design an experiment that tests the effect of caffeine on the blackworm's pulse. You can use beverages with and without caffeine in your investigation. Be sure to write a hypothesis and control all necessary variables.

8. Submit your experimental plan to your teacher for review. After making any necessary changes, carry out your experiment.

Analyze and Conclude

1. **Observing** In Part 1, what was the blackworm's pulse rate before you added adrenaline? After you added adrenaline?

2. **Interpreting Data** Use the data you collected in Part 1 to explain how you know that adrenaline acts as a stimulant.

3. **Controlling Variables** In the experiment you performed in Part 2, what was your control? Explain.

4. **Drawing Conclusions** Based on your results in Part 2, does caffeine act as a stimulant? Explain your answer.

5. **Communicating** Write a paragraph to explain how you think your body would react to drinks with caffeine and without caffeine. Use the results from this investigation to support your viewpoint.

Design an Experiment

Do you think that "decaffeinated" products will act as a stimulant in blackworms? Design a controlled experiment to find out. *Obtain your teacher's permission before carrying out your investigation.*

Chapter 6 — Study Guide

The BIG Idea
Structure and Function Structures that enable the nervous system to function include the brain, spinal cord, neurons, and sense organs, such as the eyes and ears.

1 How the Nervous System Works

Key Concepts

- The nervous system directs how your body responds to information about what is happening inside and outside your body. Your nervous system also helps maintain homeostasis.
- The three kinds of neurons found in the body are sensory neurons, interneurons, and motor neurons.
- For a nerve impulse to be carried along at a synapse, it must cross the gap between an axon and the next structure.

Key Terms

- stimulus • response • neuron
- nerve impulse • dendrite • axon
- nerve • sensory neuron • interneuron
- motor neuron • synapse

2 Divisions of the Nervous System

Key Concepts

- The central nervous system is the control center of the body. It includes the brain and spinal cord.
- The peripheral nervous system consists of a network of nerves that branch out from the central nervous system and connect it to the rest of the body.
- A reflex is an automatic response that occurs very rapidly and without conscious control.
- Concussions and spinal cord injuries are two ways the central nervous system can be damaged.

Key Terms

- central nervous system
- peripheral nervous system • brain
- spinal cord • cerebrum • cerebellum
- brain stem • somatic nervous system
- autonomic nervous system • reflex
- concussion

3 The Senses

Key Concepts

- The eyes convert light into nerve impulses that your brain interprets, enabling you to see.
- The ears convert sound into nerve impulses that your brain interprets, enabling you to hear. Structures in your inner ear control your sense of balance.
- The senses of smell and taste work together.
- The skin contains touch receptors that respond to a number of stimuli.

Key Terms

- cornea • pupil • iris • lens • retina
- nearsightedness • farsightedness • eardrum
- cochlea • semicircular canal

4 Alcohol and Other Drugs

Key Concepts

- Most abused drugs are dangerous because of their immediate effects on the nervous system. Long-term drug abuse can lead to addiction and other health and social problems.
- Commonly abused drugs include depressants, stimulants, inhalants, steroids, and alcohol.
- Alcohol use can destroy cells in the brain and liver, and lead to addiction.

Key Terms

drug
drug abuse
tolerance
addiction
withdrawal
depressant
stimulant
anabolic steroid
alcoholism

Review and Assessment

Go Online
PHSchool.com

For: Self-Assessment
Visit: PHSchool.com
Web Code: cea-4060

Organizing Information

Concept Mapping Copy the concept map about neurons and their functions onto a separate sheet of paper. Then, complete it and add a title. (For more on Concept Mapping, see the Skills Handbook.)

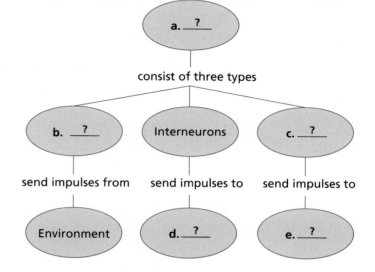

Reviewing Key Terms

Choose the letter of the best answer.

1. A change or signal in the environment that makes the nervous system react is called a
   a. stimulus.
   b. response.
   c. nerve impulse.
   d. synapse.

2. The structures that carry messages toward a neuron's cell body are
   a. axons.
   b. dendrites.
   c. nerves.
   d. nerve impulses.

3. Which structure links the brain and the peripheral nervous system?
   a. the cerebrum
   b. the cerebellum
   c. the cochlea
   d. the spinal cord

4. Which structure adjusts the size of the pupil?
   a. the cornea   **b.** the retina
   c. the lens   **d.** the iris

5. Physical dependence on a drug is called
   a. withdrawal.   **b.** response.
   c. addiction.   **d.** tolerance.

If the statement is true, write *true*. If it is false, change the underlined word or words to make the statement true.

6. A nerve message is also called a <u>synapse</u>.

7. The <u>cerebrum</u> is the part of the brain that controls involuntary actions.

8. In <u>nearsightedness</u>, a person can see distant objects clearly.

9. The <u>cochlea</u> is part of the inner ear.

10. Alcohol is a <u>depressant</u>.

Writing in Science

Descriptive Paragraph Draw a diagram of the human eye, and label the key parts. Then, write a paragraph that describes how each part helps a person "see" an image.

DISCOVERY CHANNEL **SCHOOL**™

The Nervous System

Video Preview
Video Field Trip
▶ Video Assessment

Review and Assessment

Checking Concepts

11. Compare the functions of axons and dendrites.

12. How do the cerebrum and cerebellum work together when you ride a bicycle?

13. What is the function of the autonomic nervous system?

14. What is the result if the spinal cord is cut?

15. Describe how lenses in eyeglasses correct nearsightedness and farsightedness.

16. List in order all the structures in your ear that must vibrate before you hear a sound.

17. How do anabolic steroids affect the body?

Thinking Critically

18. **Interpreting Diagrams** The diagram below shows a synapse. Explain how a nerve impulse crosses the gap.

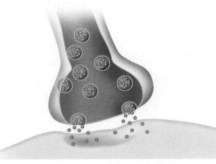

19. **Relating Cause and Effect** When a person has a stroke, blood flow to part of the brain is reduced, and some brain cells die. Suppose that after a stroke, a woman is unable to move her right arm and right leg. In which side of her brain did the stroke occur? Explain.

20. **Applying Concepts** As a man walks barefoot along a beach, he steps on a sharp shell. His foot automatically jerks upward, even before he feels pain. What process is this an example of? How does it help protect the man?

21. **Making Judgments** If someone tried to persuade you to take drugs, what arguments would you use as a way of refusing? Why do you think these arguments would be effective?

Applying Skills

Use the graph to answer Questions 22–25.

A person with normal vision stood at different distances from an eye chart and tried to identify the letters on the chart. The line graph gives the results.

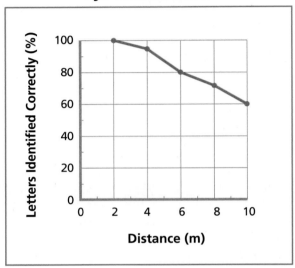

22. **Reading Graphs** What variable is plotted on the x-axis? On the y-axis?

23. **Interpreting Data** As the distance from the eye chart increases, what happens to the percentage of letters identified correctly?

24. **Controlling Variables** What was the manipulated variable in this experiment? What was the responding variable?

25. **Predicting** How would you expect the results to differ for a farsighted person? Explain.

Lab zone Chapter **Project**

Performance Assessment Explain to your classmates how you set up your experiment, which illusions you used, which senses were involved in the illusions, and why the illusions worked. Include information on how the nervous system was involved in your illusions.

Standardized Test Prep

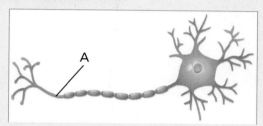
Choose the letter of the best answer.

1. A scientist studying the brain is studying part of the
   A peripheral nervous system.
   B somatic nervous system.
   C autonomic nervous system.
   D central nervous system.

Use the diagram below and your knowledge of science to answer Questions 2 and 3.

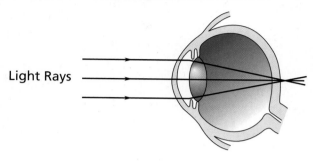

Light Rays

2. To correct the vision of the eye shown above, a lens would have to make the light rays
   F bend toward each other before they reach the eye's lens.
   G spread out before they reach the eye's lens.
   H focus on the eye's lens.
   J focus behind the retina.

3. Which of the following correctly pairs the vision problem in the eye shown above with the proper corrective lens?
   A farsightedness; convex lens
   B farsightedness; concave lens
   C nearsightedness; convex lens
   D nearsightedness; concave lens

4. The brain stem is involved in controlling
   F breathing.
   G the ability to learn.
   H movement of skeletal muscles.
   J balance.

5. You can infer that a person who has lost his or her sense of smell is also likely to have a poor
   A sense of balance.
   B sense of touch.
   C sense of taste.
   D sense of hearing.

Constructed Response

6. Outline the path of the reflex action that takes place when you step on a tack. What is the advantage of the nerve impulse not needing to go through the brain before action is taken?

Chapter 7

The Endocrine System and Reproduction

The **BIG Idea**

Regulation and Reproduction

Q How do the endocrine and reproductive systems work together?

Identical twins result when a single fertilized egg splits and forms two embryos.

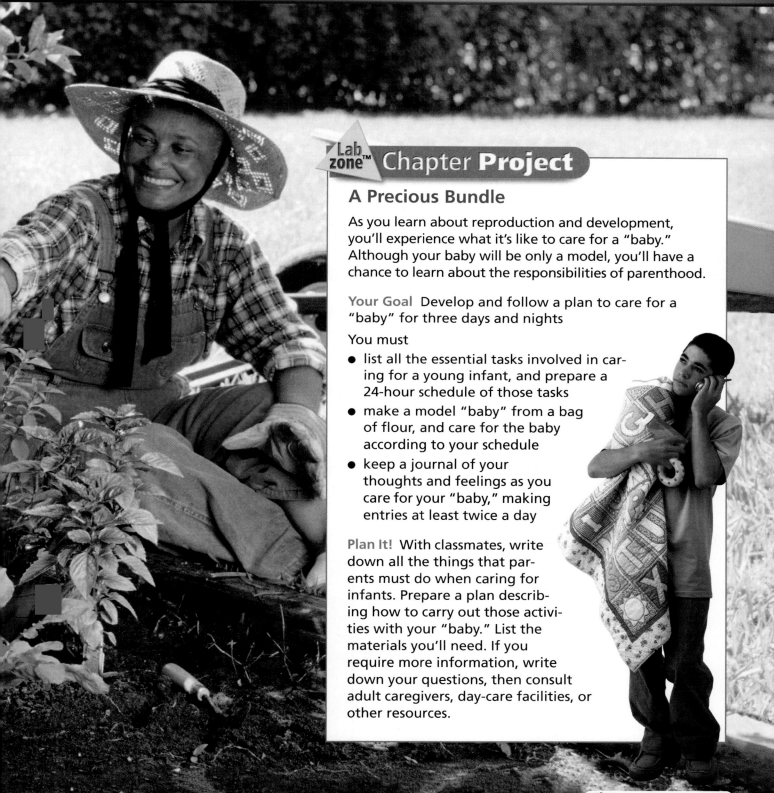

Discovery
CHANNEL
SCHOOL™

The Endocrine System and Reproduction
▶ **Video Preview**
Video Field Trip
Video Assessment

Lab zone™ Chapter **Project**

A Precious Bundle

As you learn about reproduction and development, you'll experience what it's like to care for a "baby." Although your baby will be only a model, you'll have a chance to learn about the responsibilities of parenthood.

Your Goal Develop and follow a plan to care for a "baby" for three days and nights

You must

● list all the essential tasks involved in caring for a young infant, and prepare a 24-hour schedule of those tasks

● make a model "baby" from a bag of flour, and care for the baby according to your schedule

● keep a journal of your thoughts and feelings as you care for your "baby," making entries at least twice a day

Plan It! With classmates, write down all the things that parents must do when caring for infants. Prepare a plan describing how to carry out those activities with your "baby." List the materials you'll need. If you require more information, write down your questions, then consult adult caregivers, day-care facilities, or other resources.

The Endocrine System

Reading Preview

Key Concepts
- How does the endocrine system control body processes?
- What are the endocrine glands?
- How does negative feedback control hormone levels?

Key Terms
- endocrine gland
- hormone
- target cell
- hypothalamus
- pituitary gland
- negative feedback

Target Reading Skill
Relating Cause and Effect As you read, identify the effects of pituitary hormones. Write the information in a graphic organizer like the one below.

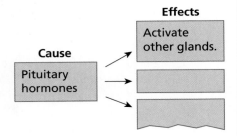

Cause

Pituitary hormones

Effects

Activate other glands.

Discover **Activity**

What's the Signal?

1. Stand up and move around the room until your teacher says "Freeze!" Then, stop moving immediately. Stay perfectly still until your teacher says "Start!" Then, begin moving again.
2. Anyone who moves between the "Freeze!" command and the "Start!" command has to leave the game.
3. When only one person is left, that person wins.

Think it Over
Inferring Why is it important for players in this game to respond to signals? What types of signals does the human body use?

Imagine that you are trapped in a damp, dark dungeon. Somewhere near you is a deep pit with water at the bottom. Overhead swings a pendulum with a razor-sharp edge. With each swing, the pendulum lowers closer and closer to your body.

The main character in Edgar Allan Poe's story "The Pit and the Pendulum" finds himself in that very situation. Here is his reaction: "A fearful idea now suddenly drove the blood in torrents upon my heart. . . . I at once started to my feet, trembling convulsively in every fibre. . . . Perspiration burst from every pore, and stood in cold, big beads upon my forehead."

Poe's character is terrified. When people are badly frightened, their bodies react in the ways that the character describes. These physical reactions, such as sweating and rapid heartbeat, are caused mainly by the body's endocrine system.

THE STORIES OF
EDGAR ALLAN POE

Hormones and the Endocrine System

The human body has two systems that regulate its activities, the nervous system and the endocrine system. The nervous system regulates most activities by sending nerve impulses throughout the body. **The endocrine system produces chemicals that control many of the body's daily activities. The endocrine system also regulates long-term changes such as growth and development.**

The endocrine system is made up of glands. A gland is an organ that produces or releases a chemical. Some glands, such as those that produce saliva and sweat, release their chemicals into tiny tubes. The tubes deliver the chemicals to a specific location within the body or to the skin's surface.

Unlike sweat glands, the glands of the endocrine system do not have delivery tubes. **Endocrine glands** (EN duh krin) produce and release their chemical products directly into the bloodstream. The blood then carries those chemicals throughout the body.

Hormones The chemical product of an endocrine gland is called a **hormone.** Hormones turn on, turn off, speed up, or slow down the activities of different organs and tissues. You can think of a hormone as a chemical messenger. Hormones are carried throughout the body by the blood. Therefore, hormones can regulate activities in tissues and organs that are not close to the glands that produce them.

FIGURE 1
Endocrine Control
The endocrine system controls the body's response to an exciting situation such as a roller-coaster ride. Endocrine glands also regulate the changes that occur as a baby grows.
Applying Concepts *What are the substances produced by endocrine glands called?*

Hormone Production What causes the release of hormones? Often, nerve impulses from the brain make that happen. Suppose, for example, a person sees a deadly, knife-edged pendulum. Nerve impulses travel from the person's eyes to the brain. The brain interprets the information and then sends an impulse to an endocrine gland. That gland, in turn, releases the hormone adrenaline into the bloodstream. Adrenaline immediately makes the heart rate and breathing rate increase.

Hormone Action In contrast to the body's response to a nerve impulse, hormones usually cause a slower, but longer-lasting, response. For example, the brain sends a signal to an endocrine gland to release adrenaline into the bloodstream. When the adrenaline reaches the heart, it makes the heart beat more rapidly. The heart continues to race until the amount of adrenaline in the blood drops to a normal level.

Target Cells When a hormone enters the bloodstream, it affects some organs but not others. Why? The answer lies in the hormone's chemical structure. A hormone interacts only with specific target cells. **Target cells** are cells that recognize the hormone's chemical structure. A hormone and its target cell fit together the way a key fits into a lock. Hormones will travel through the bloodstream until they find the "lock"— or particular cell type—that they fit.

 **Reading Checkpoint** What is a target cell?

Functions of Endocrine Glands

Each endocrine gland releases different hormones and thus controls different processes. **The endocrine glands include the hypothalamus, pituitary, thyroid, parathyroid, adrenal, thymus, and pancreas. They also include the ovaries in females and testes in males.** Figure 2 shows the locations of the endocrine glands and describes some activities they control.

The Hypothalamus The nervous system and the endocrine system work together. The **hypothalamus** (hy poh THAL uh mus), a tiny part of the brain near the middle of your head, is the link between the two systems. Nerve messages controlling sleep, hunger, and other basic body processes come from the hypothalamus. The hypothalamus also produces hormones that control other endocrine glands and organs. The hypothalamus plays a major role in maintaining homeostasis because of the nerve impulses and hormones it produces.

Lab zone **Skills Activity**

Making Models
Make a model that shows a hormone and a target cell that the hormone affects. Your model should show how the structures of the hormone and target cell enable the two to fit together. Make your model from materials such as construction paper, pipe cleaners, or modeling clay. When you have finished your model, write an explanation of how it shows the relationship between a hormone and its target cell.

FIGURE 2

Glands of the Endocrine System

Each of the endocrine glands has an important regulatory role in the body. Note the location of each gland and the functions of the hormones it produces.

Hypothalamus
The hypothalamus links the nervous and endocrine systems and controls the pituitary gland.

Thyroid Gland
This gland controls the release of energy from food molecules inside cells.

Pituitary Gland
The pituitary gland controls other endocrine glands and regulates growth, blood pressure, and water balance.

Parathyroid Glands
These tiny glands regulate the amount of calcium in the blood.

Thymus Gland
Hormones from this gland help the immune system develop during childhood.

Pancreas
The pancreas produces the hormones insulin and glucagon, which control the level of glucose in the blood.

Adrenal Glands
These glands release several hormones. Adrenaline triggers the body's response to emergency situations. Other hormones affect salt and water balance in the kidneys and sugar in the blood.

Testes
The testes release the sex hormone testosterone, which controls changes in a male's body and regulates sperm production.

Ovaries
The ovaries release female sex hormones. Estrogen controls changes in a female's body. Estrogen and progesterone trigger egg development.

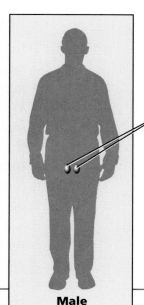

Female

Male

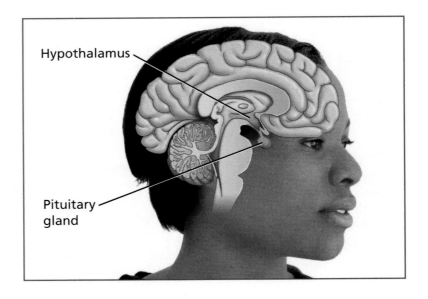

Hypothalamus

Pituitary gland

The Pituitary Gland Just below the hypothalamus is an endocrine gland about the size of a pea. The **pituitary gland** (pih TOO ih tehr ee) communicates with the hypothalamus to control many body activities. In response to nerve impulses or hormone signals from the hypothalamus, the pituitary gland releases its hormones. Some of those hormones act as an "on" switch for other endocrine glands. For example, one pituitary hormone signals the thyroid gland to produce hormones. Other pituitary hormones control body activities directly. Growth hormone regulates growth from infancy to adulthood. Another pituitary hormone directs the kidneys to regulate the amount of water in the blood.

 **Reading Checkpoint** What causes the pituitary gland to release hormones?

Negative Feedback

In some ways, the endocrine system works like a heating system. Suppose you set a thermostat at 20°C. If the temperature falls below 20°C, the thermostat signals the furnace to turn on. When the furnace heats the area to the proper temperature, information about the warm conditions "feeds back" to the thermostat. The thermostat then gives the furnace a signal that turns the furnace off. The type of signal used in a heating system is called **negative feedback** because the system is turned off by the condition it produces.

The endocrine system often uses negative feedback to maintain homeostasis. **Through negative feedback, when the amount of a particular hormone in the blood reaches a certain level, the endocrine system sends signals that stop the release of that hormone.**

You can see an example of negative feedback in Figure 4. Like a thermostat in a cool room, the endocrine system senses when there's not enough thyroxine in the blood. Thyroxine is a thyroid hormone that controls how much energy is available to cells. When there's not enough energy available, the hypothalamus signals the pituitary gland to release thyroid-stimulating hormone (TSH). That hormone signals the thyroid gland to release thyroxine. When the amount of thyroxine reaches the right level, the endocrine system signals the thyroid gland to stop releasing thyroxine.

 **Reading Checkpoint** **How is thyroxine involved in negative feedback?**

Go Online
active art
For: Negative Feedback activity
Visit: PHSchool.com
Web Code: cep-4071

Hypothalamus senses cells need more energy.

Thyroid stops producing thyroxine.

Pituitary releases TSH.

Pituitary stops producing TSH.

Thyroid produces thyroxine.

Hypothalamus senses cells have enough energy.

FIGURE 4
Negative Feedback
The release of the hormone thyroxine is controlled through negative feedback. When enough thyroxine is present, the system signals the thyroid gland to stop releasing the hormone. *Predicting What happens when the amount of thyroxine becomes too low?*

Section ❶ Assessment

Target Reading Skill

Relating Cause and Effect For Question 2, refer to your graphic organizer about the pituitary gland.

Reviewing Key Concepts

1. a. Identifying What is the role of the endocrine system?
   b. Explaining How does adrenaline affect the heart?
   c. Predicting What could happen if your body continued to release adrenaline into your bloodstream, and the amount of adrenaline did not return to normal?
2. a. Listing List the endocrine glands.
   b. Summarizing How do the hypothalamus and the pituitary gland interact?

   c. Relating Cause and Effect Explain how the hypothalamus indirectly controls growth from infancy to adulthood.
3. a. Defining Define negative feedback.
   b. Applying Concepts How does negative feedback help to maintain homeostasis?

Writing in Science

Cause-and-Effect Paragraph Explain how the nervous system and endocrine system work together when adrenaline is released.

Modeling Negative Feedback

Problem

How can you model negative feedback?

Skills Focus

observing, making models, evaluating the design

Materials

- duct tape
- round balloon
- scissors
- rubber stopper
- string, 40 cm
- large plastic soda bottle (2 L) with bottom removed
- small plastic soda bottle (1 L)
- plastic tray
- water

Procedure

PART 1 Research and Investigate

1. Figure 1 shows how a flush toilet uses negative feedback to regulate the water level. In your notebook, describe which part of the process involves negative feedback.

FIGURE 2

FIGURE 1

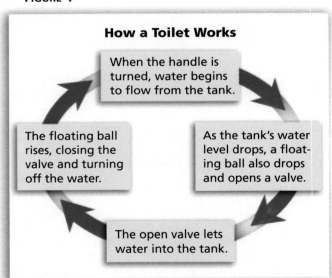

How a Toilet Works

When the handle is turned, water begins to flow from the tank.

As the tank's water level drops, a floating ball also drops and opens a valve.

The open valve lets water into the tank.

The floating ball rises, closing the valve and turning off the water.

PART 2 Design and Build

2. As you hold the open end of a balloon, push its closed end through the mouth of a small plastic bottle. Do not push the open end of the balloon into the bottle. Then, slide a straw partway into the bottle so that the air inside the bottle can escape as you blow up the balloon.

3. Partially blow up the balloon inside the bottle as shown in Figure 2. The partially inflated balloon should be about the size of a tennis ball. Remove the straw. Tie the balloon tightly, then push it into the bottle.

4. Place the large plastic bottle mouth to mouth with the small bottle. Tape the two bottles together. Make sure that the seal is waterproof.

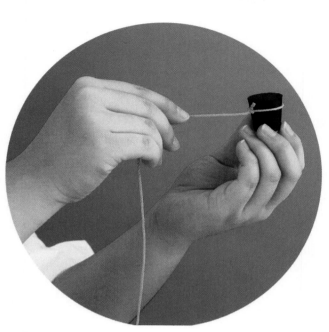

FIGURE 3

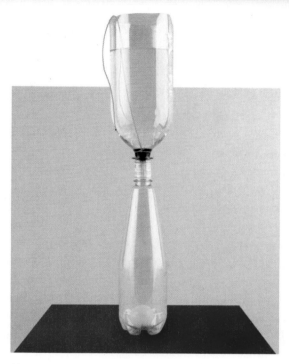

FIGURE 4

5. Tie one end of a piece of string around the top of a rubber stopper as shown in Figure 3.

6. Place the attached bottles on the tray with the smaller bottle on the bottom. Place the stopper loosely into the mouth of the larger bottle as shown in Figure 4.

7. While one partner holds the bottles upright, add water to the large bottle until it is about three fourths full. Then gently pull the string to remove the stopper. Watch what happens. Pay close attention to the following: What does the balloon do as water rises in the small bottle? Does the small bottle completely fill with water? Record your observations.

8. In your notebook, record which part of your device models negative feedback.

PART 3 Evaluate and Redesign

9. In the human endocrine system, negative feedback occurs as part of a cycle. With your partner, think of one or more ways that you could modify the model from Part 2 to show a cycle.

Analyze and Conclude

1. **Inferring** Summarize your research from Part 1 by describing an example of negative feedback.

2. **Observing** Describe the events you observed in Step 7.

3. **Making Models** In Step 7, which part of the process involves negative feedback? Explain your answer.

4. **Evaluating the Design** In a short paragraph, summarize the ideas you and your partner thought of in Step 9 to show that negative feedback can be part of a cycle.

Communicating

Suppose you are a TV health reporter preparing a program on human hormones. You need to do a 30-second segment on hormones and negative feedback. Write a script for your presentation. Include references to a model to help viewers understand how negative feedback works in the endocrine system.

The Male and Female Reproductive Systems

Reading Preview

Key Concepts
- What is sexual reproduction?
- What are the structures and functions of the male and female reproductive systems?
- What events occur during the menstrual cycle?

Key Terms
- egg • sperm • fertilization
- zygote • testis • testosterone
- scrotum • semen • penis
- ovary • estrogen
- fallopian tube • uterus
- vagina • menstrual cycle
- ovulation • menstruation

Target Reading Skill
Sequencing As you read, make a cycle diagram like the one below that shows the menstrual cycle. Write each event of the process in a separate circle.

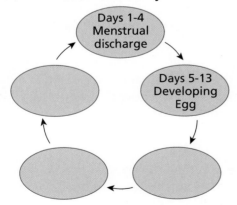

The Menstrual Cycle

Days 1-4 Menstrual discharge

Days 5-13 Developing Egg

Lab zone Discover Activity

What's the Big Difference?

1. Your teacher will provide prepared slides of eggs and sperm.
2. Examine each slide under the microscope, first under low power, then under high power. Be sure you view more than one example of each kind of cell.
3. Sketch and label each sample.

Think It Over

Observing What differences did you observe between sperm cells and egg cells? What general statement can you make about eggs and sperm?

Many differences between an adult animal and its young are controlled by the endocrine system. In humans, two endocrine glands—the ovaries and the testes—control many of the changes that occur as a child matures. These glands release hormones that cause the body to develop as a person grows older. They also produce sex cells that are part of sexual reproduction.

Hormones control growth and development.

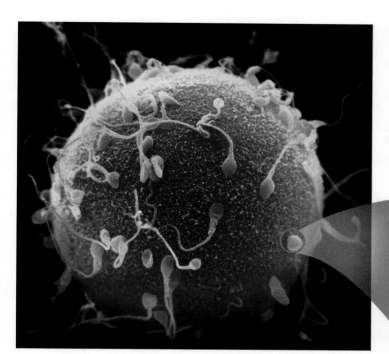

FIGURE 5
Egg and Sperm
An egg is one of the largest cells in the body. A sperm, which is much smaller than an egg, has a head (rounded end) and a tail that allows it to move. In the photograph on the left, sperm are swarming around the large egg. On the right, a sperm, which has been colored blue, has penetrated the egg.
Applying Concepts *What structure results when the sperm fertilizes the egg?*

Sexual Reproduction

You may find it hard to believe that you began life as a single cell. That single cell was produced by the joining of two other cells, an egg and a sperm. An **egg** is the female sex cell. A **sperm** is the male sex cell.

The joining of a sperm and an egg is called **fertilization.** Fertilization is an important part of sexual reproduction, the process by which male and female living things produce new individuals. **Sexual reproduction involves the production of eggs by the female and sperm by the male. The egg and sperm join together during fertilization.** When fertilization occurs, a fertilized egg, or **zygote,** is produced. Every one of the trillions of cells in your body is descended from the single cell that formed during fertilization.

Like other cells in the body, sex cells contain rod-shaped structures called chromosomes. Chromosomes (KROH muh sohmz) carry the information that controls inherited characteristics, such as eye color and blood type. Every cell in the human body that has a nucleus, except the sex cells, contains 46 chromosomes. Each sex cell contains half that number, or 23 chromosomes. During fertilization, the 23 chromosomes in a sperm join the 23 chromosomes in an egg. The result is a zygote with 46 chromosomes. The zygote contains all of the information needed to produce a new human being.

Reading Checkpoint What happens to the number of chromosomes when a male sex cell and a female sex cell join?

Male Reproductive System

The organs of the male reproductive system are shown in Figure 6. **The male reproductive system is specialized to produce sperm and the hormone testosterone. The structures of the male reproductive system include the testes, scrotum, and penis.**

The Testes The oval-shaped **testes** (TES teez) (singular *testis*) are the organs of the male reproductive system in which sperm are produced. The testes consist of clusters of hundreds of tiny coiled tubes and the cells between the tubes. Sperm are formed inside the tubes.

The testes also produce testosterone. **Testosterone** (tes TAHS tuh rohn) is a hormone that controls the development of physical characteristics in mature men. Some of those characteristics include facial hair, deepening of the voice, broadening of the shoulders, and the ability to produce sperm.

Notice in Figure 6 that the testes are located in an external pouch of skin called the **scrotum** (SKROH tum). The external location keeps the testes about 2°C to 3°C below 37°C, which is the usual temperature within the body. That temperature difference is important. Sperm need the slightly cooler conditions to develop normally.

FIGURE 6
The Male Reproductive System

In the male reproductive system, the testes produce sperm and the hormone testosterone.
Interpreting Diagrams *Trace the pathway of sperm in the male reproductive system. What structures does a sperm cell pass through before exiting the body?*

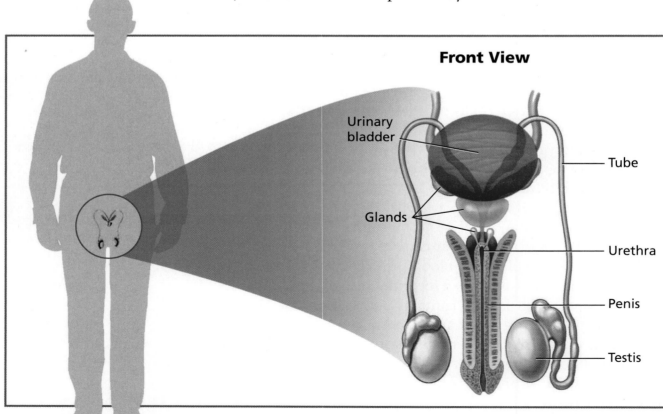

Front View

Urinary bladder

Tube

Glands

Urethra

Penis

Testis

Sperm Production The production of sperm cells begins in males at some point during the teenage years. Each sperm cell is composed of a head that contains chromosomes and a long, whiplike tail. Basically, a sperm cell is a tiny package of chromosomes that can swim.

The Path of Sperm Cells Once sperm cells form in the testes, they travel through other structures in the male reproductive system. During this passage, sperm mix with fluids produced by nearby glands. This mixture of sperm cells and fluids is called **semen** (SEE mun). Semen contains a huge number of sperm—about 5 to 10 million per drop! The fluids in semen provide an environment in which sperm are able to swim. Semen also contains nutrients that the moving sperm use as a source of energy.

Semen leaves the body through an organ called the **penis.** The tube in the penis through which the semen travels is called the urethra. Urine also leaves the body through the urethra. When semen passes through the urethra, however, muscles near the bladder contract. Those muscles prevent urine and semen from mixing.

 **Reading Checkpoint** What is the pouch of skin in which the testes are located?

Go Online
SciLINKS

For: Links on the reproductive system
Visit: www.SciLinks.org
Web Code: scn-0472

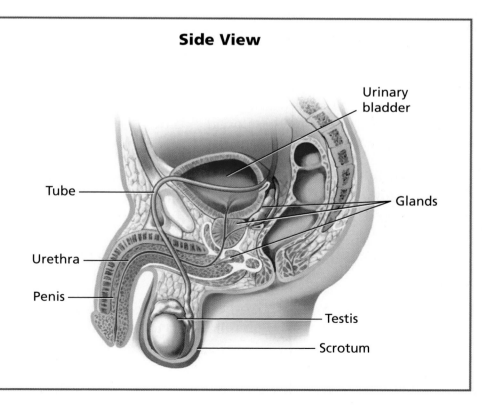

Side View

Urinary bladder

Tube

Glands

Urethra

Penis

Testis

Scrotum

Front View

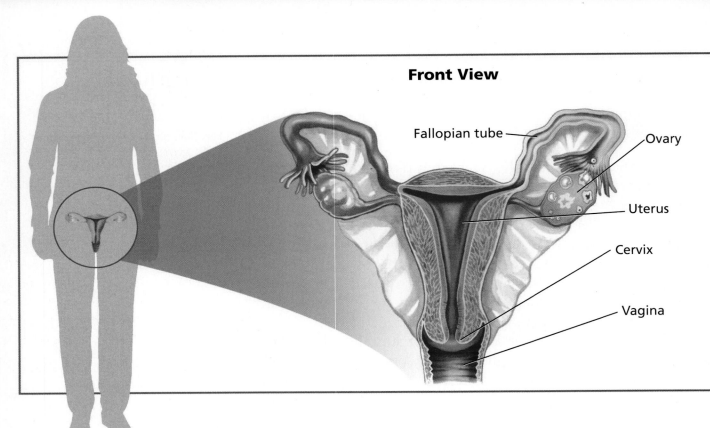

Fallopian tube

Ovary

Uterus

Cervix

Vagina

FIGURE 7
Female Reproductive System

In the female reproductive system, the two ovaries produce eggs and hormones such as estrogen.
Relating Cause and Effect *What changes does estrogen produce in a female's body?*

Female Reproductive System

Figure 7 shows the female reproductive system. **The role of the female reproductive system is to produce eggs and, if an egg is fertilized, to nourish a developing baby until birth. The organs of the female reproductive system include the ovaries, fallopian tubes, uterus, and vagina.**

The Ovaries The **ovaries** (OH vuh reez) are the female reproductive structures that produce eggs. The ovaries are located slightly below the waist, one ovary on each side of the body. The name for these organs comes from the Latin word *ova*, meaning "eggs."

Female Hormones Like the testes in males, the ovaries also are endocrine glands that produce hormones. One hormone, **estrogen** (ES truh jun), triggers the development of some adult female characteristics. For example, estrogen causes the hips to widen and the breasts to develop. Estrogen also plays a role in the process by which egg cells develop.

The Path of the Egg Cell Each ovary is located near a fallopian tube. The **fallopian tubes,** also called oviducts, are passageways for eggs as they travel from the ovary to the uterus. Each month, one of the ovaries releases a mature egg, which enters the nearest fallopian tube. Fertilization usually occurs within a fallopian tube.

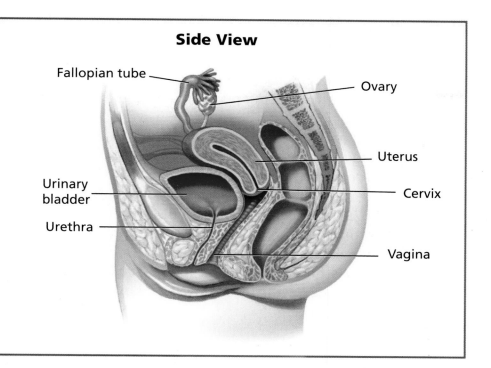

Side View

Fallopian tube

Ovary

Uterus

Cervix

Urinary bladder

Urethra

Vagina

The egg moves through the fallopian tube, which leads to the uterus. The **uterus** (YOO tur us) is a hollow muscular organ about the size of a pear. If an egg has been fertilized, it becomes attached to the wall of the uterus.

An egg that has not been fertilized starts to break down in the uterus. It leaves the uterus through an opening at the base of the uterus, called the cervix. The egg then enters the vagina. The **vagina** (vuh JY nuh) is a muscular passageway leading to the outside of the body. The vagina, or birth canal, is the passageway through which a baby leaves the mother's body.

 **Reading Checkpoint** What is the role of the fallopian tube?

The Menstrual Cycle

When the female reproductive system becomes mature, usually during the teenage years, there are about 400,000 undeveloped eggs in the ovaries. However, only about 500 of those eggs will actually leave the ovaries and reach the uterus. An egg is released about once a month in a mature woman's body. The monthly cycle of changes that occur in the female reproductive system is called the **menstrual cycle** (MEN stroo ul).

During the menstrual cycle, an egg develops in an ovary. At the same time, the uterus prepares for the arrival of an embryo. In this way, the menstrual cycle prepares the woman's body for pregnancy, which begins after fertilization.

Lab zone Skills **Activity**

Calculating

An egg is about 0.1 mm in diameter. In contrast, the head of a sperm is about 0.005 mm. Calculate how much bigger an egg is than a sperm.

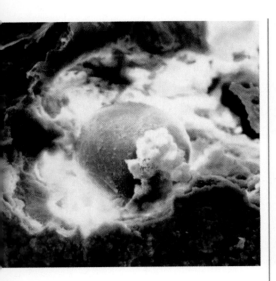

FIGURE 8
Release of an Egg
The ovary releases an egg, shown here in pink. The egg will then travel down the fallopian tube to the uterus. **Applying Concepts** *Through what opening does an unfertilized egg pass when leaving the uterus?*

Stages of the Menstrual Cycle Follow the stages of the menstrual cycle in Figure 9. Early in the menstrual cycle, an egg starts to mature in one of the ovaries. At the same time, the lining of the uterus begins to thicken. About halfway through a typical menstrual cycle, the mature egg is released from the ovary into a fallopian tube. The process in which an egg is released is called **ovulation** (ahv yuh LAY shun).

Once the egg is released, it can be fertilized for the next few days if sperm are present in the fallopian tube. If the egg is not fertilized, it begins to break down. The lining of the uterus also breaks down. The extra blood and tissue of the thickened lining pass out of the body through the vagina in a process called **menstruation** (men stroo AY shun). On average, menstruation lasts about four to six days. At the same time that menstruation takes place, a new egg begins to mature in the ovary, and the cycle continues.

Endocrine Control The menstrual cycle is controlled by hormones of the endocrine system. Hormones also trigger a girl's first menstruation. Many girls begin menstruation sometime between the ages of 10 and 14 years. Some girls start earlier, while others start later. Women continue to menstruate until about the age of 50. At around that age, the production of sex hormones drops. As a result, the ovaries stop releasing mature egg cells.

 **Reading Checkpoint** **How often is an egg released from an ovary?**

Math Analyzing Data

Changing Hormone Levels

A woman's hormone levels change throughout the menstrual cycle. The graph shows the levels of one female hormone, known as LH, during the menstrual cycle.

1. **Reading Graphs** What does the *y*-axis show?
2. **Interpreting Data** What is the level of LH on day 1? On day 17? On day 21?
3. **Calculating** What is the difference between LH levels on days 9 and 13?
4. **Drawing Conclusions** On what day does LH reach its highest level? What event takes place at about the same time?

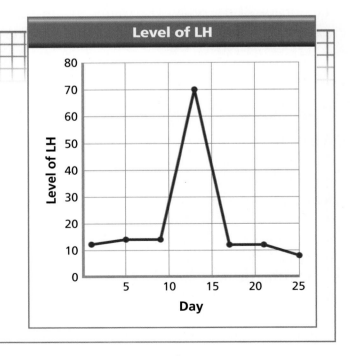

Level of LH

FIGURE 9

The Menstrual Cycle

During the menstrual cycle, the lining of the uterus builds up with extra blood and tissue. About halfway through a typical cycle, ovulation takes place. *Predicting* *What happens if the egg is not fertilized?*

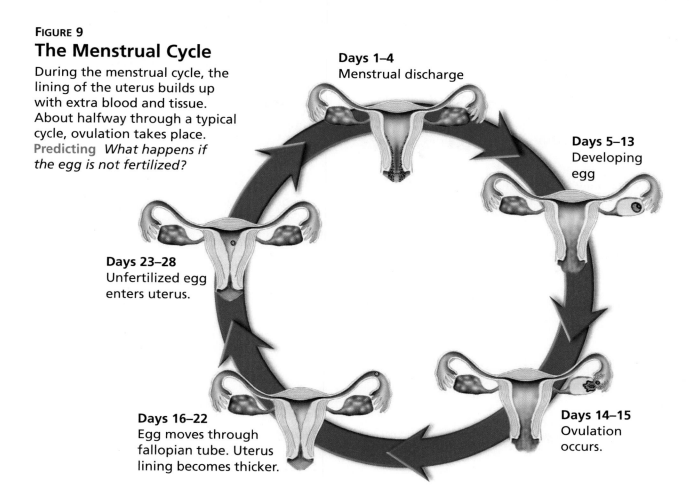

Days 1–4
Menstrual discharge

Days 5–13
Developing egg

Days 14–15
Ovulation occurs.

Days 16–22
Egg moves through fallopian tube. Uterus lining becomes thicker.

Days 23–28
Unfertilized egg enters uterus.

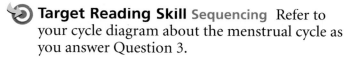

Section 2 Assessment

Target Reading Skill Sequencing Refer to your cycle diagram about the menstrual cycle as you answer Question 3.

Reviewing Key Concepts

1. **a.** Reviewing What is fertilization?
   b. Explaining Explain how fertilization produces a new individual.
   c. Comparing and Contrasting Contrast the number of chromosomes in sex cells and in a zygote. Explain why the zygote has the number of chromosomes that it does.
2. **a.** Listing List the structures of the male and female reproductive systems.
   b. Describing Describe the functions of the structures you named in Question 2a.

   c. Comparing and Contrasting In what ways are the functions of the ovaries and the testes similar? How do their functions differ?
3. **a.** Defining What is the menstrual cycle?
   b. Sequencing Events At what point in the menstrual cycle does ovulation occur?

Writing in Science

Explanatory Paragraph Write a paragraph explaining why the ovaries and testes are part of both the endocrine system and the reproductive system.

The Human Life Cycle

Reading Preview

Key Concepts
- What are the stages of human development that occur before birth?
- How is the developing embryo protected and nourished?
- What happens during childbirth?
- What changes occur from infancy to adulthood?

Key Terms
- embryo • fetus
- amniotic sac • placenta
- umbilical cord • adolescence
- puberty

Target Reading Skill
Building Vocabulary After you read Section 3, reread the paragraphs that contain definitions of Key Terms. Use all the information you have learned to write sentences using each Key Term.

Lab zone Discover **Activity**

How Many Ways Does a Child Grow?
1. Compare the two photographs. One shows a baby girl. The other shows the same girl at the age of five.
2. List the similarities you see. Also list the differences.
3. Compare your lists with those of your classmates.

Think It Over
Observing Based on your observations, list three physical changes that occur in early childhood.

An egg can be fertilized during the first few days after ovulation. When sperm are deposited into the vagina, the sperm move into and through the uterus and then into the fallopian tubes. If a sperm fertilizes an egg, pregnancy can occur. Then, the amazing process of human development begins.

Development Before Birth

A fertilized egg, or zygote, is no larger than the period at the end of this sentence. Yet after fertilization, the zygote undergoes changes that result in the formation of a new human. **The zygote develops first into an embryo and then into a fetus.** About nine months after fertilization, a baby is born.

FIGURE 10
Development of the Fetus
As a fetus grows and develops, it gains mass, increases in length, and develops all its body systems.
Applying Concepts *How large is a zygote?*

Zygote

Four-cell stage
48 hours after fertilization

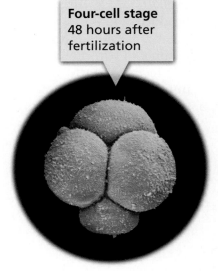

Zygote and Embryo After an egg and sperm join, the zygote moves down the fallopian tube toward the uterus. During this trip, which takes about four days, the zygote begins to divide. The original cell divides to make two cells. These two cells divide to make four, and so on. Eventually, the growing mass of hundreds of cells forms a hollow ball. The ball attaches to the lining of the uterus. From the two-cell stage through the eighth week of development, the developing human is called an **embryo** (EM bree oh).

Fetus From about the ninth week of development until birth, the developing human is called a **fetus** (FEE tus). Although at first the fetus is only the size of a whole walnut shell, it now looks more like a baby. Many internal organs have developed. The head is about half the body's total size. The fetus's brain is developing rapidly. The fetus also has dark eye patches, fingers, and toes. By the end of the third month, the fetus is about 9 centimeters long and has a mass of about 26 grams.

Between the fourth and sixth months, bones become distinct. A heartbeat can be heard with a stethoscope. A layer of soft hair grows over the skin. The arms and legs develop more completely. The fetus begins to move and kick, a sign that its muscles are growing. At the end of the sixth month, the mass of the fetus is approaching 700 grams. Its body is about 30 centimeters long.

The final three months prepare the fetus to survive outside the mother's body. The brain surface develops grooves and ridges. The lungs become ready to carry out the exchange of oxygen and carbon dioxide. The eyelids can open. The fetus doubles in length. Its mass may reach 3 kilograms or more.

 **Reading Checkpoint** At what point during development can a heartbeat be detected in a fetus?

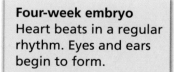

Four-week embryo Heart beats in a regular rhythm. Eyes and ears begin to form.

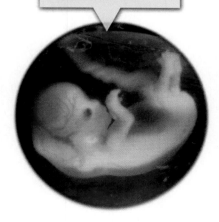

Eight-week embryo Heart has left and right chambers.

24-week fetus All parts of the eye are present. Fingerprints are forming.

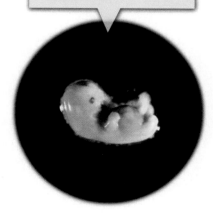

Protection and Nourishment

Just like you, the embryo and fetus need nourishment and protection to develop properly. Soon after the embryo attaches to the uterus, many changes take place. The hollow ball of cells grows inward. New membranes form. **The membranes and other structures that form during development protect and nourish the developing embryo, and later the fetus.**

Amniotic Sac One membrane surrounds the embryo and develops into a fluid-filled sac called the **amniotic sac** (am NEE aht ik). Locate the amniotic sac in Figure 11. The fluid in the amniotic sac cushions and protects the developing baby.

Placenta Another membrane also forms, which helps to form the placenta. The **placenta** (pluh SEN tuh) is the link between the embryo and the mother. In the placenta, the embryo's blood vessels are located next to the mother's blood vessels. Blood from the two systems does not mix, but many substances are exchanged between the two blood supplies. The embryo receives nutrients, oxygen, and other substances from the mother. It gives off carbon dioxide and other wastes.

FIGURE 11
The Placenta
The placenta provides a connection between the mother and the developing fetus. But the mother's and the fetus's blood vessels remain separate, as you can see in the close-up of the placenta.
Interpreting Diagrams *What structure carries nutrients and oxygen from the placenta to the fetus?*

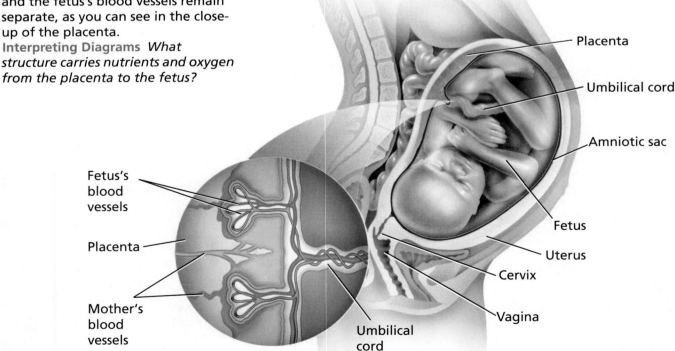

Placenta

Umbilical cord

Amniotic sac

Fetus

Uterus

Cervix

Vagina

Fetus's blood vessels

Placenta

Mother's blood vessels

Umbilical cord

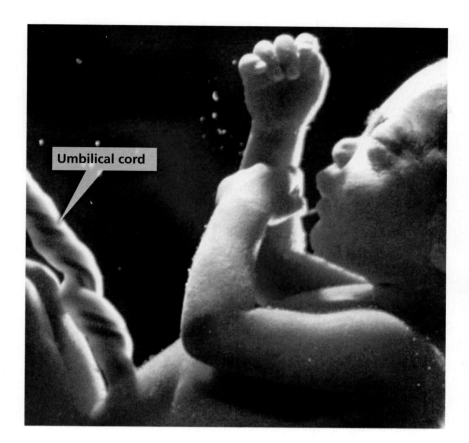

Umbilical cord

FIGURE 12
Eight-Month Fetus
This eight-month fetus is capable of surviving outside the mother. However, the fetus will remain protected within the uterus until birth, at approximately nine months.

Umbilical Cord A ropelike structure called the **umbilical cord** forms between the fetus and the placenta. It contains blood vessels that link the fetus to the mother. However, the two circulatory systems remain separated by a thin barrier.

The barrier that separates the fetus's and mother's blood prevents some diseases from spreading from the mother to the fetus. However, substances such as alcohol, chemicals in tobacco, and many other drugs can pass through the barrier to the fetus. For this reason, pregnant women should not smoke, drink alcohol, or take any drug without a doctor's approval.

 **Reading Checkpoint** How does a fetus obtain oxygen?

Birth

After about nine months of development inside the uterus, the baby is ready to be born. **The birth of a baby takes place in three stages—labor, delivery, and afterbirth.**

Labor During the first stage of birth, strong muscular contractions of the uterus begin. These contractions are called labor. The contractions cause the cervix to enlarge, eventually allowing the baby to fit through the opening. Labor may last from about 2 hours to more than 20 hours.

Lab zone Try This Activity

Way to Grow!

The table lists the average mass of a developing baby at different months of pregnancy.

Month of Pregnancy	Mass (grams)
1	0.02
2	2.0
3	26
4	150
5	460
6	640
7	1,500
8	2,300
9	3,200

1. Use a balance to identify an everyday object with a mass approximately equal to each mass listed in the table. You may need to use different balances to cover the range of masses listed.
2. Arrange the objects in order by month.

Making Models What did you learn by gathering these physical models?

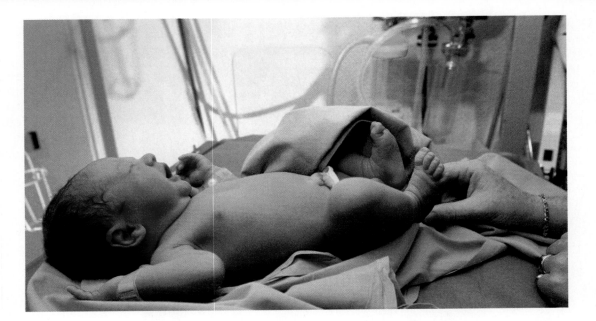

FIGURE 13
Birth
After about nine months of growth and development inside the uterus, a baby is born. You can see where the umbilical cord of this newborn was tied and cut.

Go Online
SCi*LINKS*™ NSTA

For: Links on before birth
Visit: www.SciLinks.org
Web Code: scn-0473

Delivery The second stage of birth is called delivery. During normal delivery, the baby is pushed completely out of the uterus, through the vagina, and out of the mother's body. The head usually comes out first. At this time, the baby is still connected to the placenta by the umbilical cord. Delivery of the baby usually takes less time than labor does—from several minutes to an hour or so.

Shortly after delivery, the umbilical cord is clamped, then cut about 5 centimeters from the baby's abdomen. Within seven to ten days, the remainder of the umbilical cord dries up and falls off, leaving a scar called the navel, or belly button.

Afterbirth About 15 minutes after delivery, the third stage of the birth process begins. Contractions of the uterus push the placenta and other membranes out of the uterus through the vagina. This stage, called afterbirth, is usually completed in less than an hour.

Birth and the Baby The birth process is stressful for both the baby and the mother. The baby is pushed and squeezed as it travels out of the mother's body. Muscle contractions put pressure on the placenta and umbilical cord. This pressure briefly decreases the baby's supply of oxygen.

In response to the changes, the baby's endocrine system releases adrenaline. The baby's heart rate increases. Within a few seconds of delivery, the baby begins breathing with a cry or a cough. This action helps rid the lungs of fluid and fills them with air. The newborn's heart rate then slows to a steady pace. Blood travels to the lungs and picks up oxygen from the air that the baby breathes in. The newborn's cry helps it adjust to the changes in its surroundings.

Multiple Births The delivery of more than one baby from a single pregnancy is called a multiple birth. In the United States, about 1 out of every 30 babies born each year is a twin. Multiple births of more than two babies, such as triplets and quadruplets, occur less frequently than do twin births.

There are two types of twins: identical twins and fraternal twins. Identical twins develop from a single fertilized egg, or zygote. Early in development, the embryo splits into two identical embryos. The two embryos have identical inherited traits and are the same sex. Fraternal twins develop when two eggs are released from the ovary and are fertilized by two different sperm. Fraternal twins are no more alike than any other brothers or sisters. Fraternal twins may or may not be the same sex.

 **What are the two types of twins?**

FIGURE 14
Twins
Identical twins (left) develop from the same fertilized egg. They share identical characteristics. Fraternal twins (right) develop from two different fertilized eggs. **Applying Concepts** *Why can fraternal twins be different sexes while identical twins cannot?*

Identical Twins

A sperm fertilizes a single egg.

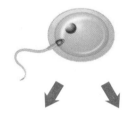

The single egg splits and forms two identical embryos.

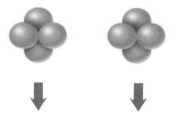

Identical twins result.

Fraternal Twins

Two different sperm fertilize two eggs.

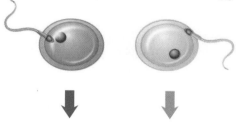

Each of the eggs develops into an embryo.

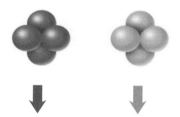

Fraternal twins result.

▲ **Infancy**

▲ **Early childhood**

▲ **Childhood**

FIGURE 15
Development
You can see the changes in development from infancy through adolescence.
Applying Concepts *What mental development takes place during childhood?*

DISCOVERY
CHANNEL
SCHOOL

The Endocrine System and Reproduction

Video Preview
▶ Video Field Trip
Video Assessment

Growth and Development

What can a newborn baby do? You might say "Not much!" A newborn can perform only simple actions, such as crying, sucking, yawning, and blinking. You can do a lot more, from playing sports to solving math problems. Many changes have taken place in you that allow you to do these things. **The changes that take place between infancy and adulthood include physical changes, such as an increase in size and coordination. They also include mental changes, such as the ability to communicate and solve complex problems.**

Infancy During infancy—the first two years of life—babies undergo many changes and learn to do many things. A baby's shape and size change greatly. When a baby is born, its head makes up about one fourth of its body length. As the infant develops, its head grows more slowly, and its body, legs, and arms begin to catch up. Its nervous and muscular systems become better coordinated. After about 3 months, it can hold its head up and reach for objects. At about 7 months, most infants can move around by crawling. Somewhere between 10 and 16 months, most infants begin to walk by themselves.

You may think that babies display feelings mostly by crying. But young infants can show pleasure by smiling and laughing. Sometime between the ages of one and three years, many children speak their first word. By the end of two years, children can do many things for themselves, such as understand simple directions, feed themselves, and play with toys.

▲ Early adolescence

▲ Adolescence

Childhood Infancy ends and childhood begins at about two years of age. Throughout childhood, children continue to grow. They become taller and heavier as their bones and muscles increase in size. They become more coordinated as they practice skills such as walking, using a pencil, and playing games.

As they develop, children show a growing curiosity and increasing mental abilities. Language skills improve rapidly. For example, most four-year-olds can carry on conversations. With the help of family members and teachers, children learn to read and to solve problems. Over time, children learn to make friends, care about others, and behave responsibly.

Adolescence The stage of development during which children become adults physically and mentally is called **adolescence** (ad ul ES uns). Adolescents gradually become able to think like adults and take on adult responsibilities. The bodies of adolescents also undergo specific physical changes.

Sometime between the ages of about 9 and 15 years, girls and boys enter puberty. **Puberty** (PYOO bur tee) is the period of sexual development in which the body becomes able to reproduce. In girls, hormones produced by the pituitary gland and the ovaries control the physical changes of puberty. The sex organs develop. Ovulation and menstruation begin. The breasts enlarge, and the hips start to widen. In boys, hormones from the testes and the pituitary gland govern the changes. The sex organs develop, and sperm production begins. The voice deepens. Hair appears on the face and chest.

Lab zone **Try This Activity**

Teenagers in Ads
In this activity, you will examine an ad taken from a teen magazine.

1. Examine an ad that shows one or more teenagers. Read the words and examine the pictures.
2. Think about how the ad portrays teenagers. How do they look and act? How accurate is this "picture" of teenagers?

Drawing Conclusions How does this ad try to influence people your age? Do you think the ad is effective? Explain your opinion.

Adulthood The mental and emotional growth of adolescence continues after puberty ends. It is difficult to say when adolescence ends and adulthood begins. And adults, like adolescents, continue to learn new things.

After about the age of 30, a process known as aging begins. As people age, the skin becomes wrinkled and muscle strength decreases. The eyes may lose their ability to focus on close objects, and hair may lose its coloring. Aging becomes more noticeable between the ages of 40 and 65. During this period, women stop menstruating and ovulating. Men usually continue to produce sperm throughout their lives. However, as men become older, the number of sperm they produce decreases.

The effects of aging can be slowed if people follow sensible diets and good exercise plans. With the help of such healthy behaviors, more and more adults remain active throughout their lives. In addition, older people have learned a lot from their experiences. Because of this learning, many older people have a great deal of wisdom. Older adults can share their knowledge and experience with younger people.

FIGURE 16
Adulthood
Young adults often enjoy helping older adults.

 **Reading Checkpoint** What are the physical effects of aging?

Section 3 Assessment

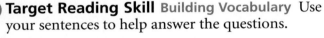 **Target Reading Skill** Building Vocabulary Use your sentences to help answer the questions.

Reviewing Key Concepts

1. a. Identifying What three steps of development does a fertilized egg go through before birth?
  b. Describing What happens to the fetus during the final three months of development?
  c. Relating Cause and Effect Explain why a baby born before the seventh month of development needs special care to survive.

2. a. Reviewing What is the general function of the membranes that surround a fetus?
  b. Explaining What is the specific function of the placenta?
  c. Relating Cause and Effect Why is it dangerous for a pregnant woman to drink alcohol or to smoke cigarettes?

3. a. Listing What are the three stages of birth?
  b. Summarizing What happens during labor?

4. a. Identifying Identify two general kinds of change that occur between infancy and adulthood. Give an example of each.
  b. Describing Describe what happens during puberty.
  c. Making Judgments Is puberty the most important process that occurs during adolescence? Explain your answer.

Lab zone **At-Home Activity**

Parenting Skills Interview a family member about what is involved in being a parent. Ask the following questions: What skills do parents need? What are some of the rewards of parenthood? What are some of the challenges?

Growing Up

Problem

How do the proportions of the human body change during development?

Skills Focus

calculating, predicting

Procedure

1. Examine the diagram below. Notice that the figures are drawn against a graph showing percentages. You can use this diagram to determine how the lengths of major body parts compare to each figure's height. Make a data table in which to record information about each figure's head size and leg length.

2. Look at Figure D. You can use the graph to estimate that the head is about 15 percent of the figure's full height. Record that number in your data table.

3. Examine Figures A through C. Determine the percentage of the total height that the head makes up. Record your results.

4. Next, compare the length of the legs to the total body height for Figures A through D. Record your results. (*Hint*: Figure A shows the legs folded. You will need to estimate the data for that figure.)

Analyze and Conclude

1. **Calculating** How do the percentages for head size and leg length change from infancy to adulthood?

2. **Predicting** If you made a line graph using the data in the diagram, what would be on the horizontal axis? On the vertical axis? What additional information could you gain from this line graph?

3. **Communicating** What can you infer about the rate at which different parts of the body grow? Write a paragraph in which you discuss the answer to this question.

Design an Experiment

Make a prediction about the relationship between the circumference of the head compared with body height. Then, design an experiment to test your prediction, using people for test subjects. *Obtain your teacher's permission before carrying out your investigation.*

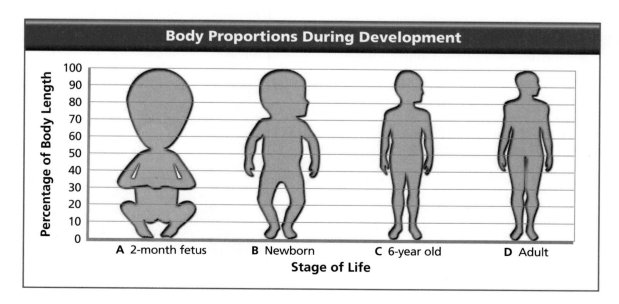

Body Proportions During Development

Percentage of Body Length

A 2-month fetus   B Newborn   C 6-year old   D Adult

Stage of Life

The **BIG Idea** **Regulation and Reproduction** The endocrine system releases hormones necessary for the development of male and female sex cells, which are needed for reproduction.

1 The Endocrine System

Key Concepts

- The endocrine system produces chemicals that control many of the body's daily activities as well as growth and development.

- The endocrine glands include the pituitary, hypothalamus, thyroid, parathyroid, adrenal, thymus, and pancreas. They include ovaries in females and testes in males.

- Through negative feedback, when the amount of a particular hormone in the blood reaches a certain level, the endocrine system sends signals that stop the release of that hormone.

Key Terms

- endocrine gland • hormone • target cell
- hypothalamus • pituitary gland
- negative feedback

2 The Male and Female Reproductive Systems

Key Concepts

- Sexual reproduction involves the production of eggs by the female and sperm by the male. The egg and sperm join during fertilization.

- The male reproductive system produces sperm and the hormone testosterone. Its structures include the testes, scrotum, and penis.

- The female reproductive system produces eggs and nourishes a developing baby until birth. Its structures include the ovaries, fallopian tubes, uterus, and vagina.

- During the menstrual cycle, an egg develops in an ovary. At the same time, the uterus prepares for the arrival of a fertilized egg.

Key Terms

- egg • sperm • fertilization • zygote • testis
- testosterone • scrotum • semen • penis
- ovary • estrogen • fallopian tube • uterus
- vagina • menstrual cycle • ovulation
- menstruation

3 The Human Life Cycle

Key Concepts

- The zygote develops first into an embryo and then into a fetus.

- The membranes and other structures that form during development protect and nourish the developing embryo and then the fetus.

- The birth of a baby takes place in three stages—labor, delivery, and afterbirth.

- The changes that take place between infancy and adulthood include physical changes, such as an increase in size and coordination, and mental changes, such as the ability to communicate and solve complex problems.

Key Terms

embryo
fetus
amniotic sac
placenta
umbilical cord
adolescence
puberty

Review and Assessment

Organizing Information

Sequencing Copy the flowchart showing the main stages that occur between fertilization and birth onto a sheet of paper. Then, complete it and add a title. (For more on Sequencing, see the Skills Handbook.)

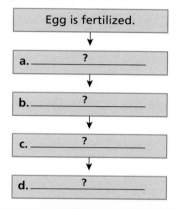

Egg is fertilized.
↓
a. _____ ?
↓
b. _____ ?
↓
c. _____ ?
↓
d. _____ ?

Reviewing Key Terms

Choose the letter of the best answer.

1. The structure that links the nervous system and the endocrine system is the
   a. thyroid gland.
   b. target cell.
   c. umbilical cord.
   d. hypothalamus.

2. The male sex cell is called the
   a. testis.
   b. sperm.
   c. egg.
   d. ovary.

3. The release of an egg from an ovary is known as
   a. ovulation.
   b. fertilization.
   c. menstruation.
   d. negative feedback.

4. The structure that protects and cushions the embryo is called the
   a. umbilical cord.
   b. scrotum.
   c. amniotic sac.
   d. ovary.

5. Sex organs develop rapidly during
   a. fertilization.
   b. ovulation.
   c. puberty.
   d. menstruation.

If the statement is true, write *true*. If it is false, change the underlined word or words to make the statement true.

6. A <u>target cell</u> recognizes a hormone's chemical structure.

7. The joining of a sperm and an egg is called <u>menstruation</u>.

8. A fluid that contains sperm is <u>testosterone</u>.

9. A <u>fallopian tube</u> is the passageway through which an egg travels from the ovary to the uterus.

10. The <u>amniotic sac</u> contains blood vessels that link the fetus to the mother.

Writing in Science

Creative Writing Imagine you just found out that you have an identical twin who was raised in another country. Write a description of what you think your twin would be like. Be sure to include information about what your twin looks like, his or her interests, and unique characteristics of your twin.

DISCOVERY CHANNEL SCHOOL

The Endocrine System and Reproduction
Video Preview
Video Field Trip
▶ Video Assessment

Review and Assessment

Checking Concepts

11. What is the function of the pituitary gland?

12. When enough thyroxine has been released into the blood, what signal is sent to the thyroid gland? How is that signal sent?

13. Identify two functions of the testes.

14. Describe the path of an unfertilized egg, beginning with its release and ending when it leaves the body.

15. What changes occur in the uterus during the menstrual cycle?

16. How does a zygote form? What happens to the zygote about four days after it forms?

17. Describe how a fetus receives food and oxygen and gets rid of wastes.

18. List five changes that a 10-year-old boy should expect to happen during the next five years. Include physical and mental changes.

Thinking Critically

19. **Inferring** Study the diagram below. Then, suggest how the two hormones, glucagon and insulin, might work together to maintain homeostasis in the body.

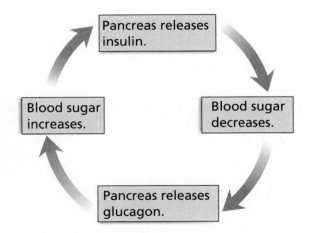

20. **Calculating** The average menstrual cycle is 28 days in length but can vary from 24 to 32 days. Ovulation usually occurs 14 days before the end of the cycle. How long after the start of a 24-day cycle will ovulation occur? A 32-day cycle?

21. **Comparing and Contrasting** Contrast the ways in which identical twins and fraternal twins form.

22. **Relating Cause and Effect** How can playing games help children develop important skills?

Applying Skills

Use the table to answer Questions 23–25.

The data table below shows how the length of a developing baby changes during pregnancy.

Length of Fetus

Week of Pregnancy	Average Length (mm)	Week of Pregnancy	Average Length (mm)
4	4	24	300
8	30	28	350
12	75	32	410
16	180	36	450
20	250	38	500

23. **Measuring** Use a metric ruler to mark each length on a piece of paper. During which four-week period did the greatest increase in length occur?

24. **Graphing** Graph the data by plotting time on the x-axis and length on the y-axis.

25. **Interpreting Data** At the twelfth week, a developing baby measures about 75 mm. By which week has the fetus grown to four times that length? Six times that length?

Lab zone Chapter Project

Performance Assessment Explain what you learned as you cared for your "baby." What did you learn about parenting that you didn't know before? Consider reading passages from your journal to the class.

Standardized Test Prep

Choose the letter of the best answer.

1. You are riding your bike when a small child suddenly darts out in front of you. Which of your endocrine glands is most likely to release a hormone in response to this situation?
   A pituitary gland
   B adrenal glands
   C thyroid gland
   D parathyroid gland

2. On day 10 of a woman's menstrual cycle, the egg is most likely
   F moving through the fallopian tube.
   G in the uterus.
   H in the ovary.
   J leaving the body.

Use the table below and your knowledge of science to answer Questions 3 and 4.

Number of Chromosomes in Body Cells of Various Animals	
Organism	**Chromosome Number**
Roundworm	2
Fruit Fly	8
Cricket	22
Mouse	40
Human	46
Pigeon	80

3. An egg cell produced by a female mouse probably contains
   A 20 chromosomes.
   B 40 chromosomes.
   C 60 chromosomes.
   D 80 chromosomes.

4. How many chromosomes will a pigeon zygote have?
   F 20
   G 40
   H 60
   J 80

5. A woman gives birth to twins that developed from a single fertilized egg that split early in development. Which of the following is a reasonable prediction that you can make about the twins?
   A They will be the same sex.
   B They will be different sexes.
   C They will not look alike.
   D They will have different inherited traits.

Constructed Response

6. What is negative feedback? Choose an example of a hormone, and describe in a general way how negative feedback regulates its release.

The Olympic Games

What event—

- **is the dream of athletes around the world?**
- **has the motto "faster, higher, stronger"?**
- **supports amateur sports?**

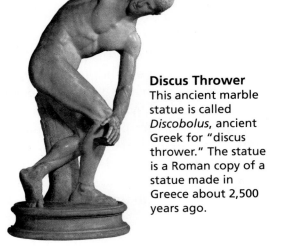

Discus Thrower
This ancient marble statue is called *Discobolus*, ancient Greek for "discus thrower." The statue is a Roman copy of a statue made in Greece about 2,500 years ago.

The Olympic games began more than 2,500 years ago in Olympia, Greece. For one day every four years, the best athletes in Greece gathered to compete. The games honored the Greek god Zeus. The ancient Greeks valued both physical and intellectual achievement. A winning athlete at the Olympic games was rewarded with a lifetime of honor and fame.

For more than a thousand years, the Greeks held the games at Olympia every four years. The games were discontinued in A.D. 394, when the Romans ruled Greece.

Centuries later, in the 1880s, Pierre de Coubertin, a Frenchman, convinced the United States and other nations to bring back the Olympic games. Coubertin hoped that the modern Olympics would promote world peace by bringing together athletes from all nations. The modern Olympics began in Athens in 1896.

Today the summer and winter Olympics alternate every two years. For several weeks, athletes from all around the world experience the excitement of competing against each other. Only a few know the joy of winning. But, all who participate learn about fair play, striving toward a goal, and becoming a little bit faster and stronger through training.

Olympic Torch, 2002
Here the flame burns in Salt Lake City, Utah. It's a symbol of the spirit of competition and fair play.

Sports in Ancient Greece

The ancient Greeks valued physical fitness as much as an educated mind. Men and boys exercised regularly by wrestling, sprinting, throwing the discus, and tossing the javelin. Greek philosophy taught that a sound mind and body created a well-balanced person. Greek art glorified the muscles and movement of the human body in magnificent sculptures and paintings.

The first recorded Olympic games were held in 776 B.C. That year a cook named Coroebus from Elis, Greece, won the only event in the games—a sprint of about 192 meters. The prize was a wreath of olive leaves. In ancient Greece, an olive wreath was the highest mark of honor.

Over the next 130 years, other events were added to the games, including longer running events, wrestling, chariot racing, boxing, and the pentathlon. *Pent-* comes from the Greek word meaning "five." A pentathlon included five competitions: a long jump, javelin toss, discus throw, foot race, and wrestling. Early records indicate that women were not allowed to compete in the games.

Ancient Greece
Rival city-states, such as Athens and Sparta, sent their best athletes to the games at Olympia.

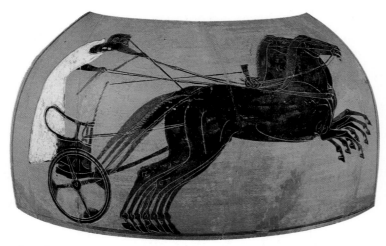

Amphora
Chariot racing became a popular sport in the ancient Olympics. This scene is painted on a Greek amphora, a pottery jar for olive oil or wine.

Social Studies Activity

The Olympics encourage peaceful competition among athletes from many nations. But political conflicts sometimes have disrupted or canceled the games. For example, the 1916 games were canceled because of World War I. Other Olympics are remembered for the achievements of certain athletes, such as Babe Didrikson in 1932. Find out what political events affected particular Olympics during the twentieth century. Or research outstanding athletes at different games. Report your findings to the class.

Jackie Joyner-Kersee
Jackie jumps to her second gold medal at the 1988 Olympic games.

Modern Olympic Games

At the 1988 Olympic games in Seoul, South Korea, Jackie Joyner-Kersee was one of the star athletes. She won two gold medals there. In total, between 1984 and 1996, she won six Olympic medals (three of them gold), making her one of the world's greatest athletes.

Jackie grew up in East St. Louis, Illinois, where she started running and jumping at age ten. Although she was a natural at the long jump, she wasn't a fast runner. But her coach, Mr. Fennoy, encouraged her. After her final Olympics, Jackie wrote an autobiography—a story of her life. Here is an excerpt from her book *A Kind of Grace*.

After school the boys' and girls' teams jogged to Lincoln Park's irregular-shaped track and makeshift long-jump pit. The track was a 36-inch-wide strip of black cinders sprinkled amid the rest of the dirt and grass. We called it the bridle path because that's what it looked like. We ran over, around and through the potholes, rocks, glass and tree limbs that littered the track. After practice, we jogged another two or three miles around the neighborhood to complete our workout.

In winter, when it was too cold to practice outside, we trained inside the Lincoln High building. Every afternoon after school and at 9:00 every Saturday morning, the team of twenty-five girls split into groups on the two floors and ran along the brown concrete corridors. When it was time for hurdling drills, Mr. Fennoy set up hurdles in the center of the hallway on the second floor, and put us through our paces. We sprinted and leaped past the doors to the math and science classrooms.

We ran to the end of the hall, turned around and repeated the drill in the opposite direction.

The running drills, exhausting as they were, eventually paid off. In 1977, between the ninth and tenth grade, I developed booster rockets and cut an astonishing four seconds off my 440 time. I surged to the front of the pack in practice heats. By the time we entered Lincoln High as tenth-graders, I was the fastest 440 runner on the team. The last was—at long last—first.

Language Arts Activity

What does Jackie mean by "the last was—at long last—first"? How did she get to be first? Some people say that Jackie was just a natural athlete. Jackie herself says, "I think it was my reward for all those hours of work on the bridle path, the neighborhood sidewalks and the schoolhouse corridors."

Think about a period in your life when you had to prepare for a math competition, a recital, a performance, a sports event, or other event. Write a short autobiographical sketch describing how you worked to improve your performance.

Yelena Yelesina
Yelena Yelesina of Russia won the women's high jump at the 2000 Olympics in Sydney, Australia. How much higher did she jump than the 1952 winner?

Women's High Jump	
Year	Height
1952	65.75
1960	72.75
1968	71.5
1976	76.0
1984	79.5
1992	79.5
2000	79.0

Olympic Records

To prepare for the Olympic games, top athletes train for years. Sometimes they even move to climates that will help them prepare to compete in their sports. Skiers, for example, might move to a mountain region where they can train year-round. Athletes also use the most advanced equipment available in their sport. This scientific approach to training has helped athletes set new records for speed, height, and distance. In addition, measurement tools such as timing clocks have become more precise. As a result, athletes can now break records by just a few hundredths of a second.

The table and graph at right show how the winning height in the women's high jump has changed over many Olympic games. Notice that the high jump measures height in inches.

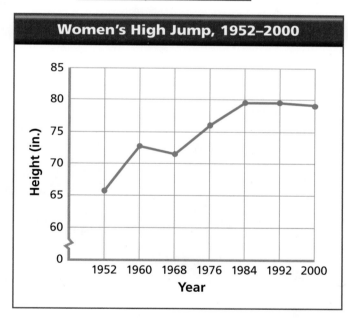

Women's High Jump, 1952–2000

Math Activity

The line graph above shows how the heights in the Olympic women's high jump have changed since 1952. Use the table at right, showing times for the men's 400-meter run, to create your own line graph.

How did the winning performance in the men's 400-meter run change over time? How does your graph differ from that of the women's high jump? Why do the graphs differ?

Men's 400-Meter Run	
Year	Time in Seconds
1952	45.90
1960	44.90
1968	43.86
1976	44.26
1984	44.27
1992	43.50
2000	43.84

High-Tech Training

Recent technology has made training for the Olympics a different process from that used in previous Olympic games. Today's high-tech equipment enables athletes to focus on specific aspects in their training.

One technology that is widely used today is video imaging. Olympic athletes such as figure skaters, gymnasts, and divers use video imaging. Using a video camera that links to a laptop computer, a coach can videotape an athlete practicing. Using software in the laptop, the coach and athlete can immediately replay a routine, like a dive, and discuss possible improvements. Some software allows the user to superimpose one video clip routine "on top" of another for comparison.

If you are a runner, you might use a watch with a chronometer, or timekeeper. But some athletes today use another new technology, sometimes called "wrist-top computers." These watches can measure an athlete's heart rate, speed, distance, and time. Many of these "mini machines" can also be connected to a computer so that athletes can compare their performances.

A third new technology, called a diagnostic system, tracks an athlete's constantly shifting body systems. Each training session can be adapted to provide enough—but not too much—of a workout. Electrodes are attached to the athlete's ankles, wrists, chest, and forehead. In 20 minutes, while the athlete is lying down, the system records and analyzes information, from heart rate and oxygen usage to how well the central nervous system, liver, and kidneys are functioning. These measurements can give all types of athletes an overall picture of their conditioning.

High-Tech Machines
The athlete on this workout machine can monitor her time, distance, speed, calories burned, heart rate, and other data (right). A transmitter attached to the chest sends data to a wrist-top computer that displays the athlete's heart rate and other data (above).

Science Activity

Athletes who are in the best shape often have very low resting heart and breathing rates. Some have resting heart rates below 40 bpm (beats per minute). Yet, while exercising, their heart and breathing rates can speed up to more than 170 bpm. Compare yourself to a top athlete.

1. In a sitting position, feel your pulse and count your heartbeats for 10 seconds. Multiply that number by 6 to get your resting bpm. Record the number. Next, count how many times you inhale and exhale in 30 seconds. Multiply that number by 2 to get your resting breathing rate. Record the data.

2. Walk up and down a staircase with at least 5 steps for 10 minutes without stopping. Keep your pace steady. As soon as the 10 minutes are up, measure your heart and breathing rates again. Record the data. **CAUTION:** *Do not do this part of the activity if you have any limiting physical and/or cardiovascular condition.*

3. What is your heartbeat range before and after exercise? How does that range compare to the top athlete described above? What is your breathing rate range?

Working Out

1. Warm-up
(5–10 minutes)
Slowly move the muscles to be used in the workout.

2. Stretch
(5–10 minutes)
Stretch the muscles to be used in the workout.

3. Workout
(20–45 minutes)
Do an activity such as walking, running, swimming, gymnastics, or riding a bicycle.

4. Cool-down
(5–10 minutes)
Move the muscles used in the workout at a reduced pace.

5. Stretch
(5–10 minutes)
Stretch the muscles used in the workout.

Tie It Together

Plan an Olympic Day!

Design a competition that can be held at your school. Decide the time, place, and kind of contests to hold. Remember that the ancient Greeks honored intellect as well as athletics. So you could include games that test the mind as well as the body.

Research the decathlon, pentathlon, heptathlon, and marathon in the ancient and modern Olympics. You could design your own pentathlon that includes athletic and nonathletic events.

To organize the Olympic day, you should

- set up the sports contests by measuring and marking the ground for each event

- find stopwatches, meter sticks, tape measures, and any necessary equipment

- locate or make prizes for first, second, and third place in each event

- enlist volunteers to compete in the events

- assign someone to take notes and to write a newspaper story on your Olympic day

Think Like a Scientist

Scientists have a particular way of looking at the world, or scientific habits of mind. Whenever you ask a question and explore possible answers, you use many of the same skills that scientists do. Some of these skills are described on this page.

Observing

When you use one or more of your five senses to gather information about the world, you are **observing.** Hearing a dog bark, counting twelve green seeds, and smelling smoke are all observations. To increase the power of their senses, scientists sometimes use microscopes, telescopes, or other instruments that help them make more detailed observations.

An observation must be an accurate report of what your senses detect. It is important to keep careful records of your observations in science class by writing or drawing in a notebook. The information collected through observations is called evidence, or data.

Inferring

When you interpret an observation, you are **inferring,** or making an inference. For example, if you hear your dog barking, you may infer that someone is at your front door. To make this inference, you combine the evidence—the barking dog—and your experience or knowledge—you know that your dog barks when strangers approach—to reach a logical conclusion.

Notice that an inference is not a fact; it is only one of many possible interpretations for an observation. For example, your dog may be barking because it wants to go for a walk. An inference may turn out to be incorrect even if it is based on accurate observations and logical reasoning. The only way to find out if an inference is correct is to investigate further.

Predicting

When you listen to the weather forecast, you hear many predictions about the next day's weather—what the temperature will be, whether it will rain, and how windy it will be. Weather forecasters use observations and knowledge of weather patterns to predict the weather. The skill of **predicting** involves making an inference about a future event based on current evidence or past experience.

Because a prediction is an inference, it may prove to be false. In science class, you can test some of your predictions by doing experiments. For example, suppose you predict that larger paper airplanes can fly farther than smaller airplanes. How could you test your prediction?

Activity

Use the photograph to answer the questions below.

Observing Look closely at the photograph. List at least three observations.

Inferring Use your observations to make an inference about what has happened. What experience or knowledge did you use to make the inference?

Predicting Predict what will happen next. On what evidence or experience do you base your prediction?

Classifying

Could you imagine searching for a book in the library if the books were shelved in no particular order? Your trip to the library would be an all-day event! Luckily, librarians group together books on similar topics or by the same author. Grouping together items that are alike in some way is called **classifying.** You can classify items in many ways: by size, by shape, by use, and by other important characteristics.

Like librarians, scientists use the skill of classifying to organize information and objects. When things are sorted into groups, the relationships among them become easier to understand.

Activity

Classify the objects in the photograph into two groups based on any characteristic you choose. Then use another characteristic to classify the objects into three groups.

Making Models

Have you ever drawn a picture to help someone understand what you were saying? Such a drawing is one type of model. A model is a picture, diagram, computer image, or other representation of a complex object or process. **Making models** helps people understand things that they cannot observe directly.

Scientists often use models to represent things that are either very large or very small, such as the planets in the solar system, or the parts of a cell. Such models are physical models—drawings or three-dimensional structures that look like the real thing. Other models are mental models—mathematical equations or words that describe how something works.

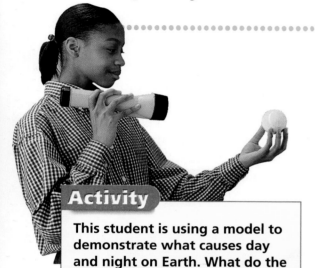

Activity

This student is using a model to demonstrate what causes day and night on Earth. What do the flashlight and the tennis ball in the model represent?

Communicating

Whenever you talk on the phone, write a report, or listen to your teacher at school, you are communicating. **Communicating** is the process of sharing ideas and information with other people. Communicating effectively requires many skills, including writing, reading, speaking, listening, and making models.

Scientists communicate to share results, information, and opinions. Scientists often communicate about their work in journals, over the telephone, in letters, and on the Internet.

They also attend scientific meetings where they share their ideas with one another in person.

Activity

On a sheet of paper, write out clear, detailed directions for tying your shoe. Then exchange directions with a partner. Follow your partner's directions exactly. How successful were you at tying your shoe? How could your partner have communicated more clearly?

Making Measurements

By measuring, scientists can express their observations more precisely and communicate more information about what they observe.

Measuring in SI

The standard system of measurement used by scientists around the world is known as the International System of Units, which is abbreviated as SI (**Système International d'Unités,** in French). SI units are easy to use because they are based on powers of 10. Each unit is ten times larger than the next smallest unit and one tenth the size of the next largest unit. The table lists the prefixes used to name the most common SI units.

Common SI Prefixes		
Prefix	Symbol	Meaning
kilo-	k	1,000
hecto-	h	100
deka-	da	10
deci-	d	0.1 (one tenth)
centi-	c	0.01 (one hundredth)
milli-	m	0.001 (one thousandth)

Length To measure length, or the distance between two points, the unit of measure is the **meter (m).** The distance from the floor to a doorknob is approximately one meter. Long distances, such as the distance between two cities, are measured in kilometers (km). Small lengths are measured in centimeters (cm) or millimeters (mm). Scientists use metric rulers and meter sticks to measure length.

Common Conversions	
1 km	=	1,000 m
1 m	=	100 cm
1 m	=	1,000 mm
1 cm	=	10 mm

Activity

The larger lines on the metric ruler in the picture show centimeter divisions, while the smaller, unnumbered lines show millimeter divisions. How many centimeters long is the shell? How many millimeters long is it?

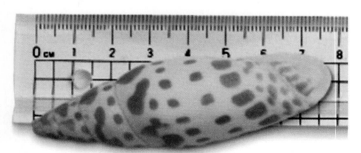

Liquid Volume To measure the volume of a liquid, or the amount of space it takes up, you will use a unit of measure known as the **liter (L).** One liter is the approximate volume of a medium-size carton of milk. Smaller volumes are measured in milliliters (mL). Scientists use graduated cylinders to measure liquid volume.

Activity

The graduated cylinder in the picture is marked in milliliter divisions. Notice that the water in the cylinder has a curved surface. This curved surface is called the *meniscus.* To measure the volume, you must read the level at the lowest point of the meniscus. What is the volume of water in this graduated cylinder?

Common Conversion
1 L = 1,000 mL

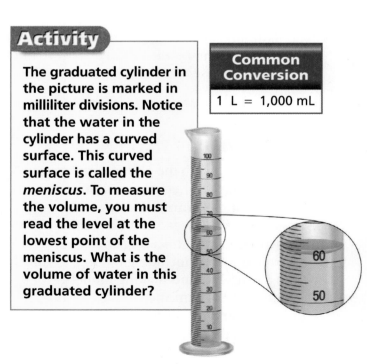

Mass To measure mass, or the amount of matter in an object, you will use a unit of measure known as the **gram (g).** One gram is approximately the mass of a paper clip. Larger masses are measured in kilograms (kg). Scientists use a balance to find the mass of an object.

Common Conversion

1 kg = 1,000 g

Activity

The mass of the potato in the picture is measured in kilograms. What is the mass of the potato? Suppose a recipe for potato salad called for one kilogram of potatoes. About how many potatoes would you need?

0.25 KG

Temperature To measure the temperature of a substance, you will use the **Celsius scale.** Temperature is measured in degrees Celsius (°C) using a Celsius thermometer. Water freezes at 0°C and boils at 100°C.

Time The unit scientists use to measure time is the **second (s).**

Activity

What is the temperature of the liquid in degrees Celsius?

Converting SI Units

To use the SI system, you must know how to convert between units. Converting from one unit to another involves the skill of **calculating,** or using mathematical operations. Converting between SI units is similar to converting between dollars and dimes because both systems are based on powers of ten.

Suppose you want to convert a length of 80 centimeters to meters. Follow these steps to convert between units.

1. Begin by writing down the measurement you want to convert—in this example, 80 centimeters.

2. Write a conversion factor that represents the relationship between the two units you are converting. In this example, the relationship is 1 meter = 100 centimeters. Write this conversion factor as a fraction, making sure to place the units you are converting from (centimeters, in this example) in the denominator.

3. Multiply the measurement you want to convert by the fraction. When you do this, the units in the first measurement will cancel out with the units in the denominator. Your answer will be in the units you are converting to (meters, in this example).

Example

80 centimeters = ■ meters

$$80 \text{ centimeters} \times \frac{1 \text{ meter}}{100 \text{ centimeters}} = \frac{80 \text{ meters}}{100}$$

$$= 0.8 \text{ meters}$$

Activity

Convert between the following units.
1. 600 millimeters = ■ meters
2. 0.35 liters = ■ milliliters
3. 1,050 grams = ■ kilograms

Conducting a Scientific Investigation

In some ways, scientists are like detectives, piecing together clues to learn about a process or event. One way that scientists gather clues is by carrying out experiments. An experiment tests an idea in a careful, orderly manner. Although experiments do not all follow the same steps in the same order, many follow a pattern similar to the one described here.

Posing Questions

Experiments begin by asking a scientific question. A scientific question is one that can be answered by gathering evidence. For example, the question "Which freezes faster—fresh water or salt water?" is a scientific question because you can carry out an investigation and gather information to answer the question.

Developing a Hypothesis

The next step is to form a hypothesis. A **hypothesis** is a possible explanation for a set of observations or answer to a scientific question. In science, a hypothesis must be something that can be tested. A hypothesis can be worded as an *If . . . then . . .* statement. For example, a hypothesis might be *"If I add table salt to fresh water, then the water will freeze at a lower temperature."* A hypothesis worded this way serves as a rough outline of the experiment you should perform.

Designing an Experiment

Next you need to plan a way to test your hypothesis. Your plan should be written out as a step-by-step procedure and should describe the observations or measurements you will make.

Two important steps involved in designing an experiment are controlling variables and forming operational definitions.

Controlling Variables In a well-designed experiment, you need to keep all variables the same except for one. A **variable** is any factor that can change in an experiment. The factor that you change is called the **manipulated variable.** In this experiment, the manipulated variable is the amount of table salt added to the water. Other factors, such as the amount of water or the starting temperature, are kept constant.

The factor that changes as a result of the manipulated variable is called the **responding variable.** The responding variable is what you measure or observe to obtain your results. In this experiment, the responding variable is the temperature at which the water freezes.

An experiment in which all factors except one are kept constant is called a **controlled experiment.** Most controlled experiments include a test called the control. In this experiment, Container 3 is the control. Because no salt is added to Container 3, you can compare the results from the other containers to it. Any difference in results must be due to the addition of salt alone.

Forming Operational Definitions Another important aspect of a well-designed experiment is having clear operational definitions. An **operational definition** is a statement that describes how a particular variable is to be measured or how a term is to be defined. For example, in this experiment, how will you determine if the water has frozen? You might decide to insert a stick in each container at the start of the experiment. Your operational definition of "frozen" would be the time at which the stick can no longer move.

Experimental Procedure
1. Fill 3 containers with 300 milliliters of cold tap water.
2. Add 10 grams of salt to Container 1; stir. Add 20 grams of salt to Container 2; stir. Add no salt to Container 3.
3. Place the 3 containers in a freezer.
4. Check the containers every 15 minutes. Record your observations.

Interpreting Data

The observations and measurements you make in an experiment are called **data.** At the end of an experiment, you need to analyze the data to look for any patterns or trends. Patterns often become clear if you organize your data in a data table or graph. Then think through what the data reveal. Do they support your hypothesis? Do they point out a flaw in your experiment? Do you need to collect more data?

Drawing Conclusions

A **conclusion** is a statement that sums up what you have learned from an experiment. When you draw a conclusion, you need to decide whether the data you collected support your hypothesis or not. You may need to repeat an experiment several times before you can draw any conclusions from it. Conclusions often lead you to pose new questions and plan new experiments to answer them.

Activity

Is a ball's bounce affected by the height from which it is dropped? Using the steps just described, plan a controlled experiment to investigate this problem.

Technology Design Skills

Engineers are people who use scientific and technological knowledge to solve practical problems. To design new products, engineers usually follow the process described here, even though they may not follow these steps in the exact order. As you read the steps, think about how you might apply them in technology labs.

Identify a Need

Before engineers begin designing a new product, they must first identify the need they are trying to meet. For example, suppose you are a member of a design team in a company that makes toys. Your team has identified a need: a toy boat that is inexpensive and easy to assemble.

Research the Problem

Engineers often begin by gathering information that will help them with their new design. This research may include finding articles in books, magazines, or on the Internet. It may also include talking to other engineers who have solved similar problems. Engineers often perform experiments related to the product they want to design.

For your toy boat, you could look at toys that are similar to the one you want to design. You might do research on the Internet. You could also test some materials to see whether they will work well in a toy boat.

Drawing for a boat design ▼

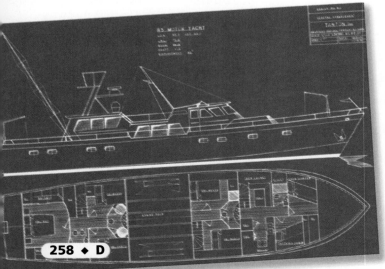

Design a Solution

Research gives engineers information that helps them design a product. When engineers design new products, they usually work in teams.

Generating Ideas Often design teams hold brainstorming meetings in which any team member can contribute ideas. **Brainstorming** is a creative process in which one team member's suggestions often spark ideas in other group members. Brainstorming can lead to new approaches to solving a design problem.

Evaluating Constraints During brainstorming, a design team will often come up with several possible designs. The team must then evaluate each one.

As part of their evaluation, engineers consider constraints. **Constraints** are factors that limit or restrict a product design. Physical characteristics, such as the properties of materials used to make your toy boat, are constraints. Money and time are also constraints. If the materials in a product cost a lot, or if the product takes a long time to make, the design may be impractical.

Making Trade-offs Design teams usually need to make trade-offs. In a **trade-off,** engineers give up one benefit of a proposed design in order to obtain another. In designing your toy boat, you will have to make trade-offs. For example, suppose one material is sturdy but not fully waterproof. Another material is more waterproof, but breakable. You may decide to give up the benefit of sturdiness in order to obtain the benefit of waterproofing.

Build and Evaluate a Prototype

Once the team has chosen a design plan, the engineers build a prototype of the product. A **prototype** is a working model used to test a design. Engineers evaluate the prototype to see whether it works well, is easy to operate, is safe to use, and holds up to repeated use.

Think of your toy boat. What would the prototype be like? Of what materials would it be made? How would you test it?

Troubleshoot and Redesign

Few prototypes work perfectly, which is why they need to be tested. Once a design team has tested a prototype, the members analyze the results and identify any problems. The team then tries to **troubleshoot,** or fix the design problems. For example, if your toy boat leaks or wobbles, the boat should be redesigned to eliminate those problems.

Communicate the Solution

A team needs to communicate the final design to the people who will manufacture and use the product. To do this, teams may use sketches, detailed drawings, computer simulations, and word descriptions.

Activity

You can use the technology design process to design and build a toy boat.

Research and Investigate

1. Visit the library or go online to research toy boats.

2. Investigate how a toy boat can be powered, including wind, rubber bands, or baking soda and vinegar.

3. Brainstorm materials, shapes, and steering for your boat.

Design and Build

4. Based on your research, design a toy boat that
   • is made of readily available materials
   • is no larger than 15 cm long and 10 cm wide

   • includes a power system, a rudder, and an area for cargo
   • travels 2 meters in a straight line carrying a load of 20 pennies

5. Sketch your design and write a step-by-step plan for building your boat. After your teacher approves your plan, build your boat.

Evaluate and Redesign

6. Test your boat, evaluate the results, and troubleshoot any problems.

7. Based on your evaluation, redesign your toy boat so it performs better.

Creating Data Tables and Graphs

How can you make sense of the data in a science experiment?
The first step is to organize the data to help you understand them.
Data tables and graphs are helpful tools for organizing data.

Data Tables

You have gathered your materials and set up your experiment. But before you start, you need to plan a way to record what happens during the experiment. By creating a data table, you can record your observations and measurements in an orderly way.

Suppose, for example, that a scientist conducted an experiment to find out how many Calories people of different body masses burn while doing various activities. The data table shows the results.

Notice in this data table that the manipulated variable (body mass) is the heading of one column. The responding variable (for

Calories Burned in 30 Minutes			
Body Mass	Experiment 1: Bicycling	Experiment 2: Playing Basketball	Experiment 3: Watching Television
30 kg	60 Calories	120 Calories	21 Calories
40 kg	77 Calories	164 Calories	27 Calories
50 kg	95 Calories	206 Calories	33 Calories
60 kg	114 Calories	248 Calories	38 Calories

Experiment 1, the number of Calories burned while bicycling) is the heading of the next column. Additional columns were added for related experiments.

Bar Graphs

To compare how many Calories a person burns doing various activities, you could create a bar graph. A bar graph is used to display data in a number of separate, or distinct, categories. In this example, bicycling, playing basketball, and watching television are the three categories.

To create a bar graph, follow these steps.

1. On graph paper, draw a horizontal, or *x*-, axis and a vertical, or *y*-, axis.

2. Write the names of the categories to be graphed along the horizontal axis. Include an overall label for the axis as well.

3. Label the vertical axis with the name of the responding variable. Include units of measurement. Then create a scale along the axis by marking off equally spaced numbers that cover the range of the data collected.

4. For each category, draw a solid bar using the scale on the vertical axis to determine the height. Make all the bars the same width.

5. Add a title that describes the graph.

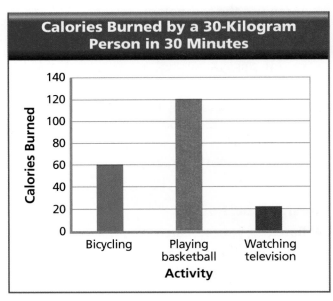

Line Graphs

To see whether a relationship exists between body mass and the number of Calories burned while bicycling, you could create a line graph. A line graph is used to display data that show how one variable (the responding variable) changes in response to another variable (the manipulated variable). You can use a line graph when your manipulated variable is **continuous,** that is, when there are other points between the ones that you tested. In this example, body mass is a continuous variable because there are other body masses between 30 and 40 kilograms (for example, 31 kilograms). Time is another example of a continuous variable.

Line graphs are powerful tools because they allow you to estimate values for conditions that you did not test in the experiment. For example, you can use the line graph to estimate that a 35-kilogram person would burn 68 Calories while bicycling.

To create a line graph, follow these steps.

1. On graph paper, draw a horizontal, or *x*-, axis and a vertical, or *y*-, axis.

2. Label the horizontal axis with the name of the manipulated variable. Label the vertical axis with the name of the responding variable. Include units of measurement.

3. Create a scale on each axis by marking off equally spaced numbers that cover the range of the data collected.

4. Plot a point on the graph for each piece of data. In the line graph above, the dotted lines show how to plot the first data point (30 kilograms and 60 Calories). Follow an imaginary vertical line extending up from the horizontal axis at the 30-kilogram mark. Then follow an imaginary horizontal line extending across from the vertical axis at the 60-Calorie mark. Plot the point where the two lines intersect.

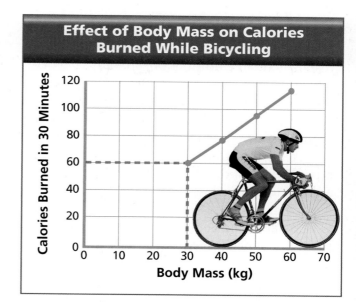

Effect of Body Mass on Calories Burned While Bicycling

5. Connect the plotted points with a solid line. (In some cases, it may be more appropriate to draw a line that shows the general trend of the plotted points. In those cases, some of the points may fall above or below the line. Also, not all graphs are linear. It may be more appropriate to draw a curve to connect the points.)

6. Add a title that identifies the variables or relationship in the graph.

Activity

Create line graphs to display the data from Experiment 2 and Experiment 3 in the data table.

Activity

You read in the newspaper that a total of 4 centimeters of rain fell in your area in June, 2.5 centimeters fell in July, and 1.5 centimeters fell in August. What type of graph would you use to display these data? Use graph paper to create the graph.

Circle Graphs

Like bar graphs, circle graphs can be used to display data in a number of separate categories. Unlike bar graphs, however, circle graphs can only be used when you have data for *all* the categories that make up a given topic. A circle graph is sometimes called a pie chart. The pie represents the entire topic, while the slices represent the individual categories. The size of a slice indicates what percentage of the whole a particular category makes up.

The data table below shows the results of a survey in which 24 teenagers were asked to identify their favorite sport. The data were then used to create the circle graph at the right.

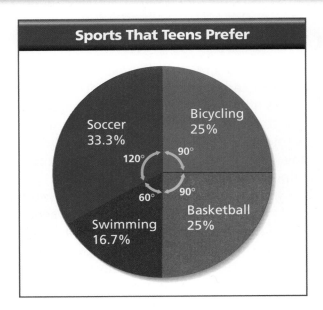

Favorite Sports	
Sport	Students
Soccer	8
Basketball	6
Bicycling	6
Swimming	4

To create a circle graph, follow these steps.

1. Use a compass to draw a circle. Mark the center with a point. Then draw a line from the center point to the top of the circle.

2. Determine the size of each "slice" by setting up a proportion where x equals the number of degrees in a slice. (*Note:* A circle contains 360 degrees.) For example, to find the number of degrees in the "soccer" slice, set up the following proportion:

$$\frac{\text{Students who prefer soccer}}{\text{Total number of students}} = \frac{x}{\text{Total number of degrees in a circle}}$$

$$\frac{8}{24} = \frac{x}{360}$$

Cross-multiply and solve for x.

$$24x = 8 \times 360$$
$$x = 120$$

The "soccer" slice should contain 120 degrees.

3. Use a protractor to measure the angle of the first slice, using the line you drew to the top of the circle as the 0° line. Draw a line from the center of the circle to the edge for the angle you measured.

4. Continue around the circle by measuring the size of each slice with the protractor. Start measuring from the edge of the previous slice so the wedges do not overlap. When you are done, the entire circle should be filled in.

5. Determine the percentage of the whole circle that each slice represents. To do this, divide the number of degrees in a slice by the total number of degrees in a circle (360), and multiply by 100%. For the "soccer" slice, you can find the percentage as follows:

$$\frac{120}{360} \times 100\% = 33.3\%$$

6. Use a different color for each slice. Label each slice with the category and with the percentage of the whole it represents.

7. Add a title to the circle graph.

Activity

In a class of 28 students, 12 students take the bus to school, 10 students walk, and 6 students ride their bicycles. Create a circle graph to display these data.

Math Review

Scientists use math to organize, analyze, and present data. This appendix will help you review some basic math skills.

Mean, Median, and Mode

The **mean** is the average, or the sum of the data divided by the number of data items. The middle number in a set of ordered data is called the **median**. The **mode** is the number that appears most often in a set of data.

Example

A scientist counted the number of distinct songs sung by seven different male birds and collected the data shown below.

Male Bird Songs							
Bird	A	B	C	D	E	F	G
Number of Songs	36	29	40	35	28	36	27

To determine the mean number of songs, add the total number of songs and divide by the number of data items—in this case, the number of male birds.

$$\text{Mean} = \frac{231}{7} = 33 \text{ songs}$$

To find the median number of songs, arrange the data in numerical order and find the number in the middle of the series.

27 28 29 35 36 36 40

The number in the middle is 35, so the median number of songs is 35.

The mode is the value that appears most frequently. In the data, 36 appears twice, while each other item appears only once. Therefore, 36 songs is the mode.

Practice

Find out how many minutes it takes each student in your class to get to school. Then find the mean, median, and mode for the data.

Probability

Probability is the chance that an event will occur. Probability can be expressed as a ratio, a fraction, or a percentage. For example, when you flip a coin, the probability that the coin will land heads up is 1 in 2, or $\frac{1}{2}$, or 50 percent.

The probability that an event will happen can be expressed in the following formula.

$$P(\text{event}) = \frac{\text{Number of times the event can occur}}{\text{Total number of possible events}}$$

Example

A paper bag contains 25 blue marbles, 5 green marbles, 5 orange marbles, and 15 yellow marbles. If you close your eyes and pick a marble from the bag, what is the probability that it will be yellow?

$$P(\text{yellow marbles}) = \frac{15 \text{ yellow marbles}}{50 \text{ marbles total}}$$

$$P = \frac{15}{50}, \text{ or } \frac{3}{10}, \text{ or } 30\%$$

Practice

Each side of a cube has a letter on it. Two sides have *A*, three sides have *B*, and one side has *C*. If you roll the cube, what is the probability that *A* will land on top?

Area

The **area** of a surface is the number of square units that cover it. The front cover of your textbook has an area of about 600 cm².

Area of a Rectangle and a Square To find the area of a rectangle, multiply its length times its width. The formula for the area of a rectangle is

$$A = \ell \times w, \text{ or } A = \ell w$$

Since all four sides of a square have the same length, the area of a square is the length of one side multiplied by itself, or squared.

$$A = s \times s, \text{ or } A = s^2$$

Example

A scientist is studying the plants in a field that measures 75 m × 45 m. What is the area of the field?

$$A = \ell \times w$$
$$A = 75 \text{ m} \times 45 \text{ m}$$
$$A = 3{,}375 \text{ m}^2$$

Area of a Circle The formula for the area of a circle is

$$A = \pi \times r \times r, \text{ or } A = \pi r^2$$

The length of the radius is represented by r, and the value of π is approximately $\frac{22}{7}$.

Example

Find the area of a circle with a radius of 14 cm.

$$A = \pi r^2$$
$$A = 14 \times 14 \times \frac{22}{7}$$
$$A = 616 \text{ cm}^2$$

Practice

Find the area of a circle that has a radius of 21 m.

Circumference

The distance around a circle is called the circumference. The formula for finding the circumference of a circle is

$$C = 2 \times \pi \times r, \text{ or } C = 2\pi r$$

Example

The radius of a circle is 35 cm. What is its circumference?

$$C = 2\pi r$$
$$C = 2 \times 35 \times \frac{22}{7}$$
$$C = 220 \text{ cm}$$

Practice

What is the circumference of a circle with a radius of 28 m?

Volume

The volume of an object is the number of cubic units it contains. The volume of a wastebasket, for example, might be about 26,000 cm³.

Volume of a Rectangular Object To find the volume of a rectangular object, multiply the object's length times its width times its height.

$$V = \ell \times w \times h, \text{ or } V = \ell w h$$

Example

Find the volume of a box with length 24 cm, width 12 cm, and height 9 cm.

$$V = \ell w h$$
$$V = 24 \text{ cm} \times 12 \text{ cm} \times 9 \text{ cm}$$
$$V = 2{,}592 \text{ cm}^3$$

Practice

What is the volume of a rectangular object with length 17 cm, width 11 cm, and height 6 cm?

Fractions

A **fraction** is a way to express a part of a whole. In the fraction $\frac{4}{7}$, 4 is the numerator and 7 is the denominator.

Adding and Subtracting Fractions To add or subtract two or more fractions that have a common denominator, first add or subtract the numerators. Then write the sum or difference over the common denominator.

To find the sum or difference of fractions with different denominators, first find the least common multiple of the denominators. This is known as the least common denominator. Then convert each fraction to equivalent fractions with the least common denominator. Add or subtract the numerators. Then write the sum or difference over the common denominator.

> **Example**
> $$\frac{5}{6} - \frac{3}{4} = \frac{10}{12} - \frac{9}{12} = \frac{10-9}{12} = \frac{1}{12}$$

Multiplying Fractions To multiply two fractions, first multiply the two numerators, then multiply the two denominators.

> **Example**
> $$\frac{5}{6} \times \frac{2}{3} = \frac{5 \times 2}{6 \times 3} = \frac{10}{18} = \frac{5}{9}$$

Dividing Fractions Dividing by a fraction is the same as multiplying by its reciprocal. Reciprocals are numbers whose numerators and denominators have been switched. To divide one fraction by another, first invert the fraction you are dividing by—in other words, turn it upside down. Then multiply the two fractions.

> **Example**
> $$\frac{2}{5} \div \frac{7}{8} = \frac{2}{5} \times \frac{8}{7} = \frac{2 \times 8}{5 \times 7} = \frac{16}{35}$$

> **Practice**
> Solve the following: $\frac{3}{7} \div \frac{4}{5}$.

Decimals

Fractions whose denominators are 10, 100, or some other power of 10 are often expressed as decimals. For example, the fraction $\frac{9}{10}$ can be expressed as the decimal 0.9, and the fraction $\frac{7}{100}$ can be written as 0.07.

Adding and Subtracting With Decimals To add or subtract decimals, line up the decimal points before you carry out the operation.

> **Example**
> ```
>   27.4          278.635
> + 6.19        - 191.4
>  33.59          87.235
> ```

Multiplying With Decimals When you multiply two numbers with decimals, the number of decimal places in the product is equal to the total number of decimal places in each number being multiplied.

> **Example**
> ```
>    46.2 (one decimal place)
>  × 2.37 (two decimal places)
> 109.494 (three decimal places)
> ```

Dividing With Decimals To divide a decimal by a whole number, put the decimal point in the quotient above the decimal point in the dividend.

> **Example**
> $$15.5 \div 5$$
> $$\begin{array}{r} 3.1 \\ 5\overline{)15.5} \end{array}$$

To divide a decimal by a decimal, you need to rewrite the divisor as a whole number. Do this by multiplying both the divisor and dividend by the same multiple of 10.

> **Example**
> $$1.68 \div 4.2 = 16.8 \div 42$$
> $$\begin{array}{r} 0.4 \\ 42\overline{)16.8} \end{array}$$

> **Practice**
> Multiply 6.21 by 8.5.

Ratio and Proportion

A **ratio** compares two numbers by division. For example, suppose a scientist counts 800 wolves and 1,200 moose on an island. The ratio of wolves to moose can be written as a fraction, $\frac{800}{1,200}$, which can be reduced to $\frac{2}{3}$. The same ratio can also be expressed as 2 to 3 or 2 : 3.

A **proportion** is a mathematical sentence saying that two ratios are equivalent. For example, a proportion could state that $\frac{800 \text{ wolves}}{1,200 \text{ moose}} = \frac{2 \text{ wolves}}{3 \text{ moose}}$. You can sometimes set up a proportion to determine or estimate an unknown quantity. For example, suppose a scientist counts 25 beetles in an area of 10 square meters. The scientist wants to estimate the number of beetles in 100 square meters.

Example

1. Express the relationship between beetles and area as a ratio: $\frac{25}{10}$, simplified to $\frac{5}{2}$.

2. Set up a proportion, with x representing the number of beetles. The proportion can be stated as $\frac{5}{2} = \frac{x}{100}$.

3. Begin by cross-multiplying. In other words, multiply each fraction's numerator by the other fraction's denominator.

   $$5 \times 100 = 2 \times x, \text{ or } 500 = 2x$$

4. To find the value of x, divide both sides by 2. The result is 250, or 250 beetles in 100 square meters.

Practice

Find the value of x in the following proportion: $\frac{6}{7} = \frac{x}{49}$.

Percentage

A **percentage** is a ratio that compares a number to 100. For example, there are 37 granite rocks in a collection that consists of 100 rocks. The ratio $\frac{37}{100}$ can be written as 37%. Granite rocks make up 37% of the rock collection.

You can calculate percentages of numbers other than 100 by setting up a proportion.

Example

Rain falls on 9 days out of 30 in June. What percentage of the days in June were rainy?

$$\frac{9 \text{ days}}{30 \text{ days}} = \frac{d\%}{100\%}$$

To find the value of d, begin by cross-multiplying, as for any proportion:

$$9 \times 100 = 30 \times d \qquad d = \frac{900}{30} \qquad d = 30$$

Practice

There are 300 marbles in a jar, and 42 of those marbles are blue. What percentage of the marbles are blue?

Significant Figures

The **precision** of a measurement depends on the instrument you use to take the measurement. For example, if the smallest unit on the ruler is millimeters, then the most precise measurement you can make will be in millimeters.

The sum or difference of measurements can only be as precise as the least precise measurement being added or subtracted. Round your answer so that it has the same number of digits after the decimal as the least precise measurement. Round up if the last digit is 5 or more, and round down if the last digit is 4 or less.

Example

Subtract a temperature of 5.2°C from the temperature 75.46°C.

75.46 − 5.2 = 70.26

5.2 has the fewest digits after the decimal, so it is the least precise measurement. Since the last digit of the answer is 6, round up to 3. The most precise difference between the measurements is 70.3°C.

Practice

Add 26.4 m to 8.37 m. Round your answer according to the precision of the measurements.

Significant figures are the number of nonzero digits in a measurement. Zeroes between nonzero digits are also significant. For example, the measurements 12,500 L, 0.125 cm, and 2.05 kg all have three significant figures. When you multiply and divide measurements, the one with the fewest significant figures determines the number of significant figures in your answer.

Example

Multiply 110 g by 5.75 g.

110 × 5.75 = 632.5

Because 110 has only two significant figures, round the answer to 630 g.

Scientific Notation

A **factor** is a number that divides into another number with no remainder. In the example, the number 3 is used as a factor four times.

An **exponent** tells how many times a number is used as a factor. For example, $3 \times 3 \times 3 \times 3$ can be written as 3^4. The exponent 4 indicates that the number 3 is used as a factor four times. Another way of expressing this is to say that 81 is equal to 3 to the fourth power.

Example

$$3^4 = 3 \times 3 \times 3 \times 3 = 81$$

Scientific notation uses exponents and powers of ten to write very large or very small numbers in shorter form. When you write a number in scientific notation, you write the number as two factors. The first factor is any number between 1 and 10. The second factor is a power of 10, such as 10^3 or 10^6.

Example

The average distance between the planet Mercury and the sun is 58,000,000 km. To write the first factor in scientific notation, insert a decimal point in the original number so that you have a number between 1 and 10. In the case of 58,000,000, the number is 5.8.

To determine the power of 10, count the number of places that the decimal point moved. In this case, it moved 7 places.

58,000,000 km = 5.8 × 10^7 km

Practice

Express 6,590,000 in scientific notation.

Reading Comprehension Skills

Each section in your textbook introduces a Target Reading Skill. You will improve your reading comprehension by using the Target Reading Skills described below.

Using Prior Knowledge

Your prior knowledge is what you already know before you begin to read about a topic. Building on what you already know gives you a head start on learning new information. Before you begin a new assignment, think about what you know. You might look at the headings and the visuals to spark your memory. You can list what you know. Then, as you read, consider questions like these.

- How does what you learn relate to what you know?
- How did something you already know help you learn something new?
- Did your original ideas agree with what you have just learned?

Asking Questions

Asking yourself questions is an excellent way to focus on and remember new information in your textbook. For example, you can turn the text headings into questions. Then your questions can guide you to identify the important information as you read. Look at these examples:

Heading: Using Seismographic Data

Question: How are seismographic data used?

Heading: Kinds of Faults

Question: What are the kinds of faults?

You do not have to limit your questions to text headings. Ask questions about anything that you need to clarify or that will help you understand the content. *What* and *how* are probably the most common question words, but you may also ask *why*, *who*, *when*, or *where* questions.

Previewing Visuals

Visuals are photographs, graphs, tables, diagrams, and illustrations. Visuals contain important information. Before you read, look at visuals and their labels and captions. This preview will help you prepare for what you will be reading.

Often you will be asked what you want to learn about a visual. For example, after you look at the normal fault diagram below, you might ask: What is the movement along a normal fault? Questions about visuals give you a purpose for reading—to answer your questions.

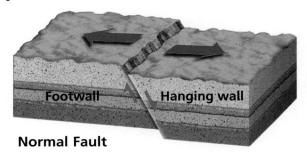

Footwall   **Hanging wall**

Normal Fault

Outlining

An outline shows the relationship between main ideas and supporting ideas. An outline has a formal structure. You write the main ideas, called topics, next to Roman numerals. The supporting ideas, called subtopics, are written under the main ideas and labeled A, B, C, and so on. An outline looks like this:

Technology and Society
I. Technology through history
II. The impact of technology on society
A.
B.

Identifying Main Ideas

When you are reading science material, it is important to try to understand the ideas and concepts that are in a passage. Each paragraph has a lot of information and detail. Good readers try to identify the most important—or biggest—idea in every paragraph or section. That's the main idea. The other information in the paragraph supports or further explains the main idea.

Sometimes main ideas are stated directly. In this book, some main ideas are identified for you as key concepts. These are printed in boldface type. However, you must identify other main ideas yourself. In order to do this, you must identify all the ideas within a paragraph or section. Then ask yourself which idea is big enough to include all the other ideas.

Comparing and Contrasting

When you compare and contrast, you examine the similarities and differences between things. You can compare and contrast in a Venn diagram or in a table.

Venn Diagram A Venn diagram consists of two overlapping circles. In the space where the circles overlap, you write the characteristics that the two items have in common. In one of the circles outside the area of overlap, you write the differing features or characteristics of one of the items. In the other circle outside the area of overlap, you write the differing characteristics of the other item.

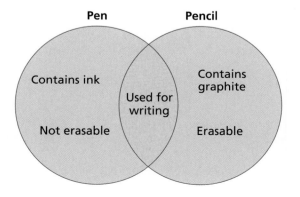

Table In a compare/contrast table, you list the characteristics or features to be compared across the top of the table. Then list the items to be compared in the left column. Complete the table by filling in information about each characteristic or feature.

Blood Vessel	Function	Structure of Wall
Artery	Carries blood away from heart	
Capillary		
Vein		

Identifying Supporting Evidence

A hypothesis is a possible explanation for observations made by scientists or an answer to a scientific question. Scientists must carry out investigations and gather evidence that either supports or disproves the hypothesis.

Identifying the supporting evidence for a hypothesis or theory can help you understand the hypothesis or theory. Evidence consists of facts—information whose accuracy can be confirmed by testing or observation.

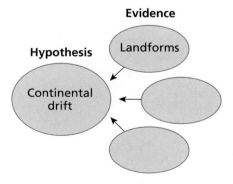

Sequencing

A sequence is the order in which a series of events occurs. A flowchart or a cycle diagram can help you visualize a sequence.

Flowchart To make a flowchart, write a brief description of each step or event in a box. Place the boxes in order, with the first event at the top of the chart. Then draw an arrow to connect each step or event to the next.

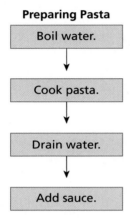

Preparing Pasta

Boil water.
↓
Cook pasta.
↓
Drain water.
↓
Add sauce.

Cycle Diagram A cycle diagram shows a sequence that is continuous, or cyclical. A continuous sequence does not have an end because when the final event is over, the first event begins again. To create a cycle diagram, write the starting event in a box placed at the top of a page in the center. Then, moving in a clockwise direction, write each event in a box in its proper sequence. Draw arrows that connect each event to the one that occurs next.

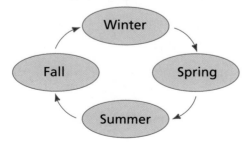

Seasons of the Year

Winter → Spring → Summer → Fall → Winter

Relating Cause and Effect

Science involves many cause-and-effect relationships. A cause makes something happen. An effect is what happens. When you recognize that one event causes another, you are relating cause and effect.

Words like *cause, because, effect, affect,* and *result* often signal a cause or an effect. Sometimes an effect can have more than one cause, or a cause can produce several effects.

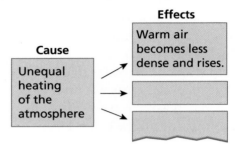

Cause

Unequal heating of the atmosphere

Effects

Warm air becomes less dense and rises.

Concept Mapping

Concept maps are useful tools for organizing information on any topic. A concept map begins with a main idea or core concept and shows how the idea can be subdivided into related subconcepts or smaller ideas.

You construct a concept map by placing concepts (usually nouns) in ovals and connecting them with linking words (usually verbs). The biggest concept or idea is placed in an oval at the top of the map. Related concepts are arranged in ovals below the big idea. The linking words connect the ovals.

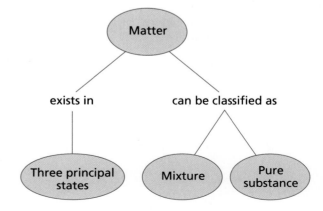

Matter
- exists in → Three principal states
- can be classified as → Mixture, Pure substance

Building Vocabulary

Knowing the meaning of these prefixes, suffixes, and roots will help you understand the meaning of words you do not recognize.

Word Origins Many science words come to English from other languages, such as Greek and Latin. By learning the meaning of a few common Greek and Latin roots, you can determine the meaning of unfamiliar science words.

Prefixes A prefix is a word part that is added at the beginning of a root or base word to change its meaning.

Suffixes A suffix is a word part that is added at the end of a root word to change the meaning.

Greek and Latin Roots		
Greek Roots	**Meaning**	**Example**
ast-	star	astronaut
geo-	Earth	geology
metron-	measure	kilometer
opt-	eye	optician
photo-	light	photograph
scop-	see	microscope
therm-	heat	thermostat
Latin Roots	**Meaning**	**Example**
aqua-	water	aquarium
aud-	hear	auditorium
duc-, duct-	lead	conduct
flect-	bend	reflect
fract-, frag-	break	fracture
ject-	throw	reject
luc-	light	lucid
spec-	see	inspect

Prefixes and Suffixes		
Prefix	**Meaning**	**Example**
com-, con-	with	communicate, concert
de-	from; down	decay
di-	two	divide
ex-, exo-	out	exhaust
in-, im-	in, into; not	inject, impossible
re-	again; back	reflect, recall
trans-	across	transfer
Suffix	**Meaning**	**Example**
-al	relating to	natural
-er, -or	one who	teacher, doctor
-ist	one who practices	scientist
-ity	state of	equality
-ology	study of	biology
-tion, -sion	state or quality of	reaction, tension

Safety Symbols

These symbols warn of possible dangers in the laboratory and remind you to work carefully.

 Safety Goggles Wear safety goggles to protect your eyes in any activity involving chemicals, flames or heating, or glassware.

 Lab Apron Wear a laboratory apron to protect your skin and clothing from damage.

 Breakage Handle breakable materials, such as glassware, with care. Do not touch broken glassware.

 Heat-Resistant Gloves Use an oven mitt or other hand protection when handling hot materials such as hot plates or hot glassware.

 Plastic Gloves Wear disposable plastic gloves when working with harmful chemicals and organisms. Keep your hands away from your face, and dispose of the gloves according to your teacher's instructions.

 Heating Use a clamp or tongs to pick up hot glassware. Do not touch hot objects with your bare hands.

 Flames Before you work with flames, tie back loose hair and clothing. Follow instructions from your teacher about lighting and extinguishing flames.

 No Flames When using flammable materials, make sure there are no flames, sparks, or other exposed heat sources present.

 Corrosive Chemical Avoid getting acid or other corrosive chemicals on your skin or clothing or in your eyes. Do not inhale the vapors. Wash your hands after the activity.

 Poison Do not let any poisonous chemical come into contact with your skin, and do not inhale its vapors. Wash your hands when you are finished with the activity.

 Fumes Work in a ventilated area when harmful vapors may be involved. Avoid inhaling vapors directly. Only test an odor when directed to do so by your teacher, and use a wafting motion to direct the vapor toward your nose.

 Sharp Object Scissors, scalpels, knives, needles, pins, and tacks can cut your skin. Always direct a sharp edge or point away from yourself and others.

 Animal Safety Treat live or preserved animals or animal parts with care to avoid harming the animals or yourself. Wash your hands when you are finished with the activity.

 Plant Safety Handle plants only as directed by your teacher. If you are allergic to certain plants, tell your teacher; do not do an activity involving those plants. Avoid touching harmful plants such as poison ivy. Wash your hands when you are finished with the activity.

 Electric Shock To avoid electric shock, never use electrical equipment around water, or when the equipment is wet or your hands are wet. Be sure cords are untangled and cannot trip anyone. Unplug equipment not in use.

 Physical Safety When an experiment involves physical activity, avoid injuring yourself or others. Alert your teacher if there is any reason you should not participate.

 Disposal Dispose of chemicals and other laboratory materials safely. Follow the instructions from your teacher.

 Hand Washing Wash your hands thoroughly when finished with the activity. Use soap and warm water. Rinse well.

 General Safety Awareness When this symbol appears, follow the instructions provided. When you are asked to develop your own procedure in a lab, have your teacher approve your plan before you go further.

Science Safety Rules

General Precautions

Follow all instructions. Never perform activities without the approval and supervision of your teacher. Do not engage in horseplay. Never eat or drink in the laboratory. Keep work areas clean and uncluttered.

Dress Code

Wear safety goggles whenever you work with chemicals, glassware, heat sources such as burners, or any substance that might get into your eyes. If you wear contact lenses, notify your teacher.

Wear a lab apron or coat whenever you work with corrosive chemicals or substances that can stain. Wear disposable plastic gloves when working with organisms and harmful chemicals. Tie back long hair. Remove or tie back any article of clothing or jewelry that can hang down and touch chemicals, flames, or equipment. Roll up long sleeves. Never wear open shoes or sandals.

First Aid

Report all accidents, injuries, or fires to your teacher, no matter how minor. Be aware of the location of the first-aid kit, emergency equipment such as the fire extinguisher and fire blanket, and the nearest telephone. Know whom to contact in an emergency.

Heating and Fire Safety

Keep all combustible materials away from flames. When heating a substance in a test tube, make sure that the mouth of the tube is not pointed at you or anyone else. Never heat a liquid in a closed container. Use an oven mitt to pick up a container that has been heated.

Using Chemicals Safely

Never put your face near the mouth of a container that holds chemicals. Never touch, taste, or smell a chemical unless your teacher tells you to.

Use only those chemicals needed in the activity. Keep all containers closed when chemicals are not being used. Pour all chemicals over the sink or a container, not over your work surface. Dispose of excess chemicals as instructed by your teacher.

Be extra careful when working with acids or bases. When mixing an acid and water, always pour the water into the container first and then add the acid to the water. Never pour water into an acid. Wash chemical spills and splashes immediately with plenty of water.

Using Glassware Safely

If glassware is broken or chipped, notify your teacher immediately. Never handle broken or chipped glass with your bare hands.

Never force glass tubing or thermometers into a rubber stopper or rubber tubing. Have your teacher insert the glass tubing or thermometer if required for an activity.

Using Sharp Instruments

Handle sharp instruments with extreme care. Never cut material toward you; cut away from you.

Animal and Plant Safety

Never perform experiments that cause pain, discomfort, or harm to animals. Only handle animals if absolutely necessary. If you know that you are allergic to certain plants, molds, or animals, tell your teacher before doing an activity in which these are used. Wash your hands thoroughly after any activity involving animals, animal parts, plants, plant parts, or soil.

During field work, wear long pants, long sleeves, socks, and closed shoes. Avoid poisonous plants and fungi as well as plants with thorns.

End-of-Experiment Rules

Unplug all electrical equipment. Clean up your work area. Dispose of waste materials as instructed by your teacher. Wash your hands after every experiment.

English and Spanish Glossary

A

absorption The process by which nutrient molecules pass through the wall of the digestive system into the blood. (p. 61)
absorción Proceso por el cual las moléculas de los nutrientes pasan a través de la pared del sistema digestivo a la sangre.

active immunity Immunity that occurs when a person's own immune system produces antibodies in response to the presence of a pathogen. (p. 154)
inmunidad activa Inmunidad que ocurre cuando el sistema inmunológico de una persona produce anticuerpos en respuesta a la presencia de un patógeno.

addiction A physical dependence on a substance. (pp. 123, 203)
adicción Dependencia física de una sustancia.

adolescence The stage of development between childhood and adulthood when children become adults physically and mentally. (p. 239)
adolescencia Etapa del desarrollo entre la niñez y la adultez cuando los niños empiezan a ser adultos física y mentalmente.

AIDS (acquired immunodeficiency syndrome) A disease caused by a virus that attacks the immune system. (p. 150)
SIDA (Síndrome de inmunodeficiencia adquirida) Enfermedad causada por un virus que ataca el sistema inmunológico.

alcoholism A disease in which a person is both physically addicted to and emotionally dependent on alcohol. (p. 207)
alcoholismo Enfermedad en la que una persona es adicta físicamente y dependiente emocionalmente del alcohol.

allergen A substance that causes an allergy. (p. 160)
alergeno Sustancia que causa la alergia.

allergy A disorder in which the immune system is overly sensitive to a foreign substance. (p. 160)
alergia Trastorno fisiológico en el cual el sistema inmunológico es extremadamente sensible a las sustancias externas.

alveoli Tiny sacs of lung tissue specialized for the movement of gases between air and blood. (p. 116)
alveolos Sacos diminutos de tejido pulmonar especializados en el intercambio de gases entre el aire y la sangre.

amino acids Small units that are linked together chemically to form large protein molecules. (p. 49)
aminoácidos Pequeñas unidades que están unidas químicamente entre ellas para formar grandes moléculas de proteínas.

amniotic sac A fluid-filled sac that cushions and protects a developing embryo and fetus in the uterus. (p. 234)
saco amniótico Saco lleno de líquido que amortigua y protege al embrión y al feto en desarrollo en el útero.

anabolic steroids Synthetic chemicals that are similar to hormones produced in the body. (p. 204)
esteroides anabólicos Sustancias químicas sintéticas que son semejantes a las hormonas producidas por el cuerpo.

antibiotic A chemical that kills bacteria or slows their growth without harming body cells. (p. 156)
antibiótico Sustancia química que mata las bacterias o frena su crecimiento sin dañar las células del cuerpo humano.

antibody A protein produced by a B cell of the immune system that destroys pathogens. (p. 148)
anticuerpo Proteína producida por una célula B del sistema inmunológico que destruye un tipo específico de patógeno.

antigen A molecule that the immune system recognizes either as part of the body or as coming from outside the body. (p. 148)
antígeno Molécula en una célula que puede reconocer el sistema inmunológico como parte del cuerpo o como un agente extraño.

anus A muscular opening at the end of the rectum through which waste material is eliminated from the body. (p. 71)
ano Abertura muscular al final del recto a través de la cual se elimina el material de desecho digestivo del cuerpo.

aorta The largest artery in the body; receives blood from the left ventricle. (p. 84)
aorta La arteria más grande del cuerpo; recibe la sangre del ventrículo izquierdo.

artery A blood vessel that carries blood away from the heart. (p. 82)
arteria Vaso sanguíneo que transporta la sangre que sale del corazón.

arthritis A disease of the joints that makes movement painful. (p. 23)
artritis Enfermedad de las articulaciones que hace que el movimiento sea doloroso.

arthroscope A slim, tube-shaped, surgical instrument that doctors use to diagnose a problem in a joint. (p. 23)
artroscopio Instrumento de cirugía con forma de tubo delgado que usan los doctores para diagnosticar un problema en una articulación.

asthma A disorder in which the respiratory passages narrow significantly. (p. 161)
asma Trastorno fisiológico por el cual las vías respiratorias se estrechan considerablemente.

atherosclerosis A condition in which an artery wall thickens as a result of the buildup of fatty materials. (p. 99)
arteriosclerosis Condición en la que la pared de una arteria se hace más gruesa debido a la acumulación de materiales grasos.

atrium Each of the two upper chambers of the heart that receives blood that comes into the heart. (p. 81)
aurícula Cada una de las dos cámaras superiores del corazón que reciben la sangre que entra en el corazón.

autonomic nervous system The group of nerves in the peripheral nervous system that controls involuntary actions. (p. 187)
sistema nervioso autónomo Grupo de nervios en el sistema nervioso periférico que controla las acciones involuntarias.

axon A threadlike extension of a neuron that carries nerve impulses away from the cell body. (p. 178)
axón Extensión con forma de hilo de una neurona que saca los impulsos nerviosos del cuerpo de la célula.

B cell A lymphocyte that produces proteins that help destroy pathogens. (p. 148)
célula B Linfocito que produce proteínas que ayudan a destruir un tipo específico de patógeno.

bile A substance produced by the liver that breaks up fat particles. (p. 69)
bilis Sustancia producida por el hígado que descompone las partículas de grasa.

blood pressure The pressure that is exerted by the blood against the walls of blood vessels. (p. 88)
presión arterial Presión que ejerce la sangre contra las paredes de los vasos sanguíneos.

brain The part of the central nervous system that is located in the skull and controls most functions in the body. (p. 183)
encéfalo Parte del sistema nervioso central que está ubicado en el cráneo y controla la mayoría de las funciones del cuerpo.

brain stem The part of the brain that lies between the cerebellum and spinal cord and controls the body's involuntary actions. (p. 184)
tronco encefálico Parte del encéfalo que se encuentra entre el cerebelo y la médula espinal, y controla las acciones involuntarias del cuerpo.

bronchi The passages that direct air into the lungs. (p. 116)
bronquios Conductos que dirigen el aire hacia los pulmones.

bronchitis An irritation of the breathing passages in which the small passages become narrower than normal and may be clogged with mucus. (p. 124)
bronquitis Irritación de los conductos respiratorios en la que los conductos pequeños se hacen más estrechos de lo normal y se pueden obstruir con mucosidad.

calorie The amount of energy needed to raise the temperature of one gram of water by one degree Celsius. (p. 45)
caloría Cantidad de energía que se necesita para elevar la temperatura de un gramo de agua un grado Celsius.

cancer A disease in which some body cells divide uncontrollably. (p. 35)
cáncer Enfermedad en la que algunas células del cuerpo se dividen descontroladamente.

capillary A tiny blood vessel where substances are exchanged between the blood and the body cells. (p. 82)
capilar Vaso sanguíneo minúsculo donde se intercambian las sustancias de la sangre y las células del cuerpo.

carbohydrate Nutrient composed of carbon, oxygen, and hydrogen that is a major source of energy. (p. 46)
carbohidrato Nutriente compuesto de carbono, oxígeno e hidrógeno, que es una importante fuente de energía.

carbon monoxide A colorless, odorless gas produced when substances—including tobacco—are burned. (p. 123)
monóxido de carbono Gas incoloro e inodoro producido cuando se queman algunas sustancias, incluido el tabaco.

carcinogen A substance or a factor in the environment that can cause cancer. (p. 162)
carcinógeno Sustancia o factor en el ambiente que puede causar cáncer.

cardiac muscle Muscle tissue found only in the heart. (p. 27)
músculo cardiaco Tejido muscular que sólo se encuentra en el corazón.

cardiovascular system The body system that consists of the heart, blood vessels, and blood; also called the circulatory system. (p. 78)
sistema cardiovascular Sistema corporal que está formado por el corazón, los vasos sanguíneos y la sangre; tambien llamado sistema circulatoria.

cartilage A connective tissue that is more flexible than bone and that protects the ends of bones and keeps them from rubbing together. (p. 15)
cartílago Tejido conectivo que es más flexible que el hueso y que protege los extremos de los huesos y evita que se rocen.

cell The basic unit of structure and function in a living thing. (p. 7)
célula Unidad básica de estructura y función en los seres vivos.

cell membrane The outside boundary of a cell. (p. 7)
membrana celular Borde externo de la célula.

central nervous system The division of the nervous system consisting of the brain and spinal cord. (p. 182)
sistema nervioso central División del sistema nervioso formado por el encéfalo y la médula espinal.

cerebellum The part of the brain that coordinates the actions of the muscles and helps maintain balance. (p. 184)
cerebelo Parte del encéfalo que coordina las acciones de los músculos y ayuda a mantener el equilibrio.

cerebrum The part of the brain that interprets input from the senses, controls movement, and carries out complex mental processes. (p. 184)
cerebro Parte del encéfalo que interpreta los estímulos de los sentidos, controla el movimiento y realiza procesos mentales complejos.

cilia Tiny hairlike extensions that move together in a sweeping motion. (p. 115)
cilios Extensiones minúsculas de las células que tienen forma de pelo y se mueven como un látigo.

cochlea A snail-shaped tube in the inner ear that is lined with receptor cells that respond to sound. (p. 197)
cóclea Tubo en forma de caracol en el oído interno que está recubierto de células receptoras que responden al sonido.

compact bone Hard, dense bone tissue that is beneath the outer membrane of a bone. (p. 16)
hueso compacto Tejido de hueso denso y duro que se encuentra debajo de la membrana externa de un hueso.

concussion A bruiselike injury of the brain that occurs when the soft tissue of the brain collides against the skull. (p. 189)
contusión Magulladura en el encéfalo que ocurre cuando el tejido suave del encéfalo choca contra el cráneo.

connective tissue A body tissue that provides support for the body and connects all of its parts. (p. 8)
tejido conectivo Tejido que da soporte al cuerpo y conecta todas sus partes.

cornea The clear tissue that covers the front of the eye. (p. 193)
córnea Tejido transparente que cubre el frente del ojo.

coronary artery An artery that supplies blood to the heart itself. (p. 86)
arteria coronaria Arteria que lleva sangre al corazón.

cytoplasm The material within a cell apart from the nucleus. (p. 7)
citoplasma Material que hay en una célula, pero fuera del núcleo.

dendrite A threadlike extension of a neuron that carries nerve impulses toward the cell body. (p. 178)
dendrita Extensión en forma de hilo de una neurona que lleva los impulsos nerviosos hacia el cuerpo de las células.

depressant A drug that slows down the activity of the central nervous system. (p. 204)
sustancia depresora Droga que disminuye la velocidad de la actividad del sistema nervioso central.

dermis The inner layer of the skin. (p. 33)
dermis Capa más interna de la piel.

diabetes A condition in which the pancreas fails to produce enough insulin or the body's cells cannot use it properly. (p. 161)
diabetes Condición en la que el páncreas no puede producir suficiente insulina o las células del cuerpo no la pueden usar adecuadamente.

diaphragm A large, dome-shaped muscle that plays an important role in breathing. (p. 118)
diafragma Músculo grande con forma de cúpula que juega un papel muy importante en la respiración.

Dietary Reference Intakes (DRIs) Guidelines that show the amounts of nutrients needed every day. (p. 59)
Ingestas de dietética referencia Pautas que muestran la cantidad de nutrientes que se necesitan diariamente.

diffusion The process by which molecules move from an area of higher concentration to an area of lower concentration. (p. 87)
difusión Proceso por el cual las moléculas se mueven de un área de mayor concentración a un área de menor concentración.

digestion The process by which the body breaks down food into small nutrient molecules. (p. 61)
digestión Proceso por el cual el cuerpo descompone la comida en pequeñas moléculas de nutrientes.

dislocation An injury in which a bone comes out of its joint. (p. 20)
dislocación Lesión en la que un hueso se sale de su articulación.

drug Any chemical taken into the body that causes changes in a person's body or behavior. (p. 201)
droga Cualquier sustancia química que se incorpora al cuerpo, que causa cambios en el cuerpo o comportamiento de una persona.

drug abuse The deliberate misuse of drugs for purposes other than medical. (p. 201)
abuso de drogas Uso indebido deliberado de drogas para fines no médicos.

eardrum The membrane that separates the outer ear from the middle ear, and that vibrates when sound waves strike it. (p. 197)
tímpano Membrana que separa el oído externo del oído medio, y que vibra cuando le llegan ondas sonoras.

egg A female sex cell. (p. 225)
óvulo Célula sexual femenina.

embryo A developing human during the first eight weeks after fertilization has occurred. (p. 233)
embrión Humano en desarrollo durante las primeras ocho semanas después de ocurrir la fecundación.

emphysema A serious disease that destroys lung tissue and causes breathing difficulties. (p. 125)
enfisema Enfermedad grave que destruye el tejido pulmonar y causa dificultades respiratorias.

endocrine gland A structure of the endocrine system which produces and releases its chemical products directly into the bloodstream. (p. 217)
glándula endocrina Estructura del sistema endocrino que produce y libera sus productos químicos directamente a la corriente sanguínea.

enzyme A protein that speeds up chemical reactions in the body. (p. 63)
enzima Proteína que acelera las reacciones químicas en el cuerpo.

epidermis The outer layer of the skin. (p. 32)
epidermis Capa más externa de la piel.

epiglottis A flap of tissue that seals off the windpipe and prevents food from entering. (p. 63)
epiglotis Extensión de tejido que sella la entrada de la tráquea impidiendo el paso del alimento.

epithelial tissue A body tissue that covers the surfaces of the body, inside and out. (p. 8)
tejido epitelial Tejido corporal que cubre la superficie del cuerpo, por dentro y por fuera.

esophagus A muscular tube that connects the mouth to the stomach. (p. 63)
esófago Tubo muscular que conecta la boca con el estómago.

estrogen A hormone produced by the ovaries that controls the development of eggs and adult female characteristics. (p. 228)
estrógeno Hormona producida por los ovarios que controla el desarrollo de los óvulos y de las características femeninas adultas.

excretion The process by which wastes are removed from the body. (p. 127)
excreción Proceso por el cual se eliminan los desechos del cuerpo.

fallopian tube A passageway for eggs from an ovary to the uterus. (p. 228)
trompa de falopio Pasaje por el que pasan los óvulos desde un ovario al útero.

farsightedness The condition in which a person can see distant objects clearly. (p. 195)
hipermetropía Condición en la que una persona puede ver claramente los objetos distantes.

fat Energy-containing nutrients that are composed of carbon, oxygen. (p. 47)
grasas Nutrientes que contienen energía y están compuestos de carbono, oxígeno e hidrógeno.

fertilization The joining of a sperm and an egg. (p. 225)
fecundación Unión de un espermatozoide y un óvulo.

fetus A developing human from the ninth week of development until birth. (p. 233)
feto Humano en desarrollo desde la novena semana de desarrollo hasta el nacimiento.

follicle Structure in the dermis of the skin from which a strand of hair grows. (p. 33)
folículo Estructura en la dermis de la piel de donde crece un pelo.

fracture A break in a bone. (p. 20)
fractura Rotura de un hueso.

gallbladder The organ that stores bile after it is produced by the liver. (p. 69)
vesícula Órgano que almacena la bilis después de ser producida por el hígado.

glucose A sugar that is the major source of energy for the body's cells. (p. 46)
glucosa Azúcar que es la principal fuente de energía de las células del cuerpo.

heart A hollow, muscular organ that pumps blood throughout the body. (p. 80)
corazón Órgano muscular hueco que bombea sangre a todo el cuerpo.

heart attack A condition in which blood flow to part of the heart muscle is blocked, causing heart cells to die. (p. 99)
infarto cardiaco Condición en la que se obstruye el flujo de sangre a una parte del músculo cardiaco, lo que causa la muerte de las células cardiacas.

hemoglobin An iron-containing protein that binds chemically to oxygen molecules; makes up most of red blood cells. (p. 92)
hemoglobina Proteína que contiene hierro y que se enlaza químicamente a las moléculas de oxígeno; con forma la mayoría de los glóbulos rojos.

histamine A chemical that is responsible for the symptoms of an allergy. (p. 160)
histamina Sustancia química responsable de los síntomas de una alergia.

HIV (human immunodeficiency virus) The virus that causes AIDS. (p. 150)
VIH (Virus de la inmunodeficiencia humana) Virus que causa el SIDA.

homeostasis The process by which an organism's internal environment is kept stable in spite of changes in the external environment. (p. 10)
homeostasis Tendencia del cuerpo a mantener un equilibrio interno, a pesar de los cambios en el ambiente externo.

hormone The chemical product of an endocrine gland. (p. 217)
hormona Sustancia química producida por una glándula endocrina.

hypertension A disorder in which a person's blood pressure is consistently higher than normal; also called high blood pressure. (p. 100)
hipertensión Trastorno en el que la presión arterial de una persona es constantemente más alta de lo normal; también se le llama presión alta.

hypothalamus A part of the brain that links the nervous system and the endocrine system. (p. 218)
hipotálamo Parte del encéfalo que une el sistema nervioso con el sistema endocrino.

immune response Part of the body's defense against pathogens in which cells of the immune system react to each kind of pathogen with a defense targeted specifically at that pathogen. (p. 148)
reacción inmunológica Parte de la defensa del cuerpo contra los patógenos en la que las células del sistema inmunológico reaccionan a cada tipo de patógeno con una defensa específica.

immunity The body's ability to destroy pathogens before they can cause disease. (p. 154)
inmunidad Capacidad del cuerpo para destruir los patógenos antes de que causen enfermedades.

infectious disease A disease caused by the presence of a living thing in the body. (p. 141)
enfermedad infecciosa Enfermedad causada por la presencia de un ser vivo en el cuerpo.

inflammatory response Part of the body's defense against pathogens, in which fluid and white blood cells leak from blood vessels into tissues and destroy pathogens by breaking them down. (p. 147)
reacción inflamatoria Parte de la defensa del cuerpo contra los patógenos en la cual los fluidos y los glóbulos blancos salen de los vasos sanguíneos hacia los tejidos y destruyen los patógenos descomponiéndolos.

insulin A chemical produced in the pancreas that enables the body's cells to take in glucose from the blood and use it for energy. (p. 161)
insulina Sustancia química que se produce en el páncreas, que permite que las células del cuerpo absorban glucosa de la sangre y la usen como energía.

interneuron A neuron that carries nerve impulses from one neuron to another. (p. 179)
interneurona Neurona que lleva los impulsos nerviosos de una neurona a otra.

involuntary muscle A muscle that is not under conscious control. (p. 24)
músculo involuntario Músculo que no se puede controlar conscientemente.

iris The circular structure that surrounds the pupil and regulates the amount of light entering the eye. (p. 193)
iris Estructura circular que rodea la pupila y regula la cantidad de luz que entra en el ojo.

joint A place in the body where two bones come together. (p. 14)
articulación Lugar en el cuerpo en donde se unen dos huesos.

kidney A major organ of the excretory system which removes urea and other wastes from the blood. (p. 128)
riñón Órgano principal del sistema excretor que elimina la urea y otros materiales de desecho de la sangre.

large intestine The last section of the digestive system, where water is absorbed into the bloodstream and the remaining material is eliminated from the body. (p. 71)
intestino grueso Última sección del sistema digestivo, donde se absorbe el agua hacia el torrente sanguíneo y los materiales restantes son eliminados del cuerpo.

larynx The voice box; located in the top part of the trachea, underneath the epiglottis. (p. 120)
laringe Caja de la voz localizada en la parte superior de la tráquea por debajo de la epiglotis.

lens The flexible structure that focuses light that has entered the eye. (p. 193)
cristalino Estructura flexible que enfoca la luz que entra en el ojo.

ligament Strong connective tissue that holds bones together in movable joints. (p. 15)
ligamentos Tejido conectivo resistente que une los huesos en las articulaciones móviles.

liver The largest organ in the body; it plays a role in many body processes. (p. 69)
hígado Órgano más grande del cuerpo; tiene una función en muchos procesos corporales.

lungs The main organs of the respiratory system. (p. 116)
pulmones Órganos principales del sistema respiratorio.

lymph The fluid that the lymphatic system collects and returns to the bloodstream. (p. 97)
linfa Fluido que el sistema linfático recoge y devuelve al torrente sanguíneo.

lymph node A small knob of tissue in the lymphatic system that filters lymph, trapping bacteria and other microorganisms that cause disease. (p. 97)
ganglio linfático Pequeña prominencia de tejido en el sistema linfático que filtra la linfa, atrapando las bacterias y otros microorganismos que causan enfermedades.

lymphatic system A network of veinlike vessels that returns the fluid that leaks out of blood vessels to the bloodstream. (p. 96)
sistema linfático Red de vasos semejantes a venas que devuelve al torrente sanguíneo el fluido que sale de los vasos sanguíneos.

lymphocyte White blood cell that distinguishes between each kind of pathogen. (p. 148)
linfocito Glóbulo blanco que reacciona a cada tipo de patógeno con una defensa específica.

magnetic resonance imaging A method for taking clear images of both the bones and soft tissues of the body. (p. 22)
imágenes por resonancia magnética Método que se usa para tomar imágenes claras de los huesos y de los tejidos blandos del cuerpo.

marrow The soft connective tissue that fills the internal spaces in bone. (p. 16)
médula ósea Tejido conectivo suave que rellena los espacios internos de un hueso.

melanin A pigment that gives the skin its color. (p. 33)
melanina Pigmento que da color a la piel.

menstrual cycle The cycle of changes that occurs in the female reproductive system, during which an egg develops and the uterus prepares for the arrival of a fertilized egg. (p. 229)
ciclo menstrual Ciclo de cambios que ocurre en el sistema reproductor femenino, durante el cual se desarrolla un óvulo, y el útero se prepara para la llegada del óvulo fecundado.

menstruation The process in which the thickened lining of the uterus breaks down and blood and tissue then pass out of the female body through the vagina. (p. 230)
menstruación Proceso en el cual el grueso recubrimiento del útero se descompone, y la sangre y el tejido salen del cuerpo femenino a través de la vagina.

minerals Nutrients that are needed by the body in small amounts and are not made by living things. (p. 52)
minerales Nutrientes que el cuerpo necesita en pequeñas cantidades y que no producen los seres vivos.

motor neuron A neuron that sends an impulse to a muscle or gland, causing the muscle or gland to react. (p. 179)
neurona motora Neurona que envía un impulso a un músculo o glándula, haciendo que el músculo o la glándula reaccione.

mucus A thick, slippery substance produced by the body. (p. 63)
mucosidad Sustancia espesa y lubricante que produce el cuerpo.

muscle tissue A body tissue that contracts or shortens, making body parts move. (p. 8)
tejido muscular Tejido corporal que se contrae o acorta, permitiendo así que se muevan las partes del cuerpo.

nearsightedness The condition in which a person can see nearby objects clearly. (p. 194)
miopía Condición en la que una persona puede ver claramente los objetos cercanos.

negative feedback A process in which a system is turned off by the condition it produces. (p. 220)
reacción negativa Proceso en el cual un sistema se apaga por la condición que produce.

nephron Small filtering structure found in the kidneys that removes wastes from blood and produces urine. (p. 128)
nefrón Estructura diminuta de filtración que hay en los riñones, que elimina los desechos de la sangre y que produce la orina.

nerve A bundle of nerve fibers. (p. 178)
nervio Conjunto de fibras nerviosas.

nerve impulse The message carried by a neuron. (p. 178)
impulso nervioso Mensaje que lleva una neurona.

nervous tissue A body tissue that carries electrical messages back and forth between the brain and every other part of the body. (p. 8)
tejido nervioso Tejido corporal que lleva mensajes eléctricos entre el encéfalo y todas las demás partes del cuerpo y viceversa.

neuron A cell that carries information through the nervous system. (p. 178)
neurona Célula que lleva información a través del sistema nervioso.

nicotine A stimulant drug in tobacco that increases the activities of the nervous system, heart, and other organs. (p. 123)
nicotina Sustancia química en el tabaco que acelera la actividad del sistema nervioso, corazón y otros órganos.

noninfectious disease A disease that is not caused by a pathogen. (p. 159)
enfermedad no infecciosa Enfermedad que no es causada por un patógeno.

nucleus The control center of a cell that directs the cell's activities and contains the information that determines the cell's form and function. (p. 7)
núcleo Centro de control de la célula que dirige las actividades de la célula y que contiene información que determina la forma y función de la célula.

nutrients Substances in food that provide the raw materials and energy the body needs to carry out all its essential processes. (p. 44)
nutrientes Sustancias en los alimentos que proveen la materia prima y la energía que necesita el cuerpo para realizar los procesos elementales.

organ A structure in the body that is composed of different kinds of tissue. (p. 8)
órgano Estructura del cuerpo compuesta de diferentes tipos de tejidos.

organ system A group of organs that work together to perform a major function in the body. (p. 8)
sistema de órganos Grupo de órganos que trabajan juntos para realizar una función importante del cuerpo.

osteoporosis A condition in which the body's bones become weak and break easily. (p. 19)
osteoporosis Condición en la cual los huesos del cuerpo se debilitan y se rompen fácilmente.

ovary Organ of the female reproductive system in which eggs and estrogen are produced. (p. 227)
ovario Órgano del sistema reproductor femenino en el cual se producen los óvulos y el estrógeno.

ovulation The process in which a mature egg is released from the ovary into a fallopian tube. (p. 230)
ovulación Proceso en el cual el óvulo maduro sale del ovario y va a la trompa de falopio.

pacemaker A group of cells located in the right atrium that sends out signals that make the heart muscle contract and that regulates heart rate. (p. 82)
marcapasos Grupo de células ubicado en la aurícula derecha que envía señales para que el músculo cardiaco se contraiga, y que regula el ritmo cardiaco.

pancreas A triangular organ that lies between the stomach and first part of the small intestine. (p. 70)
páncreas Órgano triangular ubicado entre el estómago y la primera parte del intestino delgado.

passive immunity Immunity in which antibodies are given to a person rather than produced within the person's own body. (p. 158)
inmunidad pasiva Inmunidad en la que los anticuerpos vienen de otro organismo y no del cuerpo de la propia persona.

pathogen An organism that causes disease. (p. 141)
patógeno Organismo que causa enfermedades.

penis The organ through which both semen and urine leave the male body. (p. 227)
pene Órgano a través del cual salen del cuerpo masculino tanto el semen como la orina.

Percent Daily Value A value that shows how the nutritional content of one serving of food fits into the diet of a person who consumes 2,000 Calories a day. (p. 58)
Porcentaje de valor diario Valor que muestra cómo el contenido nutricional de una porción de alimento se corresponde con la dieta de una persona que consume 2,000 Calorías al día.

peripheral nervous system The division of the nervous system consisting of all of the nerves located outside the central nervous system. (p. 182)
sistema nervioso periférico Parte del sistema nervioso formada por todos los nervios ubicados fuera del sistema central nervioso.

peristalsis Involuntary waves of muscle contraction that keep food moving along in one direction through the digestive system. (p. 63)
peristaltismo Ondulaciones involuntarias de contracción muscular que empujan el alimento en una dirección a través del sistema digestivo.

phagocyte A white blood cell that destroys pathogens by engulfing them and breaking them down. (p. 147)
fagocito Glóbulo blanco que destruye los patógenos envolviéndolos y descomponiéndolos.

pharynx The throat; part of both the respiratory and digestive systems. (p. 115)
faringe Garganta; parte de los sistemas respiratorio y digestivo.

pituitary gland An endocrine gland that controls many body activities. (p. 220)
glándula pituitaria Glándula endocrina que controla muchas actividades corporales.

placenta A membrane that becomes the link between the developing embryo or fetus and the mother. (p. 234)
placenta Membrana que se convierte en la unión entre el embrión o feto en desarrollo y la madre.

plasma The liquid part of blood. (p. 91)
plasma Parte líquida de la sangre.

platelet A cell fragment that plays an important part in forming blood clots. (p. 94)
plaqueta Fragmento de célula que juega un papel muy importante en la formación de coágulos sanguíneos.

pore An opening through which sweat reaches the surface of the skin. (p. 33)
poro Abertura a través de la cual el sudor sale a la superficie de la piel.

protein Nutrient that contains nitrogen as well as carbon, hydrogen, and oxygen; they are needed for tissue growth and repair and play a part in chemical reactions within cells. (p. 49)
proteínas Nutrientes que contienen nitrógeno, carbono, hidrógeno y oxígeno; son necesarios para el crecimiento y reparación del tejido, y juegan un papel muy importante en las reacciones químicas de las células.

puberty The period of sexual development in which the body becomes able to reproduce. (p. 239)
pubertad Período de desarrollo sexual durante la adolescencia en el que el cuerpo se vuelve capaz de reproducir.

pulse The alternating expansion and relaxation of an artery wall as blood travels through an artery. (p. 86)
pulso Expansión y relajación alternada de una pared arterial a medida que la sangre viaja por la arteria.

pupil The opening through which light enters the eye. (p. 193)
pupila Abertura por la que entra la luz al ojo.

R

rectum The end of the large intestine where waste material is compressed into a solid form before being eliminated. (p. 71)
recto Final del intestino grueso, donde el material de desecho se comprime a una forma sólida antes de ser eliminado.

red blood cell A cell in the blood that takes up oxygen in the lungs and delivers it to cells elsewhere in the body. (p. 92)
glóbulo rojo Célula de la sangre que capta el oxígeno en los pulmones y lo lleva a las células de todo el cuerpo.

reflex An automatic response that occurs rapidly and without conscious control. (p. 187)
reflejo Respuesta automática que ocurre muy rápidamente y sin control consciente.

respiration The process in which oxygen and glucose undergo a complex series of chemical reactions inside cells; also called cellular respiration. (p. 113)
respiración Proceso en el cual el oxígeno y la glucosa sufren una compleja serie de reacciones químicas en las células; también se llama respiración celular.

response What the body does in reaction to a stimulus. (p. 177)
respuesta Lo que hace el cuerpo como reacción a un estímulo.

retina The layer of receptor cells at the back of the eye on which an image is focused. (p. 194)
retina Capa de células receptoras en la parte posterior del ojo donde se enfoca una imagen.

S

saliva The fluid released when the mouth waters that plays an important role in both mechanical and chemical digestion. (p. 62)
saliva Líquido liberado por la boca que juega un papel muy importante en la digestión química y mecánica.

scrotum An external pouch of skin in which the testes are located. (p. 227)
escroto Bolsa externa de piel en donde se ubican los testículos.

semen A mixture of sperm and fluids. (p. 227)
semen Mezcla de células de espermatozoides y fluidos.

semicircular canals Structures in the inner ear that are responsible for the sense of balance. (p. 198)
canales semicirculares Estructuras en el oído interno responsables del sentido del equilibrio.

sensory neuron A neuron that picks up stimuli from the internal or external environment and converts each stimulus into a nerve impulse. (p. 178)
neurona sensorial Neurona que recoge los estímulos del medio ambiente interno o externo y convierte cada estímulo en un impulso nervioso.

skeletal muscle A muscle that is attached to the bones of the skeleton and provides the force that moves the bones. (p. 26)
músculo esquelético Músculo que está unido a los huesos del esqueleto y que proporciona la fuerza para que los huesos se muevan.

skeleton The inner framework made up of all the bones of the body. (p. 12)
esqueleto Estructura formada por todos los huesos del cuerpo.

small intestine The part of the digestive system in which most chemical digestion takes place. (p. 68)
intestino delgado Parte del sistema digestivo en la cual se produce la mayoría de la digestión química.

smooth muscle Involuntary muscle found inside many internal organs of the body. (p. 26)
músculo liso Músculo involuntario que se encuentra dentro de muchos órganos internos del cuerpo.

somatic nervous system The group of nerves in the peripheral nervous system that controls voluntary actions. (p. 187)
sistema nervioso somático Grupo de nervios en el sistema nervioso periférico que controla las acciones voluntarias.

sperm A male sex cell. (p. 225)
espermatozoide Célula sexual masculina.

spinal cord The thick column of nervous tissue that links the brain to most of the nerves in the peripheral nervous system. (p. 183)
médula espinal Columna gruesa de tejido nervioso que une el encéfalo con la mayoría de los nervios en el sistema nervioso periférico.

spongy bone Layer of bone tissue having many small spaces and found just inside the layer of compact bone. (p. 16)
hueso esponjoso Capa de tejido de un hueso que tiene muchos espacios pequeños y se encuentra justo dentro de la capa del hueso compacto.

sprain An injury in which the ligaments holding bones together are stretched too far and tear. (p. 21)
esguince Lesión en la que los ligamentos se estiran demasiado y se rompen.

stimulant A drug that speeds up body processes. (p. 204)
estimulante Droga que acelera los procesos del cuerpo.

stimulus Any change or signal in the environment that can make an organism react in some way. (p. 177)
estímulo Cualquier cambio o señal en el medio ambiente que puede hacer que un organismo reaccione de alguna manera.

stomach A J-shaped, muscular pouch located in the abdomen. (p. 64)
estómago Bolsa muscular con forma de J localizada en el abdomen.

stress The reaction of a person's body to potentially threatening, challenging, or disturbing events. (p. 11)
estrés Reacción del cuerpo de un individuo a amenazas, retos o sucesos molestos potenciales.

striated muscle A muscle that appears banded; also called skeletal muscle. (p. 26)
músculo estriado Músculo con forma de franjas; también se llama músculo esquelético.

synapse The junction where one neuron can transfer an impulse to the next structure. (p. 180)
sinapsis Unión donde una neurona puede transferir un impulso a la siguiente estructura.

T

T cell A lymphocyte that identifies pathogens and distinguishes one pathogen from another. (p. 148)
célula T Linfocito que identifica los patógenos y distingue un patógeno de otro.

tar A dark, sticky substance that forms when tobacco burns. (p. 123)
alquitrán Sustancia oscura y pegajosa producida cuando se quema tabaco.

target cell A cell in the body that recognizes a hormone's chemical structure. (p. 218)
célula destinataria Célula del cuerpo que reconoce la estructura química de una hormona.

tendon Strong connective tissue that attaches muscle to bone. (p. 26)
tendón Tejido conectivo resistente que une un músculo a un hueso.

testis Organ of the male reproductive system in which sperm and testosterone are produced. (p. 226)
testículo Órgano del sistema reproductor masculino en el cual se producen los espermatozoides y la testosterona.

testosterone A hormone produced by the testes that controls the development of physical characteristics in mature men. (p. 226)
testosterona Hormona producida por los testículos que controla el desarrollo de las características físicas del hombre maduro.

tissue A group of similar cells that perform the same function. (p. 8)
tejido Grupo de células semejantes que realizan la misma función.

tolerance A state in which a drug user needs larger amounts of the drug to produce the same effect on the body. (p. 202)
tolerancia Estado en el que un consumidor de drogas necesita mayores cantidades de la droga para que produzca el mismo efecto en el cuerpo.

toxin A poison produced by bacterial pathogens that damages cells. (p. 142)
toxina Veneno producido por patógenos bacterianos y que daña las células.

trachea The windpipe; a passage through which air moves in the respiratory system. (p. 116)
tráquea Conducto a través del cual se mueve el aire en el sistema respiratorio.

tumor An abnormal tissue mass that results from the rapid division of cells. (p. 162)
tumor Masa de tejido anormal que resulta de la rápida división de las células cancerosas.

umbilical cord A ropelike structure that forms between the embryo or fetus and the placenta. (p. 235)
cordón umbilical Estructura con forma de cuerda que se forma entre el embrión o feto y la placenta.

urea A chemical that comes from the breakdown of proteins. (p. 128)
urea Sustancia química que viene de la descomposición de proteínas.

ureter A narrow tube that carries urine from one of the kidneys to the urinary bladder. (p. 128)
ureter Conducto estrecho que lleva la orina desde cada uno de los riñones a la vejiga urinaria.

urethra A small tube through which urine flows from the body. (p. 128)
uretra Pequeño conducto a través del cual fluye la orina desde el cuerpo.

urinary bladder A sacklike muscular organ that stores urine until it is eliminated from the body. (p. 128)
vejiga urinaria Órgano muscular con forma de saco que almacena la orina hasta que es eliminada del cuerpo.

urine A watery fluid produced by the kidneys that contains urea and other wastes. (p. 128)
orina Fluido acuoso producido por los riñones que contiene urea y otros materiales de desecho.

uterus The hollow muscular organ of the female reproductive system in which a fertilized egg develops. (p. 228)
útero Órgano muscular hueco del sistema reproductor femenino en el que se desarrolla el bebé.

vaccination The process by which harmless antigens are deliberately introduced into a person's body to produce active immunity; also called immunization. (p. 155)
vacunación Proceso por el cual antígenos inocuos se introducen deliberadamente en el cuerpo de una persona para producir inmunidad activa; también se llama inmunización.

vaccine A substance used in a vaccination that consists of pathogens that have been weakened or killed but can still trigger the immune system into action. (p. 155)
vacuna Sustancia usada en una vacunación que está formada por patógenos que han sido debilitados o muertos pero que todavía pueden activar el sistema inmunológico.

vagina A muscular passageway leading to the outside of the body; also called the birth canal. (p. 228)
vagina Pasaje muscular que lleva hacia afuera del cuerpo; también llamado canal de nacimiento.

valve A flap of tissue in the heart or a vein that prevents blood from flowing backward. (p. 81)
válvula Tapa de tejido en el corazón o en un vena que impide que la sangre fluya hacia atrás.

vein A blood vessel that carries blood back to the heart. (p. 82)
vena Vaso sanguíneo que transporta la sangre de vuelta al corazón.

ventricle Each of the two lower chambers of the heart that pumps blood out of the heart. (p. 81)
ventrículo Cada una de las dos cámaras inferiores del corazón que bombean la sangre hacia afuera del corazón.

vertebrae The 26 small bones that make up the backbone. (p. 13)
vértebras Los 26 huesecillos que forman la columna vertebral.

villi Tiny finger-shaped structures that cover the inner surface of the small intestine and provide a large surface area through which digested food is absorbed. (p. 70)
vellosidades Pequeñas estructuras con forma de dedo que cubren la superficie interna del intestino delgado y proporcionan una amplia superficie a través de la cual se absorbe el alimento digerido.

vitamins Molecules that act as helpers in a variety of chemical reactions within the body. (p. 50)
vitaminas Moléculas que actúan como ayudantes en gran variedad de reacciones químicas que se producen en el cuerpo.

vocal cords Folds of connective tissue that stretch across the opening of the larynx and produce a person's voice. (p. 120)
cuerdas vocales Pliegues de tejido conectivo que se extienden a lo largo de la abertura de la laringe y producen la voz de la persona.

voluntary muscle A muscle that is under conscious control. (p. 25)
músculo voluntario Músculo que se puede controlar conscientemente.

W

white blood cell A blood cell that fights disease. (p. 93)
glóbulo blanco Célula de la sangre que protege contra las enfermedades.

withdrawal A period of adjustment that occurs when a drug-dependant person stops taking the drug. (p. 203)
síndrome de abstinencia Período de ajuste que ocurre cuando una persona adicta a las drogas deja de consumirlas.

X

X-rays A form of energy that travels in waves. (p. 21)
rayos X Forma de energía que viaja en ondas.

Z

zygote A fertilized egg, produced by the joining of a sperm and an egg. (p. 225)
cigoto Óvulo fecundado, producido por la unión de un espermatozoide y un óvulo.

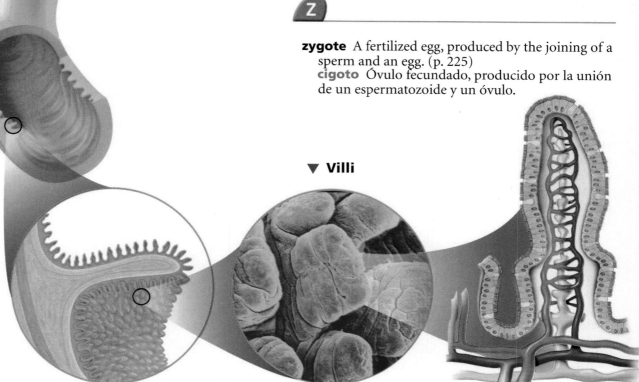

▼ **Villi**

Index

Page numbers for key terms are printed in **boldface** type.
Page numbers for illustrations, maps, and charts are printed in *italics*.

Index

Index

Acknowledgments

Acknowledgment for page 248: Excerpt from *A Kind of Grace* by Jackie Joyner-Kersee. Copyright © 1997 by Jackie Joyner-Kersee. By permission of Warner Books, Inc. All Rights Reserved. Note: Every effort has been made to contact the copyright owner.

Staff Credits
Diane Alimena, Scott Andrews, Jennifer Angel, Michele Angelucci, Laura Baselice, Carolyn Belanger, Barbara A. Bertell, Suzanne Biron, Peggy Bliss, Stephanie Bradley, James Brady, Anne M. Bray, Sarah M. Carroll, Kerry Cashman, Jonathan Cheney, Lisa J. Clark, Bob Craton, Patricia Cully, Patricia M. Dambry, Kathy Dempsey, Leanne Esterly, Emily Ellen, Thomas Ferreira, Jonathan Fisher, Patricia Fromkin, Paul Gagnon, Kathy Gavilanes, Holly Gordon, Robert Graham, Ellen Granter, Diane Grossman, Barbara Hollingdale, Linda Johnson, Anne Jones, John Judge, Kevin Keane, Kelly Kelliher, Toby Klang, Sue Langan, Russ Lappa, Carolyn Lock, Rebecca Loveys, Constance J. McCarty, Carolyn B. McGuire, Ranida Touranont McKneally, Anne McLaughlin, Eve Melnechuk, Natania Mlawer, Janet Morris, Karyl Murray, Francine Neumann, Baljit Nijjar, Marie Opera, Jill Ort, Kim Ortell, Joan Paley, Dorothy Preston, Maureen Raymond, Laura Ross, Rashid Ross, Siri Schwartzman, Melissa Shustyk, Laurel Smith, Emily Soltanoff, Jennifer A. Teece, Elizabeth Torjussen, Amanda M. Watters, Merce Wilczek, Amy Winchester, Char Lyn Yeakley.
Additional Credits Tara Alamilla, Louise Gachet, Allen Gold, Andrea Golden, Terence Hegarty, Etta Jacobs, Meg Montgomery, Stephanie Rogers, Kim Schmidt, Adam Teller.

Illustration
Articulate Graphics: 195; **Bruce Cowie:** 232–233b; **Sandy Durant:** 25; **John Edwards and Associates:** 16–17, 26–27, 32–33, 40, 61, 62, 63, 65, 69, 74bl, 79, 80, 81r, 83br, 86–87, 92–93b, 97, 108l, 178–179, 180, 185, 208, 212ml, 226–227, 228–229, 234b; **Mark Foerster:** 129; **Tom Gagliano:** 213l; **Phil Guzy:** 104–105, 115, 116, 119 120, 193, 194, 197, 199, 219, 220, **Keith Kasnot:** 129; **Richard McMahon:** 58, 100-101, 123t, 139, 155, 156–157, 218, 251; **Fran Milner:** 70, 117; **Morgan Cain and Associates:** 93tr, 95, 149, 172, 186; **Pat Rossi:** 14; **Sandra Sevigny:** 13, 25, 79, 183; **J/B Woosley Associates:** 136, 213; **Sam Ward:** 145; **All charts and graphs by Matt Mayerchak.**

Photography
Photo Research Sue McDermott
Cover top, Paul Barton/Corbis; **bottom,** Maxine Hall/Corbis
vi t, David Young-Wolff/PhotoEdit; **vi b,** Jon Riley/Stone/Getty Images, Inc.; **vii t,** Mike Peres/Custom Medical Stock Photo, Inc.; **vii b,** Richard Haynes; **viii,** Mike Powell/ Getty Images, Inc.; **ix,** Richard Haynes; **xi,** Roy Morsch/Corbis; **xii t,** Pittsburgh Steelers/ Mike Fabus; **xii b,** Doug Pensinger/Getty Images, Inc.; **1,** Pittsburgh Steelers/Mike Fabus ; **2 all,** Pittsburgh Steelers/Mike Fabus; **3 both,** Pittsburgh Steelers/Mike Fabus.

Chapter 1
Pages 4–5, Matthew Stockman/Getty Images, Inc.; **5 inset,** Richard Haynes; **6,** Richard Haynes; **7l,** Richard Haynes; **7r,** K.G. Murti/Visuals Unlimited; **8b,** Biophoto Associates/Photo Researchers, Inc.; **8bm,** James Hayden, RBP/Phototake; **8t,** John D. Cunningham/Visuals Unlimited; **8tm,** Fred Hossler/Visuals Unlimited; **9 all,** Richard Haynes; **10l,** Jon Feingersh/Corbis; **10r,** Myrleen Ferguson Cate/PhotoEdit; **11,** Mike Powell/Getty Images, Inc.; **12,** Russ Lappa; **13l,** Richard Haynes; **13r,** Dorling Kindersley; **14l,** David Young-Wolff/PhotoEdit; **14r,** Rudi Von Briel/PhotoEdit; **15l,** Journal-Courier/Steve Warmowski/The Image Works; **15r,** Peter Hvizdak/The Image Works; **16–17,** Andrew Syred/Photo Researchers, Inc.; **17l,** Prof. P. Motta/Dept. of Anatomy/University, "La Sapienza", Rome/SPL/Photo Researchers, Inc.; **17tr,** Prof. P. Motta/Dept. of Anatomy/ University, "La Sapienza", Rome/SPL/Photo Researchers, Inc.; **17br,** David Madison Sports Images, Inc 2003; **18l,** David Young-Wolff/PhotoEdit; **18r,** Marc Romanelli/Getty Images, Inc.; **19l,** Dr. Fred Hossler/Visuals Unlimited; **19r,** Dr. Alan Boyde/Visuals Unlimited; **20,** John Meyer/Custom Medical Stock Photo, Inc.; **21b,** Tom McCarthy/PhotoEdit; **21t,** ISM/Phototake; **22l,** Corbis; **22r,** Michael Acliolo/International Stock; **23,** Ted Horowitz/Corbis; **24,** Richard Haynes; **25tl,** Astrid & Hans-Frieder/Photo Researchers, Inc.; **25bl,** Eric Grave/Photo Researchers, Inc.; **25m,** Richard Haynes; **25r,** Ed Reschke/Peter Arnold, Inc.; **26t,** Richard Haynes; **26b,** Jim Cummins/Getty Images, Inc.; **27,** Jim Cummins/Getty Images, Inc.; **28,** David Madison Sports Images, Inc. 2003; **29,** Richard Haynes; **30,** Richard Haynes; **31l,** Richer Wehr/Custom Medical Stock Photo, Inc.; **31r,** David Madison Sports Images, Inc.; **32,** Richard Haynes; **33b,** Russ Lappa; **33t,** Prof. P. Motta/Dept. of Anatomy/University "La Sapienza" Rome/Photo Researchers, Inc.; **35,** Getty Images, Inc.; **36,** Richard Haynes; **37,** Richard Haynes; **38,** David Young-Wolff/PhotoEdit.

Chapter 2
Pages 42–43, Stephen Simpson/Getty Images, Inc.; **43 inset,** Jon Chomitz; **45l,** David Young-Wolff/Getty Images, Inc.; **45m,** Cindy Charles/PhotoEdit, Inc.; **45r,** Jose Luis Pelaez, Inc./Corbis; **46l,** Richard Haynes; **46m,** Matthew Klein/Corbis; **46r,** Russ Lappa; **47 all,** Royalty-Free/Corbis; **48l,** Dorling Kindersley; **48m,** Richard Haynes; **48r,** Stephen Oliver/Dorling Kindersley; **49,** Larry Lefever/Grant Heilman Photography, Inc.; **50,** Jack Montgomery/Bruce Coleman, Inc.; **51,** Jules Selmes/Dorling Kindersley; **52l,** Davies & Starr/Getty Images, Inc.; **52m,** Russ Lappa; **52r,** Russ Lappa; **53,** Joan Baron/Corbis; **55b,** David Young-Wolff/PhotoEdit; **55t,** Richard Haynes; **56t,** David Young-Wolff/PhotoEdit; **56b all,** FoodPix; **57,** Richard Haynes; **58,** Richard Haynes; **59,** David Young-Wolff/PhotoEdit; **61,** Richard Haynes; **62l,** Dorling Kindersley; **62r,** Richard Haynes; **65,** CNRI/SPL/Photo Researchers, Inc.; **67,** Richard Haynes; **68,** Richard Haynes; **69,** Richard Haynes; **70,** Prof. P. Motta/Dept. of Anatomy/University "La Sapienza" Rome/Photo Researchers, Inc.; **71,** CNRI/Photo Researchers, Inc.; **72t,** Jon Chomitz; **72b,** Davies & Starr/Getty Images, Inc.

Chapter 3
Pages 76–77, Dennis Kunkel/Phototake; **77 inset,** Richard Haynes; **79,** Richard Haynes; **81,** Photo Researchers, Inc.; **82,** ISM/Phototake; **83,** Richard Haynes; **84,** Felix Stensson/Alamy; **85b,** Dorling Kindersley; **85t,** Richard Haynes; **86,** Science Photo Library; **88,** Cabisco/Visuals Unlimited; **89,** Arthur Tilley/GettyImages, Inc.; **90,** Richard Haynes; **91,** Andrew Syred/Photo Researchers, Inc.; **93b,** Bill Longcore/Science Source/Photo Researchers, Inc.; **93m,** National Cancer Institute/PhotoResearchers, Inc.; **93t,** Andrew Syred/Photo Researchers, Inc.; **94,** Oliver Meckes/Photo Researchers, Inc.; **97,** Richard Haynes; **98b,** Joel W. Rogers/Corbis; **98t,** Bob Daemmrich/Stock Boston; **99 both,** Custom Medical Stock Photo, Inc.; **100l,** The Granger Collection, NY; **100m,** Courtesy of the Baker Institute; **100r,** Layne Kennedy/Corbis; **101l,** Getty Images, Inc.; **101m,** Richard T. Nowitz/Corbis; **101r,** Reuters NewMedia/Corbis; **102,** Nicole Katano/Getty Images, Inc.; **104;** Center for Biomedical Communications/Phototake; **106,** Oliver Meckes/Photo Researchers,Inc.

Chapter 4 **Pages 110–111,** Mario Corvetto/Evergreen Photo Alliance; **111 inset,** Richard Haynes; **112b,** Dennie Cody/Getty Images, Inc.; **112t,** Richard Haynes; **114 all,** Richard Haynes; **115,** Richard Haynes; **116,** Richard Haynes; **118,** Mark Gibson/Corbis; **119,** Richard Haynes; **120,** Dorling Kindersley; **121,** Russ Lappa; **122,** Dorling Kindersley; **124l,** Matt Meadows/Peter Arnold, Inc.; **124r,** Jonathan Nourok/PhotoEdit; **125b,** Photo Researchers, Inc.; **125tr,** SIV/Photo Researchers, Inc.; **125tl,** Michal Heron/Prentice Hall; **126,** Sonda Dawes/The Image Works; **127,** Richard Haynes; **129,** Richard Haynes; **130l,** Andy Crawford/Dorling Kindersley; **130r,** Dorling Kindersley; **131,** Ken Karp; **133,** Richard Haynes; **134,** Dennie Cody/Getty Images, Inc.; **136,** Ken Karp.

Chapter 5 **Pages 138–139,** L. Stannard/Photo Researchers, Inc.; **140,** Richard Haynes; **140–141l,** Corbis/Bettmann; **141r,** Pete Saloutos/Corbis; **142b,** Dennis Kunkel/Phototake; **142m,** Biozentrum/Photo Researchers, Inc.; 142t, CNRI/Photo Researchers, Inc.; **144b,** Mike Peres/Custom Medical Stock Photo, Inc.; **144t,** Scott Camazine/Photo Researchers, Inc.; **146l,** Science Pictures Ltd./Photo Researchers, Inc.; **146r,** Professors Motta, Correr, and Nottola/Photo Researchers, Inc.; **147,** Lennart Nilsson/Boehringer Ingelheim International GmbH; **150,** NIBSC/Photo Researchers, Inc.; **151,** Jon Riley/Getty Images, Inc.; **152,** Richard Haynes; **153,** Richard Haynes; **154,** Russ Lappa; **155,** Aaron Haupt/Photo Researchers, Inc.; **156l,** Dorling Kindersley; **156m,** Historical Picture Service/Custom Medical Stock Photo, Inc.; **156r,** Giraudon/Art Resource, NY; **157l,** Bettmann/Corbis; **157r,** Fashion Wire Daily/AP/Wide World Photo; **158,** Eyewire/Getty Images, Inc.; **159t,** Richard Haynes; **159b,** Jerome Tisne/Getty Images, Inc.; **160l,** Eye of Science/Photo Researchers, Inc.; **160m,** Andrew Syred/Photo Researchers, Inc.; **160r,** Ron Kimball; **161,** Richard Haynes;**163,** Dept. of Clinical Radiology, Salisbury District Hospital/Photo Researchers, Inc.; **164,** Richard Haynes; **166t,** Richard Haynes; **166b,** Mary Evans Picture Library; **167,** Mary Evans Picture Library; **169,** Pete Saloutos/Corbis; **170l,** Mike Peres/Custom Medical Stock Photo, Inc.; **170r,** Eye of Science/Photo Researchers, Inc.

Chapter 6
Pages 174–175, Michael Kevin Daly/Corbis; **175 inset,** Richard Haynes; **177,** Mike Blake/Reuters New Media, Inc./Corbis; **179 all,** Rolf Brudere/Masterfile; **181,** Richard Haynes; **182b,** Chet Gordon/The Image Works; **182t,** Richard Haynes; **183,** Richard Haynes; **185,** Richard Haynes; **187,** Tom Stewart/Corbis; **188 all,** Richard Haynes; **189,** Barbara Stitzer/PhotoEdit; **190t,** Ian Vorster; **190–191b,** Larry Dale Gordon/Getty Images, Inc.; **192,** Tony Freeman/PhotoEdit; **193b,** Diane Hirsch/Fundamental Photographs; **193t,** Diane Schiumo/Fundamental Photographs; **194,** Omikron/Photo Researchers, Inc.; **195,** Richard Haynes; **198l,** Lennart Nilsson; **198r,** Lee Snider/The Image **Works;** 199l, Richard Haynes; **199r,** Prof. P. Motta/Photo Researchers, Inc.; **200,** Mugshots/Corbis; **201,** Richard Haynes; **202–203,** Digital Vision/Getty Images, Inc.; **204,** David Young-Wolff/PhotoEdit; **206t,** Tom Carter/PhotoEdit; **206b,** Stacy Pick/Stock Boston; **207b,** PhotoEdit; **207t,** CNRI/Photo Researchers, Inc.; **209,** Richard Haynes; **210t,** Diane Hirsch/Fundamental Photographs; **210b,** David Young-Wolff/PhotoEdit.

Chapter 7
Pages 214–215, George Shelley/Corbis; **215 inset,** Richard Haynes; **217l,** Chad Slattery/Getty Images, Inc.; **217r,** Uniphoto; **219,** Richard Haynes; **220,** Richard Haynes; **222,** Richard Haynes; **223 both,** Richard Haynes; **224,** Tom Brakefield/Corbis; **225 both,** David M. Phillips/Photo Researchers, Inc.; **230,** Professors P.M. Motta & J. Van Blerkom/ SPL/Photo Researchers, Inc.; **232t both,** Stephen R. Swinburne/Stock Boston; **232b,** Dr Yorgos Nikas/Photo Researchers, Inc.; **233l,** CNRI/Photo Researchers, Inc.; **233m,** G. Moscoso/Photo Researchers, Inc.; **233r,** Neil Bromhall/Photo Researchers, Inc.; **235,** Petit Format/Photo Researchers, Inc.; **236,** Index Stock Imagery, Inc.; **237l,** Roy Morsch/Corbis; **237r,** Tony Freeman/PhotoEdit; **238l,** Penny Gentieu; **238m,** Tony Arruza/Corbis; **238r,** Spencer Grant/PhotoEdit; **239l,** David Grossman/The Image Works; **239r,** Myrleen Ferguson/PhotoEdit; **240,** Michael Newman/PhotoEdit; **242t,** Uniphoto; **242b,** Myrleen Ferguson/PhotoEdit. **246t,** Scala/Art Resource; **246b,** Joseph Sohm; ChromoSohm Inc./Corbis; **247,** Louvre, Dept. des Antiquites Grecques/Romaines, Paris, France. Photo by Erich Lessing/Art Resource; **248,** Tony Duffy/Allsport USA/Getty Images, Inc.; **249,** AFP/Corbis; **250l,** Pearson Education; **250r,** Robert Houser/Index Stock Imagery, Inc.; **252,** Tony Freeman/PhotoEdit; **253t,** Russ Lappa; **253m,** Richard Haynes; **253b,** Russ Lappa; **254,** Richard Haynes; **256,** Richard Haynes; **258,** Tanton Yachts; **259,** Richard Haynes; **261t,** Dorling Kindersley; **261b,** Richard Haynes; **263,** Image Stop/Phototake; **266,** Richard Haynes; **273,** Richard Haynes; **285,** Prof. P. Motta/Dept. of Anatomy/University "La Sapienza" Rome/SPL/Photo Researchers, Inc.